Accountability

for

Educational Results

EDITED BY

R. W. HOSTROP, J. A. MECKLENBURGER, & J. A. WILSON

LINNET BOOKS □ Hamden, Connecticut □ □ □ □ 1973

216299

Library of Congress Cataloging in Publication Data

Hostrop, Richard W.   comp.
  Accountability for educational results.

  Includes bibliographies.
  1. Educational accountability—Addresses, essays,
lectures. I. Mecklenburger, James, joint comp. II. Wilson,
John Alfred, 1938—   joint comp. III. Title.
LB2806.H65   379'.15   72-8809
ISBN 0-208-01275-3

CONTENTS

PREFACE

Education's several publics have raised *Accountability for Educational Results* as an issue. Government agencies, public interest groups, parents, students and critics have emphasized their concern about the results of education. Many states have written new accountability laws—more will follow. There is renewed desire for knowledge of results, for assurance of results, for *Accountability for Educational Results.*

Concise definitions of "accountability" are always inadequate. As with many of its synonyms, such as "responsibility," "liability," "openness," "intelligibility," and "answerability," the meaning of "accountability" is colored by the user of the term. The reader will recognize within the first portion of this book, "The Call to Accountability, The Struggle for Definition," that "accountability" is not so much a process as it is a concept or policy. Its implementation in different settings and for different purposes will alter its character and emphases. In "Who is Accountable?" and in "Procedures that Seek Accountability" the reader may choose among nearly two dozen approaches to thought and action that could fall within a policy of "accountability."

"Accountability," as a term associated with education, made its first significant appearance in 1970 at the annual American Association of School Administrators meeting. James E. Allen, then U.S. Commissioner of Education, explained that what has caused disillusionment and lack of confidence in the public schools is "in large measure our inability to substantiate results." "The strengthening of the concept of accountability. . .is imperative," he asserted, and he called for research to improve society's ability to assess effectiveness of educational programs.

Less than a month later, on March 3, 1970, President Nixon sent a special message on educational reform to Congress. In it he called upon school systems to "begin the responsible, open measurement of how well the educational process is working." The President firmly endorsed the concept of accountability by declaring, "School administrators and school teachers alike are responsible for their performance, and it is in their interest as well as in the interests of their pupils that they be held accountable."

These calls for accountability, by the highest educational official and the highest elected official in the land, reflect a deepening national focus upon *Accountability for Educational Results*.

As the reader will see in "Industry as the Symbol of Accountability," American education has known many of these demands before. Many of the contemporary spokesmen for accountability are urging that educators learn some of the practices industry adopted in the 1950s and 1960s with the intent to be more efficient and effective. Early in this century, there came similar demands for education to imitate industry. Others warned then and now, as Henry Dyer of Educational Testing Service has said, that "It must be constantly kept in mind that the educational process is not on all fours with an industrial process; it is a social process in which human beings are continually interacting with other human beings in ways that are imperfectly measureable or predictable."

In the fifty selections that follow, accountability is examined by foremost thinkers and practitioners in education, business, government, and the media. As many questions are raised as endorsements given or methods proposed.

Accountability for Educational Results should be a deskside companion for every practicing educator. It is a work to be studied, discussed, and used in schools of education as a basic or supplementary text. Although this book of readings has an underlying unity, the reader may profit by beginning at whatever point his interests may lie.

Demands for accountability must be reckoned within education. *Accountability for Educational Results* reveals their sources, their directions, and their significance, and it suggests many procedures appropriate to satisfying these demands.

Richard W. Hostrop
James A. Mecklenburger
John A. Wilson

Chapter One

THE CALL TO ACCOUNTABILITY, THE STRUGGLE FOR DEFINITION

I

ACCOUNTABILITY MEANS A PARTNERSHIP FOR OUR YOUTH

by Neil V. Sullivan
Commissioner of Education, Commonwealth of Massachusetts

"This Sputnik of the 70's has been given various pseudonyms by those who see it from different vantage points, but its most common name is Accountability. Though its flight has been relatively brief, it threatens to leave as marked an effect upon education as its illustrious predecessor."

The headline read "School Financial Crisis Spreading," and the article that followed carried a summary of a recent National Education Association survey that detailed a depressing commentary of our times:

Dayton, Ohio, may have to close its schools next fall as that community's funds run out. In the same state, Cincinnati will solve its fiscal plight by allowing 400 teacher vacancies to go unfilled. New York City came dangerously close to dropping 6,500 teachers and administrators and Philadelphia may have to end the school year a month ahead of schedule.

The list goes on. Kansas, California, Minnesota, Wyoming, South Carolina, Wisconsin, Oregon, Rhode Island, Vermont, New Hampshire, Montana, Colorado, Indiana and Connecticut all are faced with serious teacher layoffs and program cuts.

Here in Massachusetts it appears that the situation of our sister states has not arrived with quite the same results — perhaps due in large measure to the fiscal autonomy of our local school committees. However, there is too much evidence to indicate that the direction that we are heading should place each and every member of the profession on the alert.

Reprinted with copyright permission of *The Massachusetts Teacher,* May/June, 1971.

Superintendents report to me that this has been the most difficult period for the passage of school budgets. In the Commonwealth's capital city a $5 million cut has been announced; in one of our most prestigious suburbs the budget was reduced for the first time in its history; few communities have been spared. The list runs from the Berkshires to the Cape and from the Merrimack to the Connecticut Valley.

And throughout the discussions, be they in Town Halls or Council Chambers, the word accountability is stressed as if a new element was being introduced to education.

Well, we have been accountable and we will continue to be and we will increase our accountability, but if this concept is to function properly, then accountability must operate in more than one direction. If the future of this nation rests in her classrooms then being accountable for the achievement of our children is the responsibility of each of us — presidents, governors, legislators, mayors, councilmen, selectmen and finance board members.

I also feel that industry has a role in this. Education in this nation is a multimillion-dollar activity. When I referred to the involvement of businessmen in education in a speech earlier this year before the school committees and superintendents I suggested that if industry can recommend improvements in our management methods I do not fear its involvement, and I cannot believe that the administrators and teachers of the Commonwealth would be anything but cooperative to this help.

Sputnik to Apollo

Most of us remember, I am sure, the dramatic launch in October, 1957, of Sputnik I by Soviet Russia. Whether we were students, teachers, or administrators at that historic moment, the educational process of which we were part was to be severely tested by that first positive proof of man's ability to conquer space.

As perhaps never before in our history, the American school became the object of severe scrutiny on the part of politicians and laymen alike. Many charged that our educational system had failed to produce, and had therefore failed America. A kind of frenzied evaluation of our schools become the mania of friend and foe alike. For the first time on a national level, in my memory at least, education and educators were held to account — and were found wanting.

Incidentally, while American education became the fall guy for Sputnik I, I cannot remember any bouquets coming our way for the walk of Neil Armstrong on the lunar surface.

The results of this "national assessment" produced a mixed bag of blessings. Federal and foundation programs were written, often hastily and without regard to real needs assessments, to bolster science and mathematics education. New goals were developed for American schools, too often without the advice and consent of the teachers who would be called upon to implement them. Some of these programs and goals are still with us, 14 years later. The National Defense Education Act, one of the great euphemisms of this century, became the passport to more and more equipment, materials, laboratories, even staff indirectly, while courses geared to the "defense" aspects of the act were increasingly evaluated by the availability and sophistication of the hardware used in instruction.

Later, of course, other subjects were added to this and other Federal funding programs, even, ultimately, the so-called humane studies. But the results of that first national "calling-to-task" of the American school system remain indelibly stamped on the system we work in today. We continue to evaluate the product in terms of merit scholars, Ivy League acceptances, college board scores. This is the dubious legacy of Sputnik I.

A new Sputnik

Now, as we enter the decade of the 70's, another Sputnik has burst on the educational horizon. This one, however, was not launched from foreign soil, but from our own midst. It has been aborning, perhaps, since the "pursuit of excellence" craze of the 50's and early 60's. This Sputnik, like its predecessor, burst upon us almost without warning, although the signs were clearly present now, as in 1957. And it has soared equally as high — and seems destined to have at least as much impact on education.

This Sputnik of the 70's has been given various pseudonyms by those who see it from different vantage points, but its most common name is Accountability. Though its flight has been relatively brief, it threatens to leave as marked an effect upon education as its illustrious predecessor. Now, as then, educators are reacting in helter-skelter fashion. Some decry accountability and all it portends and proclaim that education is, somehow, sacrosanct and above scrutiny or challenge. "We don't tell doctors how to doctor," they aver. You know the rest of that argument. Others adopt a wait-and-see attitude, much like those among us who are still waiting for "all the results to come in" on such post-Sputnik I innovations as PSSC Physics, language labs, new math, and linguistics. "This, too, shall pass," seems to be their watchword.

Still others rush to embrace everything that has accountability somewhere attached to it, however emphemerally. Just as the standardized test maker found an eager market after 1957. the reading experts likewise, after *Why Johnny Can't Read* hit the stands, so too are the educational consultants, the academicians, and even industry finding a receptive market among our colleagues for all sorts of crash programs, instant innovations, or results-oriented systems that carry promises of better processes and better products. The panic is on again in some quarters, just as it was in the late fifties and early sixties.

Finally, and most fortunately, there are those among us now, as there were then, who understand and accept, even welcome, the challenge of this new Sputnik, this Accountability, and see in it the potential for new growth, new opportunity, perhaps the realization of that elusive goal of equal education for all children in all our schools.

To these educators, and I must believe they are in the majority for education to continue to survive and flourish, the call for accountability is no more than a simple recognition at last of what they have always known: that the educational community must give an account of its stewardship if it is to expect the continued and indeed expanded support which education so desperately needs at all levels.

The role of non-educators

Nor do *real* educators, who view the process as a systematized activity requiring research, assessment, planning, evaluation, all with the total involvement of society, decry participation by any segment of that society. Rather than dismiss the efforts of *all* non-educational organizations or look with jaundiced eye at those who seek to combine genuine concern and talent with making a profit (perish the thought), we would do well to learn to distinguish the sincere from the insincere, the profit-seeking from the profit-sharing among our business and industrial brethren, and earnestly solicit the very real assistance they can give us in putting our billion-dollar business on a basis that could be more accountable.

In a recent article in *Industry,* November, 1970, I urged that the new alliance begun last year between the Massachusetts Department of Education and the Massachusetts Business Task Force for School Management, under the aegis of MACE, be extended and expanded to benefit all of public education in the Commonwealth. In that alliance, leaders from the Associated Industries of Massachusetts, "learned executives," joined with leaders of the educational community in producing a document on school management practices that, if implemented, could save millions of dollars and vastly improve the management of education dollars. *This* is accountability. *This* is industry getting its feet wet. And it is certainly no hoax. All of us who shared in that joint venture, or who are now benefitting from it, look forward eagerly to more such partnerships between the professions.

The concept of accountability as I stated above is, of course, by no means a new one. We have always been held accountable on at least a one-to-one basis by the parent when son or daughter brought home the report card, when college acceptances were announced; at town meeting time when we asked for more staff or space or services "to do the job better." The term, however, became a part of educational jargon fairly recently.

During the last year-and-one-half, several state agencies and private corporations have circulated interesting documents calling for the establishment of needs assessment programs, the development of evaluation techniques, the provision for accountability in education programs. After much prodding from members of Congress who were staunch proponents of increasing Federal aid commitment but who were being hard-pressed to give evidence of demonstrable results from previous aid, the United States Office of Education developed an "accountability model" for various federally-funded programs.

The focus in USOE's model is on the assurance of performance quality in the educational project through specific factors in program design and management. The model is a good one and, with some alterations, bodes well to bring more accountability into Federal projects. Twelve factors are identified as being critical to the implementation of accountability: *community involvement,* including participation in planning and responsibilities for program facets; *technical assistance* drawn from community, business, industry, labor, etc.: *needs assessment; change strategies; management systems,* such as PPBS, PERT, CPM; *performance objectives,* including measures and means for assessing degree of attainment of goals; *performance budgeting,* i.e., allocation of resources to objectives rather than functions; *performance contracting* to provide technical assistance not available within the system; *staff development; comprehensive evaluation,* based on continuous assessment of processes and products; *cost effectiveness;* and *program auditing,* a performance control system based on external reviews conducted by qualified outside sources of both the results and the evaluation techniques employed.

Performance contracting

Some of these factors are more widely accepted than others, but taken together they form the basis for a rather decent beginning in the formation of a framework for formal accountability in a program, a school system, or a state department.

One, in particular, has been much in the news lately, performance contracting. This is the arrangement whereby a school district contracts for technical assistance in specific program operations with an outside agency or industry with compensation based upon the accomplishment of stated, specified performance objectives.

It is a practice which is becoming more widespread despite a beginning in Texarkana that I publicly deplored long before it became common knowledge in the profession. It was because of the experience in that Southwest city that I stated that in each such project the evaluation and assessment activity must be conducted by an outside and impartial agency. As perhaps many of you are aware, there is such a project currently underway within the Boston schools initiated by the teachers.

I have been interested in the potential of performance contracting for several years, long before it was widely understood as an innovation. My experience with it as an educational consultant for the Thiokol Chemical Corp. has been in the area of the Job Corps and related programs. It was not until the firm relayed a request to me from the Dallas Superintendent of Schools to visit that city and assist him with a vocational program that I was able

to view, firsthand, performance contracting projects in a public
school system.

It is unfortunate that in an article that appeared in an earlier
issue of this magazine ("Performance Contracting Is A Hoax,"
April, 1971) the author's research that carried 2,000 miles to
Dallas could not have been extended another quarter mile in Boston to ascertain the total story. The Dallas Superintendent's statement that he was unaware of the purpose of my visit was later
refuted by his Assistant Superintendent when he recalled that I
had reminded the Superintendent of my function prior to participating in a press conference that he had called.

The real potential of performance contracting, as I witnessed
it that day, is that unlike the "voucher system" an alternative outside of the public school system that I have opposed from its inception, this brings an added complement of expertise and technology to the assistance of the classroom teacher, so that, working
together, greater student performance can be achieved. Central to
the success of this liaison, however, is that the teachers, the administrators, their associations and unions, and the community
must be involved as willing partners from the beginning and must
accept the contractors as co-workers toward their common goal of
greater student achievement. In those districts where all these
forces have joined together in the effort from the inception, performance contracting is demonstrating very real potential, not as a
threat to the teaching profession, but as a viable added dimension
to the educational process.

I shall continue to lend my efforts to encouraging this sort of
meaningful relationship between industry and education. The
alternative to developing this promising innovation within the system, with all concerned, including staff, participating in the deliberations on ground rules and approaches is, I fear, that performance contracting will grow despite us, outside the system, and
will become a case of the tail wagging the dog. That this has happened in some cases should be a clear indication to us that we need
to become involved more directly from the beginning. A few
failures do *not* prove the worthlessness of the venture, any more
than the early failures we all experienced as novice teachers proved
as unworthy to become good teachers.

The role of the Department
On the State Department level, accountability has become

very much a part of our professional lives. The Board of Education
has been working for nearly a year on the development of a statement of educational imperatives which are very near fruition. The
title of the Board's preliminary report, "The Results Approach to
Education," clearly indicates the tone of its deliberations.

A companion effort has seen the Department administrators
and staff working on a statement of Educational Philosophy, including goals and objectives for the department and for education
statewide, and a statement of educational rights and responsibilities for the children of the Commonwealth. In order to insure that
all who are held accountable for education are involved, a blue-
ribbon committee of educators, business and professional leaders,
labor and civic leaders, parents, and students is working with the
Department team in this important task. Very soon the results of
this step toward accountability will be shared with the various
publics, including most especially the teachers of the Commonwealth, for their reactions and input.

Development of goals and objectives, however, is meaningless
and irrelevant unless a serious assessment of educational needs is
undertaken. To this end, the Department has established a new
Office of Planning and Evaluation and has obtained Federal funding for a needs assessment for Massachusetts. Phase I of that assessment has been recently completed by a task force from industry,
local schools, and the Department. One primary goal is the development of needs assessment techniques which LEA's can use in
assessing their own needs and doing their own planning. The
potential for this project in the immediate future in terms of
accountability is most exciting.

We recently conducted an example of accountability on a
statewide level with the enthusiastic assistance and cooperation of
many, many of you — the first complete test of basic skills ever
given to all children in the Commonwealth at a selected grade
level. The results of the fourth-grade test given in January are now
in the hands of every school district, and the Department has already begun working with principals, guidance counselors, and
teachers in seminars and workshops in our Regional Centers to
assess the meaning of those results and their implications for programs of instruction in individual school districts, schools, and
classrooms.

More good than harm

Despite the premature concerns of some that the test results would do more harm than good, it is becoming increasingly evident as our Research and Development staff develop the results in more and more comparative analyses that such testing can tell us much about what we are doing right in our classrooms and can not only enrich our teaching but can assist us to render an accounting of our stewardship more convincingly.

I can report to you that a task force has been named to study the results and to make in-depth observations of those schools which achieved well on the tests in an effort to project for the whole educational community a profile of the kinds of educational environments which lead to solid achievement. It seems obvious to all that much more than attention to basic skills must be involved.

The most striking immediate result of the state testing program, and to me the most satisfying, was that Massachusetts children are achieving at far above national norms in the basic skills. I can think of no more appropriate place to report this than in *The Massachusetts Teacher,* since this is high tribute indeed to the calibre of teacher our elementary youngsters are blessed with. Our primary teachers are to be commended for this undeniable evidence of their professional skill and competence.

The Department will continue in the business of statewide analysis. I am firmly convinced that the State Department of Education's most promising role is TO STIMULATE SCHOOLS, NOT TO CONTROL THEM. This stimulation can take several forms, but must be clearly based on goals and objectives established by the total community for its schools.

The State could take two roads to accomplish this objective — one (the route most states follow) is to develop minimum standards and enforce them vigorously; the other is to stimulate local initiative by carefully measuring and evaluating current programs and results, publishing these results, and providing assistance to the local community. We intend to be the catalyst in spotlighting good programs, good practices, good results. We shall continue to ask your assistance in this endeavor.

Much has been said and written recently about accountability and much more is in the offing. While we may disagree about techniques and practices, we must surely all agree that, if "our thing" is worth doing, it is worth doing well and in the open for all to see.

We in the profession of education accept the charge and the challenge of accountability, and we welcome all the publics whom we serve to share in that accountability. For in truth, education is the primary business of all society, and all society is accountable for its successes and its failures. The failures of education are the failures of teachers, yes. But they are also the failures of government, when it fails to provide sufficient funds; school boards, when they listen to constituents first and children last; legislators, when they worry about today's taxpayers, but not tomorrow's; parents, when they are concerned with what others think of them and forget their offspring; in short, all of society must join us in accountability for education.

　　Let's welcome the community to the team; let's get on with the task.　　　　　　　　　　　　　　　　　　　　　　　　　　□

II

PUBLIC EXPECTATIONS

by Wilson C. Riles
California State Superintendent of Public Instruction

"Far from engineering man out of education, I believe account-ability is an attempt to bring man back in. . . . I view account-ability as a process of setting goals, making available adequate resources to meet those goals, and conducting regular evaluations to determine if the goals are met."

A Gallup Poll in 1970 found that 67 percent of the people con-tacted believed teachers and school administrators should be held more accountable for the progress of their students. In the rise and fall of fads, this percentage should increase for some time to come as word gets around about the "magic" of accountability. Follow-ing much more slowly will be the practice and fact of accountab-ility, and hopefully by the time the public switches tracks to an-other destination, accountability will have settled permanently in-to our school system as a common-sense measure without the guise of a panacea.

Perhaps it takes these public exigencies to spur needed change in the education profession. The profession has the peculiar qual-ity of being able to reform others without being able to reform it-self. All the public is asking, after all, is the same high standards of responsibility with the public monies that they demand in the management of their own private affairs.

The source of the current interest in accountability is fairly well known: school needs have outrun school funds, priorities are having to be set, and the public is no longer satisfied with alloca-tions that do not clearly reflect the priorities. The public feels that

with school budgets, as with their private budgets, there ought to
be reason and priorities, the expenditures should be balanced, and
you should have "something to show" at the end of the process.
Moreover, wherever possible the factors involved should be reduced to cold hard facts — just as with the space program, just as
when an individual buys an automobile or makes a business investment. No emotion, no poetry, just cold hard facts.

Whether the analogies are directly transferable to education
or not may not be as important as whether the public thinks they
are transferable. Because the public's belief in the similarities between running a business and running a school may become the
public's expectations in accountability, those expectations may be
what educators will have to contend with most.

In my own state there are growing demands for regular evaluation of teacher performance with a prepared check-off list. There
are editorials proposing to quantify everything from the bus driver's free time to student attitudes in art. And there are people
wanting to reduce all values to a square-foot or a cent by cent expenditure. The reaction of the profession, it seems to me, can be
one of resistance and counterclaim; which I don't think is really a
plausible reaction at all. Or it can be one of greeting the new interest as a welcome enthusiasm for progress, with an invitation to the
public to help implement the precepts. This, of course, is the position I think the education profession should take. Indeed, I cannot
imagine how accountability would work otherwise. Accountability
is essentially a partnership venture.

I believe the public's expectations for accountability — whatever they may be — should be meshed with the public's participation in the accountability process. If this occurs, then for once the
hopes and the facts would be the same. Let me be specific.

I view accountability as a process of setting goals, making
available adequate resources to meet those goals, and conducting
regular evaluations to determine if the goals are met. Fundamental
to this process is that there exist an adequate "data bank" of information from which viable options can be determined. The researchers and the state departments of education should provide
this. From the available options, then, goals can be determined.

In the goal-setting stage, the broadest possible spectrum of
the community should be brought together to make the decisions.
The process should be comprehensive and cohesive, involving

students, parents, teachers, administrators, boards of education, legislators, and the public at large. Once goals have been set, the necessary resources can be allocated. The public will know what is needed from the data bank. They also will know if they do not allocate the amount needed, then it is unfair to expect the schools to meet the assigned goals later.

Finally, there's evaluation — comprehensive, in depth, and accurate. This cannot be a one-score test evaluation, but must be an ongoing, regular evaluation that is diagnostic as well as comparative, that accounts for process as well as product, and that is principally geared toward improving instruction for the individual student. Moreover, the evaluation results should be translated into terms that are clear and easily understood by the lay public. A regular "state of education" message would seem to be a must, and the terminology used should be such that the options available to the public are clearly laid out. Then the accountability process can begin again.

The thrust of this accountability system would be that the taxpayer is never asked to support inefficient schools, and that the people have a regular meaningful assessment of the quality of education in their communities. If the people have participated in establishing the goals and have a significant voice in the assessment, then there is a higher chance that their expectations will be geared into reality. Otherwise, with only an outside knowledge of education, I see no reason why the public shouldn't expect accountability to recast our schools into slide-rule perfection. If the latter persuasion takes sway, we can expect some awkward moments.

Right now in Los Angeles, serious thought is being given to decentralizing the city district into a dozen mini-districts. The reason is that many people feel local schools should be made more responsive — and hence accountable — to residents. But at the same time, and for the same reason, the Governor's Commission on Educational Reform is proposing that California abolish the 58 county superintendent positions in favor of 15 state department of education regional offices. The problem is, no one has clearly determined the influence of district size on efficiency. I know of small inefficient districts as well as small efficient ones. We still are operating largely on hunches.

Accountability, too, if improperly handled, can bring some

self-defeating results when paired with the public expectations. Administratively, the bookkeeping could be overwhelming with ineffectiveness that could pique the public anger. Or anger might come from the presence of outside research teams at the local school, evaluating the neighborhood's children. There's a very strong possibility a parent may want irgorous accountability standards used on every child but his own. Or that accountability results will be used more for comparative than diagnostic purposes. This is the case now with California's statewide testing system. It serves more as fodder in political and legislative wrestling matches than it does as a source of improved instruction for the child.

No doubt accountability does lend itself to becoming a battlefield for the "experts." Facts and counterfacts always seem to be in plentiful supply, and everyone can garner up an arsenal of experts to authenticate his case. Too, the critical process of interpreting raw data to the public is particularly susceptible to distortion, and it is the rare reporter or administrator who can penetrate into the mysterious and protected reserve of the statistician.

Politically, of course, there is a danger that school board elections might be won or lost on the basis of approximations and estimates, when in fact the figures may be generalities at best. Or legally, there may be these questions: How much power can be farmed out to private performance contracting groups; do those groups have to use state-certified personnel; who is liable for quotas set but not met?

Educationally, there may be fears of a new rigidity introduced into the system, particularly if everything is quantified and we have a series of "five-year plans." With accountability as the byword, there may be some tendency to discourage courses that don't lend themselves so readily to quantifiable measures; or to discourage services — such as counseling or health — that may not have quantifiably ascertainable results. And finally, in our rush for certitude, we might snuff out those variables in education that make for human creativity and imagination.

These possibilities are some of the reasons why I believe that if the public is not brought in on the process, they will hammer at it from the outside and eventually establish procedures devoid of the input of the profession. I do not believe, for instance, that someone who is brought into the evaluating process will demand that all values be reduced to numbers. Nor, to the contrary, will they any longer claim that no values can be reduced to numbers. Instead, I believe they will understand that some things can be quantified and that others cannot; and that those things that can be quantified should be quantified so that those things that cannot will have greater play.

Creativity and innovation are challenged today more by inefficiency and lack of direction than they are by systems analysis. Freedom is a function of your options, and today our options are precious few. Far from engineering man out of education I believe accountability is an attempt to bring man back in. What we have been squeezed out by is our own ineptitude and archaic methods that have kept us so busy we haven't had time to be human.

Thus, in summary, it seems to me our principal task is not to fret about whether the Gallup Poll registers a rise or decline in public expectations about accountability, but rather we should get busy working directly with the public to make accountability a functioning process for improving quality in our schools. Then the expectations will more likely approach what is truly possible.   □

III

MAKING SCHOOLS ACCOUNTABLE

by The President's Commission on School Finance

"If teachers are able to negotiate their pay and workload, they should be obligated to submit to output measures."

Public functions, such as education, health, welfare, environmental control, transportation and public safety are placing increasing demands on public treasuries. Education, therefore, can only seek to share in the total funds which become available for all purposes.

If education is to compete successfully with these other functions, its proponents must be able to demonstrate that whatever funds are provided are achieving the desired results. This is extremely difficult because of the intangible nature of its product—learning. It is vital, therefore, that local school systems and state agencies work to develop better methods for measuring achievement and improvement.

Educators are expected to perform functions which impart to students the knowledge of basic skills such as reading, writing and arithmetic, and they can, and should, be held accountable for their ability to teach those skills. In addition to basic skills, they must try to develop for students, a desire to learn; a socially acceptable set of values and attitudes and an ability to relate with others. These latter student attributes are not easily measured.

The attempt to determine how well students have learned basic skills is not new. What is new, and what is now seriously lacking, is the ability to determine how well the student, as an individual, has benefited from his school experience.

Several states are now using evaluation systems with this

Reprinted from *Schools, People, & Money — The Need for Educational Reform*, 1972.

broader perspective. Others ought to begin. We would suggest that all states avail themselves of the methods and experience embodied in the National Assessment Program being administered by the Education Commission of the States.

The commission recommends that state governments establish statewide evaluation systems to measure the effectiveness of educational programs. These systems should include improved techniques for measuring progress and achievement in school as well as the ability of secondary graduates to perform effectively in productive jobs or succeed in schools of higher education.

What is being addressed here is the need to make something rational out of what has often been emotion and manipulation in the guise of measurement. Consider the reaction of many parents and, for that matter, educators to the term "pupil-teacher ratio." It borders on reverence. The fewer pupils per teacher, many people believe, the better quality of the education delivered. That ratio has become a kind of instant measurement.

In a recent demonstration by parents and teachers against school budget cuts in a large city, one of the placards read: "37 pupils to 1 teacher!" That information was offered without explanation, because, it was assumed, everybody must know that a class so large had to be, prima facie, ineffective. The truth may not be so simple as that however.

In a study prepared for this commission by a distinguished research organization, all available research projects were examined in an effort to determine the effect of class size on educational effectiveness. This study — which examined the body of research in this area — found no discernible difference in student achievement even though classes ranged from 18-to-1 up to 35-to-1.

It cannot be concluded from these results that class size is irrelevant to educational quality. Large classes can increase the difficulty of dealing with discipline problems. They most certainly can create more work for teachers who must read student papers and grade tests. We may even assume that when classes are very small, children who require individual attention are more likely to receive it.

It would be wrong to conclude, based solely on the lack of evidence to the contrary, that class size has no effect whatever on student performance. But on the basis of what has been presented to us, we must caution against the use of pupil-teacher ratios as instant measures of anything remotely approaching the quality of education.

Additional studies certainly are warranted, particularly those that deal with the attitudes of teachers on class size and the effect of those attitudes, rather than size itself, on the development of children.

Despite diligent searches and widespread opinion to the contrary, the commission finds no research evidence that demonstrates improved student achievement resulting from decreasing pupil-teacher ratios.

The commission recommends that class size standards and pupil-teacher ratios be used both sparingly and selectively in the preparation of school budgets and the allocation of staff until or unless further research indicates conclusively otherwise.

The question of accountability in general raises other questions. An obvious one of who is accountable for what children learn.

Traditionally, children have been held accountable for what they learn. Success or failure in school was largely a matter of how hard the child tried. Children are often graded on such things as attitude and co-operation. We do not deny that the child's attitudes toward teachers, school and learning play a significant role in his performance. Nor would we deny that these attitudes are, to a large extent, conditioned outside the school building.

But if education is to accomplish more than it has, it seems reasonable to look to the teacher as a key factor in the development and improvement of learning ability, whatever the outside factors may be. What goes on behind the classroom door has often been considered off limits to parents and even to administrators.

To the extent that teaching is an art rather than a science and learning a mystery, other than a measurable process, we ought to continue to permit the teacher to exercise a wide degree of latitude in selecting the proper method for doing the job. But that does not mean that parents and citizens in general have no right to know the results.

Schools must do more than teach basic skills such as reading and mathematics. They must prepare children for aspects of life other than reading and doing the simple calculations. What educators call the affective aspects of education such as attitudes, values or interpersonal relationships, are of enormous importance to our children. However, it is difficult to measure them.

What can be measured is how well children acquire cognitive skills such as reading, comprehending what they read, mathematics, the ability to assemble information and make decisions based on what they know.

Schools can test the acquisition of the foregoing skills by their pupils, and many do. Far fewer make the results of these tests available to parents and to citizens in general. They fear, often with good cause, that they will be held responsible for failures for which they are not responsible and for their inability to alter patterns that are beyond their control.

A child's ability to read is simply that and nothing more. But measuring it and publishing the results for grades and schools at least provides some evidence of the effectiveness with which some educational resources are applied. Although the public cannot ascribe all successes and failures to the formal educational process, at least the air ought to be cleared by letting everybody know what the schools can do and how well they do it.

New and better methods of measuring the outputs of education are developing rapidly, covering attitudes as well as knowledge and skills. By combining these techniques with achievement tests and other existing measurement instruments, it is possible to report more accurately to the public the progress being made in improving the education of pupils.

The commission is not unaware of the potential misuse and misinterpretation of achievement test results. Historically, this has been an extremely sensitive subject. In fact, test scores indicate the severity of educational problems, rather than the ability or inability of school programs to affect learning patterns.

The commission recommends that each state, in co-operation with local school districts, systematically provide for publication and other appropriate communication to the public of the results of the assessments of achievement and improvement in education. These results should be presented on a comparative basis in relation to school, district, state, and national norms, and for such grade levels and subjects as the state may determine.

The recent increase in the organization of professional associations and teachers into unions that seek and obtain bargaining rights has created an additional requirement of accountability in the educational process. Traditionally, labor unions in many fields assume responsibility for worker compliance with work rules and production quotas of their members.

While teaching clearly involves more than safely piloting an airplane from one city to another, or acquiring all the skills of a professional football player, unions in education that demand a role in determining working conditions and workloads ought to be involved also in the process of measuring output.

It is reasonable to hold teachers responsible for whatever may be determined as the analogy to "a day's work for a day's pay" in industry, however elusive that may at first seem to be. If teachers are able to negotiate their pay and workload, they should be obligated to submit to output measures.

The whole area of the application of educational resources and investment to effective schooling is extremely complex and clearly cannot be equated directly with input-output analyses of other industries and services. But, to the extent that measures of educational need and educational effectiveness can be developed, they ought to be translated somehow into a system that permits discretion on the part of supervisors, principals and teachers in their applications.

Resources distributed to the schools are often defined in terms of days of substitute teachers' pay or other units of educational measurement. But when a principal wants to send a class of an absent teacher to a zoo or put the class in the auditorium for some special programs, he may find that all he can get for this purpose is the pay allotment for a substitute teacher, when what he needs is a chartered bus or a couple of movies and a projector.

The rigidity of such controls of educational practice demonstrates the need for translating alternative resource applications into some freely usable common denominator. One that comes readily to mind, of course, is money, which has a transferability as a resource that surpasses anything any state or district board could possibly devise.

In the hands of a principal or teacher, it can provide a variety of educational experience that could not possibly be anticipated by anybody who writes rule books. We urge that this kind of flexibility be made available throughout school systems, districts, and schools, with proper checks and balances.   □

IV

ACCOUNTABILITY FOR STUDENT LEARNING

by Ervin L. Harlacher and Eleanor Roberts

If educators undertake to provide "Guaranteed Accountability,"
they will need the technological know-how of which private
industry has been the sole source.

Ever since the Texarkana experiment in "guaranteed learning"
made its appearance on the national education scene in April of
1969, boards of education and college boards of trustees have been
wondering about the accountability of their institutions for the
learning that does (or does not) take place there. Certainly, there
is no question that simply to make programs of learning available
and, by sometimes heavy-handed and didactic methods, to cram as
many facts into young heads as possible (the tell 'em-and test 'em
system) does not vindicate an educational institution's attrition
and failure rates. Neither does such a procedure advance the pre-
sumable cause of education; namely, to produce a maximum number of self-confident, self-reliant, self-motivating, and self-fulfilling
citizens for active participation in the mainstream of American
life.
        The old notion that only the so-called "best brains" are
worthy of development because only these can effectively be used
in the economy has long since become obsolete. Similarly, the idea
that a majority of students represent pint-sized containers into
which it is impossible to pour quart-sized content has been proved
erroneous, both empirically and through careful research. Classroom activities have, nevertheless, reamined teacher and teaching
centered (rather than learner and learning centered), with the
teacher sitting or standing before his students presenting them

with facts, much as he did in the Middle Ages. The result has been that too many educators have succumbed to the illusion that only a small percentage of students have the capacity to learn what is being taught.

In some respects, this may be true; for "what is being taught" is not necessarily synonymous with "what is being learned." As a profession, we have talked for years about individual differences among learners, without having done much about trying to understand the relationship of those differences to strategies that promote learning. We have come now to that point in time when it is necessary to realize, along with Benjamin Bloom, that:

. . . highly developed nations must seek to find ways to increase the proportion of the age group that can successfully complete both secondary and higher education. The problem is no longer one of finding the few who can succeed. The basic problem is to determine how the largest proportion of the age group can learn effectively those skills and subject matter regarded as essential for their own development in a complex society.[1]

Bloom is convinced that fully 90 percent of all students can master learning tasks. But, he cautions:

If the schools are to provide successful and satisfying learning experiences for . . . [this] 90 per cent . . ., major changes must take place in the attitudes of students, teachers, and administrators; changes must also take place in teaching strategies and in the role of evaluation.[2]

The implications here seem clear. Behaviors change only when a realistic set of goals and sub-goals has been formulated for the institution as a whole, and when practical objectives for implementing these goals at the classroom level have been posed and tested to determine their relevance. But, in all cases, each individual involved in the total process must be accountable for the satisfactory performance of his role in the overall scheme.

Brookdale's Philosophical Platform

At Brookdale, before the college opened in September 1969, the board of trustees adopted a philosophical platform covering broadly the philosophy and objectives of the institution. But more specific guidelines were needed if the college was to fulfill its mission of "bringing higher educational opportunities within geographic and financial reach of all citizens" in its host community, the entire county of Monmouth in New Jersey. Thus, during the ensuing summer, Brookdale administrators conducted a two-day workshop on institutional goals and performance objectives. Working from the phiosophical platform, the group developed a more precise mission statement, institutional goals and subgoals, and tentative activities for implementation.

Declaring that the college would fulfill its mission as effectively and/or economically as would a traditional educational institution, the mission statement further avowed that accomplishment would come about through achievement of ten specific institutional goals:

1. Institute the concept of accountability by defining outcomes, differentiating processes, and evaluating results for all undertakings

2. Prepare students for entry into and appreciation of actual careers

3. Provide educational opportunities that facilitate human development

4. Facilitate the development of the broadly educated person

5. Develop an instructional program that accommodates individual differences in learning rates, aptitudes, prior knowledge, etc.

6. Engender in each student a concern for excellence and a desire for continuous learning

7. Develop an institution whose total environment is dedicated to learning and is open to those who desire to learn

8. Utilize the total community as a laboratory for learning

9. Contribute to the educational, economic, social, and cultural development of the host community

10. Provide for continuous institutional evaluation.

Most of the few cautious excursions into the realm of accountability that have been taken in recent months have occurred at the classroom level. Certainly, the classroom is where accountability should begin for, as John Roueche remarked at a recent conference on improvement of teaching, "It's the teacher, not the student, who should be held accountable for the student's failure to learn." But does this concept go far enough? Should not administrators, too, be held accountable for student achievement of predetermined learning objectives? Not to do so is rather like

holding the bookkeeper in a corporation's business office accountable for his president's embezzlement of funds, while the president
himself skips off to South America with the loot. Accountability
should be demanded not at one level but at all institutional levels,
especially in the college—the demand originating with the board of
trustees as a board policy. The Brookdale board of trustees recently approved the following policy on accountability:

> Consonant with its philosophy to provide equal opportunity for all
> citizens to gain post high school educational experiences that will prepare
> them for meaningful participation in the social and economic life of the con-
> temporary world. Brookdale Community College subscribes to the concept
> that accountability for student learning is an accepted responsibility of the
> entire college community.

> Therefore, the President shall implement a process of periodic evalua-
> tion of the instructional program, and shall report his findings to the board of
> trustees on an annual basis, to include:

> 1. The success of students in attaining learning objectives, including
> student attrition rates
> 2. The success of students in occupations entered into upon leaving the
> college, including employer's perceptions of the efficacy of the college's
> career programs
> 3. The success of students who transfer to other institutions
> 4. The extent to which the college programs are fulfilling the stated
> overall philosophy and objectives of the college
> 5. The responsiveness of the college programs to a student's initial
> and/or changed career aspirations.

Corporate Organization

Going back to the corporation for an analogy, it seems
obvious that corporate organization differs very little from the
organization of a college. There is (1) a board of directors, which
is responsible to the stockholders; there are (2) the executive
officers, who are responsible to the board; (3) division managers
and department heads who are responsible to one or more of the
executive officers; and (4) under each of these, the "performers"—
those whose expertise in executing specialized segments of the
total endeavor helps to move the enterprise toward achieving its
goals. These performers, in our analogy, may be equated with
teachers. The executive officers compare with administrators, and
the board of directors with the college board of trustees.

Corporate quotas (goals in our terminology) for any given period are not self-producing. They are developed by management after careful consideration of the corporation's past performance, its current operational design, its future potential—and account-ability for the achievement of the overall goals rests with the executive officers.

Carrying the analogy a little further, the corporation recog-nizes that all stockholders have the right to a guaranteed share in the overall profits, proportional to the amount of their investment. Similarly, the college must recognize that students—the stockhold-ers in the educational enterprise—are entitled to fair returns for their investment of time, effort, and ability in the learning process.

Many educators have been accustomed to think of ability in terms of aptitude for particular kinds of learning, so that John Carroll's assertion that "aptitude is *the amount of time* required by the learners to attain mastery of a learning task"[3] seems some-what startling. Yet, in point of fact, it is merely a restatement of the principle on which self-paced learning is based. And several re-cent studies[4] have verified that although most students eventually reach mastery on each learning task, some achieve it much sooner than others. Thus, it becomes the responsibility of the teacher to discover, on an individual basis, the amount of time each student requires to master the learning experiences provided in any set of objectives governing the units of knowledge to be acquired in a given course of study, and to provide more effective learning con-ditions for those who need more time.

Developing Learning Objectives

It would appear obvious, then, that insofar as the instruction-al program is concerned, the development of learning objectives is the first step in the total process of accountability. Such objectives represent a unit of production and make it possible to verify whether the production occurred or not. But, although it is easy enough to recommend the development of learning objectives and perhaps to enumerate the steps in the process, it is *not* an easy matter to get viable objectives.[5] This means that learning objec-tives require periodic "internal audit" to determine how well they are guiding the student toward salient activities and changed be-haviors. Thus, in the process of accountability, evaluation becomes a highly important factor.

Accountability cannot be limited to teachers, however. Each administrative unit must develop performance objectives and evaluative techniques by which to ensure accountability in the noninstructional activities. To this end, it is recommended that program planning procedures be instituted. In essence, each activity (office, department, etc.) of the institution is assigned a set of functional responsibilities, in addition to the institutional goals which have priorly been evolved. Each administrator takes these two documents—the goals and functional tasks—and plans a set of programs within his functional area that serve to accomplish some aspects of the institutional goals. These programs then provide a basis upon which to assign accountability in the noninstructional areas. Coupled with this program planning is a costing process that leads into program planning budgeting, and this brings to full cycle the concept of management by objectives for the total institution.

The Texarkana Experiment

In the Texarkana experiment, which has been variously evaluated during the time it has been in existence, it was decided to bring in "big business" to execute a plan which could have been implemented by those in charge of the school system, had management by objectives been operative. Weaknesses in the educational program might early have been discovered and corrected instead of being allowed to accumulate. Ongoing evaluation of each learning objective and each performance objective would have welded the entire organization into a cohesive whole, accountable for the individual mastery of specific learning tasks by the children in the system.

Actually, under conditions of the experiment, there is little accountability involved, except in terms of monetary bonuses or penalties accruing from the firm's success or nonsuccess in producing student learning that is "guaranteed." But for how long? The editor of *Phi Delta Kappan* raised that very question the June 1970 issue:

> One of our early disappointments in Texarkana was the discovery that the schools' contract with Dorset [Educational Systems, who are conducting the experiment] does not include a clause, discussed at the negotiations stage, which would have provided penalties should initial gains disappear after six months. Thus temporary spurts so familiar to educational researchers . . . may fade away without anybody noticing.[6]

On the positive side, Texarkana may be just the right catalyst to stimulate constructive action on the part of educators—self-preserving, if you will, but certainly long overdue. Is there any reason why educators can't develop and put into action the same kind of technological know-how of which industry boasts? Is there any reason why schools of education cannot develop courses of study that will fit generations of educators to meet the challenges of current educational needs? It is one thing to make an administrator accountable if he has the modern tools with which to work; it is quite another to hold him accountable if he's using a hand plow to do a job that requires a bulldozer.

Accountability: A Privilege

That accountability should be built into every college program there is little doubt. But accountability must be regarded a privilege—not a burden, nor a checkrein on teachers and administrators alike. Rather, it should be considered a kind of self-scoring quiz that will reveal how far-fetched our institutional goals are—or how realistic; how nebulous our learning objectives are—or how well structured; how successful our programs are in motivating students to remain in college—or in suggesting that they might as well drop out.

But accountability for the programs offered and the results produced cannot be based on an M & M reward system. When colleges set up goals and objectives, they don't require monetary or stock issue incentives. Their goals and objectives merely describe the purpose for which they are in business. And, as in any profitable business, they must be accountable for the quality of their end product. What kind of human being will a student be when, after two years, he walks again through the open door into the world of work or advanced study?

It is the responsibility of the community college to offer as many educational opportunities to as many citizens of its community as they may find useful. It is its equal responsibility to see that the maximum number of students who enter its doors— 90 per cent of them, if Professor Bloom's projection is accurate—leave again with learnings mastered and a clear knowledge of how to apply those learnings to life in the real world. The excellent institution is not the one that flunks out 60 per cent of its students. The excellent institution—the accountable institution—is the one that can declare, "When students finish their studies here, 90 per cent of them can do these things."

If educators undertake to provide "guaranteed accountability" (not guaranteed performance, for there are too many ways of covering up mistakes in this area), they will be forced to acquire and execute the technological know-how of which private industry now appears to be the sole source. This is the only course open to them if they are to preserve the enormous gains education has made over its long history and, at the same time, apply the technology that can facilitate accomplishment of their goals. In such circumstances, faith in the community college's seriousness of purpose and determination to fulfill its mission within its community will be revitalized, and those who are involved in the teaching-learning process will acquire new vigor.

An educational credo for the nation's community colleges might well include the following nine articles of belief:

1. We believe that both administrators and teachers ought to be accountable for student failures

2. We believe that an individual educational plan or prescription ought to be developed for each student, utilizing a wide variety of learning experiences

3. We believe that an educational institution ought to be judged on the basis of what it does for and with students and not on the basis of their opening handicaps

4. We believe in learning for mastery by all students—not just a chosen few

5. We believe that the instructional program ought to accommodate individual differences in learning rates, aptitudes, and prior knowledge, for a college exists, not to measure the extent of its students' failures, but to evaluate the depth of their successes

6. We believe that the individualization of instruction requires the provision of optional paths to learning, and the utilization of a highly diversified teaching/learning team composed of full-time teachers, part-time teachers, media specialists, counselors, paraprofessionals, peer tutors, and community volunteers

7. We believe that education must be learner and learning centered, measured by performance criteria—not teacher and teaching centered

8. We believe that teachers ought to be managers of the

learning process—change agents, guides, mentors, questioners—not feeders of information.

9. And we believe that each learner ought to be able to start where he is and become all that he is capable of becoming.   □

Ervin L. Harlacher is President of Brookdale Community College and Eleanor Roberts is Administrative Assistant in the Department of Research.

[1,2] Bloom, Benjamin S. "Learning for Mastery." *UCLA Evaluative Comment,* May 1968, p. 2.

[3] Carroll, John A. "A Model of School Learning." *Teachers College Record,* 1963, pp. 723-33.

[4] Atkinson, R. C. *Computerized Instruction and the Learning Process.* Report No. 122, Stanford, California: Institute for Mathematical Studies in the Social Sciences, 1967. Glaser, R. "Adapting the Elementary School Curriculum to Individual Performance." *Proceedings* of the 1967 Invitational Conference on Testing Programs, Princeton, New Jersey: Educational Testing Service, 1968.

[5] Mager, Robert F. *Preparing Instructional Objectives.* Palo Alto, California: Fearon Publishers, 1962. Also Johnson, Stuart R. and Johnson, Rita B. *Developing Individualized Instructional Material.* Palo Alto, California: Westinghouse Learning Press, 1970.

[6] Elam, Stanley. "The Age of Accountability Dawns in Texarkana." *Phi Delta Kappan,* LI, June 1970, p. 509.

V

ACCOUNTABILITY

by Albert V. Mayrhofer

"The public has a right to know what they are getting for their money. . .Accountability is the result of reporting student accomplishment to the public and taking the consequences of that accomplishment."

The first applications of the concept of accountability by the U.S. Office of Education were undertaken by the Bureau of Elementary and Secondary Education. The applications were made within the Drop-Out Prevention and Bilingual Education Programs, Titles VII and VIII of the Elementary and Secondary Education Act.

Basically the concept means "answerability for student progress as expressed in the local project," funded under these programs. The public and its representatives in Congress have the right to know the extent to which money allocated to achieve student accomplishment, as developed by the local school people themselves, has actually resulted in improved student performance.

Accountability is the result of reporting student accomplishment to the public and taking the consequences of that accomplishment.

Performance contracting is not synonymous with accountability though it *can be* an important tool for achieving accountability.

Evaluation is not synonymous with accountability though *it is* a tool for achieving it.

The outside, independent educational accomplishment audit is not synonymous with accountability *but is the anchor tool* for achieving it.

Reproduced with permission of the author.

The public has a right to know what they are getting for their money. In addition to knowing the resources purchased — such as personnel, facilities and material, which we have always reported — accountability also calls for information regarding the effect of these resources on actual student gain.

Accountability has implications which go beyond the applications instituted in the Drop-Out and Bilingual Education Programs. The people have a right to expect the schools to constantly seek ways to improve student performance with available resources. This means that all levels of education must improve capability to meet burdens, on a cost effective basis. This means that experimentation must be documented and evaluated. This means that education must institutionalize those cost effective improvements. Institutionalize means the replacement of less cost effective programs with the more cost effective programs resulting from research and development.

While these are not easy tasks, we are not without resources. Education is far from the state of desolation which some would infer.

The shift from emphasis on resources applied to the improvement of student performance resulting from resource allocation gives us guidance for increasing the relevance, responsiveness, and cost effectiveness of our efforts. It gives us direction in spelling out our burdens and assessing our capabilities as well as the lack of them. It justifies the educational accomplishment audit as a management tool. It changes our mode from response to "felt need" or by crisis to a planned problem solving mode.

A management plan for achieving results has been suggested by Corrigan and Kaufman. A very similar approach was recommended by Forum 9 of the recent White House Conference on Children. This approach holds real promise of assisting schools to become more accountable. The approach has six components.

The first component requires identification of problem, using documented needs as criteria. A need is simply the discrepancy between what is and what should be. The statement of the problem also requires the specification of requirements for problem resolution, or a definition of terminal product or behavior. This is the component which documents that for which we will be held accountable. For this reason, statement of the problem must also identify conditions such as time, materials, personnel, and funds.

It should include the managed input of *all* levels of the community in sufficient *numbers* to make it statistically equivalent to vox populi. By doing this, one knows what the people want — a socially responsible action which creates a virtually impregnable political stance.

The second component involves the determination of solution requirements and solution alternatives. An analysis is performed which determines the detailed requirements for proceeding from the current conditions to the required conditions — or what should be.

These requirements *must* be stated in measureable performance terms. Possible solution stragegies and tools are identified to meet the requirements. Their advantages and disadvantages relative to producing the required outcomes are documented.

The third component involves the *selection* of stragegies and tools from among the documented alternatives. Criteria for selection should certainly contain cost *effectiveness* indicators. All too often cost efficiency is used in its stead. Basing "how to do it" discussions on what will do the job for the least expenditures of time, resources, and effort of both learner and educator makes good sense.

The fourth component involves implementation. Based on needs, solution requirements, the selected tools and strategies, a plan is designed and followed. The tools and strategies are obtained and utilized. This is the "doing" component in which the tools and strategies are utilized and performance data is collected.

The fifth component involves the determination of performance effectiveness. The application of the implementation plan to the solution of the problem is *evaluated* to determine the extent to which results are achieved. Data on terminal *performance and process utility* are collected, analyzed, compared to requirements and used to determine revision requirements.

The independent review and public report of this evaluation component is the major function of the *outside, independent educational accomplishment auditor.*

The sixth component involves *revision as required.* Any time a performance requirement *is not met,* either during or at the end, revision is required. If it is not accomplished, the planned relationships among and between the tools and strategies will be changed. Without control and redirection of this change, the program will

be limited in achieving the resolution of the problem. This component applies to all of the other components, individually and
collectively.

And now, a word about the performance contract. The performance contract, as a tool for increasing the capability of our
schools to meet their burdens, has great *potential.* It might be an
option one would select in the third component. It might not. Its
social utility will depend on the criteria for its selection as a tool,
from among other options, and how skillfully it is orchestrated,
within the educational technology process. The success or lack of
it, achieved by this tool, should be verified and reported by the
outside, independent, educational auditor. The delivery of this
educational audit, to the people, is the cornerstone of accountability in education. It is the document which answers the question: What student progress occurred as the result of the application of public resources?   □

_____

Albert V. Mayrhofer is an official of the U.S. Office of Education.

VI

THE NEW RULES OF BOARDMANSHIP

by Nolan Estes

"The name of the game is conflict, and those who cannot accept the prospect of entering into public debate to argue for programs which they are convinced will improve public education, and to submit fact, rational analysis, and empirical evidence to buttress their convictions, would do well to leave the public education arena before they get hurt."

The reign of boardmen-kings and administrator-kings is just about over. If most board members and administrators aren't yet aware of precisely that, they surely recognize already, and at the very least, that something strange and disturbing is taking place in public education. Not only has the calm that once characterized board relationships with citizens and teachers been shattered by strikes, picketings, walk-outs and sit-ins, but the unaccustomed bitterness between those legally responsible for the schools and the clientele of public education shows no signs of abating.

This does not mean that power is lost to school boardmen and administrators; indeed, they're being handed more power than ever before, albeit of a different and more challenging kind. How they use that power will depend, I submit, on how well they understand what is happening and, as important, what they must *make* happen.

The first question that any school board member or administrator might ask, then, is *what has gone wrong?*

Difficult as it might be for a board member or for equally beleaguered school superintendents to accept this answer, I think a lot in public education is suddenly going *right*. American

education is finally coming of age as an American institution —
read political institution. Having been sheltered for more than 100
years from the realities of power — from conflict, from debate,
from victory and defeat — public education has been forced out of
its neutral corner and into the ring with all the other boxers.
Boardmen and superintendents must learn how to defend themselves. It's about time.

Until the decade just ended, school boards had had a very
limited constituency. Technically, of course, they were responsible
to all the citizens who paid taxes and sent their children to the
schools. Yet this legal responsibility tended to be a democratic
fiction, largely for economic reasons. Fifty years ago, even 25
years ago, if a youngster was failing in school, he could drop out
and still get some kind of a job. Employment requirements began
inching up after World War I, but first the Depression and then
World War II concealed most of the deficiencies in the schools that
might have been revealed by the inability of uneducated Americans to get jobs. The Depression hid such deficiencies behind a
breakdown in our economy (even educated persons couldn't find
employment, so nobody blamed the schools), and the war created
a market for manpower of every description regardless of quality.

The result was that public education had nothing but satisfied
customers, because the dissatisfied ones usually could be counted
on to leave without complaining. The children of the affluent
could seek educational improvement in private schools or other
communities, and the children of the poor could ignore educational failure by seeking employment. Like the telephone company,
public education had a captive market and no competition; it was
a benign monopoly and, like the telephone company, it dismissed
its occasional critics as cranks.

That may not have been a very healthy state of affairs; even
so, what changed it?

The list is so familiar that, rather than attempting to explain
the major factors, I will simply name them: more demanding job
requirements, stemming from the increased intellectual and technological complexity of modern employment; a new militance
among ethnic minorities, proceeding from the tension between
extraordinary affluence among some Americans and continuing
poverty for others; a new perception of social injustice, rising from
a communications explosion that brought the squalor of Harlem

into the living rooms of Winnetka and the comfort of the suburbs onto the TV sets of the ghetto. These factors have operated across the spectrum of our national concerns, producing a new demand for "participatory democracy," for a layman's voice in making decisions that were formerly reserved to professionals and officials.

In elementary and secondary education, of course, we have a rash of demands for participation in the decision-making process: teacher power, student power, black power, flower power. These power blocs, each with specific interests that sometimes coincide but often conflict, constitute a new electorate in education. Indeed, they constitute a new politics of education.

How does this new politics affect the boardman? It complicates his job by injecting the probability of political conflict — and most school boardmen and superintendents are unequipped for politics. For decades we have said, "Let's keep politics out of education, and education out of politics." This axiom stemmed from the day when teaching jobs were regarded as political plums, to be handed out by a victorious party to unemployed supporters. Thus it made good sense at one time.

As long as we have public schools, however, and as long as public funds support the education of our young, politics will affect, if not absolutely dictate, school policy and practice. The hundreds of bond issues offered local voters every year, community attitudes toward federal aid, the response of state legislators to the specific needs of densely populated cities and sparsely populated rural areas — all reinforce the point that education is in politics up to its neck.

Yet our revered piety about keeping politics out of education has had its effect, by deflecting educational controversy away from politicians; at the first sign of public uproar about the schools, mayors and aldermen hoist the banner of political purity and proclaim their staunch refusal to dictate educational policy. The school board and the superintendent are on the spot, left alone in the middle of a highly charged political situation without any political weapons.

What can a board member do about this situation? Two things. First, he ought to develop a sense of perspective that balances political necessity against legal prerogatives.

Second, he'd best develop political weapons of his own. Right away.

Boardmen cannot, on the one hand, flatly reject the demands from their new electorate for a voice in making decisions that affect the lives of their children; on the other hand, they must not abandon their legal responsibilities for making final policy. Even though there is room for a new democracy in education — indeed, we *must* make room for it — we cannot go to the extreme of regarding educational policy-making as a populist free-for-all in which every man has equal say. The perhaps nasty but nonetheless solid truth is that every man should not have equal say.

Democracy can go only so far in any professional concern. We respect the skill of the surgeon, and the years of education and experience he has invested in refining his ability. We do not argue, "Look here, I'm as American as you are, and this is a democratic country; give me the scalpel and let me take out that appendix." Knowledge is not democratic: we do not determine the square root of three by taking a vote on it.

In the same way, while the new educational electorate is entirely within its rights in complaining about school deficiencies, it remains the task of the school board members and their appointed deputy, the superintendent, to translate *complaints* about educational deficiencies and *demands* for school improvement into a *program* — just as a doctor translates a patient's complaints about the symptoms of poor health into a prescribed therapy. But just as the doctor does not allow the patient to write the prescription, so the school board and the superintendent cannot abdicate their legal obligation to make the final decisions about *prudent public policy* and *effective educational plans.*

The problem facing boardmen is to make their just claims to experience and knowledge stick. After doing their level best to give citizens' demands an honest hearing, they must have the courage to choose an unpopular view when necessary, and must develop the public support to make that view prevail as often as possible.

And that, in turn, brings up the second challenge facing boardmen in their dealings with the new educational electorate: They must develop political weapons of their own.

How? Political power flows from numbers. Boardmen and superintendents are outnumbered by parents, by teachers, by students; no matter how exalted their position in a community, no matter how strong their traditional influence, each boardman and superintendent has only one vote at the ballot box. How are they to convert their minority voice into a persuasive sentiment representing the wishes of a majority?

By proof of performance. Just as a surgeon upholds his claim to expert, specialized knowledge by operating successfully on the sick and an attorney maintains his claim to expertise by winning favorably verdicts, so those responsible for public education must be able to *prove* that they know more about running effective schools than any other citizen chosen at random.

Yet those involved in public education are poorly prepared to argue the just claims of professionalism, because we've resisted time and again the one and only test of specialized competence: proof of results.

Our public schools enroll more than 44 million students, employ nearly two million teachers, and account for the expenditure of at least $30 billion in tax funds each year. We have all kinds of measurements of where this money goes: We can pin down per-capita expenditures to the penny, state how much any school district in the country spent for construction and debt service, and enumerate pupil-teacher ratios until the sun goes down.

But we have virtually no measurement of the results that such an enterprise yields. We do not know, for example, what it costs on the average to increase a youngster's reading ability by one year; all we know is what it costs to keep him seated for one year. All the indices we have measure the skill of boardmen and superintendents as financial managers; not a single one evaluates our skill as educational managers.

If we are to make the new democracy in public education function properly, we must provide proof of performance to our constituents. We must move beyond showing the public where its educational expenditure went (teacher salaries, textbooks, new buildings) to showing the public what it *received* for those expenditures — youngsters who moved from one level of scholastic achievement to a higher one.

And if our analyses of performance show that this achievement is lacking, then we must take our medicine like men and, if the public will give us another chance, go back to the old drawing board and revise our blueprints for education.

The name of the game, in short, is *conflict,* and those who cannot accept the prospect of entering into public debate to argue for the programs which they are convinced will improve public education, and to submit fact, rational analysis, and empirical evidence to buttress their convictions, would do well to leave the public education arena before they get hurt. And those who remain must learn to accept with good grace the defeats that will inevitably come their way, and must refuse to abandon the fight for public support because their pride has been hurt.

Remaining a board member in our time requires, in essence, an act of faith in the capacity of the democratic process to operate effectively in a specialized endeavor. How nicely that faith was summed.up by Jerome Bruner when he said this:

"Whatever I know about policy making reinforces the conviction that technicians and scientists often lack the kind of follow-up commitment that is the prerequisite of wise social policy. I cannot work up much enthusiasm for philosopher-kings, doctor-kings, or even mixed-committee kings. The political process . . . is slow, perhaps, but it is committed to the patient pursuit of the possible."

Those of us in policy-making positions in public education can either sigh for the good old days when the humble voter had no voice in designing educational policy, or we can realize that our new electorate gives us a power we never had before. Whether we learn to live with that power, to channel it as well as live with it, depends on our skill in blending a responsiveness to the public will with an assertion of the rights of expertise.

"The trouble with Congress," H. L. Mencken once said, "is that it *does* represent the American people." While all of us may sometimes share Mencken's exasperation with Congress and the democratic process in general, let us hope that all our institutions continue to be infected with this democratic malady. Judging from the results since Congress first sat in 1787, neither the people of the United States nor their representatives have done such a bad job.

Nor, I am convinced, will they do a bad job now that they have forced their way into the throne-room of public education. We boardmen-kings and administrator-kings, having been forced to abdicate our autocratic rule, must now join the rest of our fellow-citizens in the patient pursuit of the possible.   □

Nolan Estes is Superintendent of Schools, Dallas, Texas.

VII

WHAT IS ACCOUNTABILITY?

by Kenneth P. Mortimer

"Evaluation is concerned primarily with educational effectiveness, whereas accountability is concerned with effectiveness and efficiency."

What is meant by accountability? How is the term used as it applies to problems in higher education? Pleas for increased accountability in the expenditure of funds, for the effectiveness of education and for holding faculty members and students accountable for their actions and behavior are commonplace. The multiplicity of uses of the term accountability has resulted in a situation in which it is difficult to ascertain what reforms are necessary to achieve it and what activities should be revised.

The confusion results from three different areas of concern which will be classified as managerial accountability; accountability versus evaluation; and accountability versus responsibility. These three classifications are not mutually exclusive, as will be shown, but summarize a good deal of the content of the literature dealing with accountability in higher education.

Managerial Accountability

Control is one of the functions of management in almost any organization.[1] The mechanics of organization control are rooted in the basic elements of classic organization theory (Koontz and O'Donnell, 1959).

> The control function includes those activities which are designed to compel events to conform to plans. It is thus the measurement and correction of activities of subordinates to

Reprinted from *Accountability in Higher Education,* ERIC Clearinghouse on Higher Education – The George Washington University, February, 1972.

> assure the accomplishment of plans. . . . Compelling events to
> conform to plans really means locating the persons responsible
> for negative deviations from standards and making certain that
> the necessary steps are taken to ensure improved performance.
> Thus, the control of things is achieved through the control of
> people (pp. 38-39).

The optimum control situation for organizational accountability is one in which rewards and sanctions are distributed so
that those whose performance deviates from the plan will be pun-
ished (Etzioni, 1964). Holding organizations and their actors accountable for performance is one of the prime purposes of managerial control.

According to Spiro (1969) there are two basic schools of
thought as to the best means of enforcing the accountability of
administrators in public administration: the legal view and the
constitutional view.

> [Legalists tend] to advocate accountability which is clearly de-
> fined as to both its content and the means and routes by which
> it can be enforced. The logic of this position leads to advocacy
> of a very clear chain of command and enforcement of account-
> ability through two channels only: first, the courts and discip-
> linary control of departments; and second, the authority exer-
> cised over public servants by ministers who are accountable to
> a representative assembly (p. 83).

This is a rather simplistic view of accountability and is chiefly
relevant where there is a unitary line of accountability to a single
recognized authority such as a dictator, a monarch, or a body poli-
tic which derives its authority through coercion, heredity or elected representatives. In this situation the administrator is clearly accountable, at least in theory, to one entity.

The constitutional view of accountability gives wider latitude
to administrative discretion as an integral part of the organizational environment. Adherents of this view tend to argue that a rigid
definition of managerial accountability is neither possible nor desirable. Administrators need to exercise discretion in performing
their duties and should be held accountable in terms of several
mutually complementary standards. These standards emanate from
a variety of sources including the people as organized into pressure
or interest groups. The legislature, the chief executive, a profesion
and the courts.

The constitutional view recognizes that duly elected representatives of the people are often in conflict over what is in the public interest and that administrators clearly exercise a good deal of discretion in interpreting the laws passed by a legislature, signed by a chief executive, and interpreted, when necessary, by the courts. The administrator also is held accountable for the exercise of this discretion by those intimately concerned with the issue involved. Individual citizens or organized interest groups attempt to get administrators to exercise discretion in favor of the interests they represent (Mortimer and McConnell, 1970). Finally, administrators who are members of professions, e.g., accountants, lawyers, or engineers, are held accountable for implementing the canons of that profession.

The debate over organizational accountability and control in higher education reflects this contrast between the legal and constitutional views of accountability. Some of the advocates of collective bargaining believe that legally binding contracts will result in imposing accountability to a rule of law (Sherman and Loeffer, 1971). "By the emergence of a rule of law in the university, we mean the evolution of a system of accountability and a concomitant pattern of standards that attempt to govern the behavior of the institution and its agents." The emphasis is in limiting the discretionary power of administrators and faculty performing administrative functions to deviate from the terms of a legal contract. Although the scope of the contract varies among institutions, such issues as salaries, qualifications for rank, tenure, and other academic personnel policies, grievances, selection of certain administrators, and selected decisionmaking procedures may be involved.

Quite another view of accountability is suggested by Kingman Brewster, Jr., President of Yale (1971). He suggests presidential accountability be achieved through a periodic and explicit renewal of his tenure. Rather than being held accountable for each specific decision, the president would be evaluated and held accountable for his overall performance for a specified period of time. This would allow him to exercise discretion and leadership in interpreting and implementing the various goals of the institution and the demands of its many constituents.

In practice, both the legal and constitutional view of accountability are present in institutions of higher education. Neither view should be regarded as the ultimate answer.

Accountability versus Evaluation

There is, admittedly, a great deal of overlap between the concepts of accountability and evaluation as they are used in the literature. Harnett (1971) says there are some basic distinctions between evaluation and accountability.

Evaluation is concerned primarily with educational effectiveness, whereas accountability is concerned with effectiveness *and efficiency.* Effectiveness is the degree to which the organization succeeds in whatever it is trying to do; efficiency is an organization's capacity to achieve results with a given expenditure of resources. The accountability expert is involved in assessing both effectiveness and efficiency.

Second, evaluation tends to be a process which is internal to the organization with respect to the stimulus for the evaluative effort and who participates in it. The process of institutional self-study, for example, provides an opportunity for the organization to assess its own strengths and weaknesses and thereby to improve its operations and educational programs. Accountability, on the other hand, carries with it the notion of external judgment. Accountability has the connotation of vindictive rather than affirmative judgment about the institution's activities, i.e., "the public has to know how its money is being spent."

Another distinction which Harnett makes between evaluation and accountability is the skills and orientations of those who perform each process. Evaluators are often psychologists or educational researchers, whereas those who assess accountability tend to have backgrounds in business and finance. The latter group tend to stress efficiency-oriented criteria, such as output models; whereas educational researchers often stress inputs, like admissions criteria and teaching. Those who are arguing that the accountability of *institutions* is crucial tend to favor evaluating institutional *outputs,* e.g., student learning, degrees awarded. The emphases are diametrical, with one likely to evaluate teaching and the other likely to evaluate student *learning,* while in the process attempting to hold the institution accountable for what is learned rather than what is taught. The latter emphasis is illustrated by the following statements of what accountability should mean to community colleges (Roueche, Baker, and Brownell, 1971).

Accountability accentuates results—it aims squarely at what comes out of an educational system rather than what goes into it.

It assumes that if no learning takes place, no teaching has taken place.

Accountability requires measurement:

> ... modern educational techniques enable us to achieve accept-
> able evidence of learning. The concept of accountability is
> based on specifically defined objectives, measurement tech-
> niques that determine exactly what the teacher intends to ac-
> complish, and the instructional methods that guarantee most
> students will obtain the objectives.

Accountability assumes and shifts responsibility— it assumes responsibility for the success or failure of individual schools and pupils and shifts primary learning responsibility away from the student to the school.

Accountability permeates the college community:

> Accountability implies that two-year colleges must be account-
> able externally to the community and that colleges must be ac-
> countable internally to the students who pass through their
> doors. This state is achieved when students from the commun-
> ity enter the college, find a program that is compatible with
> their goals, persist in college until the goal is reached and then
> become productive members of the community.

Accountability versus Responsibility

There is a growing concern in higher education about the distinction between accountability and responsibility. For example, the American Association of University Professor's Statement on Government of Colleges and Universities (1966) speaks of operating responsibility and authority, delegating responsibility, the faculty's primary responsibility, of students who may desire to participate responsibly in the government of the institution and of the special obligations of the president. Arp (1969) proposes that a university accept "the unequivocal responsibility for not producing or communicating knowledge without at the same time exploring and communicating the limits of completeness of that knowledge and its probable consequences applied in current contexts."

Neff (1969) proposes a useful distinction between the terms accountability and responsibility. "I would propose that 'responsibility' be used to refer only to the voluntary assumption of an obligation, while 'accountability' be used to refer to the legal liability assigned to the performance or nonperformance of certain acts or duties".

The distinction between *a legal or formal liability* and *assuming a voluntary obligation* is crucial. Most social systems can enforce standards of accountability, while responsibility is often not enforceable because it is closely allied with individual freedom. The organization must decide, either collectively or otherwise, for which behavior it will hold its citizens accountable—but the individual has the freedom, in a democracy, to decide which obligations he will assume. Responsibility "consists of two distinct relations: the act of responding to something and the assumption of an obligation."

While the essence of responsibility is individual judgment, the concept provides for collective judgment, or what Neff terms academic responsibility, which is a "common responsiveness within a university to institutional and professional norms and values, and the collective voluntary assumption of the obligation of furthering these norms and values." Many colleges and universities are adopting codes of professional ethics or statements of rights and responsibilities so as to define the differences between individual and collective or academic responsibility. There appear to be certain manifestations of academic responsibility for which individual faculty members can be held accountable; for example, teaching loads, meeting their classes, holding office hours, and publication output. Presumably the institution is justified in asking an individual to leave if he does not meet some of these standards. The current furor over administrative supervision of academic programs illustrates the kinds of activities for which many believe faculty can legitimately be held accountable (Hitch, 1970).

> Our experiences have shown that it is necessary to provide more specifically and in detail for the prevention and correction of abuses in the conduct of courses. I think it is essential to state some principles about responsibility and authority.
>
> 1. The format of the conduct of a course. Methods for determining and authorizing justifiable changes in format need to be made clearer and more specific. . . .
>   (a) Classes and examinations are to be held at the times and places officially scheduled by the department chairman and the Registrar. . . .
>   (b) Each instructor and teaching assistant is responsible for keeping his instructional appointments at the assigned times and places. . . .

2. The subject matter of a course and the use of time in class. The instructor in a course is obligated to teach the course in reasonable conformity with the subject and course description. . . .

The purpose of such guidelines is not to restrict the legitimate freedom of the faculty member to teach his courses according to his best judgment but to establish common understanding of reasonable limits on what is and what is not professionally ethical and to provide checks against illegitimate practices.

The preceding is an example of an attempt to specify behavior for which faculty members can be held accountable. Should such a statement be adopted it would constitute an example of academic responsibility and be used as a guide to control excessively deviant behavior.

The term accountability has at least three major applications to higher education. First, in the management of higher education there is the view that accountability be defined in legal terms. In practice administrators are accountable to a variety of nonlegal but equally demanding interests and constituents. Second, evaluation is part of accountability but the latter term is more encompassing. Third, while responsibility and accountability are often used interchangeably, Neff urges a distinction between voluntarily assuming an obligation and the legal liability attached to the performance of certain acts.   □

Kenneth P. Mortimer is a Research Associate at the Center for the Study of Higher Education and Assistant Professor of Education at the Pennsylvania State University.

---

[1]Organizational control is a far more complicated subject than indicated here. See Tannenbaum (1968) for a more complete discussion.

VIII

ACCOUNTABILITY DEFINED

by Marvin C. Alkin
University of California, Los Angeles

It is over simplistic to say that schools are accountable or they are not. Different areas of participation and negotiated responsibility suggest the need to consider different accountability "types." In this article we propose to view accountability as composed of three types: goal accountability, program accountability, and outcome accountability. These derive from an attempt to answer the question, "Who is accountable to whom and for what?"

Introduction

The public has lost faith in educational institutions. Traditional acceptance of educational programs on the basis of their past performance and apparent but unsubstantiated worth is no longer the rule. The public has demanded that schools demonstrate that resources are being utilized "properly". But this has meant far more than mere financial accounting, to ensure that funds have not been illegally spent or embezzled. What is demanded instead is that schools demonstrate that the outcomes they are producing are worth the dollar investment provided by communities. In short, what has been called for is a system of "educational accountability."

But educational accountability is very much like other abstract virtues such as patriotism and truthfulness: which are universally acknowledged but not amenable to facile description. Lack of adequate description has been one of the major shortcomings of accountability. The reader investigating the subject for the first time becomes immediately innundated with a plethora of

Reprinted from Accountability Defined, *Evaluation Comment,* 3 (3), 1972. Center for the Study of Evaluation, University of California, Los Angeles.

of views, schemes, mechanisms and, for that matter, a multitude of definitions.

To say that discussion of accountability has been confusing and that definitions of accountability have been amorphous and imprecise is to understate the problem. Barro (1970) says that the basic premise of accountability is that "professional education should be held responsible for educational outcomes—for what children learn." Many teachers and teacher organizations have a negative connotation such as "is for punishment." Some school administrators feel accountability can be used to eliminate some of the "deadwood" in teaching. Boards of trustees frequently feel the same way about eliminating the "deadwood" and "overstaffing" in administration. Some economists view accountability as a panacean information system which will cure educational ills by ensuring the wisest allocation of scarce resources. To many people, then, *accountability* is the answer. It is "in", however, in a variety of ways for different kinds of proponents.

Popham (1970) asserts that "Educational accountability means that the instructional system designer takes responsibility for achieving the kinds of instructional objectives which are previously explicated." Lopez (1970) casts the definition in a social context: "Accountability refers to the process of expecting each member of an organization to answer to someone for doing specific things according to specific plans and against certain timetables to accomplish tangible performance results." Lieberman (1970) asserts that the objective of accountability is to relate results to resources and efforts in ways that are useful for policy making, resource allocation, or compensation.

Smith (1971) suggests three kinds of accountability; program accountability, process accountability, and fiscal accountability. *Program* accountability is concerned with the quality of the work carried on and whether or not it met the goals set for it. *Process* accountability asks whether the procedures used to perform the research (teaching) were adequate in terms of the time and effort spent on the work, and whether the experiments (lessons) were carried out as promised. *Fiscal* accountability has to do with whether items purchased were used for the project, program, etc.

Lessinger (1970) has said, "Accountability is the product of a process; at its most basic level, it means that an agent, public or private, entering into a contractual agreement to perform a service will be answerable for performing according to agreed-upon terms, within an established time period, and with a stipulated use of resources and performance standards."

Definition

In this paper we will tentatively settle on a definition of accountability as:

Accountability is a negotiated relationship in which the participants agree in advance to accept specified rewards and costs on the basis of evaluation findings as to the attainment of specified ends.

— The essence of this definition is that a negotiated relationship exists in which each of the participants agree in advance as to the criteria (evaluation findings) that will be used to determine acceptability. Furthermore, the level of attainment on those criteria in order to achieve acceptability is pre-specified. Finally, the negotiants stipulate a set of rewards and penalties that will attach to compliance/non-compliance.

At the heart of all of the above noted elements is the concept of "negotiation". Negotiation, for example, is suggested in the kind of dialogue which leads to mutual acceptance of a position, or in the acceptance of a negotiated, specified end. Negotiation frequently involves the allowable constraints, such as the students to be worked with and the instructional materials to be utilized. One major form of negotiated relationship, although not the only one, is the written contract. A contractual agreement will specify the locus of problem solving and areas of responsibility between the negotiants. To establish these relationships, a contract will provide with utmost explicitness and clarity, the following:

- A set of stated constraints
- The negotiated ends in light of the constraints
- Designation of responsibility in terms of who is responsible for what, to whom, and when
- Criteria for judging attainment of ends
- Specification of the rewards and costs to include payment and penalty schedules

Before such contractual explicitness can be achieved in terms of relationships between negotiants in a system of accountability, we must first address some contextual considerations and discuss the major segments within that context. Without such specification it is virtually impossible to adequately address the locus of problem solving and areas of responsibility in any manageable form.

We view the three major segments of the accountability context as: (1) goals and objectives, (2) programs, (3) program outcomes. A system of accountability can be functional only in those educational sub-systems which have clearly defined goals and objectives. These goals and objectives derive from interactions with various constituencies whose views are thought to be relevant and whose priorities are reflected in the specified outcomes. For these objectives, which in turn are related to the broader goals, there are specific, clearly defined, and validated instructional programs or strategies. The instructional programs or strategies have been validated to the extent that there are specific product specifications demonstrating the success of the programs relative to the stated objectives of the program for various kinds of population groups, one of whom is the group for which it will be employed. A further element of this context is a specific procedure for measuring the program's outcomes in terms of the stipulated objectives. To the extent that the school context approaches such a rational effort, it is possible to have an accountability system.

Accountability types

Part of the differing conceptions of accountability undoubtedly stem from our insistence that accountability is unidimensional. It is over simplistic to say that schools are accountable or they are not. For each area of the context there can be different role participants. Different areas of participation and responsibility suggest the need to consider different accountability "types"; the three components outlined above suggest that there are perhaps three types of accountability.

We propose to designate the three types of accountability as: *goal accountability, program accountability,* and *outcome accountability.* These three accountability types derive from an attempt to answer the question, "Who is accountable to whom and for what?" When this question is considered with respect to the context areas

noted on the preceding page, we note that different participants
are involved on various occasions.

The first area to be considered is *goal accountability*. School
boards are accountable (or should be) to the public for everything
that they do. But the foundation of this accountability relationship is in educational goals. School boards are accountable to the
public for the proper selection of goals. After all, school boards
are legally supposed to function as the lay group expressing the
desires and wishes of a broader constituency as to what should be
the goals and objectives of the educational program. This determination is clearly within the domain of the public's review responsibility. In goal accountability, school boards are accountable
to the public for ensuring that the proper goals and objectives are
being pursued in the school program.

After goals and objectives are selected, responsibility rests
somehwere for the selection of instructional strategies deemed
most effective for achieving the stipulated goals and objectives.
This responsibility for *program accountability* rests generally with
the school administration and other school personnel designated
by administration. If we conceive of the teachers as being program
operators and intend to hold them accountable for the outcomes
of their activities, then clearly they may only be held accountable
within the constraints of the programs with which they have been
provided. The responsibility for program accountability rests with
administrators and other members of the professional staff engaged in the process of program selection, modification, and
adoption.

In program accountability these administrators and other district personnel, though again ultimately responsible to the public,
are specifically accountable to the school board for maintaining a
program which is appropriate for meeting a set of stipulated objectives. We cannot hold a machine operator responsible for his
products until we have demonstrated that the machine he has been
provided with has the capability for producing that outcome. We
cannot expect a printing press operator to produce 100 copies a
minute on a machine whose maximum output is 50 copies per
minute. We cannot expect a racetrack driver to push 300 miles an
hour out of an automobile whose limit is far below that standard.

If we are to follow this line of argument to its logical conclusion, then clearly, producers of program components (let us refer

to these as instructional products) must be held accountable for the products they produce. This is an area of accountability about which we have heard very little. While there is considerable demand that the classroom teacher be accountable, where is the outcry for accountability on the part of textbook producers? Who demands that producers of film strips, films, and supplemental materials present the specifications of their products in terms of outcomes that may be anticipated?

As part of the standards implied in program accountability, a demand should be placed on those to be held accountable for instructional programs that the producible program outcomes be stipulated in terms of the various sets of constraints and the varying inputs that might be encountered. That is, one cannot merely stipulate, without a considerable loss of accuracy in description, that a given product will produce objectives A, B, and C at a given level of achievement. It is also necessary to indicate what the expectations would be for different characteristics of student inputs (for different student groups). This is similar to the example previously discussed in which a printing press operator might be expected to produce 100 copies a minute on a given machine. It is important in that example to consider such things as the quality and weight of the paper to be used, color of the ink, type of marker plate, etc. In the racecar example it is necessary to be aware of the performance standards for different kinds of roads and weather conditions. Similarly, in educational accountability it is important to have an indication of the performance standards for each program in terms of a variety of input constraints.

With respect to program accountability a difficult and confused area is the role of teachers in, and as part of, instructional programs. The confusion is amply demonstrated by the diverse views as to what is meant by "teacher accountability". For example, there are those who maintain that teacher accountability is determined on the basis of input standards for teachers. That is, a teacher is accountable if he demonstrates that he is an able teacher in terms of his ability to teach and by satisfactory application of his skills in terms of the amount of effort put forth on his job. This view of the teacher's role basically considers the teacher as a program component, a part of the instructional program. Under such a definition of teacher accountability one merely looks at teachers as a potential input or program component. Here teacher accountability is judged, in the same way that a textbook, film, or a film strip is considered; the accountability task under such a viewpoint is to ensure the quality of the teacher input. Thus, we may use teacher performance tests as a basis for determining whether teachers participating in the program meet a standard of accountability in terms of their ability to teach.

Within this same definition of the role of teachers, but beyond certification of teacher-input quality, there is a further consideration of the accountability task. This area of accountability responsibility relates to the proper utilization of teacher input. That is, accountability requirements demand that there be an assurance that the inputs (teachers) are working an appropriate number of hours using those skills considered to be appropriate. The notion of teachers *as part of* instructional programs requires accountability examination in terms of input and process evaluation.

A second view of teacher accountability is one in which the teacher is urged to be responsible for the quality of student outputs. In this view the teacher is considered as an instructional manager utilizing a program whose capabilities have already been determined. Here the teacher is held responsible for the outcomes of his management of that program. This type of accountability we will refer to as *outcome accountability.* In this framework we do not question the teacher on process characteristics such as score on a teacher performance test, or the amount of time spent in the classroom, or the processes used. Instead, what is said is, "Here is a program whose capabilities have been demonstrated. Show that you are able to produce student outcomes of the desired type and standards using that program."

In *outcome accountability,* an instructional leader (usually a teacher) is accountable to administration for specified pupil outcomes thought to be a function of teacher management of the instructional program. That is, a teacher manages an instructional program which has certain product capabilities; the job is to determine whether the teacher has managed the program in such a way as to achieve standards or criteria that might be expected from the program.

We have previously said, however, that teachers may only be held accountable within the constraints of the program with which they have been provided. There are those who would maintain, however, that the accountability concern should not focus upon these constraints, since the teacher, to a great extent, *is* the program. In this light, in terms of financial outlay for program operation, those costs incurred directly by the teacher amount to the major portion of the available budget. Further, there is sufficient evidence that program constraints have minimal, impact upon student outcomes. One would not deny that the teacher incurs the greatest amount of cost in program operation or that program constraints have only a small effect. Yet teachers do work with constraints, such as type of students, kind of text, size of classroom, etc. Though the effects of these constraints may be small, they do, to varying degrees, affect the management of the program and to that extent must be considered in outcome accountability.

Accountability Types: Summary

We have already discussed three major accountability types (goal, program, and outcome) and have indicated a response for each relative to the question, "Who is accountable to whom and for what?" A summary description of each of these types, along with three sets of factors, is presented in Chart 1: (1) Who is accountable — the specific individual or group bearing the responsibility, (2) To whom — the individual or group demanding accountability, (3) For what — specific tasks required.

Chart 1:			
Accountability Types			
	Who is Accountable	**To Whom (Primary Responsibility)**	**For What**
Goal Accountability	School Board	Public	Goal & Objective Selection
Program Accountability	School District Management	School Board	Development and/or Selection of Instructional Programs Appropriate for Stated Objectives
Outcome Accountability	Instructional Manager (i.e., Teacher)	School District Management	Producing Program Outcomes Consistent with Pre-Selected Objectives at a Performance Standard Appropriate for the Instructional Program

Implications of Various Accountability Schemes

A number of schemes have been presented for achieving greater accountability in schools. Many of these, such as the voucher plan or performance contracting, have been thought of as almost synonymous with accountability. It is important to recognize, however, that these accountability schemes cannot be understood properly without considering to which accountability types they are addressed (e.g., goal accountability, program accountability, outcome ability) and how they fit within the accountability context previously described.

We will consider three accountability schemes that are fairly exemplary of the kinds of proposals presently made and which cover a broad range of accountability types. These three schemes are the voucher plan, performance contracting with an external contractor, and performance contracting with a teacher.

Under the voucher plan the school passes on the responsibility for all three kinds of accountability. By giving fund grants directly to parents for their expenditure on a program of their own choosing, the school is in essence relieving itself of the full accountability responsibility. No longer must schools be accountable for goals, because parents with funds in hand will choose educational institutions or programs having goals compatible with their preferences. By such a choice parents and not public schools will be holding their own contractor responsible for both program and outcome accountability. Thus the voucher plan represents a complete irresponsibility on the part of public schools in terms of accountability.

Under performance contracting with an external contractor, while the school retains the responsibility for goal accountability, the contractor becomes responsible for program and outcome accountability. In essence, appropriate goals have been decided upon for a program; the school has consulted with various constituencies about the relevance of various goal areas and has selected a goal or set of goals most worthy of consideration. The external performance contractor is held responsible for the creation of a program to meet these goals as well as for the implementation and management of that program. That is, the external contractor must show both program and outcome accountability. If the community complains about the program and feels that the schools have not achieved the desired outcomes, it is the responsibility of the external contractor; he has obviously failed to do his job. The only way the school can be held accountable is if there is criticism that the goals being pursued are incorrect or inappropriate.

In a system of performance contracting in which the teacher rather than the external contractor is the instructional manager, the school delegates the responsibility only of outcome accountability. That is, the goals have been determined within the school; the program has been determined within the school, including a specification of its capabilities, and the teacher as an instructional manager is to be held accountable for program outcomes. If the teacher is unable to attain educational outcomes equal to a pre-specified standard, and that standard is considered appropriate for the given program and students, then it is the teacher who is held accountable. On the other hand, if there is a question about the adequacy of the program itself for achieving the specified goals and objectives, then the school itself (or the school administrator) is found short on the accountability criteria.

What we have demonstrated is that there are three types of accountability and there are various schemes that have been presented whereby different agencies or individuals take the responsibility for various types of accountability. In developing a total accountability program, apparently the first decision to be made is the locus of the responsibility for each of the three accountability types.   □

IX

APPLIED ACCOUNTABILITY

by William A. Deterline

"Many companies, both large and small, many government agencies, and instructional projects on schools of all kinds have demonstrated that accountability can be implemented on an efficient, cost-effective basis, and made a way of life. None of it is easy, but hell, the things that we are doing now aren't easy either, so we might as well do it right!"

Objectives

Upon completion of this article, including the search for answers to the questions at the end of the work, you should be able to do the following:

1. Explain what "accountability" means in the broad sense.
2. Describe what impact accountability would have on your training/education setting; or, if you are not involved full time in training or education, describe the impact that accountability would have on a hypothetical training/education operation.
3. Explain what is meant by the "information presentation" approach to instruction, and describe briefly three objections that the author expresses to that approach. Prepare at least a 100-word rebuttal to one of his objections.
4. Clarify the distinction the author makes between *training* and *education.* From your own experience—either as an instructor or student—describe an example of each, without going back to your elementary or secondary school courses.
5. Describe each of the three accountability "directives." Describe, in terms of a real or hypothetical course, how each of these directives might be implemented.

6. In terms of your own involvement with instructional design, development, implementation, or management, describe the following:

   a. Changes that you could make now, under present conditions, with your present skills, to utilize any aspect of the accountability approach.
   b. Changes that could not be made because of existing constraints; and describe those constraints.
   c. Skills or methodologies that appear to be required, but which you do not understand, or do not think are feasible.
   d. Procedures, techniques, skills that appear to be a necessary part of applied accountability that probably do not exist where you are, and which would have to be obtained or developed.

7. Considering your answer to 6a, above, prepare a plan detailing the steps that you would take, and then, ideally, *go take them.*

Subject Matter Experts, Skilled Performers and Instruction

Consider a group of people all doing basically the same job. The group might be a group of surgeons in a hospital, a group of assembly line workers in a factory, or a group of white collar workers doing related but not completely similar activities. One day it becomes necessary to appoint a supervisor or coordinator for the group: a chief surgeon, a foreman or a chief clerk. Too often, what happens is that the best performer gets the job, and sometimes the hospital loses its best surgeon to administrative detail, which he fouls up; the plant loses an excellent worker and gets an incompetent foreman; and the office loses a highly skilled clerk and gets a lousy supervisor. This is one example of the Peter Principle in action: people tend to be promoted out of jobs they do well, and eventually they end up in a job they don't do well; there is, therefore, no reason to promote them, and there they sit, having risen to the level of their own incompetence!

That sad example is all too familiar. There is another, related kind of problem that is neither as obvious nor as well-known. There is a myth that says, "Any competent subject matter expert and/or skilled performer of a job or activity is, by the nature of that competence alone, automatically a highly competent teacher

of the competence." Often—but not always—those two competen-
cies *do* go together. And because we see that happen frequently,
we apparently assume that it is true all the time. But we have all
encountered many exceptions: The instructor of whom we have
said, "He knows his subject, but he is way over my head," or "It is
obvious that he knows his stuff, but he sure can't teach it!" So,
sometimes, for one reason or another, a competent subject matter
expert is assigned the task of participating in the design, development and implementation of a course of instruction. And sometimes we lose a competent worker or supervisor, and find him
operating at a level of relative incompetence in the training field.

There is another myth, perpetuated by much of the training
and education community, that says that teaching means a competent subject matter expert *presenting information,* and then,
through testing, identifying learning deficiencies—and blaming
them on the students.

Some people believe those myths—really *believe* them. Other
people act as if they believe them, because it is certainly easier
that way. But those myths are not true. Being an effective teacher
requires more than subject matter expertise, and consists of more
than a technically accurate and clear and interesting presentation
of information.

Visit schools, colleges, universities, industrial, military and
government training facilities, and you will find many people acting out the myths. What sense does a lecture make? If the students
need the information being presented by the lecturer, why make
them try to take accurate and complete notes while the lecturer is
talking? Why not record and transcribe them, and pass out copies?
If the lecture is actually a lecture/discussion, with considerable
participation by the students, again, why not eliminate the lecture
—the information presenting part of it—and concentrate on interactive discussion? Get the information to the students by more
effective and efficient means, and use the discussion periods for
diagnostic, remedial application, implication and practical con-
sideration-types of discussion. The most obvious thing for us to
do, when, as subject matter experts we are asked to become involved in course development or teaching, is to do what our teachers did to us. So we do, and it doesn't work very well. But since all
failures and ineffective aspects of our instruction are slyly laid on
the students, in the form of a grade or rating, we never really have
to face the facts of our own incompetence in the field of instruction.

Consider your own job, whatever it might be: would you expect a brand new person—a cook, nuclear physicist, accountant, mechanic, bank president, clerk, or confidence man—to be able to walk in and do your job without any training, or without being taught any tricks of the trade? Would you expect him to sit at the desk next to yours and with little direction do the same thing that you are doing? Not very likely. *Yet we do exactly that* and perpetuate those myths when we say, "Hey, subject matter expert, sit down here and design and develop a course to teach something." Where is he supposed to get the skills, and procedures, and techniques to do it with? That's where the first myth comes in: if he can do a job, we assume that he has all the necessary instructional skills, and that isn't fair to him or to his students. So he relies on the other myth: he prepares barrages of information to present to the students.

How does he decide *what* information to present? Intuitively, from his own experience, or from reference materials that also present information. And there is a very real limiting factor. In education and training for scores of years we have attempted to present information as skillfully as possible, using a great number of methods, audiovisual devices, games, demonstrations, all designed toward the impossible, ultimate form of the second myth: that there is a *perfect* presentation or information possible, such that every student will learn everything, understand everything, and remember it all. When we concentrate on the presentation of information, we strive for that unattainable *perfect presentation.* No one has ever gotten there; most fall far short.

Accountability

Most of us are held accountable for our work. We are expected to earn our salaries by producing results, by carrying out the tasks assigned to us with at least a minimum acceptable level of competence. Certainly we tend to look for and give excuses when our performance is less than it should be, but that only works a little bit, sometimes. Basically, we are accountable and are held to be accountable. There is, however, a never-never quality about the instructional world that says, "You are the professional, you are the competent person here, and the students are dependent upon you. Yet we won't hold you accountable if they fail to learn from you; we'll blame them. We will hold them accountable for any failures, deficiencies and incompetence in your teaching. And we will use the instructional setting as a screening device: if the students can not learn in spite of what goes on here, we will penalize them. Their records will show that their intelligence and motivation were not enough; and sometimes those records will haunt them, and affect their careers, and their lives. You will not be affected in any way. You are not accountable for the results of your activities."

Now, however, we find education talking about "accountability" in teaching and in the operation of schools. Teachers and schools are to be held accountable for the results of instruction, and rewarded or not rewarded depending on those results. What is a teacher to do? Suppose a teacher had worked very hard, very conscientiously, trying to achieve perfect presentations. That teacher learned the hard way that there are limiting factors—constraints—and that reality and practicality prevented that ideal from being attained. Why should that teacher welcome the notion of accountability?

Some parts of the training world have been able to avoid accountability because of the nature of the subject matter being taught. Some topics are so ill-chosen, so irrelevant, that it doesn't really matter what happens—whather the students learn or not! A training manager who is involved in the training of flight crews for jets told me recently that, in the past, although the cockpit procedures trainer and flight simulator provided very relevant practice, much of what went on in the classroom was largely irrelevant to anything the crews needed to know, or had to be able to do. For example, when an aircraft manufacturer sent the airline all of the specifications and information about the construction and operation of the aircraft and all of its systems, the trainers attempted to teach the crews how the plane was built, and how it worked. Some of that is relevant, of course, and some is critical, but no attempt was made to separate the relevant and critical from the irrelevant. So pilots were trying to learn the dimensions and capacity of tiny flutter values, and components and systems of many kinds that were irrelevant to the requirements of flying the aircraft. And the irrelevant got in the way of the critical things, making the course harder, duller and longer, and, most important of all, less effective. Fortunately, following the classroom sessions, the other methodologies did adequately prepare the crews to do their jobs! For those results the training staff has always been held accountable. They have never been able to do a poor job, and then blame it on the students if any deficiencies slipped through.

Some training courses have avoided accountability because no one has bothered to follow-up to see if the training really accomplishes anything. Sometimes the course examinations are so simple—far less complex than the job performance requirements for which the course was to prepare the student—that most of the students are able to demonstrate high levels of competence on the examinations, and this is a fine feather in the cap of the training staff. Occasionally a surly malcontent on the line or in the field will scream that the newly trained people assigned to him are incompetent, but often his is only a single voice. The "silent majority"—like any silent majority—can be interpreted as expressing—through their silence—approval, and a lack of criticism. Often, however, line supervisors and managers are silent because they have learned not to expect anything better; they have learned that the training courses will turn out some skills, but with many holes, many deficiencies that will have to be repaired on the job, through direct and close supervision, and on-the-spot correction and guidance. Why make a fuss, they reason, next year it might be their turn in the barrel, assigned to the training department!

In training there is usually an external criterion that can be used to evaluate the results of training: job effectiveness. An analysis of the job performance requirements can improve the relevance and effectiveness of instruction, and that same analysis permits a very precise analysis of the effectiveness of instruction. But if the training instructors have also learned about the very limited features of information presentation as a teaching method, then why should *they* welcome or seek accountability if they can avoid it?

So we can conclude that both teachers in educational settings and instructors in training settings might be expected to cry "foul and unfair" when faced with the notion of accountability. And I don't blame them a bit. Unless someone else accepts accountability for teaching those teachers relevant skills beyond those they already possess, and unless the conditions that limit their effectiveness can be changed, then there is no justification for expecting them to do better, or for holding them accountable for doing so. They need more effective techniques, procedures, methods, materials and other components of instruction. And then, when new components are added, no matter how innovative, how effective, there will be a limit to the overall effectiveness of that totality, probably still short of that ideal of all students learning everything. That new limit will have to be determined empirically, and then additional research and development efforts can be aimed at raising that ceiling.

The foregoing is *not* intended to imply that accountability is not feasible, or that it would be premature to explore the concept in action. It *would* be a mistake to attempt to impose accountability within the existing system of information-oriented instruction, where it would be, in effect, nothing more than a punitive structure. Teachers and students fail, not because they don't try hard enough, but because of the limitations imposed on them by the way they are forced to go about it! Students are presently held accountable for failures; accountability does not mean—although it has often been interpreted to mean—simply assigning accountability to teachers and arranging some form of reward system for teachers based on results. Accountability must start at the top, and must be applied to everything that has an instructional or instructional management function. The purpose is not punitive; the purpose is—to use a manufacturing term—quality control. The systems approach—and we are all tired of hearing about the systems approach—is basically a methodology which requires exact specifications of what is to be accomplished by each component, and the use of techniques to see that each specification is achieved; meeting specifications is quality control. Seeing to it that specifications and quality control work—at all levels—is accountability.

I recently heard a prominent educator refer to accountability as a "new theory of education." It is not. There is nothing theoretical about it. While discussing accountability with a group of industrial training specialists, who were involved in sales training that might or might not have been having an effect on sales skills, I suggested that they do some follow-up studies to find out what impact—if any—their instruction made on the real-world activities of the salesmen they trained. One member of the group exclaimed, "Wow, that would really be laying it on the line, wouldn't it!" Yes, it would, and that seems only fair, because the salemen they train are laying it on the line, presumably assisted by skills learned during training. Again, what I was suggesting was not a fault-finding procedure, but an empirical approach to developing, implementing and managing instruction. We may *think* that we are accomplishing something; if we are wrong, we need to find it out as quickly as possible, so we can do something about it.

Applied Accountability

There are many examples of accountability in training, not because someone thought that accountability sounded like a good idea, but because of the criticality of the job performance requirements. Obviously the punitive interpretation of accountability would make no sense in the airline setting, where flight crews must, as a result of training, meet very precise performance standards: holding the training department accountable for pilot error accidents is not much of a solution. The training department must do everything necessary to provide relevant and effective training, and identify any deficiencies in time to correct them, both in their trainees and in their training methods and materials. They have to know what they are trying to accomplish in precise and measurable terms; they have to have effective methods for determining when they have or have not been successful; they have to be as empirical as possible in their approach in order to identify problems and deficiencies; they have to have effective diagnostic and remedial methods available for trainees who for any reason are in difficulty; and they must collect relevant data, and use the data to revise, improve and maintain the resulting instructional effectiveness.

How does one introduce accountability into instruction where it did not formerly exist? The easiest setting, relatively speaking, is in a training environment, preparing trainees to perform a specific job, all components of which are readily identifiable. The job itself is the criterion. The job can be analyzed as a basis for instructional design. Later the job serves as the source of quality control data for determining how well the instruction works, and where it must be improved. A non-accountable approach to training in that setting—difficult to justify, but all too common—pays very little attention to the job itself *as it really exists.* Instead, rather vague job descriptions and subjective judgments are used as a basis for selecting information that is to be presented, probably in a lecture setting. Gathering information and lecturing about it is the easiest and most convenient method available, so, whether or not it is the most appropriate approach, some training staffs make very little contact with the job itself, with people who can do it, or with those who supervise those who can do it. A non-accountable approach can afford to ignore the job and make intuitive rather than empirically-based judgments about the design of instruction. Moving one step closer to the job, using subject matter experts as sources of information, or even going so far as having them design or assist in the design of the content, does not solve all of the problems. It obviously does not solve the problems created by the information-presenting approach; nor does it adequately replace the missing empirical and objective analysis of the job performance requirements.

The first step in introducing accountability is setting some basic standards or rules or specifications. The first directive says that no trainee will proceed from training to the job until we have complete and objective evidence that he can do the job according to the established criteria. There are many implications of that prime directive, which applies—incidentally—to education as well, although couched in different terms and involving slight modifications in methodology. One implication is the dependence on *established criteria,* which may never have been established beyond the level of vague and ambiguous job descriptions. Who is to establish the criteria, the descriptions of the job performance requirements in objective, measurable terms? We might do several kinds of task analyses: an observation task analysis, observing people doing the job in order to see what they do and the way in which they do it; a consensus analysis, asking workers, supervisors, equipment designers and anyone else who purports to know how the job should be done; or a content analysis, determining what the manufacturers of equipment put into the directions for operation, and so on. The consensus and content analyses would probably yield very similar kinds of information, but both might disagree markedly with the results of the observation tasks analyses. Suppose we find that the job, as it is being done, does not agree with the experts' descriptions of the way they think that it should be done? Which description is "right?" The establishment of objective criteria in the form of performance specifications is a complex problem in itself. Some training departments operate without such specifications; some apparently never hear of such things. Sometimes the responsibility for establishing such specifications is left to the training staff; sometimes there is a separate department responsible for performance specifications and job simplification. It should be obvious at this point that this is a complex requirement, but the complexity and difficulty are not justification for ignoring the problem, hoping that it will go away or take care of itself!

What form does the prime directive take in education, or in the education portions of training? First of all, consider the distinction that has just been implied, between education and training. Many people have made such a distinction, which in its harshest form becomes: when we know what we are doing, that's training; when we don't, that's education. A less critical—and more sympathetic—distinction is made mere: training implies objective criteria in the form of job performance requirements; education is instruction of a more general nature, possibly specifically job-related, but also "general knowledge" and skills relevant to many kinds of jobs, or to activities outside of job settings. Some academic subjects have certain aspects of training, in that objective criteria are available, and the performance components are relatively unchanging no matter what kind of job or real world application is involved (e.g., reading, mathematical skills, language skills, including foreign languages, operation or use of measuring devices, etc.). A course in "principles of electricity" would fall under the heading of *education,* whether taught in a training or education environment, but the specific application of those principles as job performance activities would be the *training* part of the course. In any case, and regardless of the nature of an appropriate distinction, or in the absence of any distinction, one requirement stands out: the prime directive, independent of any job referent, states that no student will be considered to have completed a course of instruction until we have complete and objective evidence that he has achieved the objectives according to the established criteria. The common denominator for training and education is the use of established criteria and evidence of attainment.

Education requires some form of commitment to a set of criteria. Unless we are willing to commit ourselves to a specific set of criteria, no "complete and objective evidence" can be obtained indicating that our students have or have not attained them! If we don't care about all of our students attaining at least some uniform minimum level of competence, then we can do without criteria, and quality control and accountability. We can then

continue to present information and grade on a curve and let it go
at that. Once we commit ourselves, however, and agree on a set of
criteria—even if it is necessary to establish a tentative set of criteria,
planning to improve that set as we collect relevant data—we can
make accountability a viable concept and methodology. Obviously, I am referring here to the use of instructional objectives.

The second directive says that we have to assemble a set of
"learning experiences" and evaluation and management procedures that will allow and assist every student to reach that specified criterion or set of criteria. We can start by assembling components intuitively, using our own best judgment about the requirements of each objective. We might develop or select conventional text materials, programmed materials, audiovisual materials
of various kinds, hands-on practice materials and simulators, and
we might schedule field trips, use both individualized and group
instruction, and a variety of methods. We should use past experience, not just our own, but the vast applied and methodological
research, media, training and learning research data, and the practical know-how collected as part of thousands of developmental and
implementation projects. And that is only a start. All we have so
far is an experimental version of a course of instruction; we do not
know whether it will meet the requirements of the first two objectives. Total accountability means that each component has a specified function; we have to determine how well each component succeeds, and revise and improve where necessary. Accountability also
means that we must identify the weaknesses and provide corrective
back-up so that no student is lost to us. This is also part of the
game specified by the first two directives.

The third directive says that we must rely on data. Too many
courses are considered to be "finished, polished, and perfect," because a group of subject matter experts or instructional specialists
pronounced them so. In their best judgment, the course *should*
teach. An empirical approach requires more than that. The subjective, intuitive and experiential judgments of the experts are interesting, encouraging and nice to have. But the final judges are the
students. The data they produce as they proceed through the
various components of the course, and the evaluation data, and
any available follow-up data tell the story. We are accountable for
the data; if the data are not adequate in comparison with the data
we had hoped for, we have not met the requirements of the first

two directives, so now we must act on the third directive as our only hope for attaining the first two!

The teachers, the instructors, in an accountability setting, have to function effectively as tutors, diagnosticians, remediators, managers, counselors, advisors, conversationalists and stimulating consultants. These skills are not part of most teacher-training or instructor-training curricula. Some will have to be learned by experience on the job, and some people will be able to develop higher levels of proficiency at one skill than another. Eventually we will have to learn how to analyze and teach these skills, and be accountable for doing so, to at least a minimally adequate level. At that time we will be able to establish and implement a reasonable merit reward system. The teacher or instructor who can "service" the most students with the best results deserves to be rewarded.

At present, education and training are *time-oriented,* not *performance-oriented:* a student completes a course at the end of a fixed period of time, not when he reaches a specified level of proficiency; instructional staff members are promoted and given salary increases on the basis of longevity, or for credits accumulated for spending specified numbers of hours, days, or years in training courses, workshops, or graduate courses. All that can be changed, and changed now.

Only a vocal minority sees much need for accountability and its requirements. The instructional world is primarily structured on subject matter content and presentations of information. In effect, that world doesn't seem to care about results, about learning, about student competence. Yet those are all that count. I have collected a number of objections to accountability, from representatives of all parts of the instructional world:

- A teacher asked, "Are we then to stop educating the whole child?"
- Another teacher said, a bit sadly, I thought, "It sounds exciting, but it is obviously impractical, or immoral, or something, or we'd be doing it already."
- A training director growled, "We don't have time for all that."
- Another training director said, "If I tried to sell that idea to our management, they would either think I had lost my my mind, or would accuse me of admitting that everything we had done previously was wrong, incompetent, or irrelevant!"

- A dean told me, "Those activities would get in the way of the scholarly activities of our faculty."
- A college professor, avoiding the term "scholarly activities," was more blunt when he said, "We are *not* accountable and never will be. The system specifies that the student is responsible and accountable in higher education. I must talk to them about what I know, help them, try to interest them, and guide and steer their curiosity and interests. And I help them in their career decisions if they commit themselves to my field. But my profession, my professional advancement, and my professional activities come first. That's the name of this game!"
A harassed instructor cried, "What the hell are you talking about? I have to squeeze an hour or two out of each day for the next week in order to put together a one-day course on something I'm still learning about myself!"

If all of the real world, the practical world, indicated that accountability is not feasible, or that universal constraints make it impossible, then we would have to assign accountability to the pipe-dream category. But the constraints are *not* universal; the system can be changed or the constraints by-passed. Many companies, both large and small, many government agencies, and instructional projects in schools of all kinds have demonstrated that accountability can be implemented on an efficient, cost-effective basis, and made a way of life. As I said above, none of it is easy, but hell, the things that we are doing now aren't easy either, so we might as well do it right!

Summary
Instruction too often relies on subject matter expertise and information-presentation methods to be the primary—or entire—set of resources and tools of design, development and implementation. Sometimes this is the only approach possible, but most of the time alternatives are available. Accountability imposes three directives: specified performance capability will be produced; the instructional components must produce those results; and an empirical development and management process must be employed. Accountability is not a punitive method of assigning blame for failure, or a method of rewarding teachers who work harder. An

overhaul of the entire instructional environment—its components and its methods—is a basic requirement. The entire operation must become results-oriented, results measured in terms of students' performance capabilities stemming from the instructional events arranged for them.

Questions

1. The "accountability" concept does not hinge on a punitive and/or reward system for instructors. What then is its basis?
2. Accountability requires several new implementation procedures and criteria. Describe them.
3. Industry does training, and also provides education. The educational community educates, and also does some training. How are "training" and "educating" defined in this article?
4. Describe each of the accountability "directives" and their implications for both training and education, not in the abstract, but in terms of the procedures necessary to act on these directives.   □

William A. Deterline is President of Deterline Associates.

Chapter Two

PROCEDURES THAT SEEK ACCOUNTABILITY

A. Accountability as "Systems Approaches"

B. Accountability as Institutional Change

I

THE GREEKS HAD A WORD FOR IT: TECHNOLOGIA

by Gerald M. Torkelson

"Instructional technology, technologia, "systematic treatment" of instructional problems can lead the way towards more rewards for teachers and learners and towards a science of teaching and learning."

I.   Meaning of Instructional Technology

During 1970 the major national organization of professionals in "audiovisual" education, The Department of Audiovisual Instruction, National Education Association, changed its name to the Association for Educational Communications and Technology (AECT). This may suggest to some that the organization has sharpened the focus of its title to reflect more concern with communicative processes in education while still retaining, in the word *technology,* its identification with the traditional tools and machines of the old audiovisual concept. This might be a common conclusion were one to equate "technology" with the hardware of teaching, that is, projectors. record players, recorders, and other kinds of instructional equipment. Certainly the intent of AECT is to broaden its function and image. However, there looms a much larger problem than a new name, even though a new name is meant to reflect a new direction or a maturation of an older concept.

The real problem of AECT, and of this discussion, is to bring some objectivity and accuracy to the meaning of instructional technology. Prejudgments, based on superficial analysis and misconceptions, have caused some skepticism about the advantages of instructional technology. A typical criticism is that learners are dehumanized by being subjected to control by machines. Machines

---

create automatons rather than creative, thinking people. It is this writer's intent to provide a viewpoint on this controversy, as well as to focus more sharply on the meaning of technology. It will also attempt to: (1) place "machines" in their proper perspective with respect to the instructional process, (2) discuss the implications of instructional technology for education generally, and (3) conclude with some basic problems which still remain.

The root of technology may be found in the Greek word *technologia,* meaning "systematic treatment." Or this meaning might be extended to the application of scientific methods to the solution of instructional problems. The actual and intended meaning of instructional technology thus encompasses the *process* for solving instructional problems rather than the simple application of machines to those problems. This does not exclude traditional and newer technological developments identified as the hardware or equipment associated with instruction. It is meant to place them in proper relationship to the process.

Confusion about the use and meaning of the term "instructional technology" stems in part from what Paul Saettler contends are two different theoretical persuasions.

> The physical science concept of instructional technology usually means the application of physical science and engineering technology, such as motion picture projectors, tape recorders, television, teaching machines, for group presentation of instructional materials. Characteristically, this concept views the various media as aids to instruction and tends to be preoccupied with the effects of devices and procedures, rather than with the differences of individual learners or with the selection of instructional content.[1]

> ... the behavioral science concept of instructional technology is that educational practice should be more dependent on the methods of science as developed by behavioral scientists in the broad areas of psychology, anthropology, sociology, and in the more specialized areas of learning, group processes, language and linguistics, communications, administration, cybernetics, perception and psychometrics. Moreover, this concept includes the application of engineering research and development (including human factors engineering) and branches of economics and logistics related to the effective utilization of instructional personnel, buildings (learning spaces), and such new computerized systems as data processing and information retrieval.[2]

Comparing these opposing views historically, it would appear that many professionals in the older audiovisual field emphasized the applications of machines as a primary solution to instructional problems. Fewer individuals perceived of instruction as a problem of mixing content, machines, and methods to meet learner needs, previously identified as requiring such a combination of instructional elements. There is abundant evidence[3] of "no significant differences" between treatments in studies of the comparative effects of educational media versus more traditional methods of instruction. An "educated" speculation suggests that many of the nonsignificant differences could be attributed to a physical science concept of instructional technology. Whenever experimental treatments were superimposed upon existing instructional matrices, the experimental effects of using "machine" instruction were diffused by the influence of underlying problems. The physical science concept of mediating agents in instruction as described above tended to perceive problems as less global than is inherent in the behavioral science concept. It is interesting to note that the President's Commission on Instructional Technology reflects the behavioral scientist's viewpoint. It defines instructional technology as:

> A systematic way of designing, carrying out, and evaluating the total process of learning and teaching in terms of specific objectives, based on findings from research in human learning and communication, and employing a combination of human and nonhuman resources to bring about more effective instruction.[4]

Note that this definition emphasizes the *total* process of learning, a view not prominent in the physical science concept. One might conclude that the more simplistic "application of hardware to instruction" approach does not deal with the interaction of other significant variables. Studies of this sort were in essence just "scratching the surface," not viewing instructional components as interrelated parts.

The President's Commission also commented upon the pervasive nature of instructional technology and the need to view the totality of the instructional process. It stated that:

> . . . instructional technology is integrally involved with the process of learning and the genuine individualization of learning. Any sharp distinction, then, between research and development in instructional technology, on the one hand, and research and

development in the basics of education, on the other, appears to
be arbitrary. In fact, this very decision has contributed to the
disappointing impact thus far of instructional technology—so
frequently heralded, so seldom realized down the years since
1913 when Edison proclaimed the motion picture as the prospective agent of complete school reform.[5]

The definition of instructional technology expressed by the
President's Commission and the behavioral scientist's orientation
are consistent with *technologia,* a "systematic treatment" of *all*
the factors which impinge upon teaching-learning processes. The
"machine" concept must be separated from the true meaning of
technology and recognized as only one factor in determining the
best conditions for learning.

A related concept has been expressed as *machine dependent*
versus *machine independent* systems of instruction. Machine dependent refers to the use of machines for instructional purposes
which are integral with the total instructional process. An example
would be the use of a computer for purposes of student scheduling
as well as for use as interactive instruction. The latter refers to the
computer program designed to shape student learning on the basis
of how he responds to questions from the computer. In a machine
dependent system, the removal of the computer and other kinds
of instructional hardware would cause a breakdown both in administration and in teaching procedures.

The machine independent system of instruction is characterized as using machines as "frills" or "appendages" which if removed would make no essential difference in the instructional program. Even with the greater accessibility to machines and materials
provided by greater numbers of education industries, machine independent systems of instruction persist. They may be characterized as superimposing a layer of machine mediated instruction,
that is, programmed instruction, self-instructional *packages,* over a
program essentially unchanged from teacher dominance and conducted largely with groups of students in a highly verbal, symbolic
framework. In this setting, innovative procedures and newer tools
of instruction tend to be superficial in that they generally attack
small problems without influencing fundamental arrangements or
procedures of the large problem, as if it were an educational ice-
berg with its significant mass submerged beneath the surface.

Of these two alternative systems of instruction, the machine dependent system would be consistent with the meaning of *tech-nologia,* whether by deliberate design or by the gratuitous circum-stance of educators having incorporated machines incidentally into the instructional process to a point where their advantages have been realized through practice. Having become a machine depen-dent system does not automatically mean, however, that the ma-chines are used to their best advantage nor that decisions to use a particular machine or procedure was based upon a *systematic treatment* of all of the variables involved.

A popular and useful way to analyze the elements in a *sys-tematic treatment* is to apply *systems* concepts for identifying and solving instructional problems. *Systems concept* may be regarded as synonomous with *systematic treatment.* It includes many non-machine aspects, such as logistics, environments for instruction, methodology, content organization and analysis, refinement of the purposes of instruction, and careful identification of learner char-acteristics. In a larger sense, any instructional system is man-made with a number of interrelated parts, all contributing to the fulfill-ment of stated educational goals. An instructional system may be viewed as organismic. That is, each part supports and interacts with all other parts, a sort of dynamic balance of learners, teacher, administrators, parents, school boards, local and national agencies, procedures, instructional materials and hardware. A desirable goal for this kind of instructional system, particularly as viewed from a behavioral scientist's concept of instructional technology, is for it to be open-ended and interactive, where feedback to the system reshapes its directions and characteristics.

Thus, instructional technology must be interpreted as being concerned with the systematic treatment of instructional prob-lems, with the machine aspects regarded as only part of a larger problem. To ignore this interrelationship of machines to other factors influencing the effectiveness of instruction would result in the perpetuation of the more limited benefits of a physical science concept of instructional technology. To pursue the implications of a behavioral science concept would begin to get at some of the un-answered questions about the interrelationships of man-machine arrangements for learning.

II.   Implications of the Behavioral Scientist's Concept of Instructional Technology

The implications of the behavioral scientist's concept of instructional technology are far reaching. Taken in concert they get at the very roots of the educational system, its purposes and its procedures.

There is probably little disagreement among educators that the primary focus of an educational system should be to assist each learner to achieve his potentials. This has been voiced in many ways from the early days of organized education. Many educational institutions, however, reflect conditions which deny this objective. As Charles E. Silberman has written recently:

> The public schools are the kind of institution one cannot really dislike until one gets to know them well. Because we all take the schools so much for granted, we fail to appreciate what grim, joyless places most American schools are, how oppressive and petty are the rules by which they are governed, how intellectually sterile and esthetically barren the atmosphere, what an appalling lack of civility obtains on the part of teachers and principals, what contempt they unconsciously display for children as children. And a society whose schools are not humane is not likely to be humane itself.[6]

Silberman's attack is not directed at the teachers, who, in his estimation, are destroyed in spirit as much by the school system as learners are. His attack is upon those institutions which have become so encrusted with the impedimenta of routine and unthinking educational procedures that they have stifled both learners and teachers.

The following points suggest some areas for the systematic treatment of instructional variables as ways to diminish the stifling aspects of educational systems as described by Silberman. There has been no attempt to suggest priorities among them.

A.   Focus Attention Upon the Needs of Individual Learners

The nature of the world today requires that the school system be dynamic and changing. Even a generation ago learners were much less mobile, less well informed, subject to fewer pressures (such as the international situation) than they are today. Auditory-pictorial persuasion, instant problems, and instant solutions are more ubiquitous today than before. Members of the "now" generation demand excitement and current information. They have been weaned on television, they observe distant conflict while they eat their dinner, they are assailed by the stimulation of music, psychedelic art, and avant garde films which test social mores. This is a generation living in the midst of rapid change and rapid dissemination of information. These young people seriously question the relevancy of what is being done in schools. They are demanding all sorts of solutions to their problems. The critical question for educators relates to the retention of the main threads of man's development while striving for relevancy and appeal. For example, how much of the tremendous information load generated every day in the world should the learner be required to remember? Most observers would conclude with Clifford F. S. Bebell that:

> The future will demand citizens who have been trained to *think* rather than primarily to remember. Increasingly, the information available to an individual in school may become outmoded, irrelevant, or superseded before his working life is over. His continuing effectiveness should reside in his ability to solve problems and continue learning, rather than be based on his prior training and the knowledge acquired in formal schooling.[7]

Emphasis upon the individual and the kinds of skills, knowledge, and attitudes he will need in the future is apt to generate what Alvin Toffler[8] has described as "future shock." This is the phenomenon resulting from rapid changes in the society in which a person lives, as distinct from "culture shock" which is related to that experienced in a foreign land from which a person can return. A return to familiar ways is not possible under "future shock." There may be no security except in the ability to change with and to anticipate the future. This pehnomenon undoubtedly relates to much of the general unrest experienced by people today, although not generally recognized as such. Teachers as well as students must reckon with it.

The implications of such a condition are pervasive. If educators are to prepare learners for the inevitability of change, they must also search for ways to provide security in a recognition of the universals in man's needs and desires, regardless of historic age, as a substitute for the comfortable feeling that one may seek refuge in old ways. Old ways may be wiped out by the inevitable results of man's genius for instant communication and interchange.

For the curriculum worker who has responsibility for mapping future content and activities, this becomes a critical factor. Perhaps some of the universals are inherent in the curricular focuses suggested by June Grant Shane and Harold G. Shane:[9]

- the integrity and dignity of the individual
- the dynamics of group behavior
- the learning process and qualities in the home and school environment that help mediate experience
- social trends that influence a student's present world and the world he will enter
- the economic, political, and technological developments that help shape people's life, their work, and their leisure activities

It is interesting to note how the individual and his personal involvements and interests pervade the emphases above. A companion need, implied but not expressed directly, is to build in individuals the respect for others and the desirability of maintaining the rights of the group.

B.   *Examine Instructional Procedures and Arrangements*

To realize the potentials of each individual learner and to prepare him to become a productive member of society, those responsible for schools must develop procedures and arrangements to support such an emphasis. Charles E. Silberman comments on the value of considering informal kinds of schools to foster the adjustment to learners and situations.

> Advocates of informal education begin with a conception of childhood as something to be cherished, a conception that leads in turn to a concern with the quality of the school experience in its own right, not merely as preparation for later schooling, or later life. There is, in addition, a conviction that learning is likely to be more effective if it grows out of what interests the learner, rather than what interests the teacher. This is a truism to any adult: we *know* how rapidly we can learn something that really interests us, and how long it takes to master something which bores us, or for which we have a positive distaste.[10]

In this setting of sensitivity to individuals and flexibility in curriculum and methods, the scientific approach to the use of mediating agents with learners raises three questions: What are the real contributions of mediating agents to instruction; what are

appropriate methods for utilizing mediating agents; and what are
the characteristics of environments necessary to support their use?

Mediating Agents

In responding to the question about the best kinds of mediating agents for given learners and purposes, it is important to consider what is meant by a mediating agent. It is also useful to structure a method for judging characteristics of mediating agents.

In using the word teaching to encompass group presentations
by the teacher as well as the preparation of self-instructional materials, mediation represents the interposition of some substitute or
surrogate between the learner and his environment. To state it another way, the learner in or out of school perceives his world
through the response of his senses to objects and situations. He responds to what may be called perceptual stimuli, which I define as
"initiators of sensory awareness." Thus, anything which causes the
learner to attend may be called a stimulus. The problem for the
teacher is to select, organize, and make available appropriate perceptual stimuli. Once the learner has attended to the stimulus, he
processes what he perceives in proportion to the acuity of his
senses, his intelligence, his maturation level, his biases, and experiences. In essence, what the teacher does is to provide the learner
with opportunities for various kinds of experiences. She cannot
predict exactly the effects of those experiences, but by providing a
wide variety of stimuli she enhances opportunites for broader
experience.

In the context of the older audiovisual concept of communication, or the physical science concept, mediating agents tended to
be equated with traditional motion pictures, symbols, objects, and
other agents usually available in most schools. Little thought was
given to the global meaning of mediating agent, particularly to include the teacher, although some studies have proved the relevance
of teacher characteristics to learner responses. Critical analysis suggests that mediating agents must be considered to encompass *all*
agents interposed between the learner and his environment, particularly when one wishes to be inclusive about determining which
agents influence learners. Thus the teacher must be regarded as a
mediating agent in the same sense as one would regard a motion
picture. More than some teachers realize, they are "gatekeepers"
through which learners gain impressions of many concepts outside

their own personal experiences. If the teacher is relatively unin-
formed or prejudiced, to what extent does this gatekeeping affect
learner perceptions? Certainly educators who focus on questions
such as this are applying instructional technology to the process of
communicating with learners.

Three terms which the author has found useful in refining a
differentiation among mediating agents are *message, medium,* and
channel. Defined as being interrelated and yet discrete, they offer
a system for bringing more precision to the selection of mediating
agents.

Message refers to content that a learner is to acquire, be it
understandings, knowledge, skills, or feelings. When the teacher
determines that there is a given body of information to be learned,
this content may be called the *message.* When a teacher wishes to
shape attitudes and determines the nature and qualities which are
to be evidence of attitude acquisition or change, that content is
the *message.* When the purpose is to have a learner acquire a motor
skill, the content necessary for teaching that skill is the *message.*
All of these messages refer to the content to be conveyed to the
learner, content determined prior to giving it form or shape for
transmission to the learner.

A *medium* may be described as the "shape of the message."
As the message is determined, the teacher must decide the form it
is to assume for presentation to the learner. Familiar shapes of
messages, or message systems, are words, symbols, drawings, pictures, objects, models. Note that the shapes of messages were not
described as filmstrips, motion pictures, or television. The reason
for this is that the latter terms to dnot necessarily describe the
characteristics of the *media* they contain. A motion picture may
contain a combination of mediums, such as words, pictures, and
graphics. Simply selecting a motion picture because it is a motion
picture does not identify the shape of its content or message. For
precision in teaching, examining such medium for its characteristics, that is, verbal, symbolic, pictorial, color, motion, static, and
so forth are critical to a decision about the appropriateness of a
medium for a given learner. This conclusion is based on the notion
that mediating agents, *media,* vary in their ability to represent the
world in a realistic fashion. For example, how many ways may one
present the concept "moon landing" and what are the prerequisites for using certain kinds of media with certain kinds of learners

to explain this concept? If a learner has a high level of verbal skill, one might expect that presenting messages in verbal form would be much less a challenge for him than using the same type of medium with a retarded child. Motion pictures with such features as time-lapse photography or cinémicrography require some knowledge of filmic techniques for full appreciation and understanding of the phenomenon shown. This brief discussion is simply to point out that this aspect of instructional technology, utilizing the best mediating agents, must be subject to "systematic treatment" the same as other factors affecting the learning situation.

Channel is sometimes used interchangeably with *medium* and hence causes some confusion. Questioning the validity of this interchangeability is not the purpose of this discussion. By using *channel* in the arbitrary manner to be described, attention may be drawn to another aspect of developing precision in selecting mediating agents. Channel is used here to mean conveyance systems for media. Television is a channel because it is an electronic conveyance for messages which may take the form of pictures, graphics, words, or a variety of forms. The problem of the learner is to interact with the media carried by the television system. While Marshall McLuhan suggests that there may be some aura to messages presented via television, the learning problem of responding to words, symbols, pictures, and so on, as substitutes for the world is essentially the same as responding to those media without television. If television, in fact, does add another dimension to learning, besides the element of immediacy which results when events are observed as they occur, then evidence is needed to support this view.

The word channel would also apply to such common experiences as the field trip, the exhibit, the bulletin board. In each instance, the problem for the learner is to interact with the media each contains as representing objects or phenomena. To pursue this point even more minutely, a field trip is not a channel but an administrative device for placing learners in juxtaposition with mediating agents in the field. Granted, there are good and poor field trips. The basic reason for a poor field trip are most likely to be poor administration and inadequate preparation of learners to respond to the mediating agents observed or manipulated on the trip.

Greater Variety of Methods

In order to make an instructional system more responsive to
a variety of learners, it follows that much more attention needs to
be paid to methods used. Traditional methods have favored group
instruction in preference to the more difficult task of providing individualized experiences. Where group instruction is used it should
preferably be justified as being effective for specified instructional
purposes and not used simply as an expedient way to handle large
groups of students simultaneously.

Ideally, instructional experiences should range from various
sorts of group experiences to individualized instruction. There is
some logic to this need for variety apart from the idiosyncracies of
individuals. This logic is based upon the notion that certain kinds
of learning require certain kinds of methods, inherent in the content and purpose rather than inherent in the type of learner involved. For example, one of the major functions of any educational system is to provide learners with information. Much of this information is imparted through the expository function, the sheer
telling, explaining, demonstrating activity which seems to occupy
such a great portion of the school day. Not enough study has been
made, however, of the mediating agents best adapted to the process of exposition. Perhaps most people would suggest that the
teacher is best in this role. This may be true only for limited purposes, such as the explanations a teacher can give on the spur of
the moment, or where the teacher must synthesize information unavailable in any other form. However, when the teacher engages in
imparting content which could just as well be put in writing, or
some other retrievable form, one can readily question the effectiveness or wisdom of using the teacher as a live information dispenser. How many occasions have there been where a teacher has
adlibbed through five classes in the same subject, expecting that
the content for each class was to be identical, only to have the
disturbing feeling that the content had changed during the course
of the day? By and large, teachers are not effective agents for presenting repetitive kinds of information. This is particularly true
where words are woefully inadequate to describe processes, places,
phenomena. How much better that the instruments of a technological society be put to use, that is, film loops, tape and video re-
cordings, picture sets, artifacts. The teacher thus released from
some unrewarding and ineffective activities can devote time and

energies to the role of counselor, diagnostician, evaluator, synthesizer, instructional systems builder. In this redirection of roles, the teacher will not be the only one to benefit. The learner will have the advantage of experiences with more avenues for learning than the printed word.

In addition to the expository process, another universal teaching-learning act may be labeled the investigative function. This requires the student to interact with experiences and materials for purposes of arriving at his own conclusions. In this instance, expository functions are only supplementary, usually provided by lab manuals, direction sheets, and other written and pictorial materials. Except for the infrequent instances where the teacher needs to give instructions to a group, most of this activity is individualized in nature. A critical point relevant to the investigative function is to determine the extent to which the teacher should remain vicarious in student projects.

Promising steps toward individualized instruction are evident in the growing use of performance-based objectives for designing educational environments and for creating proper educational experiences. Admittedly, there are problems with this aspect of instructional technology, particularly in specifying behaviors of a more esoteric nature than the simpler tasks associated with certain kinds of "tool" subjects. However, as more sophistication is gained in determining proper kinds of behaviors and experiences for learners, determinations may be made about the nature of experiences necessary for more complex behaviors. A case in point may be the task of developing convergent versus divergent thinking. Critics of programmed and other individualized instruction formats point to conformity of thinking and convergence as an inherent evil. This criticism has an element of truth in it, as well as containing an overgeneralization about the dangers of carefully designed learning packages where learners proceed from A to Z in linear, largely unquestioning fashion. Fundamental criteria for using sequenced instruction are: (1) to provide such formats for those areas of learning where the nature of the content is amenable to programming, and (2) where the content involved has some value to the general population. Such areas as computational skills, language-use proficiency, vocabulary building, and basic rules of logic lend themselves to the programmed format and are generally non-controversial from a philosophical point of view. To assume that programmed sequences are equally effective for all areas of instruction is a myopic view.

At the beginning of this paper, reference was made to the criticism of some that individualized instruction in the programmed format may lead to a dehumanization of the individual and the creation of automatons rather than thinking, creative individuals. This criticism usually stems from assumptions that learners must not be subjected to experiences which restrict their latitude for response and free choice and that somehow one or several uses of the programmed format will lead to an entire curriculum devoted to this instructional approach.

In response to the first assumption, there are many experiences that have been part of the traditional school where learners have had to engage in exercises which were geared for mastery of given content. Examples are the acquiring of skills in language arts and computation. In many cases this was accomplished by the teacher holding flash cards before a group of learners, or similar techniques which were essentially repetitive in nature. This tended to be boring and dehumanizing for the teacher. It certainly did not support those children who, for psychological or intellectual reasons, were either behind or ahead of the pace set by the teacher. If dehumanization means that the needs of the individual were not met at the moment the need was present, then many non-programmed techniques used by teachers could be classified as dehumanizing. What could be more dehumanizing to learners than to be in a large group of students listening to a lecture where no oppotunities existed for interacting with the lecturer? Even in a somewhat homogenous, selected group, as may be typical of college students, how many in any given group are actually at a state of readiness for a given lecture? The fact that so little information remains from the many hours of sitting in lectures ought to suggest something about the effectiveness of the lecture as a basic means for "fixing" information. It ought to suggest something also about the tremendous dehumanization of students who have lost many precious hours of time when equated on a standard of the residual gains from lectures.

In response to the second assumption, no serious advocate of programmed instruction suggests that all subjects should be in programmed format, or that such a feat is even possible. Rather, any "systematic treatment" of instruction, the application of an instructional technology, is concerned with the uniqueness of modes and methods of instruction. Subject matter which has an inherent hierarchical pattern and sequence usually lends itself to the programming format and to an expository mode, whether by book or in a computer is immaterial. Usually the intent of such programming is to ensure mastery of conetent and skills to provide for individually paced learning, although some evidence supports forced pacing under some circumstances as beneficial. On the other hand, where the intention is to develop divergence in thinking and skills of synthesis and discussion, there are obvious limits to the use of programmed sequences. It is possible, of course, to provide learners with programmed sequences which lead them through exercises in recognizing the characteristics of divergent thinking. But this would only be for purposes of building skills needed in the spontaneity of a seminar situation.

Perhaps the best answer to criticisms about dehumanization is that the contrary may actually be true. When instructional processes, learning styles, various modes for the presentation of content, and learner needs are carefully researched and documented, the result will be predictably more humane to the learner than traditional methods and systems which do not engage in or permit realistic attempts to meet each learner's needs.

Supportive Learning Environments

The key word a few years ago in referring to modern educational facilities was that they were designed to be flexible, meaning that they could meet a variety of needs with minimal adjustment. More recently the term has been modified to become *changeability,* among others, referring to the practice of shifting walls and other aspects of the physical facilities to meet a changing need. Proper design of educational facilities or learning spaces is another aspect of instructional technology. It has become even more important with the adoption by schools of electronic-mechanical instructional equipment. Because a more complete discussion of this subject is in another section of this publication, it is sufficient here to point out that it is equally important to design facilities which support the learner as it is to determine the unique characteristics of various mediating agents.

C.   Gather Information About Learners and Learning Practices
One important advantage of instructional technology is the
opportunity it affords for gathering data about learners and learning procedures on a systematic basis, particularly when utilizing
the capabilities of the computer to provide almost instant feedback on learner progress. A model for systems analysis by Launor
F. Carter[11] offers a pattern:

1. State the real NEED you are to satisfy.
2. Define the educational OBJECTIVES.
3. Define the real-world limiting RESTRAINTS.
4. Generate many different ALTERNATIVE systems.
5. SELECT the best alternative(s) for testing.
6. IMPLEMENT the alternative(s) for testing.
7. Based on experimental and real-world results, FEEDBACK
   the required MODIFICATIONS and continue this cycle until
   the objectives have been attained.

While offering such a solution, Carter also is realistic about the
conditions which must prevail.

> The careful application of systems analysis leads to a better
> understanding and a more disciplined, scheduled approach to
> the solution of the problem. But unless the context within
> which the problem is being approached is sufficiently flexible so
> that systems analysis can be applied well, it may not lead to any
> particularly valuable results. The particular problem must have
> sufficient flexibility and resources to allow for a serious imple-
> mentation, evaluation and revision. If these steps are not pos-
> sible, then neither systems analysis nor any other technique can
> be particularly helpful in trying to solve the problem.[12]

III. Problems Which Remain

It is important to discuss instructional technology as a systematic treatment of instructional problems and to suggest that
the behavioral scientist's approach offers great possibilities for
building a science of instruction. Several large problems remain before such a promise may become a reality.

One major problem concerns the difficulties of moving a
bureaucratic organization, such as a school, to adopt innovative
practices at a substantive enough level before it is too late to make
any difference. Unused instructional equipment gathering dust on

school shelves give mute evidence that fundamental changes in instructional methods have not been influenced perceptibly by the presence of new hardware. There must be a change of perception about what it means to deal with individuals instead of groups. There must be a shift of sensitivity from the needs of teachers and administrators to the real needs of *individuals.* There must be a greater knowledge about and expertise in producing and evaluating professional information about learners and instructional procedures. There must be a greater focus upon how to organize and present information. More experimentation needs to be directed toward freer schedules, more flexibility in handling the continually changing needs of learners. More needs to be known about the technology of instruction and ways to differentiate teacher roles. Instructional technology, *technologia,* "systematic treatment" of instructional problems can lead the way towards more rewards for teachers and learners and towards a science of teaching and learning.   □

---

[1]Paul Saettler, *A History of Instructional Technology.* (New York: McGraw Hill Book Co., 1968). p. 2.

[2]*Ibid.,* p. 5.

[3]J. Christopher Reid, and Donald W. MacLennan, *Research in Instructional Television and Film.* U. S. Department of Health, Education, and Welfare, Office of Education, Bureau of Research. (Washington, D.C.: Government Printing Office, 1967). (See Chapter I by Greenhill.)

[4]U. S. Congress, House, Commission on Instructional Technology, Committee on Education and Labor. *To Improve Learning.* (Washington, D.C.: U. S. Government Printing Office, 40-715 0), p. 59. (A Report to the President and the Congress of the United States), p. 38.

[5]*Ibid.,* p. 40.

[6]Charles E. Silberman, "The United States Has the Kinds of Schools Its Citizens Have Thus Far Demanded." *Washington Education,* 82, (November, 1970): 4.

[7]*Designing Education for the Future: Rationale, Procedures and Appraisal.* An Eight State Project. Denver, Colorado: 1362 Lincoln Street, June, 1969.

[8]Alvin Toffler as cited in June Grant Shane, and Harold G. Shane, "Cultural Change and the Curriculum 1970-2000 A.D." *Educational Technology,* 10, No. 4 (April 1970): 13.

[9]Shane and Shane *op. cit.,* p. 13.

[10]Charles E. Silberman, *op. cit.,* p. 5.

[11]Launor F. Carter, "The Systems Approach to Education: Mystique and Reality." *Educational Technology,* 9, No. 4 (April 1969): 22-3.

[12]*Ibid.,* p. 31.

Gerald M. Torkelson is Professor of Education at the University of Washington.

II

PPBS: PLANNING FOR SCHOOLS OF THE FUTURE

by Gerald L. Robinson

"PPBS should be considered as a replacement for planning methods that don't do the job. It's not a cost-cutting tool. It offers a way of improving a school system's ability to reach its objectives within its limited resources."

Many school systems face crises in the 1970's. Teachers demand higher salaries and more voice in decisions. Students protest for more freedom and for representation in curriculum planning. Minorities seek local control of their schools; they believe that they can educate their children better than the established system can. School requests for funds are getting chilly receptions; defeats of school bond issues have increased 70 percent in the last 5 years. Deep, far-reaching changes are called for.

How will schools manage these changes without being crippled? Solving problems of such scope and magnitude calls for skillful planning and agressive methods for putting plans into action. Planning today must look beyond the next year. School administrators must plan with vision that is broad enough to encompass all aspects of the system. Above all, they need to set a positive direction with long-term goals and carefully specified objectives that will serve as steps to those goals.

Budgeting will be part of this planning for change. A budget should represent a means for using funds to reach goals and objectives. It's not enough just to generate a list showing the cost of salaries, textbooks, maintenance, and other inputs to the school system. Who can tell from such a budget what the spending will accomplish? Good planning calls for consideration of outputs—

Reprinted with copyright permission of *Battelle Research Outlook,* Volume 2, Number 2, 1970.

what can be gained from various expenditures—before funds are budgeted. Committing funds now for new buildings, textbooks, courses of study, and the like can affect educational programs for years ahead. The school administrator who plans for only one year at a time leaves himself with little leeway to consider alternatives in the future—he spends himself into a corner. Long-range planning, on the other hand, puts him in a position where he can pick from a wider range of alternatives, some of which have long lead times.

Finally, planning must provide for feedback so that better plans can be laid next year and the years after. If budget allocations merely take care of rising costs, no real planning is being done. It is much more important to make sure that desirable, but troubled, programs are strengthened effectively and get the funds needed to bolster them. Certainly funds must be spent for those efforts that will benefit the whole system most.

Today, few schools are equipped to plan adequately. The kind of comprehensive planning outlined here calls for a system. Many educators hope that planning systems that have succeeded in industry and government will serve school management, too. Of those methods that now are under discussion, PPBS (Planning-Programming-Budgeting System) seems to have generated the greatest interest. PPBS was first applied in the early 1960's in the U.S. Department of Defense although its roots go back much earlier. Currently, a number of school districts and educational agencies are working to adapt it to school systems. Let's look at what PPBS is and how it applies.

7 Steps To Good Planning

The key element in PPBS is "planning". Basically, PPBS is a systems approach to planning that considers the costs and the consequences of using various alternatives, or options, in order to achieve the desired goals and objectives. To accomplish a school system's stated purposes, PPBS breaks down the total effort into programs, which combine related activities and resources to attain clearly stated objectives.

Budgeting in PPBS is output-oriented rather than input-oriented. This means that instead of just setting aside certain funds for teacher salaries, textbooks, building maintenance, and other goods and services, spending is planned on the basis of the results it will buy—a better driver training program, a more effective mathematics program, or a more responsive communications program. Battelle-Columbus and other specialists in PPBS are generally convinced that this planning method will improve the overall operations of a school system. However, it's not easy to set up a completely operable PPBS. This system is best adopted in steps, some of which may be expensive. Among the requirements for applying PPBS are: (1) clearly defined authority and responsibility; (2) recognition by administrators and teachers that considerable effort will be required from them; and (3) collection and analysis of substantial amounts of data. PPBS is not a programmed system to be bought off a shelf and used like many other tools. It is a systematic, rational way of planning and administering that must be learned.

PPBS should be considered as a replacement for planning methods that don't do the job needed. It's not a cost-cutting tool, per se. Rather, it offers a way of improving a school system's ability to reach its objectives within its limited resources. PPBS doesn't replace judgment; it encourages more effective use of judgment. Best of all, it can increase the effectiveness of any organization whose major concern is human values, by building these values into the goals and objectives of the organization.

What's involved in employing PPBS? For a school system, these are the basic steps:

1. Develop broad goals and objectives
2. Design a program structure.
3. Define objectives for each program—including the means for measuring or indicating program effectiveness.
4. Identify or design alternative approaches for attaining program objectives.
5. Make cost-effectiveness analyses of the alternative approaches for each program.
6. Select the best approach for attaining program objectives and allocate funds.
7. Evaluate the results of operating each program and provide feedback to the planning process.

If PPBS is to work well, these steps have to be retraced, to some extent, each year. For the first three steps, it's mainly a matter of checking to see if any changes of direction are needed each year. The last four steps require more incisive review. For each, one major question must be answered: Are all of the involved elements still pertinent to current operations?

Adopting PPBS also makes other demands. Program budgets must be prepared for the upcoming year, and a long-range plan must be drawn up to project financial and other needs for several years. Finally, administrative structures and procedures must be organized.

The seven steps on the preceding page outline the major efforts involved in instituting a complete PPBS from scratch, as a newly formed school district might. However, an established district might well approach PPBS by taking just a few programs and applying Steps 3 through 7. After gaining experience with these individual programs, it might extend PPBS into other ones and also implement Steps 1 and 2 for the entire school system. Such gradual adoption often is prudent; it allows PPBS to be established smoothly and permits the staff to be trained at a rate that keeps pace with the changes made. Each school district has to decide how best to apply PPBS. There is no one optimum way of putting it into practice.

Develop Goals and Objectives

As discussed here in earlier articles, goals are broad general statements of a school system's long-range purposes. Goals are not quantifiable; they tend to be idealistic, and serve as a guide and inspiration for the school system's personnel and activities. All groups involved in and with the system should help set the goals to be sure that they reflect the overall needs and interests, and that they express the broad purposes of the system in terms that point the way to ultimate accomplishment. Goals must be relevant—not merely glittering generalities to distract people while the system goes off in other directions.

Objectives, on the other hand, are more specific statements that relate to shorter-term, attainable ends; they represent planned steps to be taken to achieve the set goals. They should be drawn up with the full participation of all concerned groups. Typical objectives would be: to reduce the dropout rate of a high school to a specified percentage, or to increase the average student score to a specific level on a particular achievement test.

Goals, then, ultimately shape the content of the curriculum, standards for the teaching staff, priorities for expenditures, and other matters so that the school system moves in the desired direction. Objectives must be carefully set to ensure the attainment of those goals.

Design the Program Structure

A program is a collection of activities and resources that contribute to the accomplishment of specified goals and objectives. A program structure, in the terminology of PPBS, is the organized listing of the titles of all the programs that comprise the school's total activities.

In designing the program structure, the planner determines the programs that will be needed to fulfill the broad goals and objectives, and he organizes the titles of these programs into an integrated structure. Related programs often are grouped into three major areas:

1. Instructional—e.g., English, mathematics, and kindergarten.
2. Administrative—e.g., central administration, planning and research, and purchasing.
3. Service—e.g., student transportation, food services, and building maintenance.

The program structure makes it possible to accomplish a number of things that are essential to applying PPBS. First and foremost, it classifies the man, varied activities of a school system into clearly identified programs that help attain specific objectives. Second, it provides a coherent basis for ultimately examining all of the programs and for allocating funds to each. It enables management to group activities and associated expenditures, so that the funding for programs can be tied to effectiveness in achieving the objectives. Third, it facilitates the assignment of responsibility for a particular program to a specific person or organizational entity.

When PPBS has been adopted for an entire school system, all of the system's activities and resources are intermeshed and pointed toward pursuing its broad goals and objectives. However, when some programs have not been organized on a PPBS basis, these must be distinguished clearly in the planning/budgeting process to ensure that they get adequate consideration.

Define Each Program's Objectives

Here, the focus shifts from the integrated program structure to the individual programs. This step begins by setting up the program objectives, including the level of performance the programs will shoot for.

Posing and answering four questions can assist in defining program objectives. The questions and typical answers based on a driver training program are these:

1. *What are the goals of the program?* To train all students to drive cars safely and not be a menace to others.

2. *How is the effectivensss of the program to be measured?* By determining the percentage of students who pass the state driving test on the first try and the proportion of graduates who have been cited for traffic violations over a certain period.

3. *What level of effectiveness should be sought?* To have at least 95 percent of the students pass the state driving test on the first try, and to have the rate at which graduates are cited for traffic violations during their first licensed year be no more than half the rate for the local driving population.

4. *What constraints are likely to limit program effectiveness?* Perhaps a limited number of instructors or of cars, which, in turn, would restrict the amount of training that could be given to each student.

The relevant objective might be stated, finally, as this: to provide driver training that assures that at least 95 percent of the students will pass the state driving test on the first attempt, and to train drivers whose rate of violating traffic regulations will be no more than half that of the local driving population.

Always, the more specific the measure of effectiveness, the more useful the objective. However, since goals are not quantifiable, there always will be doubts about how far we have moved to achieve a goal when we have attained a well-defined objective. The driver training example above represents a good objective, and we can be fairly confident that the student who passes the test and seldom gets a ticket is a good driver. Nevertheless, there is the

possibility that the student hasn't learned to respect the traffic
laws; rather, that he has learned only to look out for the police.
Judgment will always be necessary in assessing the achievement of
goals; neither PPBS nor any other approach can do the evaluating
automatically.

Generate Alternative Approaches

Once program objectives have been defined, the next step is
to identify or design various possible approaches for implementing
each program. This is where the success of PPBS depends on the
planner's ingenuity. Having a number of possible options does not,
of course, guarantee anything, but it does give management a
chance to pick the best available course of action.

Here's an example of how alternative approaches may be
generated. In Ohio, approved driver education courses must provide 36 hours of classroom instruction, plus either 24 hours of in-
car training or a combination of 12 hours in a car and 12 hours in
a driving simulator. The following are some of the possible ways of
handling the nonclassroom training for a driver education program:

- 24 hours in-car with certificated teacher
- 24 hours in-car with commercial driver-training-school
  instructor
- 24 hours in-car with paraprofessional instructor
- 12 hours in-car with certificated teacher and 12 hours of
  simulator
- 12 hours in-car with commercial driver-training-school instructor and 12 hours of simulator
- 12 hours in-car with paraprofessional staff instructor and
  12 hours of simulator.

Other possibilities also might be considered. For example,
when permitted by law, in-car training could be conducted on a
driving range. This would allow simultaneous use of a number of
cars, with a single instructor supervising the range. The student/
teacher ratio would be increased, thereby reducing the costs for in-
car training.

Legal limitations, public attitudes, political considerations,
school policy, staff capabilities, available funds, and other factors
must be considered carefully in designing alternatives. Ingenuity
and creativity are essential in providing the best possible options
from which to choose.

Analyze Approaches/Select One

Now, how does the planner pick the best way of implementing each program? The systematic examination of the possible
courses of action for achieving program objectives is of major importance in applying PPBS. Feasibility, costs, and effectiveness
must be given prime consideration in judging and in selecting from
the alternatives; this process is called cost-effectiveness analysis.

Analyzing the cost-effectiveness of possible courses of action
can be a complicated task, requiring trained and skillful analysts.
The process cannot begin until criteria have been set for evaluating
the alternatives. If both cost and effectiveness are allowed to vary,
comparing options becomes very complex and selection becomes
largely a matter of judgment. Practically, the judging usually is
done by setting either a tolerable cost or a desirable effectiveness
level; then, the option that either (1) will achieve the most at the
set cost or (2) will cost the least for the set level of effectiveness is
picked as the best one.

Suppose, however, that the administrators haven't the data or
experience of their own on which to base predictions of effectiveness—a frequent case. What then? The most obvious step is to use
specialists who are familiar with the various courses of action. Another approach is to study data and reports on the experiences of
other school systems. When these are used as a basis for the analysis, consideration must be given to how a comparable program was
conducted and to differences in the students, teachers, equipment,
and other resources.

Costs naturally are easier to predict than effectiveness because they reflect resources used whereas effectiveness is based on
results achieved. For this reason, there is likely to be a tendency to
base the assessment on set financial limits. The prediction of effectiveness often depends on subjective judgment. With experience,
better techniques for assessing such subjective matters will evolve;
until they do, such prediction is a matter for specialists. In any
case, the last move in evaluating possible courses of action is to
rank the alternatives on the basis of assigned values, so that the
best option will stand out clearly.

An increasingly promising way to predict costs and effectiveness more precisely is to use mathematical models. Such models
can be powerful tools once they have been validated. They can be
used to calculate output variables as a function of input and

THE PLANNING-PROGRAMMING-BUDGETING SYSTEM (PPBS) IN THE MANAGEMENT CYCLE OF SCHOOLS

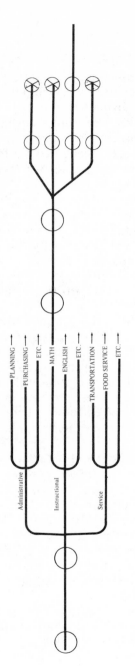
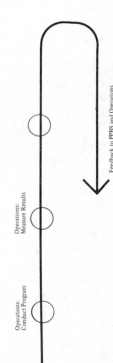

PPBS, Step 1: Develop Broad
Goals and Objectives

PPBS, Step 2: Design
Program Structure

PPBS, Step 3: Define Objectives
for Each Program

PPBS, Step 4: Prepare
Alternative Approaches
for Each Program

PPBS, Step 5: Analyze
Cost-Effectiveness
of Each Approach

PPBS, Step 6: Select Best
Approach; Allocate Funds

PPBS, Step 7: Review
and Evaluate Results

Administrative

PLANNING →
PURCHASING →
ETC. →

Instructional

MATH →
ENGLISH →
ETC. →

Service

TRANSPORTATION →
FOOD SERVICE →
ETC. →

Operations:
Conduct Program

Operations:
Measure Results

Feedback to PPBS and Operations

process variables, thereby aiding management in choosing effective and efficient alternatives.

Cost-effectiveness analysis does not make decisions. It does supply information that increases the decision-maker's knowledge, and it sharpens his judgment by reducing uncertainties. But other unmeasurable factors must be considered—e.g., political climate, community goals, and economic conditions. Only the individual or group that ultimately is responsible for results—like the superintendent or the board of education—should make the final decisions.

Evaluate Each Program's Results

Though review or evaluation of a program's operation is not always listed as a part of PPBS, it is essential. It is this feature that makes PPBS responsive and flexible. Moreover, it must be done by the end of each planning period since it provides the feedback that is needed to adjust and improve goals, objectives, program structure, or the programs themselves during the next planning period. Without this review, management lacks effective control over operations.

Management review and evaluation are basically a matter of comparing actual results with the stated objectives. The results must be measured using the same standards that were employed in defining the objectives. If a program's results are unsatisfactory, either the program must be redesigned or the aspirations stated by the program objectives must be trimmed. Wherever possible, management should exercise control of programs by evaluating them frequently or continually, rather than only at the end of the planning cycle.

PPBS and The Schools

PPBS is really only beginning to enter the school scene. Battelle-Columbus specialists recently surveyed over 40 school districts throughout the nation that have started to use PPBS. Although none of the 32 school districts that returned completed questionnaires is operating completely under PPBS, several districts are well on their way.

The evolution of PPBS for use by many school districts is moving forward. The Research Corporation of the Association of School Business Officials is conducting a project for the U.S. Office of Education, to develop a "program-planning-budgeting-evaluation system design" for local schools. Under a U.S. Office of Education grant, the University of Pennsylvania has developed an education-planning-programming-budget system for the public schools of 6 counties in Pennsylvania. The California State Department of Education is sponsoring work on a conceptual PPBS design for California school districts. Battelle-Columbus currently is investigating PPBS for 90 Ohio school districts; one district has joined with Battelle in a pilot study, and a number of other districts will participate through an advisory council.

In spite of the problems associated with setting up PPBS, school systems are expected to employ it increasingly in the years ahead. As the top people in school systems realize, management and planning are difficult at best. PPBS will not make these activities easy, but it will make them more fruitful. With PPBS, school leaders not only can plan more effectively, but also can be much more successful in reaching the goals and objectives.

As more schools turn to PPBS, approaches to implementing it are expected to improve. Moreover, developments in such areas as learning theory, educational indicators, measurement techniques, organization theory, and predictive models will ease the rigors of implementation and increase the value of PPBS to the schools.   □

Gerald Robinson is Senior Systems Analyst, Management Systems Group, Battelle, Columbus Laboratories.

III

BRINGING MANAGEMENT BY OBJECTIVES TO SCHOOLS

by William D. Hitt

"How can taxpayers know where the schools are trying to go or how well they are getting there unless proper goals are defined and communicated? Consider a school system recently studied: The school board had said: 'Evaluate the program, facilities, and personnel of our system.' The research team began its study by asking, 'What are your goals—what are you trying to accomplish? The answer was an embarrassed silence.'"

We hear a great deal today about "management by objectives", especially in business and industry. Success in directing a commercial enterprise usually is based on skillfully designing useful objectives that mark progress toward the fulfillment of worthwhile goals, and on developing and carrying out procedures for attaining those objectives, and thus the goals. Can a management approach that is so successful in business and industry help education as well? Let's take a look.

Like businesses, school systems need clearly defined statements of what they want to accomplish. Basically, such statements are of two types: *goals,* which are long-term and may be philosophical, idealistic, and even visionary, and *objectives,* which are short-term and attainable, and function as steps to the goals.

A goal of the U.S., according to the Declaration of Independence, is to guard the inalienable rights of the individual to ". . . Life, Liberty, and the pursuit of Happiness." Some years ago AT&T's board chairman cited as a company goal "good, cheap, fast worldwide service for everyone." For school systems a typical goal would be "to develop in each student the ability to acquire and use knowledge effectively."

Reprinted with copyright permission of *Battelle Research Outlook,* Volume 2, Number 2, 1970.

Objectives, on the other hand, are likely to be more sharply focused and down-to-earth. School systems might work toward objectives such as improving the reading achievement of disadvantaged students by a specific amount or decreasing the student dropout rate by a certain percentage. Objectives, unlike goals, can be measured quantitatively and thus can serve as milestones of progress.

Our concern here centers on using proper goals and objectives in managing educational systems—nominally, management by objectives. This is not a simple matter. School systems involve many types of activities. Consider the kaleidoscope of responsibilities facing the school superintendent. He must deal with the curriculum, the staff that administers and teaches it, the facilities and buildings that house and serve the schools, the long- and short-range financing, and not the least, the relations of the school system to the parents and taxpayers. Somehow, the superintendent must pull all these elements together—coordinate, organize, and direct them—so that the system will move toward its goals.

Goals and Education Today

No organization, much less an educational system, can operate meaningfully unless all of its components are working toward common goals. These goals must be stated lucidly and publicized widely so that all concerned will understand and hopefully will accept them; they must come through loud and crystal-clear. The goals for school systems should be tailored specifically, because each system is unique and must set its own direction. And when the time for evaluation comes, there is only one way to determine how the school system is doing, and that is by measuring its progress against its own goals.

Goals should be challenging. They should not be so idealistic and so far out that they are completely unrealistic; nor should they bo so pedestrian that little or no real effort is needed to attain them. The ideal goal for a school system is one that is just beyond its grasp.

Consider a school system recently studied by Battelle-Columbus staff members. The school board had said: "Evaluate the program, facilities, and personnel of our system." The research team began its study by asking: "What are your goals—what are you trying to accomplish?" The answer was an embarrassed silence.

This made life difficult for the research team. They had no definite basis for evaluating the effectiveness of the system under study. In the absence of stated goals, the question arose: Should this school system be compared with some ideal system or some general set of guidelines not specifically tied to the school system itself?

Some bases for evaluation finally were set up. Two were chosen to give ballpark indications: how that system met the state's minimum requirements, and how it compared with the study team's conception of a high-quality educational organization. Neither criterion permitted a meaningful evaluation.

Such lack of goals also comes back to haunt school systems when they go to taxpayers for more funds. What answers can be given when the voters ask, "What are you trying to achieve? Can you give us a good reason for requesting more of our money?" The skepticism underlying such questioning has now become an important factor in voting, as schoolmen know. During a 4-month period in Ohio last year, out of 201 school tax levies and bond issues voted on, 108 were turned down. Many of these lost out because the voters either disagreed with the school system's goals or didn't understand what they were. How can taxpayers know where the schools are trying to go or how well they are getting there unless proper goals are defined and communicated?

Setting Goals

Who should formulate the goals? Even when the system recognizes the importance of goals, the efforts to establish them and subsequently to implement them often are handled ineffectively. In some systems, goals are handed down from on high—by the superintendent's office, the school board, or a specially appointed committee. When this happens, those who must work to attain them, as teachers, or those who are affected by them, as students and parents, are likely to be unhappy and might even refuse to accept them.

Yet, when the task of setting a school system's goals is placed in the hands of those who must live with them, confusion can result. Recently, PTA members and teachers of an elementary school met to lay out broad goals for the school in order to provide guidelines for developing the curriculum and for communicating with parents. As the effort began, teachers said, in effect, "Tell us what

you want, and we'll try to carry it out." Parents replied, "You're
the educators. Tell us what is best for our children."

Because schools exist basically to teach the young and to prepare them for life in the world, the entire community has a real
stake in the school system. Therefore, all those who have children
to be educated, who must finance the schools, and who genuinely
care about the future of their community should have a voice in
determining the direction of the schools. Their right, and responsibility, to participate in formulating goals must be recognized.
This, in turn, calls for creating the means for getting all of these
groups to contribute to the development of worthwhile goals and
for clearly communicating what role each might be expected to
play. The wise school administrator will take the steps needed to
handle this task successfully.

Emphasizing the Important Goals
Establishing priorities for various goals and selecting appropriate means for accomplishing the objectives are critical to the effectiveness of the school system. For example, of goals relating to
buildings, equipment, and facilities dominate a school system's
operation, then that system is being led down a primrose path;
when concern for the student and his involvement in learning gets
pushed aside, the net accomplishments of the system will be questionable. If covering the work plan for that day's class session pre-
cludes the student from participating in life situations where true
learning can occur or if there is no leeway for exploiting an unexpected learning experience, then something is wrong with the way
the goals are being pursued.

It is essential to give precedence to the most important goals.
A school system may be committed to helping each student achiev
achieve a successful life and also to creating the best possible
school plant. When the superintendent is organizing his plans for
attacking these two goals, he may give more attention to the latter,
because it is easier to pin down. Thus, the more important goals
often must play second fiddle, because they generally are more
elusive.

The situation is indeed soriest where excellent goals have
been set up, but are disregarded in actual operations. At the beginning of a study to design a model prison education and training
program, the Battelle-Columbus research team was informed with

great emphasis that the primary goal of the prison system is to help inmates become productive members of society. When asked "On what basis is your performance evaluated?", the warden listed these: (1) the number and severity of disturbances, (2) his ability to stay within the budget, and (3) the profit generated by the prison industries. Real-life circumstances denied the true importance of the stated goal for the prison system. Obviously, preoccupation with goals that should be low in priority, or should not exist at all, will dilute or even negate efforts to achieve what should be the prime goals.

Objectives As Steps To Goals

Reaching a goal is usually a long-term process that involves several intermediate steps. To insure that these steps go in the right direction, each must be carefully defined and oriented. If we take objectives to be synonymous with these steps, then this process calls for setting up and implementing a limited number of achievable objectives. These may be designed to cover the school system as a whole, one educational program (e.g., vocational education), or one course (e.g., auto mechanics). If the system's goals are to be achieved, the objectives for any part of the system must be consistent with those goals.

Objectives should meet three standards. They should: (1) clearly state the type of behavior that is desired; (2) specify the criteria of acceptable performance; and (3) state the conditions. Let us take, for example, an objective that relates to increasing the reading ability of disadvantaged youngsters. If it specifies that after 16 hours of instruction, 90 percent of all students should have 75 percent accuracy on a standardized reading test, achievement can be measured effectively. If any one element were omitted, say, the term of instruction or the kind of test to be used, then the objective would be too vague, and the extent to which it was attained could not be evaluated.

Flexibility is essential in the establishment of an objectives-based curriculum. For example, we cannot expect the same type of performance from every student. Therefore, objectives should recognize variances in abilities and allow each person to be evaluated on the basis of his abilities. In the classroom situation, moreover, the teacher's daily lesson plan should not be so inflexible that it is limited to prescribed materials, which, of necessity;

disregard what is happening in the world at that moment. Many of
these happenings, like the moonshot, have direct relevance to the
student's life and learning situation, and must be dealt with. Objectives, therefore, must give the teacher latitude to take advantage
of the unanticipated.

When objectives are being set, resources and constraints also
must be considered. What funds are available to finance desirable
activities? Can the students afford to pay something toward worthwhile activities—for materials, trips, or extra equipment? Which
local people might volunteer to assist in enriching the educational
program? What public facilities—museums, arboretums, etc.—are
accessible? In another direction, those establishing objectives must
consider legal requirements and the community's social, economic,
and political conditions.

Managing School Systems

Reaping the real advantages of managing by objectives requires careful consideration of the organizational structure that
will be used in applying it. Agreeing on goals and objectives demands the cooperation of many groups. The ability to accomplish
the established objectives depends upon having people who are dependable, capable, and willing to work on the task. As is typical of
all management methods, managing by objectives is successful
only when coordination is maintained with many people and co-
operation is obtained from them, when responsibilities can be
assigned with the assurance that they will be assumed, and when
there is genuine commitment to the desirability of pursuing the
objectives using all available resources and talents.

Generally, four basic types of organization are seen in school
systems:

1. *Authoritarian.* With this type, information and direction
   flow from the top down. The boss gives the orders and
   calls out the goals and objectives. Subordinates are expected to carry them out. The teaching staff, students, and
   people in the community have little or no voice in shaping
   the system. Therefore, they are likely to have little interest
   in achieving the goals and objectives that are specified for
   them.

2. *Laissez-faire.* Here, each staff member pretty much goes

his own way. If objectives are formalized, they are likely to have little relation to the system's goals—if these are even stated. And since communications are likely to be sporadic or non-existent, little or no attempt is made to reach agreement on ultimate purposes or on any other facet of the system.

3. *Management-labor.* Under such management, school matters are likely to be polarized between the administrators and the teachers. As a result, there will be differences in goals and conflicts in objectives, and the school system will be pulled in different directions.

4. *Participative.* This type of management is based upon co-operation by all concerned groups—supervisors, teaching staff, students, and parents. Goals and objectives are established in concert, and all parties work together to attain them. All these people aprticipate actively in the communication process, which operates both up and down and outside the school system. Within the framework of participative management, a formal structure of responsibilities is agreed upon and accepted; those who make the final decisions are also accountable for the results.

The participative type of organization is best fitted to managing by objectives. It incorporates what the philosopher Hegel pointed out years ago, "If I am to exert myself for any object, it must, in some way, be my object." The message for the educational manager is this: get your people immersed in formulating and working toward achieving goals and objectives. The school system and everyone associated with it will benefit. When teachers, parents, and students as well as the superintendent, other administrators, and the school board join forces in designing the basic framework, the school system becomes an authentic *community* educational system; it is a true extension of the participants.

Organizing The School System
The superintendent or manager of a school system will find that managing by objectives will be a refreshing experience, but not an easy one. He will be able to develop schools that meet the needs of the community and that, in turn, elicit a response from

the community. At the same time, he will have evolved a system that will adjust continually to changes in the community and that will reach out to sense and to employ measures that will keep the schools alive and forward-looking.

In general terms, these are the steps that management by objectives calls for:

First, the community's needs and desires should be assessed. This requires inputs from all elements of the community. To provide proper balance, information also should be obtained from the students—directly. Assessment of these inputs will lead to an educational program that will fit the community and the student. This process should be repeated periodically. These inputs will point the way to the instructional, social, ethical, and economic goals that should be established.

With the goals formulated, the next step is to specify the objectives that, when attained, will most effectively accomplish the desired ends. Following this, the type of staff members needed to achieve the objectives, and also the matter of supplementary training for those people, should be considered.

The budgeting of funds is, of course, another major consideration. Each part of the overall program should be reviewed to decide how much financial support it should receive. The balancing of priorities among the various goals and objectives is a critical step in the total process.

Finally, the program should be evaluated in regard to the cost-effectiveness of its various elements. In terms of the stated objectives, these kinds of questions should be asked: What has been accomplished? How much did it cost to achieve that much? What should be done to help the system better achieve its objectives? Answers that are based on both cost and effectiveness must be sought.

The Advantages

Managing by objectives entails an effort that cannot merely be added to the regular, everyday activities of a school administrator, because it represents an approach that is basically different from other approaches to school management. Although managing by objectives will require time for implementation, it should reduce the time that the administrator has to spend in putting out fires.

Properly administered, this management approach will provide several benefits to a school system:

1. Orderly growth of each school's educational program, together with the facilities for implementing it

2. Better recognition and understanding of alternative courses of action

3. A systematic and rational basis for evaluating the program

4. Sensitive means for alerting administrators to drift in the system or its parts

5. An effective mechanism for communicating job responsibilities to all staff members in the system

6. A sound basis for further development of the staff

7. A solid foundation for bringing about cooperation among all those concerned with the educational system.

The net result will be a school system that is geared to the community's needs and desires, to the student's hopes and ambitions, and to the world's trials.   □

William D. Hitt is Director, Center for Improved Education, Battelle, Columbus Laboratories.

IV

ACCOUNTABILITY IN EDUCATION

by Sidney P. Marland, Jr.

"The art of drafting objectives is still quite young and unrefined in education, and this is not surprising. We are dealing with human beings — teachers, parents, children, Congress, the public. And we are dealing with politics and legislation."

Accountability is a relatively new term in the language of education. It is not, however, a completely original concept. As far back as 1649, the Great and Central Courts of Massachusetts Bay Colony required that each town teach its children to read the Scriptures. Noncompliant towns were fined five pounds. That was a form of accountability.

As our modern system of education developed, board of education members, school administrators, and teachers were required by the people to perform certain duties. When today we see a board of education changed, or a teacher asked to resign, that too is a form of accountability.

Accountability as we have known it thus far, however, has been a relatively fumbling, ad hoc process. The new dimensions of accountability which appear to be emerging bring better organized and more precise methods of measurement to the practice of accountability. Efforts are being made to establish objectives in more systematic ways. Management by objective has been recognized as an important key to the smooth operation of our contemporary educational institutions.

Office of Education Objectives
One way to illustrate the management by objective concept is

to describe its operation within the United States Office of Education.

Major educational objectives are established. Though these are called the "Commissioner's Objectives," many other people share in their selection and definition. Some objectives may derive from the law, some from the direction of the White House or the Secretary of Health, Education, and Welfare, but far outweighing these external persuasions is the inner commitment of responsible people at all levels in the Office of Education itself

Eight objectives for fiscal year 1972 were determined and refined over a period of several months last year. They will undoubtedly be further refined and modified as we progress toward their fulfillment, but, simply stated, as they stand today they are:

1. Career Education: To encourage the establishment of school organization, curricula, and educational methods that will enable all students to leave school prepared either to continue their education or to enter the job market with a truly saleable skill.
2. Racial Integration: To achieve between 1972 and 1977 equal educational opportunity for all racial, ethnic, and cultural minorities.
3. Innovation: To promote more responsive alternatives to existing forms of education and pursue significant improvements and modifications of current educational practices.
4. Education of the Handicapped: To obtain a national commitment to specialized training and other essential educational services for all handicapped children.
5. Education of the Disadvantaged: To assure, at all levels of education, equal access to educational opportunities and similar patterns of educational attainment to persons of all economic circumstances by targeting federal dollars on the dissemination and installation of programs that will help to accomplish this goal.
6. The Right to Read: To assure that 99 percent of all people in the United States who are 16 years old and 90 percent of all over 16 will be functionally literate by 1980. This will necessitate the development of procedures by which to determine a community's reading

problems, the evaluation of promising programs and an
analysis of the resources required for each, and the design
and placement of a technical information system regarding
these programs.

7. Special Revenue Sharing: To assist in the passage and implementation of legislation for Special Revenue Sharing for
Education and to prepare for necessary organizational and
administrative changes once this legislation is enacted.

8. Management: To improve the overall management of the
Office of Education, particularly to coordinate financial
and manpower resources, simplify program administration,
and systematize program responsibilities.

Subparts

It is laudable to establish objectives in a radiant atmosphere
of consensus and make confident statements of our good intentions. But that is only the very first and relatively modest step in
the management by objectives process. Once large objectives have
been hammered out, each must be broken into specific and carefully defined subobjectives. Accountability is implicit from day to
day and from month to month as all echelons in the Office of Education focus their energies on the objective and its subobjectives
and perform the various tasks which lead to their completion.

To use a concrete example, let us look at a subcomponent of
the Education of the Handicapped Objective which calls for the
training in 1972 of 17,000 teachers of the handicapped. The goal
was clear as the year began and there was a specific timetable for
its accomplishment. In July, the Office selected the training institutions according to carefully defined criteria. In August, the students to receive special training were chosen. In October, field
trips were made to each institution to assess the progress of their
training program. The programs will be conducted throughout the
remainder of the school year, and evaluated upon their termina-
tion by each participating institution.

The complexities of training 17,000 special education teachers can perhaps best be illustrated by describing some of the work
involved in choosing the teacher training institutions. The Office
of Education disseminates materials it has prepared to inform institutions of higher education and state education agencies of the
possibilities open to them in the area of special education training.

When a university or state education agency applies for funding, it uses these informational materials and the OE program administration manual as guidelines in outlining its plans to prepare special education teachers. The Office of Education, in conjunction with consultants who are sensitive to the needs in the field of education of the handicapped, studies the staffing and other characteristics of the applicant, as well as its specific program proposal. OE not only chooses those institutions which have proven their excellence, but also assists those which could help to meet the great demand for specialists in educating the handicapped if their programs were upgraded. From this careful review system, this year three hundred universities and fifty-five state education agencies (SEAs) and territorial education agencies were selected and have received awards.

The financial aspects of the awarding process are also intricate. Some colleges and SEAs choose to apply for funding through the traineeship system. These institutions receive $2,000 for program support for each undergraduate student receiving a traineeship, and up to $2,500 for each post-graduate student receiving aid. The second form of funding for whcih universities and SEAs can apply is the block grant. Block grant funds are used at the discretion of the institutions which receive them, and separate scholarships are not awarded. The entire process involves many long hours of planning, establishing criteria, designing financial formulas, and otherwise assuring that selection of training institutions will be carried out efficiently and in accord with the criteria for meeting the overall goal. Each step of the process is tracked on a management-by-objectives system, to insure accountability from one echelon of responsibility to the next higher.

When one person in the Bureau of Education for the Handicapped involved in any part of the teacher training effort completes his task—for example the observation of an institutional program—he informs his immediate supervisor. The supervisor then informs his bureau chief, and reports of completed acts are compiled and transmitted from level to level, culminating in a progress report presented by a deputy commissioner to the Commissioner of Education. This check-up occurs at least monthly. Where there are shortfalls, these must be explained, and by discussing ways to avoid future shortfalls, the entire effort of the Office is upgraded. The accountability process does not end with the Commissioner, of course, for he accounts monthly to the Secretary of Health,

Education, and Welfare, who is accountable to the Congress and the President and, through them, to the people.

The major point here is that goals are established, broken into their subparts, and defined as specifics which can be measured. These measurements tell us whether the objectives have been met.

Having defined by illustration a form of accountability which has translatable parts in other institutions of education, I must hasten to add that not all things in education can be easily measured and tracked through a systems approach. The art of drafting objectives is still quite young and unrefined in education, and this is not surprising. We are dealing with human beings—teachers, parents, children, Congress, the public. And we are dealing with politics and legislation.

All these considerations have, until now, made educators reluctant to adopt real accountability. The development of a sound educational system is unlike the development of a scientific product like the Salk vaccine which, complex and elusive as it might have been, was still dealing with something relatively tangible and capable of definition. But who is to say what happens in the heart and mind of a 10-year-old when he perceives for the first time the breach, let us say, of a democratic ideal? An unintended brush-off by his teacher? The academic failure or triumph of a friend? How does it affect him and his view of life, of truth, his home, his school, his community? These are vague concepts, difficult to apply yardsticks to. Nevertheless, the theory of accountability calls for us, if we establish goals such as "the socialization of the child," to verbalize these goals in measurable terms, and we must seek ways to do so.

Accountability Through Objectives

As we define accountability as the process of establishing objectives and assessing the degree to which those objectives have been fulfilled, we must be rational in establishing our methods of measurement and realistic in setting our goals for fulfillment at a given time. Yet we must also know what the people want, for we are ultimately accountable to them. It is, after all, they who own the schools.

Leon Lessinger, sometimes called the high priest of accountability, has said, "Without decision-making responsibility, accountability is a hollow concept." The only way to ensure the account-

ability system's responsiveness to individuals is to involve as many
people as possible in the decision-making process. This is not to
say that the schools will be turned over altogether to the people of
the communities in which they are located without professional
leadership. To advocate that would be to deny the education profession and to say that no expertise is required for excellent
schooling. But it is to say that we must encourage as many persons
as possible—represneting a broad spectrum of interests and backgrounds—to become involved, through the boards of education, in
the work of the schools.

One of the programs administered by the Office of Education
which seeks to match the talents of community people with the
needs of the schools is the Career Opportunities Program. This
program combines work opportunities with study opportunities
for those adults, mostly young, interested in the borad field of
education as a career, in a blending of talent and interest which results in a stronger school and a fulfilled community. Program participants, often from disadvantaged circumstances, are enrolled as
part-time students in colleges in order to gain more expertise in
their fields of interest while they receive practical knowledge in
those fields through work experience. The emphasis is on long-
term study, as opposed to the kind of once-in-a-lifetime study
which has been common.

The Career Opportunities Program places great confidence in
the individual school district and its community instead of looking
to teacher colleges to solve all educational problems. It places confidence in the people, and as a result the 8,000 COP participants
have responded with new self-confidence, with increased trust in
the schools, and with a willingness to help their schools be accountable to the needs of the children they were designed to serve.

Humane Goals

As we pursue the practice of management by objective, we
must always remember the basic imperative of education: the
eternal and transcending obligation to be humane. Our *primary*
concern must always be the fulfillment of individual human beings
rather than the fulfillment of managerial concepts.

Yet even our commitment ot individuals can often be stated
in measurable terms. Consider the very complex and challenging
goal of ending racial isolation. Our objective is to end the dreadful

curse upon our land that is inherent in the separation of races, either by law or by fact. It is an overriding goal, perhaps the most humane of all the goals we have set for ourselves, and yet in its subparts it may appear to be inhumane. Counting children, counting buses, counting houses, counting teachers (and recording the color of their skin)—how cold, how callous, this numbers game appears to be! Yet the impersonal numbers play an important part in the achievement of the broad humane goal. Wise people, creative people, conscientious leaders blending together the implied inhumaneness of the subparts can relate them to the greater good of the major goal. This is a challenge to the wisest and best school leaders, and calls for the involvement of as many people from the community as possible. Again, to bring accountability into full force and avoid the possibility of its being reduced to a mere structure, we must solicit in-depth participation in decision-making from the very start.

Close to $77.6 billion—8 percent of our Gross National Product—was spent on education in the United States in academic year 1970-71. This is double that portion of the GNP devoted to education in 1956, and double the actual dollars spent in 1963. Never before have we invested so heavily in education, and never before has our society so sorely needed the reform which only education can bring. It is apparent that education must find new ways to respond to the public more systematically and meaningfully than it has in the past.

Indeed, within our time—perhaps within the next ten years—there could well be a nationwide accounting process or institution which would act like a certified public accountant in business, objectively assessing the success and failure of our schools and reporting the findings to the public. This agency would find ways to assess both the structure and the content of the educational process. We must know, for example, not only how many teachers are being trained, but how well they are being trained, and we must be able to judge whether the curriculum in the institutions in which they serve is truly relevant to the lives of students and to the needs of the society into which they will graduate.

There are other issues which we must explore, and which a systems approach can elucidate. We need to know how to move from a mass teaching approach to a highly individualized approach, how to go about the important work of treating each child

as an individual human being, how to succeed with those youngsters who have never before experienced success. How do we substitute a vigorous, enjoyable classroom atmosphere for one that
has too often been marked by competition and pain and fear of
failure?

How productively are our teachers being used, and how effectively is their time and wisdom being applied to the needs of the
learner? What technology is available to multiply greatly the teacher's talent? What is the full scope of the university professor's mission? There is typically a ratio of one faculty member to seven or
eight students; is the professor using his time and talents in such a
way as to change the lives of his students—and of how many?
These are pertinent questions of accountability, and as our schools
and colleges face economic crisis, the questions become even more
crucial.

The answers to these questions elude us now, but we can
draw indications of answers by studying which kinds of schools
have holding power as opposed to those with high absenteeism and
dropout rates.

By looking at what happens to people when they leave
school, by looking at the stereotypes which non-schooled people
have placed upon the institutions, and by talking with people who
have been in the system and are now in a position to judge their
own experience, we can begin to define objectives which will help
us to evaluate the less tangible aspects of education, an evaluation
of which is essential to educational success.

A System for Change

In the meantime, I laud such elements of accountability as
are present in performance contracting and the independent audit
of performance. Crude as they are, these are beginnings toward the
kinds of assessment instruments which we must have if our educational system is to be truly responsive to the needs of the society
which it was created to serve. I do not hold that performance contracting is likely to transform the traditional ways of structuring
education, that is, that education firms will set objectives and will
strip teachers, superintendents, and school boards of their decision-making powers. The beauty of a systems approach is that it
will reveal new methods, new techniques, new materials, new
ways to motivate young people, and indeed, new ways to define

objectives. The advent of performance contracting and other profit-making systems approaches may also help us to develop the science of evaluation, for this is an important tool in ascertaining the success of the contractor. Few contractors would resort to chicanery in an effort to increase their profits, but some might built into their curricula techniques which would ensure the correct responses without necessarily ensuring the child's actual assimilation and application of the subject matter. The science of educational evaluation must over time become more refined and exact. This, along with other elements essential to accountability, will continue to challenge our social scientists, our theoreticians, and our educational philosophers so that progress will continue as education accounts to the people in more and more systematic ways.

Accountability, then, is concerned with both people and process. In order to attain the best critique of the process of education, we must weigh educational goals against the needs and goals of all our country's people. We are being severely criticized by many who have not had the opportunity to join in our search for new and better ways to educate. We are even more harshly criticized by some who would not join with us if they were presented with the opportunity. But let us invite everyone to assist in some way in the process of systematically tailoring education to the needs of our rapidly changing society. Together let us consider such elements as the changing structure of the family, the information explosion, the mobility of our citizenry, and the express need for disadvantaged and minority children to learn effectively.

It is true that accountability has always been with us. Until now it did not have a name. While our instruments for its realization are still very blunt, they are gradually being sharpened and refined. One thing seems clear—the expectations of the American people now call for accountability, and that call will not go away.   □

Sidney P. Marland, Jr. is U.S. Commissioner of Education.

V

AN APPROACH TO DEVELOPING ACCOUNTABILITY MEASURES FOR THE PUBLIC SCHOOLS

by Stephen M. Barro

"Each participant in the educational process should be held responsible only for those educational outcomes that he can affect — and only to the extent that he can affect them."

The Concept of Accountability

Although the term "accountability" is too new in the educational vocabulary to have acquired a standard usage, there is little doubt about its general meaning and import for the schools. The basic idea it conveys is that school systems and schools, or, more precisely, the professional educators who operate them, should be held responsible for educational outcomes — for what children learn. If this can be done, it is maintained, favorable changes in professional performance will occur, and these will be reflected in higher academic achievement, improvement in pupil attitudes, and generally better educational results. This proposition — that higher quality education can be obtained by making the professionals responsible for their product — is what makes accountability an attractive idea and provides the starting point for all discussion of specific accountability systems and their uses in the schools.

The unusual rapidity with which the accountability concept has been assimilated in educational circles and by critics of the schools seems less attributable to its novelty than to its serviceability as a unifying theme. Among its antecedents, one can identify at least four major strands of current thought and action in education: 1) the new, federally stimulated emphasis on evaluation of school systems and their programs; 2) the growing tendency to look at educational enterprises in terms of cost effectiveness;

3) increasing concentration on education for the disadvantaged as a priority area of responsibility for the schools; and 4) the movement to make school systems more directly responsive to their clientele and communities, either by establishing decentralized community control or by introducing consumer choice through a voucher scheme. Under the accountability banner, these diverse programs for educational reform coalesce and reinforce one another, each gaining strength and all, in turn, strengthening already powerful pressures for educational change.

How the Schools Can Be Made Accountable

Accountability in the abstract is a concept ot which few would take exception. The doctrine that those employed by the public to provide a service — especially those vested with decision-making power — should be answerable for their product is one that is accepted readily in other spheres and that many would be willing to extend, in principle, to public education. The problems arise in making the concept operational. Then it becomes necessary to deal with a number of sticky questions:

> To what extent should each participant in the educational process — teacher, principal, and administrator — be held responsible for results?
> To whom should they be responsible?
> How are "results" to be defined and measured?
> How will each participant's contribution be determined?
> What will be the consequences for professional educators of being held responsible?

These are the substantive issues that need to be treated in a discussion of approaches to implementing the accountability concept.

Various proposals for making the schools accountable differ greatly in the degree to which they would require existing structures and practices to be modified. In fact, it is fair to say they range from moderate reform to revolution of the educational system. The following paragraphs summarize the major current ideas that, singly or in combination, have been put forth as approaches to higher quality education through accountability:

Use of improved, output-oriented management methods.

What is rapidly becoming a new "establishment" position – though it would have been considered quite revolutionary only a few years ago – is that school district management needs to be transformed if the schools are to become accountable and produce a better product. The focus here is on accountability for effective use of resources. Specific proposals include articulation of goals, introduction and output-oriented management methods (planning-programming-budgeting, systems analysis, etc.), and – most important – regular, comprehensive evaluation of new and on-going programs. Mainly internal workings of the school system rather than relations between school and community would be affected, except that better information on resource use and educational outcomes would presumably be produced and disseminated.

Institutionalization of external evaluations or educational audits. Proposals along this line aim at assuring that assessments of educational quality will be objective and comparable among schools and school districts and that appropriate information will be compiled and disseminated to concerned parties. They embody the element of comparative evaluation of school performance and the "carrot" or "stick" associated with public disclosure of relative effectiveness. A prototype for this function may be found in the "external educational audit" now to be required for certain federal programs. However, the need for consistency in examining and comparing school districts suggests that a state or even a federal agency would have to be the evaluator. This would constitute a significant change in the structure of American public education in that it would impose a centralized quality-control or "inspectorate" function upon the existing structure of autonomous local school systems.

Performance incentives for school personnel. Perhaps the most direct way to use an accountability system to stimulate improved performance is to relate rewards for educators to measures of effectiveness in advancing learning. One way to do this is to develop pay schedules based on measured performance to replace the customary schedules based on teaching experience and academic training. An alternative approach would be to use differentiated staffing as the framework for determining both pay and promotion. The latter is a more fundamental reform in that it involves changes in school district management and organization as well as changes in the method of rewarding teachers. Professional organizations have tended to oppose such schemes, partly out of fear that performance criteria might be applied subjectively, arbitrarily, or inequitably. Although this may not be the only objection, if a measurement system could be developed that would be widely recognized as "objective" and "fair," the obstacles to acceptance of a system of performance incentives might be substantially reduced.

Performance or incentive contracting. Performance contracting rests on the same philosophy as the proposals for incentives, but applies to organizations outside the school system rather than individual professionals within it. A school district contracts with an outside agency — a private firm or, conceivably, a nonprofit organization — to conduct specified instructional activities leading to specified, measurable educational results. The amount paid to the contractor varies according to how well the agreed-upon objectives are accomplished, thereby providing a very direct incentive for effective instruction. At present, there is too little experience with performance contracting to support conclusions about its potential. However, a large number of experiments and several evaluation efforts are under way.[1] Should they prove successful, and should this very direct method of making the purveyor of educational services responsible for his product become widely used, there would undoubtedly be substantial and lasting effects on both the technology and organization of American public education.

Decentralization and community control. These are two conceptually distinct approaches to accountability that we lump together under one heading only because they have been so closely linked in recent events. Administrative decentralization, in which decision-making authority is shifted from central administrators to local area administrators or individual school principals, can itself contribute to accountability. The shift of authority should, for example, favor greater professional responsiveness to local conditions and facilitate the exercise of local initiative. Also, it allows responsibility for results to be decentralized and, in so doing, provides the framework within which various performance incentives can be introduced.

The movement for community control of the highly bureaucratized, big-city school systems aims at accountability in the sense of making the system more representative of and responsive to its clientele and community. In the context of community control, accountability can be defined very broadly to include not only responsibility for performance in achieving goals, but also for selecting appropriate or "relevant" goals in the first place. Most important, community control provides the means of enforcing accountability by placing decision-making and sanctioning powers over the schools in the hands of those whose lives they affect.

Alternative educational systems. Probably the most radical proposal for achieving better education through improved accountability is this one, which would allow competing publicly financed school systems to coexist and would permit parents to choose schools for their children. Usually this is coupled with a proposal for financing by means of "educational vouchers,"[2] although this is not the only possible mechanism. The rationale for this "consumer-choice" solution is that there would be direct accountability by the school to the parent. Furthermore, there would be an automatic enforcement mechanism: A dissatisfied parent would move his child — and funds — to another school. Of course, the burden of becoming informed and evaluating the school would be on the individual parent. At present, there is very little experience with a system of this kind and little basis for judging how well it would operate or what effect it would have on the quality of education.

The Need for Accountability Measures

These proposals, though not mutually exclusive, are quite diverse both with respect to the kinds of restructuring they would imply and the prospective educational consequences. However, they are alike in one important respect: Each can be carried out only with adequate information on the individual and the collective effectiveness of participants in the educational process. At present, such information does not exist in school systems. Therefore, a major consideration in moving toward accountability must be development of information systems, including the data-gathering and analytical activities needed to support them. This aspect of accountability — the nature of the required effectiveness indicators and the means of obtaining them — will be the principal subject of the remainder of this paper.

Progress in establishing accountability for results within school systems is likely to depend directly on success in developing two specific kinds of effectiveness information: 1) improved, more comprehensive pupil performance measurements; and 2) estimates of contributions to measured pupil performance by individual teachers, administrators, schools, and districts. As will be seen, the two have very different implications. The first calls primarily for expansion and refinement of what is now done in the measurement area. The second requires a kind of analysis that is both highly technical and new to school systems and poses a much greater challenge.

The need for more extensive pupil performance measurement is evident. If teachers, for example, are to be held responsible for what is learned by their pupils, then pupil performance must be measured at least yearly so that gains associated with each teacher can be identified. Also, if the overall effectiveness of educators and schools is to be assessed, measurement will have to be extended to many more dimensions of pupil performance than are covered by instruments in common use. This implies more comprehensive, more frequent testing than is standard practice in most school systems. In the longer run, it will probably require substantial efforts to develop and validate more powerful measurement instruments.

But no program of performance measurement alone, no matter how comprehensive or sophisticated, is sufficient to establish accountability. To do that, we must also be able to attribute results (performance gains) to sources. Only by knowing the contributions of individual professionals or schools would it be possible, for example, for a district to operate an incentive pay or promotion system; for community boards in a decentralized system to evaluate local schools and their staffs; or for parents, under a voucher system, to make informed decisions about schools for their children. To emphasize this point, from now on the term "accountability measures" will be used specifically to refer to estimates of contributions to pupil performance by individual agents in the educational process. These are described as "estimates" advisedly, because, unlike performance, which can be measured directly, *contributions* to performance cannot be measured directly but must be *inferred* from comparative analysis of different classrooms, schools, and districts. The analytical methods for determining individual contributions to pupil performance are the heart of the proposed accountability measurement system.

A Proposed Approach

In the following pages we describe a specific approach that could be followed by a school system interested in deriving accountability measures, as they have just been defined. First, a general rationale for the proposed approach is presented. Then the analytical methodology to be used is discussed in more detail.

For what results should educators be held responsible? Ideally, a school system and its constituent parts, as appropriate, should be held responsible for performance in three areas: 1) selecting "correct" objectives and assigning them appropriate priorities, 2) achieving all the stated (or implicit) objectives, and 3) avoiding unintentional adverse effects on pupils. Realistically, much less can even be attempted. The first of the three areas falls entirely outside the realm of objective measurement and analysis, assessment of objectives being an intrinsically subjective, value-laden, and often highly political process. The other two areas can be dealt with in part, subject to the sometimes severe limitations to the current state of the art of educational measurement. The answer to the question posed above must inevitably be a compromise, and not necessarily a favorable one, between what is desirable and what can actually be done.

Any school system aims at affecting many dimensions of pupil performance. In principle, we would like to consider all of them — appropriately weighted — when we assess teacher, school, or district effectiveness. In practice, it is feasible to work with only a subset of educational outcomes, namely, those for which (a) objectives are well defined and (b) we have some ability to measure output. The dimensions of performance that meet these qualifications tend to fall into two groups: first, certain categories of cognitive skills, including reading and mathematics, for which standardized, validated tests are available; second, certain affective dimensions — socialization, attitudes toward the community, self-concept, and the like — for which we have such indicators or proxies as rates of absenteeism, drop-out rates, and incidence of vandalism and delinquency. For practical purposes, these are the kinds of educational outcome measures that would be immediately available to a school system setting out today to develop an accountability system.

Because of the limited development of educational measurement, it seems more feasible to pursue this approach to accountability in the elementary grades than at higher levels, at least in the short run. Adequate instruments are available for the basic skill areas — especially reading — which are the targets of most efforts to improve educational quality at the elementary level. They are not generally available — and certainly not as widely used or accepted — for the subject areas taught in the secondary schools. Presumably, this is partly because measurement in those areas is inherently more difficult; it is partly, also, because there is much less agreement about the objectives of secondary education. Whatever the reason, establishing accountability for results at the secondary level is likely to be more difficult. Pending further progress in specifying objectives and measuring output, experiments with accountability measurement systems would probably be more fruitfully carried on in the elementary schools.

Fortunately, existing shortcomings in the measurement area can be overcome in time. Serious efforts to make accountability a reality should, themselves, spur progress in the measurement field. However, for the benefits of progress to be realized, the system must be "open" — not restricted to certain dimensions of performance. For this reason, the methodology described here has been designed to be in no way limiting with respect to the kinds of outcome measures that can be handled or the number of dimensions that can ultimately be included.

Who should be accountable for what? Once we have determined what kinds of pupil progress to measure, we can turn to the more difficult problem of determining how much teachers, principals, administrators, and others have contributed to the measured results. This is the key element in a methodology for accountability measurement.

The method proposed here rests on the following general principle: *Each participant in the educational process should be held responsible only for those educational outcomes that he can affect by his actions or decision and only to the extent that he can affect them.* Teachers, for example, should not be deemed "ineffective" because of shortcomings in the curriculum or the way in which instruction is organized, assuming that those matters are determined at the school and district level and not by the individual teacher. The appropriate question is, "How well does the teacher perform, given the environment (possibly adverse) in which she must work and the constraints (possibly overly restrictive) imposed upon her?" Similarly, school principals and other administrators at the school level should be evaluated according to how well they perform within constraints established by the central administration.

The question then arises of how we know the extent to which teachers or administrators can affect outcomes by actions within their own spheres of responsibility. The answer is that we do not know *a priori;* we must find out from the performance data. This leads to a second principle: *The range over which a teacher, a school principal, or an administrator may be expected to affect outcomes is to be determined empirically from analysis of results obtained by all personnel working in comparable circumstances.* Several implications follow from this statement. First, it clearly establishes that the accountability measures will be relative, involving comparisons among educators at each level of the system. Second, it restricts the applicability of the methodology to systems large enough to have a wide range of professional competence at each level and enough observations to permit reliable estimation of the range of potential teacher and school effects.[3] Third, it foreshadows several characteristics of the statistical models needed to infer contributions to results. To bring out the meaning of these principles in more detail, we will explore them from the points of view of teachers, school administrators, and district administrators, respectively.

Classroom teachers. We know that the educational results obtained in a particular classroom (e.g., pupils' scores on a standard reading test) are determined by many other things besides the skill and effort of the teacher. The analyses in the Coleman report,[4] other analyses of the Coleman survey data,[5] and other statistical studies of the determinants of pupil achievement[6] show that a large fraction of variation in performance levels is accounted for by out-of-school variables, such as the pupils' socioeconomic status and home environment. Another large fraction is attributable to a so-called "peer group" effect; that is, it depends on characteristics of a pupil's classmates rather than on what takes place in the school. Of the fraction of the variation that *is* explained by school variables, only part can be attributed to teachers. Some portion must also be assigned to differences in resource availability at the classroom and school level and differences among schools in the quality of their management and support. Thus, the problem is to separate out the teacher effect from all the others.

To illustrate the implications for the design of an accountability system, consider the problem of comparing teachers who
teach very different groups of children. For simplicity, suppose
that there are two groups of pupils in a school system, each internally homogeneous, which we may call "middle-class white" and
"poor minority." Assume that all nonteacher inputs associated
with the schools are identical for the two groups. Then, based on
general experience, we would probably expect the whole distribution of results to be higher for the former group than for the latter.
In measuring gain in reading performance, we might well find, for
example, that even the poorest teacher of middle-class white children obtains higher average gains in her class than the majority of
teachers of poor minority children. Moreover, the ranges over
which results vary in the two groups might be unequal.

If we have reason to believe that the teachers associated with
the poor minority children are about as good, on the average, as
those associated with the middle-class white children — that is, if
they are drawn from the same manpower pool and assigned to
schools and classrooms without bias — then it is apparent that
both the difference in average performance of the two groups of
pupils and the difference in the range of performance must be
taken into account in assessing each teacher's contribution. A
teacher whose class registers gains, say, in the upper 10% of all
poor minority classes should be considered as effective as one
whose middle-class white group scores in the upper 10% for that
category, even though the absolute performance gain in the latter
case will probably be much greater.

This illustrates that accountability measures are relative in
two senses. First, they are relative in that each teacher's contribution is evaluated by comparing it with the contributions made by
other teachers in similar circumstances. In a large city or state
school system, it can safely be assumed that the range of teacher
capabilities covers the spectrum from poor to excellent. Therefore,
the range of observed outcomes, after differences in circumstances
have been allowed for, is likely to be representative of the range
over which teacher quality can be expected to influence results,
given the existing institutional framework. It may be objected that
the range of outcomes presently observed understates the potential range of accomplishment because present classroom methods,
curricula, teacher training programs, etc., are not optimal. This

may be true and important, but it is not relevant in establishing teacher accountability because the authority to change those aspects of the system does not rest with the teacher.

Second, accountability measures are relative in that pupil characteristics and other nonteacher influences on pupil performance must be taken fully into account in measuring each teacher's contribution. Operationally, this means that statistical analyses will have to be conducted of the effects of such variables as ethnicity, socioeconomic status, and prior educational experience on a pupil's progress in a given classroom. Also, the effects of classroom or school variables other than teacher capabilities will have to be taken into account. Performance levels of the pupils assigned to different teachers can be compared only after measured performance has been adjusted for all of these variables. The statistical model for computing these adjustments is, therefore, the most important element in the accountability measurement system.

School administrators. Parallel reasoning suggests that school administrators can be held accountable for relative levels of pupil performance in their schools to the extent that the outcomes are not attributable to pupil, teacher, or classroom characteristics or to school variables that they cannot control The question is, having adjusted for differences in pupil and teacher inputs and having taken account of other characteristics of the schools, are there unexplained differences among schools that can be attributed to differences in the quality of school leadership and administration? Just as for teachers, accountability measures for school administrators are measures of relative pupil performance in a school after adjusting the data for differences in variables outside the administrators' control.

Consideration of the accountability problem at the school level draws attention to one difficulty with the concept of accountability measurement that may also, in some cases, be present at the classroom level. The difficulty is that although we would like to establish accountability for individual professionals, when two or more persons work together to perform an educational task there is no statistical way of separating their effects. This is easy to see at the school level. If a principal and two assistant principals administer a school, we may be able to evaluate their relative proficiency as a team, but since it is not likely that their respective administrative tasks would relate to different pupil performance measures there is no way of judging their individual contributions by analyzing educational outcomes. Similarly, if a classroom teacher works with a teaching assistant, there is no way, strictly speaking, to separate the contributions of the two. It is conventional in these situations to say that the senior person, who has supervisory authority, bears the responsibility for results. However, while this is administratively and perhaps even legally valid, it provides no solution to the problem of assessing the effort and skills of individuals. Therefore, there are definite limits, which must be kept in mind, to the capacity of a statistically based accountability system to aid in assessing individual proficiency.

District administrators. Although the same approach applies, in principle, to comparisons among districts (or decentralized components of larger districts), there are problems that may limit its usefulness in establishing accountability at the district level. One, of course, is the problem that has just been alluded to. Even if it were possible to establish the existence of overall district effects, it would be impossible to isolate the contributions of the local district board, the district superintendent, and other members of the district staff. A second problem is that comparisons among districts can easily fail to take account of intangible community characteristics that may affect school performance. For example, such factors as community cohesion, political attitudes, and the existence of racial or other intergroup tensions could strongly influence the whole tone of education. It would be very difficult to separate effects of these factors from effects of direct, district-related variables in trying to assess overall district performance. Third, the concept of responsibility at the district level needs clarifying. In comparing schools, for example, it seems reasonable to adjust for differences in teacher characteristics on the grounds that school administrators should be evaluated according to how well they do, given the personnel assigned to them. However, at the district level, personnel selection itself is one of the functions for which administrators must be held accountable, as are resource allocation, program design, choice of curriculum, and other factors that appear as "givens" to the schools. In other words, in assessing comparative district performance, very little about districts can properly be considered as externally determined except, perhaps, the total level of available resources.[7] The appropriate policy, then, seems to be to include district identity as a variable in comparing schools and teachers so that net district effects, if any, will be taken into account. Districts themselves should be compared on a different basis, allowing only for differences in pupil characteristics, community variables, and overall constraints that are truly outside district control.

A Proposed Methodology

The basic analytical problem in accountability measurement is to develop a technique for estimating the contributions to pupil performance of individual agents in the educational process. A statistical method that may be suitable for that purpose is described here. The basic technique is multiple regression analysis of the relationship between pupil performance and an array of pupil, teacher, and school characteristics. However, the proposed method calls for two or three separate stages of analysis. The strategy is first to estimate the amount of performance variation that exists among classrooms after pupil characteristics have been taken into account, then, in subsequent stages, to attempt to attribute the interclassroom differences to teachers, other classroom variables, and school characteristics.[8] This methodology applies both to large school districts, within which it is suitable for estimating the relative effectiveness of individual teachers and schools in advancing pupil performance, and to state school systems, where it can be used, in addition, to obtain estimates of the relative effectiveness of districts. However, as noted above, there are problems that may limit its utility at the interdistrict level.

Pupil performance data. Since we are interested in estimating the contributions of individual teachers and schools, it is appropriate to use a "value-added" concept of output. That is, the appropriate pupil performance magnitudes to associate with a particular teacher are the *gains* in performance made by pupils while in her class. Ideally, the output data would be generated by a program of annual (or more frequent) performance measurement, which would automatically provide before and after measures for pupils at each grade level.

It is assumed that a number of dimensions of pupil performance will be measured, some by standardized tests and some by other indicators or proxy variables. Specific measurement instruments to be used and dimensions of performance to be measured would have to be determined by individual school systems in accordance with their educational objectives. No attempt will be made here to specify what items should be included.[9] The methodology is intended to apply to any dimension of performance that can be quantified at least on an ordinal scale. Therefore, within a very broad range, it is not affected by the choice of output measures by a potential user.

Data on pupils, teachers, classrooms, and schools. To conform with the model to be described below, the variables entering into the analysis are classified according to the following taxonomy:

1. Individual pupil characteristics (ethnicity, socioeconomic status, home, family, and neighborhood characteristics, age, prior performance, etc.).

2. Teacher and classroom characteristics.
   a) Group characteristics of the pupils (ethnic and socioeconomic composition, distribution of prior performance levels, etc., within the classroom).
   b) Teacher characteristics (age, training, experience, ability and personality measures if available, ethnic and socioeconomic background, etc.).
   c) Other classroom characteristics (measures of resource availability: class size, amount of instructional support, amount of materials, condition of physical facilities, etc.).

3. School characteristics.
   a) Group characteristics of the pupils (same as 2a, but based on the pupil population of the whole school).
   b) Staff characteristics (averages of characteristics in 2b for the school as a whole, turnover and transfer rates; characteristics of administrators — same as 2b).
   c) Other school characteristics (measures of resource availability: age and condition of building, availability of facilities, amount of administrative and support staff, etc.).

No attempt will be made to specify precisely what items should be collected under each of the above headings. Determination of the actual set of variables to be used in a school system would have to follow preliminary experiementation, examination of existing data, and an investigation of the feasibility, difficulty, and cost of obtaining various kinds of information.

Steps in the analysis. The first step is to determine how different pupil performance in each classroom at a given grade level is from mean performance in all classrooms, *after* differences in individual pupil characteristics have been allowed for. The procedure consists of performing a multiple regression analysis with gain in pupil performance as the dependent variable. The independent variables would include (a) the individual pupil characteristics (category 1 of the taxonomy), and (b) a set of "dummy" variables, or identifiers, one for each classroom in the sample. The latter would permit direct estimation of the degree to which pupil performance in each classroom differs from pupil performance in the average classroom. Thus, the product of the first stage of the analysis would be a set of estimates of individual classroom effects, each of which represents the combined effect on pupil performance in a classroom of all the classroom and school variables included in categories 2 and 3 of the taxonomy. At the same time, the procedure would automatically provide measures of the accuracy with which each classroom effect has been estimated. Therefore, it would be possible to say whether average performance gains in a particular classroom are significantly higher or lower than would be expected in a "typical" classroom or not significantly different from the mean.

Heuristically, this procedure compares performance gains by pupils in a classroom with gains that comparable pupils would be likely to achieve in a hypothetical "average" classroom of the system. This can be thought of as comparison of class performance gains against a norm, except that there is, in effect, a particular norm for each classroom based on its unique set of pupil characteristics. It may also be feasible to carry out the same analysis for specific subgroups of pupils in each class so as to determine, for example, whether there are different classroom effects for children from different ethnic or socioeconomic groups.

Estimation of teacher contributions. The second stage of the analysis has two purposes: 1) to separate the effects of the teacher from effects of nonteacher factors that vary among classrooms; and 2) to determine the extent to which pupil performance can be related to specific, measurable teacher attributes. Again, the method to be used is regression analysis, but in this case with a sample of classroom observations rather than individual pupil observations. The dependent variable is now the classroom effect estimated in stage one. The independent variables are the teacher-classroom characteristics and "dummy" variables distinguishing the individual schools.

Two kinds of information can be obtained from the resulting equations. First, it is possible to find out what fraction of the variation in performance gains among classrooms is accounted for by nonteacher characteristics, including group characteristics of the pupils and measures of resource availability in the classroom. The remaining interclassroom differences provide upper-bound estimates of the effects that can be attributed to teachers. If there is sufficient confidence that the important nonteacher variables have been taken into account, then these estimates provide the best teacher accountability measures. They encompass the effects of both measured and unmeasured teacher characteristics on teacher performance. However, there is some danger that such measures also include effects of group and classroom characteristics that were inadvertently neglected in the analysis and that are not properly attributable to teachers. This problem is referred to again below.

Second, we can find out the extent to which differences among classrooms are explained by measured teacher characteristics. Ideally, of course, we would like to be able to attribute the whole "teacher portion" of performance variation to specific teacher attributes and, having done so, we would be much more confident about our overall estimates of teacher effectiveness. But experience to date with achievement determinant studies has shown that the more readily available teacher characteristics — age, training, experience, and the like — account for only a small fraction of the observed variance. It has been shown that more of the variation can be accounted for when a measure of teacher verbal ability is included.[10] Still more, presumably, could be accounted for if a greater variety of teacher ability and personality measurements were available. At present, however, knowledge of what teacher characteristics influence pupil performance is incomplete and satisfactory instruments exist for measuring only a limited range of teacher-related variables. This means that with an accountability information system based on current knowledge, the excluded teacher characteristics could be at least as important as those included in determining teacher effectiveness. For the time being, then, the interclassroom variation in results that remains after nonteacher effects have been allowed for probably provides the most useful accountability measures, though the danger of bias due to failure to include all relevant nonteacher characteristics must be recognized.

The principal use of these estimates would be in assessing the relative effectiveness of individual teachers in contributing to gains in pupil performance. More precisely, it would be possible to determine whether each teacher's estimated contribution is significantly greater or significantly smaller than that of the average teacher. At least initially, until there is strong confirmation of the validity of the procedure, a rather stringent significance criterion should be used in making these judgments and no attempt should be made to use the results to develop finer gradations of teacher proficiency.

The analysis will also make it possible to determine the extent to which measured teacher characteristics are significantly correlated with teacher effectiveness. Potentially, such information could have important policy implications and impacts on school management, resource allocation, and personnel practices. A number of these potential applications are noted at the end of th paper.

Estimation of contributions by school administrators. The same analytical techniques can be used in estimating the relative effectiveness of different schools in promoting pupil performance. Conceptually, a school accountability index should measure the difference between pupil performance in an individual school and average pupil performance in all schools after all pupil, teacher, and classroom variables have been accounted for. Such measures can be obtained directly if school dummy variables are included in the regression equation, as described earlier. Of course, the results measure *total* school effects, without distinguishing among effects due to school administration, effects of physical attributes of the school, and effects of characteristics of the pupil population. It may be feasible to perform a third-stage anlaysis in which the results are systematically adjusted for differences in the latter two categories of variables, leaving residual effects that can be attributed to the school administrators. These would constitute the accountability measures to be used in assessing the effectiveness of the principal and his staff. The results may have policy implications with respect to differential allocation of funds or resources among the different schools and, of course, implications with respect to personnel. Also, as would be done for teachers, an attempt could be made to relate measured characteristics of the school administrators to the estimated school effects. By so doing, it might be possible to learn whether administrator training and experience and other attributes are reflected in measured school output. Even negative results could provide important guidance to research on administrator selection and assignment.

Comparisons among districts. For reasons that have already been stated, it would probably be desirable to treat comparisons among districts separately from comparisons among classrooms and schools. This could be done by means of yet another regression analysis, with individual pupil performance gain as the dependent variable and with independent variables consisting of pupil and community characteristics, measures of resource availability, and a dummy variable or identifier for each district being compared. The purpose would be to determine whether there are significant differences in results among districts once the other factors have been allowed for. If there are, the findings could be interpreted as reflections of differences in the quality of district policy making and management. But as pointed out earlier, there would be uncertainty as to the causes of either shortcomings or superior performance. Nevertheless, the results could have some important, policy-related uses, as will be noted shortly.

The Need for Experimental Verification of the Approach

The methodology described here carries no guarantee. Its success in relating outcomes to sources may depend both on features of the school systems to which it is applied and on the adequacy of the statistical models in mirroring the underlying (and unknown) input-output relationships in education. The validity and usefulness of the results must be determined empirically from field testing in actual school systems. Experimental verification, possibly requiring several cycles of refinement and testing, must precede implementation of a "working" accountability system.

Potential problems. Three kinds of technical problems can threaten the validity of the system: intercorrelation, omission of variables, and structural limitations of the models. None of these can be discussed in detail without mathematics. However, a brief explanation of each is offered so that the outlook for the proposed approach can be realistically assessed.

Intercorrelation. This is a problem that may arise where there are processes in a school system that create associations (correlations) between supposedly independent variables in the model. An important example is the process — said to exist in many systems — whereby more experienced, better trained, or simply "better" teachers tend to be assigned or transferred to schools with higher socioeconomic status (SES) pupils. Where this occurs, pupil SES will be positively correlated with those teacher characteristics. On the average, high SES children would be taught by one kind of teacher, low SES children by another. This would make it difficult to say whether the higher performance gains likely to be observed for high SES pupils are due to their more advantaged backgrounds or to the superior characteristics of their instructors. There would be ambiguity as to the magnitude of the teacher contribution and a corresponding reduction in the reliability of estimates of individual teacher effectiveness. Thus, the quality of accountability information would be impaired.

This problem can take many forms. There may be strong correlations between characteristics of pupils and characteristics of school staffs, between teacher characteristics and nonteacher attributes of the schools, between classroom-level and district-level variables, and so on. The general effect is the same in each instance: ambiguity resulting in diminished ability to attribute results to sources.[11]

There are several things that can be done to mitigate the effects of intercorrelation. One is to stratify the data. For example, if teacher characteristics were linked to pupil SES, it would be possible to stratify the classrooms by pupil SES and to perform separate analyses for each stratum. This would eliminate some of the abmiguity *within* strata. One the other hand, comparisons of teachers *across* strata would be precluded. Another possible solution would be to take account of interdependence explicitly in the statistical models. Some attempts along this line have been made in studies of determinants of school performance. However, this solution is likely to raise a whole new array of technical problems as well as questions about the feasibility of routine use of the methodology within school systems.

The problem of omitted variables. The validity and fairness of the proposed approach would depend very strongly on inclusion of all major relevant variables that could plausibly be cited by teachers or administrators to "explain" lower-than-average estimated contributions. This means that all variables would have to be included that (a) have significant, independent effects on performance and (b) are likely to be nonuniformly distributed among classrooms and schools.

It will never be possible to demonstrate in a positive sense that all relevant variables have been included. Many intangible, difficult-to-measure variables, such as pupil attitudes, morale, "classroom climate," etc., can always be suggested. What can be done is to determine as well as possible that none of the additional suggested variables is systematically related to the estimated teacher and school contributions. In an experimental setting, administrators could be interviewed for the purpose of identifying alleged special circumstances, and tests could be carried out to see whether they are systematically related to performance differences.

Structural limitations of the models. The models described here may be too simple to take account of some of the important relationships among school inputs and outputs. One such shortcoming has already been noted: The models do not allow for possible interdependencies among the various pupil and school characteristics. Another, whcih may prove to be more troubling, is that interactions among the various output or performance variables have also not been taken into account.

Researchers have pointed to two distinct kinds of relationships. First, there may be trade-offs between performance areas.[12] A teacher or school may do well in one area partly at the expense of another by allocating resources or time disproportionately between the two. Second, there may be complementary relationships. Increased performance in one area (reading, for example) may contribute directly to increased performance in others (social studies or mathematics). Therefore, treatment of one dimension of output at a time, without taking the interactions into account, could produce misleading results.

Econometricians have developed "simultaneous" models, consisting of whole sets of equations, specifically to take account of complex, multiple relationships among variables. Some attempts have been made to apply these models to studies of determinants of educational outcomes.[13] It may prove necessary or desirable to use them in an accountability measurement system, despite the complexity they would add, to eliminate biases inherent in simpler models.

Validity. Another important reason for thoroughly testing the accountability measurement system is that its validity needs to be assessed. Some of the procedures mentioned above contribute to this end, but more general demonstration would also be desirable. Two procedures that may be feasible in an experimental situation are as follows:

Replication. A strong test of whether the method really gets at differences in effectiveness instead of differences in circumstances would be to apply it to the same teachers and schools during two or more years. Consistence in results from year to year would strongly support the methodology. Lack of consistency would show that major influences on performance remained unmeasured or neglected. Certainly, if the results were to be used in any way in connection with personnel assignment, reward, or promotion, the use of several years' estimates would be an important guarantee of both consistency and fairness.

An external test of validity. The most direct way to test the validity of the statistical approach is to compare the results with alternative measures of teacher and school effectiveness. The only measures that are likely to be obtainable are subjective assessments by informed and interested parties. Though such evaluations have many shortcomings, it could be valuable in an experimental situation to see how well they agreed with the statistical results. Two important questions that would have to be answered in making such a comparison are: 1) Who are the appropriate raters – peers, administrators, parents, or even pupils? and 2) What evaluation instruments could be used to assure that subjective assessments apply to the same dimensions of performance as were taken into account in the statistical analysis? It may not be possible to provide satisfactory answers. Nevertheless, the feasibility of a comparison with direct assessments should be considered in connection with any effort to test the proposed accountability measurement system.

Potential Uses of Accountability Measures

Space does not permit a full review of the potential uses of an accountability measurement system. However, an idea of the range of applications and their utility can be conveyed by listing some of the main possibilities.

Identification of effective schools. The most rudimentary use of the proposed accountability measures is as an identification device. Once relative school effectiveness is known, a variety of actions can follow, even if there is ambiguity about causes. As examples, less formal evaluation efforts can be more precisely targeted once school effectiveness with different kinds of children is known and campaigns can be initiated to discover, disseminate, and emulate good practices of high-performing schools.

Personnel assignment and selection. Accountability measures may help to improve both staff utilization and selection of new personnel. Personnel utilization could be improved by using information on teacher effectiveness in different spheres and with different types of students for guidance in staff assignment. Selection and recruitment could be aided by using information from the models as a guide to performance-related characteristics of applicants and as a basis for revising selection procedures and criteria.

Personnel incentives and compensation. An accountability measurement system can be used to establish a connection between personnel compensation and performance. One use would be in providing evidence to support inclusion of more relevant variables in pay scales than the universally used and widely criticized training and experience factors. Another possibility would be to use accountability measures as inputs in operating incentive pay or promotion systems. The latter, of course, is a controversial proposal, long resisted by professional organizations. Nevertheless, putting aside other arguments pro and con, the availability of objective measures of individual contributions would eliminate a major objection to economic incentives and help to make the idea more acceptable to all concerned.

Improved resource allocation. An accountability measurement system could also contribute to other aspects of resource allocation in school systems. Analytical results from the models could be of value, for example, in setting policies on class size, supporting services, and similar resource variables. More directly, school accountability measures could provide guidance to district administrators in allocating resources differentially among schools according to educational need. Similarly, state-level results could be used in determinging appropriate allocations of state aid funds to districts.

Program evaluation and research. Models developed for accountability could prove to be valuable tools for program evaluation and research. They could be readily adapted for comparing alternative ongoing programs simply by including "program" as one of the classroom variables. Also, "norms" provided by the models for specific types of pupils could be used as reference standards in evaluating experimental programs. This would be preferable, in some cases, to using experimental control groups. Viewed as research tools, the models could help to shed light on one of the most basic, policy-related problems in education, the relationship between school inputs and educational output. The process of developing the models could itself be very instructive. The results could add substantially to our knowledge of how teachers and schools make a difference to their pupils.

In sum, there are many potential uses of the proposed measures and models, some going well beyond what is generally understood by "accountability." If the development of a system is undertaken and carried through to completion, the by-products alone may well prove to be worth the effort.   □

Stephen M. Barro is an economist with the Rand Corporation, Santa Monica, California. Any views expressed in this paper are those of the author. They should not be interpreted as reflecting the views of the Rand Corporation or the official opinion or policy of any of its governmental or private research sponsors.

---

[1] An experiment involving 18 districts and testing several different forms of performance contracting is being carried out in 1970-72 under sponsorship of the Office of Economic Opportunity. Also, the Department of Health, Education, and Welfare has contracted with the Rand Corporation to carry out an evaluation of other efforts to plan and implement performance contracts.

[2] See *Education Vouchers: A Preliminary Report on Financing Education by Payments to Parents,* Center for the Study of Public Policy, Cambridge, Mass., March, 1970.

[3] This does not mean that accountability cannot be established in small school districts. It does mean that the analysis must take place in a broader context, such as a regional or statewide evaluation of performance, which may encompass many districts.

[4] James S. Coleman *et. al., Equality of Educational Opportunity.* Washington, D.C.: Office of Education 1966.

[5] George W. Mayeske *et al.,* "A Study of Our Nation's Schools" (a working paper), Office of Education, 1970.

[6] E.g., Eric A. Hanushek, "The Education of Negroes and Whites," unpublished Ph.D. dissertation, M.I.T., 1968; and Herbert J. Kiesling, "The Relationship of School Inputs to Public School Performance in New York State," The Rand Corporation, P-4211, October, 1969.

[7] In addition, of course, there are constraints imposed by state or federal authorities, but these are likely to be the same across districts.

[8]The statistical method described here is essentially the same as that used by Eric A. Hanushek in a study, *The Value of Teachers in Teaching,* to be published in late 1970 by the Rand Corporation.

[9]Realistically, however, almost every school system will be likely to include reading achievement scores and other scores on standardized tests of cognitive skills among its output variables. Also, it will generally be desirable to include attendance or absenteeism as a variable, both because it may be a proxy for various attitudinal output variables and because it may be an important variable to use in explaining performance. Otherwise, there are innumerable possibilities for dealing with additional dimensions of cognitive and affective performance.

[10]Hanushek, *The Value of Teachers in Teaching, op. cit.*

[11]The existence of this type of ambiguity in analyses of the Coleman survey data is one of the principal findings reported in Mayeske, *op. cit.*

[12]See Henry M. Levin, "A New Model of School Effectiveness," in *Do Teachers Make a Difference?* Washington, D.C.: Office of Education, 1970, pp. 56-57.

[13]*Ibid.,* pp. 61 ff.

VI

A SYSTEMS APPROACH
TO STUDENT PERSONNEL SERVICES

by Richard W. Hostrop

"Good instructional faculty would not think of entering a class-room without at least a lesson plan and increasingly would not think of entering their classrooms without clearly spelled out measurable learning objectives. Contrast this with the state of affairs with all too many student personnel offices where the staff waits for students to 'drop in.' "

Those of us in the two-year colleges solemnly state we consider the counseling and guidance function of our institutions of equal (or near equal) importance to the curricular functions of our institutions. Yet our actions appear to "speak platitudes" rather than facts.

With but few exceptions, counseling programs across the land have no well-thought-out, planned or organized program. In short, most student personnel offices have failed to have any clearly defined objectives. Is it any wonder then that on so many campuses the instructional faculty views the counseling faculty with less respect than their own peers?

Good instructional faculty would not think of entering a classroom without at least a lesson plan and increasingly would not think of entering their classrooms without clearly spelled out measurable learning objectives. Contrast this with the state of affairs with all too many student personnel offices where the staff waits for students to "drop in" or at best uses "tripping counseling" by means of dispersing counselors throughout various geographical locations on campus. Certainly, student personnel offices should be commended for seeking varied solutsion ofr ministering to the curricular and noncurricular needs of their students. However, these and similar solutions, by and large, are desperation measures. Such offices know there *is* a problem but, rather than ask the "right" questions, they persist in putting out "fires." Until student personnel professionals begin to ask the right questions and take the necessary actions as a result of the answers to these questions, they will continue to function at less than an optimum level.

Though a number of questions ought to be asked, I believe almost every list needs to include the following:

1. How can we improve our recruitment of the economically disadvantaged?
2. How can we assist every student to choose realistic career goals?
3. How can we reduce attrition?
4. How can we assist students in improving their academic performance?
5. How can we assist students in making the college experience more relevant — both the curricular and noncurricular aspects?

Turning these questions into objectives, each student personnel office needs to establish the following or similar achievement goals:

Task 1:   Recruit economically disadvantaged students.

Some
Possible
Means: (1)   provide store-front counseling centers in the heart of the neighborhoods where such potential students reside;
             (2)   offer courses in these neighborhoods;
             (3)   work with business and industry in cooperative learning-working arrangements for the so-called hard core unemployed; and,
             (4)   especially, seek out such students in the feeder high schools of the district.

*Suggested
Criterion:*   The percentage of the student body coming from economically disadvantaged homes (family income below $6,000 annually) will increase at a percentage rate of not less than twice the enrollment rate of those not

coming from this category as compared to the previous academic year.

Task 2: Assist every student to choose realistic career goals.

Some Possible Means:

(1) Employ one or more *high school* counselors in each feeder high school on a part-time basis after thorough inservice training to assist the current high school senior in planning a realistic curriculum offered by the college;

(2) have some college counselors available to students throughout the entire summer on campus; and

(3) have roving college counselors at various times of the day and evening spend a portion of their time at various key centers throughout the district (libraries, schools, churches, etc.) — one or two days at a time.

Suggested Criterion: The percentage of students who enroll solely in baccalaureate oriented courses will *decrease* by not less than 5 percent over the previous academic year as compared to those enrolled in career curricula who will *increase* proportionately by not less than 5 percent over the previous year (we know that more than two thirds of our students avow they are transfer students when in reality less than one third actually do transfer).

Task 3: Increase the number of students who complete a program (reduce attrition).[1]

Some Possible Means:

(1) By means of Task 2, assist the student to choose realistic career goals — and hence a realistic curriculum;

(2) require enrollment in an orientation credit course as part of the general education program since such courses reduce attrition;

(3) establish a procedure requiring students to see a counselor for assistance who at midterm receive two or more grades below satisfactory performance;

(4) eliminate the present punitive grading system (no F's); and

(5)   establish an exit interview requirement for all students who state they wish to drop out of college in
order to dissuade them, when appropriate, and to
ascertain their reasons for wishing to drop out so
as to improve the relevancy of the college experience for present and future students.

Suggested
Criterion: The percentage of students who complete a program will
increase by not less than 5 percent over the previous
academic year; hence, the dropout rate will be reduced
by not less than 5 percent over the previous year.

Task 4:   Increase the learning results of students.

Some
Possible
Means: (1)   Work closely with the instructional faculty in assisting them to become more fully aware of the impor-
tance of developing clearly stated measurable learning tasks, conditions, and criteria for each course
so that students will know the exact instructor-
specified standard of learning mastery expected for
each course offering;
(2)   require enrollment in a Learning Skills Center as
needed; and
(3)   require that students receiving two or more grades
below satisfactory performance see a counselor for
special guidance and assistance on a regular basis as
long as needed.

Suggested
Criterion: The overall grade point average of the student body will
increase by not less than .05 in addition to an increase
of program completion of not less than 5 percent and a
cropout rate reduction of not less than 5 percent. Library transactions shall also increase at a rate of not less
than 5 percent over the percentage of increase in student
enrollment as compared to the previous academic year
(since there is a positive relationship between the use of
library materials and academic and class standing).[2]

Task 5:   Assist students to achieve a relevant college experience.

Some
Possible
Means: (1)   Assist the instructional faculty in establishing and

writing measurable learning objectives concerned
with the relating of academic learning to the "real
world";

(2)   establish convenient hours and locations for providing counseling services;

(3)   establish an exit evaluation interview and/or form
to complete for *all* students with respect to how
they viewed their college experience — what was
good — what needs improving;

(4)   establish a follow-up program on students giving a
longitudinal view of the apparent successes and
failures of the institution; and

(5)   establish a feedback program to pertinent staff to
correct deficiencies and to make appropriate
improvements.

Suggested
Criterion: The percentage of positive comments over defensible
negative ones will increase at a rate of not less than 2
percent a year over the previous academic year.

Without the articulation of cyrstal-clear objectives, stated in
measurable performance terms by the student personnel staff, and
the resultant determination to overcome the inertia of "business as
usual," that office on our campuses will remain only a bright
promise of what it could be.

The first thing our student personnel offices need to do is to
clearly determine their objectives — and in *measurable performance terms.* In short, they, like the instructional faculty, need to
become accountable. The time is long since past in which accountability for a satisfactory college experience is solely the responsibility of the student. In a two-year college, especially, the accountability for a successful college experience for *each* student is as
much, if not more, the responsibility of the total professional staff
as it is the student's.

If we are to be accountable, we need to establish measurable
objectives around an orientation program core where they do not
exist and strengthen those that do exist. And the teacher-counselor
needs to be held accountable for the success of the counselees enrolled in the group guidance classes he teaches.

It has been estimated that 700,000 students each year in our

two-year colleges fail to complete any kind of program whatsoever.[3] This is a national disgrace that we can no longer conveniently sweep under the rug. Teachers need to clearly specify the learning tasks students are expected to achieve in each course and under
what conditions and criteria. Moreover, punitive grading practices
by the faculty must cease. We need to award excellence in achievement when learning mastery is achieved — not before. However if
learning mastery does not occur, it simply should go unrecognized
insofar as transcripts are concered rather than be recognized as a
"failure." Since it is essentially the faculty who are accountable
for superior teaching to ensure learning mastery, the measure of
their success should not be the number of students who fail, *but
the number who succeed!*

Counselors and other student personnel workers, like faculty,
need to form the "right questions" into objectives which are clearly spelled out and formulated into measurable terms. They also
need to exercise the requisite leadership to change teaching faculty attitudes on punitive grading practices. They must also become
accountable for guiding students into realistic curricula since that
is the only way teaching faculty can realistically hold up their end
of this partnership. And, finally, counselors and others on the student personnel staff need to teach orientation classes, with well-
thought-through content, and to provide group guidance in order
to reach far more students than is possible with the drop-in or
tripping-method of counseling.[4]

This is not only the Age of Aquarius but the Age of Accountability. It is time that we accept more of the burden of failure for
our students. Only by so doing will there be any real hope of re-
versing the mockery of our revolving door two-year colleges.   □

---

[1] Gerber, Sterling K. "Four Approaches to Freshman Orientation," *Improving College
and University Teaching:* 57-60; Spring 1970.

[2] Hostrop, Richard W. *Teaching and the Community College Library,* Hamden,
Connecticut: Shoe String Press, 1968.

[3] Based on the assumption that at least 30 percent of our students are not back for a
second year (Clark, Collins, Knoell, Medsker, et al.) and that our present student population is over two million.

[4] E.g., Hostrop, Richard W. *Orientation to the Two-Year College — A Programmed
Learning Text,* Homewood, Illinois: Learning Systems Company, 1970.

VII

THE RELEVANCE OF THE CIPP EVALUATION MODEL
FOR EDUCATIONAL ACCOUNTABILITY

by Daniel L. Stufflebeam
The Ohio State University

"Evaluation systematically supports decision-making and provides the basic data for accountability."

The CIPP Evaluation Model was originally developed to provide timely information in a systematic way for decision making which is a proactive application of evaluation. This article examines whether the CIPP Model also serves the retroactive purpose of providing information for accountability. Specifically, can the CIPP Model adequately assist educators, after the fact, to account for their decisions and actions? If so, the CIPP Model is a powerful tool both for making and implementing decisions and for *post hoc* accounting for those decisions and actions. The remainder of this article describes the CIPP Model, presents a conceptualization of accountability, and analyzes the potential of the CIPP Model for meeting the information requirements of accountability.

The CIPP Evaluation Model

The CIPP Model defines evaluation as the *process of delineating, obtaining, and providing useful information for judging decision alternatives.* This definition contains three important points: First, evaluation is a systematic, continuing process; second, the evaluation process includes three basic steps: the delineating of questions to be answered and information to be obtained, the obtaining of relevant information, and the providing of information to decisions and thereby to improve ongoing programs; and, third, evaluation serves decision making.

Reprinted with permission of the author and copyright permission of the *Journal of Research and Development in Education,* Fall, 1971.

Since evaluation should serve decision making, the decisions to be served must be known. Four kinds of decisions are specified by the CIPP Model. *Planning* decisions determine objectives. *Structuring* decisions project procedural designs for achieving objectives. Decisions in executing chosen designs are *implementing* decisions, and *recycling* decisions determine whether to continue, terminate, or modify a project.

These decision types are served by four types of evaluation. *Context* evaluation provides information about needs, problems, and opportunities in order to identify objectives. *Input* evaluation provides information about the strengths and weaknesses of alternative strategies for achieving given objectives. *Process* evaluation provides information about the strengths and weaknesses of a strategy during implementation so that either the strategy or its implementation might be strengthened. *Product* evaluation provides information for determining whether objectives are being achieved and whether the procedure employed to achieve them should be continued, modified, or terminated. Basically, the CIPP Model answers four questions: What objectives should be accomplished? What procedures should be followed? Are the procedures working properly? and, Are the objectives being achieved? (More detailed descriptions of the CIPP Model are referenced at the end of this article).

Accountability

Accountability is defined in this article as *the ability to account for past actions in relationship to the decisions which precipitated the actions, the wisdom of those decisions, the extent to which they were adequately and efficiently implemented, and the value of their effects.*

Using this definition, those responsible for a program must be able to answer questions concerning both the *ends* and *means* of their program. The answer should be defensible with respect to present scientific and technological knowledge, some explicit set of moral, social, institutional, and individual values, and appropriate performance data.

Several questions apply to *ends*. What objectives were chosen? Why? How adequately did program personnel pursue the chosen objectives? How well were the objectives achieved?

Questions concerning *means* refer especially to program

designs. What designs were chosen? Were they chosen for good and sufficient reasons? To what extent were they properly implemented? Of what value were their primary, secondary, and tertiary effects?

Relevance of the CIPP Model to Accountability

Figure 1 relates evaluation and accountability as defined in this article. The main decisions served by the CIPP Model are recounted in the first row of the matrix, and the second row identifies the main accountability needs that are served by each evaluation type.

EVALUATION TYPES

	Context	Input	Process	Product
Decision Making U S E S	Objectives	Solution strategy Procedural design	Implementation	Termination, continuation, modification, or installation
Accountability	Record of objectives and bases for their choice	Record of chosen strategy and design and reasons for their choice	Record of the actual process	Record of attainments and recycling decisions

Figure 1: The Relevance of the CIPP Model to Decision Making and Accountability

Context evaluation, through assisting in the choice of objectives, provides a record of the objectives chosen and the bases for their choice. This kind of accountability is fundamental. When outsiders including the community, representatives of funding agencies, and external evaluators pose questions about objectives, educators must be able to identify their objectives and the supporting rationale. What are the objectives? Who chose them? Why? What assumptions do they make, especially about the needs of children to be served? Are those assumptions internally consistent? Are they true? Are they morally, socially, and scientifically valid? These are critical questions that educators must be prepared to answer. Context evaluation assists in choosing objectives and in defending them.

Input evaluation, through assisting in the choice of a procedural strategy for achieving specified objectives, provides a record of the alternative strategies considered and the reasons for choosing one of them. What strategies were considered? Which one was chosen? Why? Was it the most promising approach for achieving the specified objectives? Was its choice dictated by some influential funding agent? Was it better than the other alternatives? Was it cheaper? What information was available to rank the alternatives? Did it reveal the past effectiveness of the competing strategies? Were cost data available? Were there indications of the feasibility of implementing the various strategies in the adopting system? Educators must be prepared to answer these questions if they are not to be subject to charges of irresponsible spending or of being too responsive to current fads and political pressures. Input evaluation supports this kind of accountability by recording data that compare the chosen procedural strategy with the competitors that were considered.

Process evaluation, through assisting in implementing a project design, provides a record of the actual process as it occurred. If a particular procedure was not successful, was this because the project design was never implemented, or was the design, though implemented correctly, simply inadequate to achieve the objectives? The controversy that surrounded the early experiments with modern mathematics illustrates the importance of process evaluation for accountability. Many persons asked whether the "no significant difference" findings comparing modern and traditional mathematics curricula were because modern mathematics curricula were no better than traditional curricula or because teachers had never implemented the new modern math curriculum. Process evaluation was needed to certify whether the modern math experiments had been implemented as designed.

Finally, product evaluation, through comparing attainments with objectives, supplies a record of outcomes and of decisions about a procedure based on outcome information. If a procedure was continued year after year, was it because it in fact has been effective in achieving its objectives or was it merely because someone interested in the procedure was still in the system and wanted to continue the procedure's use? Or was it because more Federal

money was available for that procedure, irrespective of its effectiveness? On the other hand, if a procedure was terminated, was it
terminated merely because of a lack of outside funds, or because it
in fact had not worked? These are important accountability questions that can be supported by product evaluation.

Based upon the analysis of Figure 1, the CIPP Model has relevance for accountability. Figure 2 further considers the ability of
the CIPP Model to meet the data requirements implied in the conceptualization of accountability being presented here.

Data Requirements for Accountability	Evaluation Types			
	Context	Input	Process	Product
What objectives were chosen?	√			
Why?	√			
Were they adopted?		√	√	
Were they achieved?				√
What designs were chosen?		√		
Why	√	√		
Were the implemented?			√	
What were their effects?				√

**Figure 2: Data Requirements for Accountability That Can Be Met
By The CIPP Evaluation Model**

Figure 2 is a matrix comprised of two dimensions: the four
kinds of evaluation and the basic data requirements for accountability. Check marks in the matrix indicate the basic data requirements that are met by each kind of evaluation.

As shown, all specified data requirements are met by the
CIPP Model. Context evaluation identifies objectives that were
chosen, the reasons for their choice, and the goal related reasons
for the choice of procedural designs. Input evaluation indicates
whether stated objectives were the ones that were actively pursued,
what particular designs were selected, and why they were chosen
over other alternatives. Process evaluation confirms further whether stated objectives were actually pursued and whether procedural
specifications were actually implemented. Product evaluation

reveals whether objectives were achieved and what main and side effects resulted from the implementation of a project.

Implementation

The preceding analysis argues that the CIPP Model provides a powerful framework for meeting decision-making and accountability needs. Two final points need to be made concerning the implementation of the CIPP Model.

First, both internal evaluation and external evaluation are required. Internal evaluation systematically supports decision making and provides the basic data for accountability. External evaluation periodically brings outsiders in to ask important questions and make objective assessments. In general the outsiders provide an independent, summative evaluation of the system's goals, designs, procedures, and results. Outside evaluations require much data that are best obtained by the internal evaluation group. Likewise the internal evaluator's credibility is enhanced when outsiders attest to the adequacy of internal evaluation data. The interdependence of internal and external evaluation requires that both be implemented by an institution.

The second and final point regarding implementation of the CIPP Model is that there must be a cybernetic relationship between evaluation and all decision-making levels in the system. Evaluators must serve decisions and record accountability data at all levels of the system and, the information provided must not be screened and filtered through one particular bureaucratic level. This relationship between evaluation and decision making can increase openness and responsibility throughout the system, since evaluation both assists and accounts for decisions at all levels.

Conclusion

The preceding analysis supports the thesis that the CIPP Evaluation Model provides both proactive support for decision making and retroactive support for accountability. Proper implementation of the model will yield significant improvements over typical social accounting and standardized test information systems in providing information for a wide range of decision making and accountability questions.   □

References

Adams, James A. A. manual of policies, organization, and procedures for evaluation. School District of the City of Saginaw, Michigan, mimeo.

Austin, Gilbert R. Evaluation of 1968 Summer Institute on Evaluation. University of New Hampshire, 1968.

Barbadora, Bernard M. Report of the EPDA 1969 Summer Institutes on Evaluation. The Ohio State University Evaluation Center, 1970.

Dickson, George E. *et al., Educational Specifications for a Comprehensive Elementary Teacher Education Program.* The University of Toledo, Final Report, Project No. RFP OE-68-4, Contract No. OEC-0-8-089026 3310 (010), 1968.

Findlay, Donald C. Application of the CIPP Model to a center with multiple program areas and levels, *Educational Technology* (in press).

Gidney, Dolores, Merriman, Howard O., Smith, Calvin, and Overholt, George, Evaluation report to The Columbus Public School System, Regional Service Centers Project. The Ohio State University Evaluation Center, mimeo, September 1967.

Griessman, B. Eugene, An approach to evaluating comprehensive social projects, *Educational Technology,* IX, February 1969, pp. 16-19.

Guba, Egon G. Report of results of a follow-up evaluation of two institutes for training education professions development act project personnel in educational evaluation. Report prepared under contract with The Ohio State University Evaluation Center, mimeo, September 1970.

Guba, Egon G. and Stufflebeam, Daniel L., *Evaluation: The Process of Stimulating, Aiding, and Abetting Insightful Action.* Bloomington, Indiana: Monograph Series in Reading Education, Indiana University, No. 1, June 1970.

Hammond, Robert L., Context evaluation of instruction in local school districts, *Educational Technology,* IX, January 1969, pp. 13-18.

Marks, Walter L., Progress report no. 2, context-evaluation. The Ohio State University Evaluation Center, RFP No. 70-12, September 10, 1970.

Merriman, Howard O., From evaluation theory into practice, *Journal of Research and Development in Education, 3,* Summer, 1970, pp. 48-58.

Owens, Thomas R., Suggested tasks and roles of evaluation specialists in education, *Educational Technology, VIII,* November 30, 1968, pp. 4-10.

Randall, Robert S., An operational application of the CIPP Model for evaluation, *Educational Technology, IX,* July 1969, pp. 40-44.

Rankin, S. C., Design for evaluation of the elementary program of the Detroit Public Schools. Detroit Public Schools, mimeo, April 1970.

Stufflebeam, Daniel L., The use and abuse of evaluation in Title III, *Theory Into Practice, VI,* June, 1967, pp. 126-133.

Stufflebeam, Daniel L., Evaluation as enlightenment for decision-making, *Improving Educational Assessment & An Inventory of Measures of*

Affective Behavior, edited by Walcott H. Beatty, Washington, D.C.: The Association for Supervision and Curriculum Development, NEA, 1969, pp. 41-73.

Stufflebeam, Daniel L., Toward a science of educational evaluation, *Educational Technology, VIII,* July 30, 1968, 11. 5-12.

Stufflebeam, Daniel L., Foley, Walter J., Gephart, William J., Guba, Egon G., Hammond, Robert L., Merriman, Howard O., Provus, Malcolm, *Educational Evaluation and Decision Making,* Itasca, Illinois: F. E. Peacock Publishers, Inc., 1971.

Worthen, Blaine R., Toward a taxonomy of evaluation designs, *Educational Technology, VIII,* August 15, 1968, pp. 3-9.

Worthen, Blaine R., Kean, Michael H., and McLaughlin, Nancy, Evaluation of a process for selecting and testing educational innovations, A report to the Xenia Center for Educational Programming, Title III, The Elementary and Secondary Education Act of 1965. The Ohio State University Evaluation Center, 1969.

VIII

TESTING FOR ACCOUNTABILITY

by Ralph W. Tyler

"To measure educational outcomes requires tests designed for this purpose—and the problem for administrators is that most tests currently available are not very suitable."

The growing concern about accountability has put new emphasis on measuring what and how much a student has learned in a short period of time. To measure educational outcomes in such a period requires tests designed for this purpose — and the problem for administrators is that most tests currently available are not very suitable.

A good example of the problem is in the area of performance contracting, where schools contract for instruction with private companies on a fee arrangement based on student performance. Since it appears that performance contracts will generally be let to cover students considered to be low achievers from disadvantaged environments, the standard achievement tests in common use do not furnish a dependable measure of how much these children have learned during one school year or less.

They were not constructed to do so.

A typical achievement test is explicitly designed to furnish scores that will arrange the pupils on a line from those most proficient in the subject to those least proficient. The final test questions have been selected from a much larger initial number on the basis of tryouts and are the ones which most sharply distinguished pupils in the tryouts who made high scores on the total test from those who made low scores. Test questions were eliminated if most pupils could answer them or if few pupils could answer them, since these did not give much discrimination.

As a result, a large part of the questions retained for the final form of a standard test are those that 40 to 60 per cent of the children were able to answer. There are very few questions that represent the things being learned either by the slower learners or the more advanced ones. If a less advanced student is actually making progress in his learning, the typical standard test furnishes so few questions that represent what he has been learning that it will not afford a dependable measure for him. The same holds true for advanced learners.

This is not a weakness in the test in serving the purpose for which it was designed. The children who made lower scores had generally learned fewer things in this subject than those who made higher scores and could, therefore, be dependably identified as less proficient. Furthermore, a good standard test has been administered to one or more carefully selected samples, usually national, regional or urban samples, of children in the grade for which the test was designed. The scores obtained from these samples provide norms for the test against which a child's score can be related.

These tests — called *norm-referenced tests* — thus provide dependable information about where the child stands in his total test performance in relation to the norm group. But when one seeks to find out whether a student who made a low score has learned certain things during the year, the test does not include enough questions covering the material on which he was owrking to furnish a dependable answer to that question.

This leads to another problem encountered when one attempts to measure what a child learns in a school year or less. In the primary grades, particularly, each child's learning is dependent on what he had already learned before the year began and what sequence he follows. For example, in reading, some children enter the first grade already able to read simple children's stories and newspaper paragraphs. Measures of what they learn during the first year should be based on samples of reading performance that go beyond this entry level.

On the other extreme, some children enter the first grade with a limited oral vocabulary and without having distinguished the shapes of letters or noted differences in their sounds. Measures of what such a child learns during the first year must take off from his entering performance and be based on the learning sequence used in his school to help him acquire the vocabulary and language skills that are involved in the later stages of reading instruction.

A standardized test, however, is designed to be used in schools throughout the nation, despite the different learning sequences they have and with children coming from a variety of backgrounds and at various stages of learning in the field covered by the test. For this reason, it cannot include enough questions appropriate to each child's stage of development to measure reliably what he has learned during a single school year.

Recognizing that norm-referenced tests can provide dependable information on the relative standing of children, but cannot reliably measure what a child has learned or how much he has learned in a year or less, efforts are now under way to construct and utilize tests that are designed to sample specified knowledge, skills and abilities and to report what the child knows and can do of those matters specified. Since the criterion for a performance contract is that each child will learn specified things, a test that samples them is called a *criterion-referenced* test.

For example, in primary reading, the children who enter without having learned to distinguish letters and sounds might be tested by the end of the year on letter recognition, association of letters with sounds, and word-recognition of 100 most common words. For each of these specified "things to be learned," the child would be presented with a large enough sample of examples to furnish reliable evidence that he could recognize the letters of the alphabet, he could associate the appropriate sounds with each letter, alone and in words, and he could recognize the 100 most common words. A child has demonstrated mastery of specified knowledge, ability or skill when he performs correctly 85 per cent of the times. (Some small allowance, like 15 per cent, is needed for lapses common to all people.)

At a higher level of initial performance, a group of children may be expected to read and comprehend typical newspaper paragraphs, simple directions for making or doing something, etc. Similar specifications are made in arithmetic and in writing. Science and the social studies represent greater problems because of the variations in content and the lack of agreement on essential objectives.

The National Assessment of Educational Progress utilizes criterion-referenced tests and reports to the public about the performance of various categories of children and youth rather than individuals. The public is given the percentage of each group — 9

year olds, 13 year olds, 17 year olds, and young adults — who
know certain facts, can use certain principles in explaining phenomena, are able to do certain things. The reports reveal the exercises that were used and give the per cent of each group who answered the question correctly or who demonstrated the ability or
skill involved. The public can get a better grasp of what children
and youth are learning by these reports than by trying to interpret
abstract scores.

The need for criterion-referenced tests is particularly acute
when a contractor undertakes to aid the education of disadvantaged children. Currently used standard tests are not satisfactory
tools to appraise the learning of disadvantaged children that can be
expected in a single school year. Because most of the disadvantaged begin the year at much earlier stages than a majority of
pupils, the standard tests developed for that grade include very few
questions that represent what these children are learning.

For this reason, when such a test is given at the beginning of
the year and a second test at the end of the year, the changes in
score for an individual child may largely be chance variations, since
both scores are based on very small samples of knowledge, abilities
or skills to which these children could respond. Furthermore, since
the number of questions on which the initial score is based is small,
coaching for these particular items can give a large relative gain.
For example, if a child answered four questions correctly in the
initial test, being able to answer four more in the final test will
place him very much higher on the relative score of a standard test
than would a gain of four points when his initial score was 40.

This fact increases the temptation for coaching in the case of
contracts involving disadvantaged children. Criterion-referenced
tests constructed for the learning sequences actually being followed will include a much larger sample of appropriate questions.

Although there are few criterion-referenced tests presently
available, if performance contracting continues to expand rapidly,
both schools and contractors will soon recognize that they do not
have the tests they need to furnish dependable measures of performance. Publishers may well respond by a crash program of
criterion-referenced test development.   □

Dr. Tyler is director emeritus, Center for Advanced Study in the Behavioral
Sciences, Palo Alto, Calif.

IX

HOW EDUCATIONAL AUDITS MEASURE PERFORMANCE

by Leon M. Lessinger

"The Independent Accomplishment Audit is a process similar to that used in a fiscal audit. The emphasis, however, is on learning— on student performance as a result of financial outlays."

Independent fiscal reports have been applied to the fiscal side of education for many years with great success. These audits have not only resulted in the virtual abolition of shady financial practice but the professional recording, classifying and interpreting of the economic facts of the enterprise have been done in a manner designed to produce data which encourages effective management.

The Independent Accomplishment Audit is a process similar to that used in a fiscal audit. The emphasis, however, is on learning — on student performance as a result of financial outlays. The IAA is designed as a "management feedback loop," a reliable and objective report to local personnel, commending accomplishments realized and recommending procedures for getting results missed.

It is designed to put local school personnel and the clients they serve in a problem-solving mode of thinking, and although it is built around a financial core — since money is a common denominator for the heterogeneous elements of inputs — its focus is upon student attitudes, skills and knowledge in specific areas.

Out of the IAA a whole range of useful byproducts may be anticipated. First, it may lead to a knowledge of optimum relationships between outputs and inputs, *i.e.* those that are cost effective or otherwise to be valued.

Second, it can form a basis for the discovery and improvement of good practice in education.

Finally, it can renew credibility in the educational process, effect more responsiveness to the needs of children, and supply the understanding needed for change.

The electorate is the most powerful of all our political agencies. If technics can be developed to convince its members of the benefits of responsible leadership through accountability for results, those interested in furthering education can better and more increasingly support the educational enterprise.

IAA relies upon outside judgment of results or accomplishments, primarily in terms of student accomplishment. It has six essential parts: the pre-audit; the translation of local goals into demonstrable data; the adoption/creation of instrumentation and methodology; the establishment of a review calendar; the assessment process; and the public report.

I.   The Pre-Audit: The auditor selected by the school system, in a manner similar to that used in selecting personnel for fiscal accounting, starts the IAA process by discussing with the staff (students and community can be involved at this stage) the objectives and plans of the particular program to be reviewed. This phase produces a list of local objectives and a clear description of the programs in some order of priority. It is anticipated that auditors will come from the ranks of professional educators, the laity, universities and private enterprise. Training will be essential.

II.   The Translation: In concert with local people, the auditor determines a clear formualtion of the evidence that will be used by the local people to indicate that the objectives have been met and the conditions that will be used to elicit the evidence. This phase produces a set of specifications revealing what the student will be able to do as a result of the educational experience, the manner in which the evidence will be secured, and the standards which will be applied in interpreting the success of the student in meeting the objectives.

III.   Instrumentation: Along with the translation, the auditor determines the instruments, such as tests, questionnaires, standardized interviews, and the like — which will be developed or secured to gather the evidence agreed upon in the translation phase. The product of this activity is a set of defined technics and procedures for data gathering.

IV. Review Calendar: An agreement is secured in writing which indicates the nature of the reviews where they will be held, how long they will take, when they will occur, who is responsible for arrangements, the nature of the arrangements, and other logistical considerations. It is essential that the calendar be determined in advance and that all concerned be a party to the agreement and competent to honor the agreement.

V. The Audit Process: This is a responsibility of the auditor. In this phase, he carries out the procedures agreed upon in the pre-audit translation and instrumentation phases as codified in the review calendar.

VI. The Public Report: The auditor files a report at an open meeting giving commendations and recommendations as they relate to the local objectives. The report is designed to indicate in specific terms both accomplishments and ways the program may be made more effective and efficient.   □

Dr. Lessinger, until January 1 of this year U.S. Associate Commissioner of Education for Elementary and Secondary Education, is presently Dean of The College of Education, University of South Carolina.

X

FROM INNOVATIONS TO ALTERNATIVES:
A DECADE OF CHANGE IN EDUCATION

by Ronald Gross

"Schools themselves can benefit from the creation of many options and alternatives to the present monolithic system. But the chief benefit will be for our children, who will have the chance to grow up in a society of autonomous men rather than coercive institutions."

For the past 10 years, first at the Ford Foundation, later with the Academy for Educational Development, I've been acting as a kind of Typhoid Mary of education, picking up new ideas and practices whereever I found them, then spreading them around to the susceptible.

This experience has given me a chance both to examine the state of American education and to make my own judgments about the new ideas and programs. Some of the things I've learned are small and simple. From Herb Kohl in Berkeley, for instance, I learned how teachers can start off in moving toward a freer class-room by devoting only 10 minutes a day to new ideas. Nothing frightening in that — despite Kohl's insistence that his revolutionary strategy comes straight out of Che Guevera!

From John Holt I found out how students sabotage their own education, learning to please the teacher by "psyching out" the tests. And from Neil Postman I discovered that students and teachers can use "judo" rather than violent confrontation to get their schools to change.

The movement for change in recent American education has moved through three phases: first, "innovation"; second, "radical reform"; and the phase just emerging, "alternatives" to traditional concepts of schooling.

When I first entered the field of education in the mid-fifties, it was in the midst of a flurry of what came to be called "innovations." I'm thinking of the various new curricula exemplified by the new math — ideas like team teaching and programmed instruction, the use of technologies such as television and the language laboratory, the first serious experiments with nongrading.

These innovations were sparked by a fresh concern with educational quality, both personally and nationally. Every parent was concerned about whether his child was getting a good enough education; the "sheepskin psychosis" was hitting high gear. And for the nation as a whole, that superb visual aid called Sputnik had made many citizens look down from the skies and into the classrooms — with dismay at the supposed educational causes of our technological failure. So a corps of master plasterers was recruited to patch up the intellectually disreputable facade of American education.

These "innovative" programs were undertaken in well-established schools with fairly conventional philosophies. They were not based on new ideas about the role of education, or the nature of the child, or the place of culture in a democratic society. They focused on practical methods of achieving the traditional end of schooling — the mastery of basic skills and subject matter.

These innovative approaches changed the climate of American public education in the late fifties and early sixties. What they achieved has been important, but what they failed to achieve, unfortunately, has been even more important.

A Deeper Malaise

For even as those innovations relieved the rigid programs and teaching practices in many schools, a deeper malaise was developing, unnoticed, in American education. The seemingly enlightened educators who had pressed these changes toward flexibility and enrichment had focused their energies entirely on making the process of learning in school more lively and rewarding. But they had not perceived that larger social forces were calling into question the relevance of education.

In the urban ghetto schools, starvation budgets, the impact of the slum environment, teacher indifference and sometimes unconscious racism had reduced the schools to mere disciplinary or custodial institutions. And in the suburbs, the shadow of college preparation and social conformity had blighted the process of growing up — less brutally but with comparable efficiency.

By the mid-sixties black parents in the ghettos and white students on the campuses and in the suburban high schools began to revolt against the educational system. The riots of the big-city slums and the demonstrations on the campuses of the multiversities made it shockingly clear that the educational and social system had reached a point where it could no longer continue without basic, radical changes in its structure, control, and operation.

As a result, over the past five years a new breed of radical theorists and teachers has emerged in American education.

True learning and healthy growth are sabotaged in most American schools today, these critics argue, because of an authoritarian atmosphere in which the emphasis is on the teacher teaching rather than on the student learning. The whole process of schooling is frozen into a rigid lockstep through the grades, chopped up mechanically into blocks of time and different subjects, dominated by a curriculum fixed in advance and imposed from above. There is no real regard for the students as individual regard for the students as individual people, with real concerns of their own and inherent drives to know, understand, and create.

For John Holt, "To a very great degree, school is a place where children learn to be stupid." Paul Goodman "would not give a penny to the present administrators, and would largely dismantle the present school machinery." Jonathan Kozol demonstrates that the schools of one of our major cities destroy the minds and hearts of black children. George Leonard, Peter Marin, and Edgar Friedenberg see schools stifling the finest and most passionate impulses of young people. The igh school students who formed the Montgomery County (Maryland) Student Alliance testified that "From what we know to be true as full-time students it is quite safe to say that the public schools have critically negative and absolutely destructive effects on human beings and their curiosity, natural desire to learn, confidence, individuality, creativity, freedom of thought, and self-respect."

These charges, which were considered beyond the pale of "responsible criticism," have been officially substantiated by such recent reports as Charles Silberman's *Crisis in the Classroom* and the *Schools for the Seventies* publications project of the NEA's Center for the Study of Instruction.

The Radicals' Platform

On what principles would the radical reformers reconstitute education? Here the diversity of such an individualistic group of writers makes it difficult to generalize, but among the propositions most frequently found in these writings, and embodied in radical programs, are:

1. Students, not teachers, must be at the center of education.

2. Teaching and learning should start and stay with the students' real concerns, rather than with artificial disciplines, bureaucratic requirements, or adults' rigid ideas about what children need to learn.

3. The paraphernalia of standard classroom practice should be abolished: mechanical order, silence, tests, grades, lesson plans, hierarchial supervision and administration, homework, and compulsory attendance.

4. Most existing textbooks should be thrown out.

5. Schools should be much smaller and much more responsive to diverse educational needs of parents and children.

6. Certification requirements for teachers should be abolished.

7. All compulsory testing and grading, including intelligence testing and entrance examinations, should be abolished.

8. In all educational institutions supported by tax money or enjoying tax-exempt status, entrance examinations should be abolished.

9. Legal requirements which impede the formation of new schools by independent groups of parents — such as health and safety requirements — should be abolished.

10. The schools' monopoly on education should be broken. The best way to finance education might be to give every consumer a voucher for him to spend on his education as he chooses, instead of increasing allocations to the school authorities.

Based on some of these new principles, positive, fresh starts have developed throughout the country. Silberman, in his book, focuses on one such trend at the elementary level: the adoption here of the so-called British infant school approach. He also cites impulses toward reform at the high school level, in such schools as Murray Road in Newton, Massachusetts, Parkway in Philadelphia, and John Adams in Portland. In my books, *High School* and *Radical School Reform*, I provide case studies written by participants or close observers of all of these schools. I report on many other promising experiments throughout the nation: Herb Kohl's Other Ways School in Berkeley; Harlem Prep in New York City; George Dennison's First Street School; the CAM Academy in Chicago; Shule ya Uhura, a freedom school in Washington, D.C.; a middle-class free school in suburban Montgomery County, Maryland; the super-free public school called Fernwood in rural Oregon; and others.

The New Ultra-Radicals

In the last years, a new viewpoint has emerged in this continuing debate over American education. More radical than radical school reform, this viewpoint asserts that reforming schools is impossible.

One practicing teacher who came to this conclusion is James Herndon, who teaches in a suburban junior high school outside of San Francisco. Some years back when Herndon wrote the best book about ghetto teaching, *The Way It Spozed To Be,* he was fired. For the past 10 years he has been trying his damndest to humanize his school. He and his *simpatico* colleagues began by pushing the idea of freedom as far as it would go. They made classes voluntary, had the kids decide what would go on when they came, gave no grades. But the students didn't turn on; the teachers realized that the children couldn't tell them what and how to teach. "We were both waiting around. Together, we amounted to zero."

Then suddenly, out of this zero, out of reaching bottom, it all came together: a school-within-the-school in which they concentrated on teaching reading, found their own answer, and succeeded handsomely. They simply recreated the convivial, "inefficient," noncompetitive atmosphere in which kids learned to read before schools made it such a big deal. The story of their success shows stunningly what can be achieved when teachers seriously re-examine what they are doing and why — as Charles Silberman has urged so eloquently.

But the experiment was murdered. The successful reading approach they demonstrated was rejected by the school bureaucracy, which preferred to follow mindlessly the latest state education ukase. "Public education is a game you can't whip," said the principal when he delivered the *coup de grâce.*

Herndon'c conclusions are dark. He believes the U.S. public school blights the whole learning process, that it is hopelessly hung up on ramming children into bureaucratic categories, dividing them destructively at every level into winners and losers.

He rests his hopes, therefore, not on the possibility of changing education, but on just getting it off people's backs. "There is no law any more that people must go to church or pay attention to the church," Herndon writes, "and so many people don't, while others do. That is the best you can expect, and good enough. . . . The public school is the closest thing we have in America to a national established church, Getting-an-Education the closest thing to God, and it should be possible to treat it and deal with it as the church has been treated and dealt with."

At the center of this line of thought is Ivan Illich, that extraordinary mastermind who works out of the Center for Intercultural Documentation in Cuernavaca, Mexico. Illich seems to be having the same kind of impact on social criticism in this country that Marshall McLuhan had, operating out of Toronto in the late fifties. Illich argues that the reason our schools seem to be doing everything wrong these days is that schools *are* basically wrong, *per se.* He believes that schools and all the other service institutions by which we have sought to maintain and enhance our lives actually oppress and degrade us. Schooling, in Illich's view, has little to do with learning. Each of us has learned most of the useful, lovely, or engaging things he knows from his life rather than from his teachers. Learning comes about through association with people and books and things and institutions, through trying to grow up.

Illich demands the "dis-establishment" of schooling: the repeal of compulsory education laws, provision of constitutional guarantees against discrimination on the basis of possession of a high school or college diploma or advanced degree, rollback of public support of public schools, and an "edu-credit" card which each individual may use to receive his equal share of public education resources (broader than the voucher plan, because Illich would not confine its use to schools).

My Own View

I do not see deschooling coming to America the way the de-schoolers would like. Rather, I envisage a various, halting, impulsive, sometimes troubled groping toward more diverse options, finer possibilities. My hope is that through the gradual erosion of those constraints of place, time, age, and mode of learning which now define schooling, it will gradually become impossible to tell where school begins and life stops — a more feasible goal which would reinstate, under more benign conditions, the preindustrial unity of learning and living.

Already there are "schools without walls," free universities, human potential growth centers, the *Whole Earth Catalog,* and a myriad of other initiatives, inside and outside the formal education system, for enabling what I call "free learning" to commence. Many educators seem reconciled to the fact that the present generation of 10- to 20-year-olds is just about the last one that will voluntarily trudge through the lockstep from kindergarten to college. Something has got to be done — or many, many things.

I have seen too many good classrooms in the past 10 years to agree that the schools are going to shrivel up and die, or should. Many, many children are spending many, many happy and fruitful hours in our schools at every level. Particularly heartening is the emergence of a new spirit among some groups of teachers, joining together through what Joseph Featherstone calls "a common conviction of what it means to do a good job." Once teachers and students together begin to take themselves seriously, to ask what they are really doing in school, why they are doing it, and what they could and should do, I think we will see some extraordinary changes.

But at the same time I would like to see a real flowering of other options, other avenues to growing up, other milieu in which youngsters and grownups could learn from each other. Institutions that have a monopoly, like schooling, grow impervious to reform. The church was oppressive and rigid when it had a monopoly and could force people to heed its dicta. Now it is more enterprising in defining its authentic role in the modern world.

Alternatives can do the same for education. Schools themselves will benefit from the creation of many options and alternatives to the present monolithic system. But the chief benefit will be for our children, who will have the chance to grow up in a society of autonomous men rather than coercive institutions.   □

Ronald Gross is a teacher and poet whose books include *Radical School Reform, High School, The Teacher and the Taught,* and *Pop Poems.* He is currently adjunct associate professor of social thought at New York University, on leave from his position as vice-president of the Academy for Educational Development. This article is drawn from a talk delivered at a workshop sponsored by the Educational Press Association of America at Detroit on June 26, 1971.

XI

STATES AND HAMSTERS: THE VOUCHER SYSTEM

by John R. Coyne, Jr.

Why is it that educationists go red in the face when you mention the voucher system? Could it be that if parents are offered a choice they might opt out of the public schools?

American Education is, we all agree, in rotten shape.

We spend about $40 billion per year on education — more, writes Peter Drucker in *The Age of Discontinuity,* "than on all other nondefense community services together — health care, welfare, farm subsidies . . ."

What do we get for this massive investment? No one really knows. There is no comprehensive published information on how school children are faring nationwide. Why not? Because, some critics contend, the educationist establishment doesn't dare release available figures. The nearest thing to a national report yet issued, compiled in 1966 for the Defense Department, shows that one out of every four American men fails the Armed Forces Qualifying Tests because he can't read an elementary passage, write a simple sentence or add a basic sum. One-quarter of our population, in other words, after at least ten years of spending five hours or more per day in American classrooms, is functionally illiterate. The percentage in the ghettos is much worse: There, two out of three flunk the qualifying tests.

We all know the schools are doing a dismal job. The question is: How do we make them better? Restructure the classroom itself, runs one of the hoariest reformist recipes. But how? Liberals argue that classrooms are structured too rigidly. Charles E. Silberman, for instance, author of *Crisis in American Education,* says that schools stifle children by tending "to confuse day-to-day routine with purpose and to transform the means into the end itself." If the emphasis were on "creative" learning rather than on order, children would *want* to learn and therefore would do so.

But such ideas offend conservative parents who believe that the schools aren't structured tightly enough. Imagine for instance the reaction of Max Rafferty were he to wander into that North Dakota school celebrated by Silberman, where rabbits, chickens, hamsters, children and white rats all learn together in cardboard boxes. Most conservative parents would probably react similarly, insisting that if schools just forgot about such fripperies and returned to the three Rs, fifth graders would once again be conjugating irregular Latin verbs, just as they did back in 1906 when things were good.

Now it well may be that there is nothing wrong with either approach. Perhaps your little Gwendolyn will one day win a Nobel Prize in zoology because of those hours spent in a cardboard box with a hamster. And perhaps Waldo will eventually hold a chair in classics at Harvard because he learned to conjugate Latin verbs on his slate in the fifth grade at East Overshoe grammar school. But the problem is this: If Waldo lives in Minot, North Dakota, he will not be conjugating, for, unless his parents have a good deal of money, they will send him to the public school to which he is assigned. And if Gwendolyn's parents live in East Overshoe, the same will be true for her. Thus Waldo will be paired with the hamster, Gwendolyn will scribble unhappily on her slate. And the parents will be able to do nothing whatsoever about it, even though East Overshoe may lie only five miles from Minot.

Everyone Revolting

And yet Waldo and Gwendolyn are lucky. Imagine in the plight of destitute black parents in places such as New York or Newark, where ghetto schools are daily torn by violence, where white unionized teachers, quite obviously more concerned with paychecks than teaching, strike at will, where children seldom reach the eighth grade able to read. Such schools have given up even the pretense of attempting to educate. Yet when frustrated parents try to act, as they did in New York in Ocean Hill-Bronsville, for instance, they are crushed by the self-serving educationist bureaucracy. And so ghetto-school parents have no options. They

are denied a voice in running their schools and because they are
poor they are unable to vote with their feet. The result? A generation of sub-literate black children. And violence. The brutal beat-
ing of a striking group of white Newark teachers by a crew of
blacks should surprise no one familiar with the frustrations of
ghetto parents.

And it is not only black parents who are in revolt against the
educationist structure. Middle- and upper-middle-class parents are
also rebelling by firmly closing their pocketbooks. In the *Phi Delta
Kappan,* George Gallup writes: "Budgets and bond issues are being
voted down in increasing number . . . in the last year (fiscal 1969)
school bond issues were voted down by voters at a record rate. By
dollar value, voters approved less than 44 per cent of the $3.9 bil-
lion in bond issues put to the electorate. The $1.7 billion that
passed comprise the lowest total since 1962. A decade ago 80 per
cent of such bond issues were approved." And this before the re-
cession. If the trend persists, we will see wisespread closings of
public schools.

Educationists Lobby

It becomes increasingly clear that the American public has
lsot faith in its system of public education. To borrow a phrase
currently in vogue, the system is unresponsive to the needs of the
people. "The same thing is wrong with the school system that is
wrong with the Post Office," says Milton Friedman. "The government monopoly tends to be inefficient and costly, and most important of all, it is not responsive to the wishes of its customers."
And how to make the system responsive? According to psychologist Kenneth Clark, the key is "aggressive competition." Let
schools compete for students by promising to educate them better
than other schools. And if they fail to keep their promise, let them
close down. "We need a spectrum of educational institutions giving
families a variety of schools," writes Dean Theodore Sizer of the
Harvard education school. A responsive system, said OEO Director Donald Rumsfeld, must be one in which "poor parents would
be able to exercise some opportunity to choose similar to that
now enjoyed by wealthier parents who can move to a better public-school district or send their children to private schools." Responsiveness, competitiveness, flexibility, mobility, free choice,
variety. Slates and hamsters. Almost all critics believe that these

are the necessary ingredients of a successfully restructured school system. And an increasing number of them, no matter what their ideological or political hue, agree that this restructuring can best be accomplished by adopting the voucher system.

Although the basic idea can be traced back to Adam Smith, the voucher plan was first proposed in contemporary from by E. C. West in 1965 in *Education and the State.* West, an English economist, believed that education should be removed from the direct control of the state and that the poor as well as the rich should be able to exercise some measure of control over the education of their children. In America the plan is lauded by conservatives such as Milton Friedman, left-radicals such as Christopher Jencks, and numerous Administration officials.

There has been an unusual amount of academic haggling over the details of the plan's administration, so that many have come to view it as hairily complex. But actually it's a simple scheme. An issuing agency—state, city, town, school board—gives to the parents of a school-age child a chit approximately equal to the amount it takes to educate that child during the school year, say about $800. The parents then hand over this voucher to the school—public or private—in which they want to enroll their child. The school turns the voucher in to the issuing agency, and the agency reimburses the school. Advocates of the system believe that it would encourage competition among public schools and would also encourage the growth of a network of private innovative schools competing with the public schools for students, such competition providing an incentive for both public and private schools to maintain high standards. Gwendolyn's parents, in other words, wouldn't have to move from East Overshoe to give her her hamster.

Despite the attractiveness of the voucher plan, it has so far been given little chance to prove itself. Virginia put it into effect statewide in 1958, but it never really worked out, operating as it did in the shadow of the Supreme Court desegregation decision. And in addition to racial complications, the stipends were never quite large enough, so that by 1967 the experiment was largely deemed a failure. In Maine and New Hampshire, about two thousand children are involved in plans roughly similar to proposed voucher plans, but their situation is the result of demographic expediency (they live outside organized school districts). New York legislators have proposed a modified voucher plan for parochial

school students in New York, a governor's commission has come
out for vouchers in Maryland, and voucher bills have been introduced in the California legislature.

The voucher system has trouble getting a trial, primarily because it is vehemently opposed by the educationist establishment.
It is no coincidence that on the day the OEO expressed interest in
trying it out in Kansas City, an educationist coalition, led by the
American Federation of Teachers, was formed in Washington "to
work against the implementation of the education voucher plan
anywhere in the United States."

Anyone can figure out why the educationists fear the voucher system. It would force them to produce or lose their cushy benefits. Still, several of their objections to vouchers merit consideration, for some of them are also shared by people with honest
doubts. There are four general arguments against vouchers: 1) the
voucher plan would turn public schools into "dumping grounds,"
serving only children rejected by all other schools; 2) the plan
would encourage racial segregation; 3) the plan would make
"hucksterism" the order of the day: private schools would dazzle
parents with fads and gimmicks and parents would be too bewil-
dered to choose schools wisely; 4) vouchers would encourage the
growth of parochial schools at the expense of others, and vouchers
cashed in by church schools would violate the constitutional principle of separation of church and state.

Jencks' Plan

Dr. Jencks, architect of the voucher plan favored by OEO,
addresses himself to the first two arguments. "Dumping grounds"
is boviously code for all-black schools: Blacks would stay in public
schools, everyone else would flee to private schools, and the result
would be, objection 2), segregation. To prevent this Jencks has
worked out an involved system. His voucher agency, which would
disperse all local, state and federal funds for the sole purpose of
redeeming vouchers, would include a certain number of blacks.
Schools would be required to accept vouchers as full payment and
would not be allowed to raise tuition above voucher level, thereby
insuring that the poor would not be penalized for poverty. Schools
would choose students partly by processing applications and partly
by lottery, and financial supplements would be offered to those
schools choosing low-income children, thereby making it profitable to take poor blacks.

Milton Friedman, who finds the Jencks plan unnecessarily complex and fears that it will result in a bureaucracy just as complex as the present one, gives the first tow objections short shrift. In the first place, he says, the city schools are *already* dumping grounds, and there is nothing on the horizon, given the present system, that promises to change this. New York City schools are among the most segregated in the world, and the flight to the suburbs simply strengthens the pattern. Conceivably, says Friedman, as a variety of schools develops catering to special talents and needs, the voucher system could lessen the white exodus from the cities and might even bring some people back. Things could certainly get no worse.

No matter what angle you examine it from the "dumping ground" argument seems a curious one, almost as if the educationists hadn't quite thought their argument through. For what they are saying is that public schools are so wretched that no one with any ability at all would stay in them if there were alternatives.

An Alternative

The "hucksterism" charge, leveled most frequently by AFT President David Selden, seems anchored in the notion that parents are incapable of choosing wisely for their children, that they must be led by the hand by those wiser than they, in this case, presumably, the AFT. Parents surely know at least as much about education as they do about, say, medicine. Yet no one seriously champions the creation of some elite body that would dictate to Mrs. Garkle which doctor should remove Gwendolyn's tonsils.

The church-state argument is the most complex. Voucher defenders claim that there is no constitutional problem involved, since if parents sent their children to parochial schools the government would not be making payment to the schools but to the parents. This, of course, is an argument that will have to be resolved by the courts. But to those critics who believe that the voucher system would benefit church schools at the expense of the public, Milton Friedman offers an ingenious answer. At present, says Friedman, in most parts of the country, parents send their children to parochial schools not because they're religious but because they're *private.* Parochial schools, in other words, offer the only alternative to public schools that middle- and working-class parents can afford. The voucher system, Friedman argues, would create a new kind of public school that every middle-class family could afford.

Closely related to this argument is the contention that the price of land and construction would prevent private secular schools from coming into existence in sufficient number to compete with the parochial. Tuition in the form of vouchers can keep a school running, but before you collect tuition, you have to build the school. This objection is one of the most telling, but it touches upon things we as yet have no way of evaluating, and it is invalid insofar as it rests on the false assumption that the quality of education is somehow directly related to the cost and effectiveness of the physical plant. Why couldn't a small experimental school in a tenement, renovated by teachers, parents and students, provide just as rewarding an education as some $5-million concrete-and-glass complex? Or why couldn't a remodeled Victorian house in Westport do the same? The quality of education can't be measured by the number of feet of carpeting in the library.

It remains doubtful whether the voucher system will get a chance to prove itself. The word out of Washington until very recently was that it is dead as an OEO project. But on January 20, in a speech in Wilkes-Barre, Pennsylvania, Frank Carlucci, new OEO acting director, announced that his agency would award preliminary planning grants to school districts in Indiana and California interested in setting up experimental voucher programs. And San Francisco, San Diego and Seattle have also expressed strong interest in similar grants.

Crusade To Stifle

But there's tough going ahead, for the educationist lobby is digging in. "The critics," said Rumsfeld, "are certain, or so they say, of their own concern for education and they deny that anyone else is concerned or can have any reason to be dissatisfied. They fear experimentation because it may call into question their own dogmas and orthodoxies. They seem to be embarked on a crusade to stifle efforts . . . to improve." Some of these critics, theorized Rumsfeld, "think their profession must be insulated from change. They fear the consequences of new techniques because, I suspect, they doubt their ability to adapt to them. They conceal their fear in the fog of educational jargon and claim that only they can evaluate themselves. They reject the idea of

accountability and want to ensure that their paychecks and per-
quisites are maintained regardless of what is achieved in the
classroom."

   The hard truth, of course, is that education is under the control of a monopoly which, although perhaps the single most powerful lobbying group in Washington, is much less adept at educating
than lobbying. When the teachers' groups become just one more
special-interest group with a vested interest in protecting themselves at the expense of the people they supposedly serve, then we
must view with suspicion the misgivings they express over experimentation. When they call the idea of a voucher system "a tragic
mistake," as does the AFT, then we must wonder whether they
mean a tragic mistake for the country or for the AFT. Says Harvard's Dean Sizer: "Given the condition of the schools that serve
poor youngsters, it takes a depressing amount of paranoia to suggest that we should not even give the voucher plan a reasonable
trial."   □

John R. Coyne, Jr. is presently Special Assistant to Vice President Agnew.

XII

THE YEAR-ROUND SCHOOL:
A RESPONSE TO ACCOUNTABILITY

by Richard W. Hostrop

"One way to reduce the tax load is to build one-third fewer class-rooms by the adoption of a year-round school plan."

Valley View School District 96 in Illinois on June 28, 1970 became the first entire school district in the nation to embark upon a modern day, computer-assisted, year-round school calendar.[1]

The calendar revision was dictated by seemingly insurmountable conditions. Zooming from less than 100 students in 1953 to more than 5,000 only a decade-and-a-half later, the school district had completely exhausted its bonding power to build more classrooms. In addition to an almost unbelievable geometric growth in enrollments, and a concomitant plunge into financial impoverishment, it was faced with a new crisis created by the Illinois Legislature. In 1968, the 75th General Assembly made kindergarten mandatory in all public schools in the State commencing with the 1970-71 school year. To District 96 this meant imposition of an additional classroom load of more than 800 kindergarten age children on already overburdened school facilities. Without further bonding power to build more classrooms to reduce already overcrowded classrooms, and further faced with the need for an additional 20 kindergarten classrooms mandated to house 800 kindergarteners two years hence, the board passed a formal resolution prepared by district superintendent Kenneth L. Hermansen. The August, 1968 resolution read:

> I (Harold Lindstrom) move that the Board of Education, School District 96 of Will County, hereby directs the administrative team to begin forthwith the investigation procedures for updating the school calendar,

utilizing more calendar days of the year, staff, and equipment, and giving periodic reports to the Board of Education. The new calendar designed shall be recommended to the school board, and instituted on or before the 1971-72 school year.

The Valley View Year-Round School Plan is known more familiarly as simply the "45-15" plan. This is because four nearly equally divided teams of children in grades K-8 attend school year-round for 45 days and then are on vacation for 15 days. Children within the same families and same neighborhoods are on the same team. The result of this innovation is that one team is always out of school while three teams are in school. The economic results of this innovation has been to increase building utilization by one-third. In the case of Valley View, this calendar revision meant obtaining the benefits of a $5 million school plant which the district could not have bonded to build in the first place. Moreover, even if Valley View had had the bonding capacity to build more classrooms there would have been no assurance it could have secured voter approval. Double sessions would have been the only alternative. In recent times considerably more than half of all bond referenda have failed and the record for passing rate hikes is even worse. In short, homeowners are demanding greater fiscal accountability to their perceived already overburdened tax load. One way to reduce this onerous tax load is to build one-third fewer classrooms by the adoption of a year-round school plan. District 96 opted for a year-round school plan over the alternative of "permanent" double sessions.

The year-round school plan not only reduces the need for additional school buildings, but also reduces operating costs. Cost-Ed analysis reveal that the operating costs of year-round schools vis-a-vis traditional calendar schools is decreased by approximately 7.2 percent.[2]

Calendar Reform as a Catalyst for Innovations

Though the 45-15 continuous school plan grew out of economic necessity, the year-round calendar has served as a catalytic change agent in spurring an open-ended cycle of innovations on the part of individual teachers and small groups of teachers.

Some changes initiated by the faculty include the following:

1. Formation of groups of teachers into cooperative or team teaching corps. The 45-15 plan has made this a logical outcome since teacher requested contracts range in length from 184 to 244 days (with proportionate pay).

2. A sweeping reorganization of the whole curriculum in which materials have been developed into units of 45 days or less. This has increased individualization of instruction and has also made it possible to provide quarterly student progress reports to the students and their families before each 15-day off period. This reorganization has also made it possible to more readily facilitate the acceleration of gifted students. Likewise, it has made it possible for less gifted students to spend more time on the clearly defined objectives at home during the off 15 days. For slower students needing still more time, the 45-15 plan enables such students to cycle in to the succeeding group in which case they would lose only 45 days of school progress rather than an entire year.

3. Organization of "repeater," "catch-up," or "tutoring classes" in which lagging students can continue with their group by taking a few classes during their regular 15-day vacation.

The "15-45" Performance Contract

The use of the 15-day vacation periods for special tutoring was quickly recognized by the Welch Learning Systems Company of Skokie, Illinois. The company contacted the Valley View administration shortly before the 45-15 plan went into effect requesting the district's blessing on opening a "15-45" tutoring school.

Several weeks before Group A students were scheduled to complete their first cycle of 45 days Welch opened its "Tutoring Center" in the district. In its first year of operation approximately 200 students took advantage of the tutoring services offered. The Welch plan calls for keeping the students in the Tutoring Center for about 4 hours a day during vacation weeks, and for about 3 hours a week during the regular 45 days of school. Tutoring is provided in English, remedial and developmental reading, and mathematics.

The Welch Tutoring Center makes extensive use of programmed materials and learning machines and concentrates on individual and small group instruction. Tuition is on a flat 2 dollar hourly rate, with most programs calling for a contract of 35 hours. In keeping with the current trend of accountability via performance contracts, the Welch Tutoring Center makes the following guarantee: "We guarantee to improve Reading, Math, or English skills by at least *one full grade level* upon completion of 35 hours of study. Additional instruction as may be necessary to achieve that level will be provided free of charge by Welch Learning Systems — or a full refund of tutoring fees will be made."

Toward Accountability

The 45-15 year-round program, growing out of an economic imperative, has served as a catalytic change agent. District 96 faculty are reshaping the curriculum, individualizing instruction, matching students in accordance with cognitive learning styles, moving toward ungraded schools and differentiated staffing, all within the framework of educational excellence.

Just as the faculty have been forced to reappraise the purpose of education by a vitalizing year-round school calendar, so has the administration. The teachers are becoming more accountable for their students' success. And the administration made it happen by accepting the challenge of accountability mandated by the board of education by implementing year-round schooling a year ahead of the time established in the board's resolution.

Within 2 years of District 96's successful implementation of year-round schooling nearly a thousand school districts across the width and length of America are in the process of reexamining their agrarian age school calendar and examining District 96's fiscally and educationally accountable urban age school calendar. ☐

---

[1] Hermansen, Kenneth L., Gove, James R. *The Year-Round School.* Hamden, Conn.: Linnet Books, The Shoe String Press, Inc., 1971.

[2] Blaschke, Charles. "Performance Contracting Costs, Management Reform, and John Q. Citizen," *Phi Delta Kappan,* December, 1971, p. 247.

XIII

CONTRACTING FOR EDUCATIONAL REFORM

by Reed Martin and Charles Blaschke

"Performance contracting should not be viewed as a way of linking a new outside force onto the existing educational process. It is a way to rearrange the relationships of all the participants in the educational process, new and old."

Educators have had a year of debate on the Texarkana performance contract experiment, and, with allegations of teaching to the test at the end of that experiment, testing and measurement specialists are now having their day. But beneath all the controversy, a change is taking place, with legal ramifications which will long outlive the educational innovation being considered. The application of contractual principles to educational performance is going to pervade every relationship schools now have. Schools were excited by the idea that under performance contracting they could purchase new packages of instruction; what they are now discovering is that they are contracting for educational reform.

The education of our nation's children is a responsibility carefully delegated in constitutions, statutes, and laws. Those who assume that responsibility — whether teachers or parents or private companies — will find legal consequences to all that they do. The most dramatic current attempt to assume responsibility for education is the involvement of private instructional firms which are willing to be paid on the basis of student performance. The relationship established between a public school and a private company takes the form of a so-called performance contract — a legal document. Thus from the very moment a school becomes interested in performance contracting it must consider the many legal questions involved.

The first such question is whether a local school district is *able* to contract with a private organization to perform instructional tasks. Local education agencies, as creations of the state, are given very limited power to contract. Any contract in excess of that power is void even though both parties may agree to it.

Most schools may contract with outside parties to provide certain services, but those generally are services not imposed upon it by constitutional declaration or by state delegation. As Dean Ringel, of Yale Law School, has observed, where the school is under a *duty* to perform a task, then an attempt to contract out for its performance may be void. Although there are as yet no judicial decisions directly on educational performance contracting, cases on the general problem indicate that a controlling factor may be that a school cannot contract for an extended period of time to employ private individuals when public employees have been retained to perform a comparable job.[1]

Thus, having a private company take over the full operation of the school, even with a purpose of doing a "better" job than employees already retained on the public payroll, may raise this legal barrier. This has occurred in one city, and the state attorney general has indicated his misgivings. A more limited contract for services which cannot be provided by the school should come closer to meeting legal requirements.

Assuming, then, that there is the authority to contract for the type of services desired by the school, a second legal obstacle may arise: improper delegation of policy-making powers. States delegate certain educational policy-making functions to the local school, and these powers cannot be further delegated to a private group without an abdication of responsibility on the part of the local school. Cases seem to indicate that courts will examine a school's policy-making role even more closely than its authority to contract. It is not clear where a court might draw the line between policy and other roles in regard to the various educational tasks a school might ask a company to perform, but policy roles must be controlled by the school and not delegated to a company.[2]

Three factors might be considered important in determining whether a school is retaining control of policy matters. First is the school's role in developing the program. If the school invites bids on the basis of specifications which are vague and subject to the bidder's own interpretation, then the school may be allowing the

bidder to exercise too much authority. If there is not a bidding
process, and the school signs a sole-source contract, there are still
problems. A company may convince a school to adopt a certain
approach which changes school policy, thus assuming too much
authority and really nullifying the contractual relationship.

A second area to consider in the question of control is staff
expertise. The school must provide a monitoring and management
function during the program in order to retain authority and protect policy-making prerogatives. If the staff does not have the
requisite expertise, the company will in reality be in control and
the school will have abdicated its responsibility. Many schools
secure outside management support not only to increase their capability in planning but also to retain control over the program and
all its policy ramifications.

A third area indicating policy control is the basic purpose of
the contract. Some schools, unfortunately, perceive performance
contracting as a way to contract out their problem students, shrug-
ging responsibility for failure off their backs and onto an outside
party which is willing to be paid on the basis of student performance. One cannot really blame overburdened schools for finding
such a notion so attractive. One can also understand why performance contracting is viewed as a market development and penetration device by new firms and by firms that have had trouble getting their foot in the door of the local schoolhouse. But contracting out as an end in itself may be a delegation of too much authority. If a program were to be conducted for a specified period of
time, then evaluated and either abandoned or absorbed by the
school, the school would obviously be retaining full authority.
However, if a program might be extended indefinitely, always
under contract to an outside agency, then effective control of decisions with policy implications might have passed to the contractor.

The state commissioner of education in Texas, which has four
performance contracts under way, drew that line clearly in posing
a question recently to the attorney general of the state:

> May a school district enter into performance contracts
> with private corporations where such a program is pri-
> marily proposed for a study in depth of the utilization
> of the capability of the private sector as one strategy
> to facilitate desirable educational reforms as distin-
> guished from any general plan or movement to contract

to private corporations the education of regular public
school children?[3]

The attorney general's opinion answered the question in the
affirmative.[4] One may assume that a school is on safest legal
ground when it specifies in the original contract the procedures for
taking over the operation of a successfully demonstrated instructional program. This process has come to be called the *turnkey*
phase — when the contractor turns the keys over to the school so
that the school can run the program thereafter.

This step also has important educational consequences, for
the turnkey phase is what will distinguish the performance contracting movement, hopefully, from past educational panaceas.
The "crisis" in public education and particularly Johnny's inability
to read has long been with us. Suggestions from the private sector,
and even demonstration programs which promise dramatic break-
throughs, have been numerous over the last few years. With billion-
dollar federal funding, virtually every school district in America
has had the opportunity to participate in some experiment. But
few approaches, no matter how successfully they were demonstrated, seem to be able to have a continuing impact.[5]

The reason is that at the end of a program demonstration
there are many reasons why the approach may or may not be
adopted by the school system: financial, legal, social, political, and
even educational reasons. More important, a variety of parties
must cooperate if that adoption is to have impact: administrators,
teachers, supervisors, school boards, business officers, taxpayers,
and even students. Finally, and most important, changes will have
to be made in the way people relate to each other and to an overall goal for the adoption to fit into the system. Unless the right
questions are considered by the right people, with the correct
changes accompanying the answers to those questions, no program
will be able to survive. This has been the history of research and
demonstration in education over the last few years — highly successful demonstration of programs which have absolutely no trace-
able impact as they are spread throughout the system. This could
be the history of performance contracting if it were not coupled
with the turnkey approach.

The idea of turnkey, both legally and educationally, is to
demonstrate a program which can be successfully adopted by the

school system. Therefore, the first step is to consult decision makers, beginning with teachers, to see what conditions and constraints they would place upon the program. Why pursue the demonstration of an approach which, if successful in educational terms, would not be acceptable to local decision makers for political, social, or economic reasons? Why demonstrate an approach that would require a facility modification the taxpayers would not underwrite or a use of noncertified instructional personnel which the teacher union would not accept?

The second step, after a successful demonstration, is to ascertain what changes need to be made to adopt the approach and maintain its success. Teachers may need to be retrained; administrators may have to develop new staff relationships; students may have to be rescheduled; a new type of diagnostic testing, found to be effective, might have to be employed; measurable performance outcomes, having proven their value as incentives, might have to be developed.

The third step is to make these changes. Thus, performance contracting plus turnkey determines the terms upon which a school system will accept change. demonstrates the effect change can have, and uses that successful demonstration as leverage to have change adopted.[6]

Legal and educational requirements and ramifications appear to merge in the performance contracting-turnkey process. In any one jurisdiction or a specified set of circumstances the case may differ, but a general set of principles may be stated: The test of an adequate contract is the retention of policy control; the test of policy control is the conclusion of the outside relationship and the adoption of successful approaches; and the test of turnkey is the adoption of reforms that must accompany successful adoption of the new approach. *Thus the principal legal consequence of performance contracting is educational reform.*

As stated in an earlier section, staff capabilities become crucial to the fulfillment of legal responsibilities. A turnkey analysis must be performed which shows what, if any, demonstrated approach is worth adopting; the changes which must accompany and facilitate adoption must be indicated; a strategy for accomplishing those changes must be stated; and a continuing monitoring system must be established to feed new information into this dynamic process of self-renewal. Staff must be trained to perform those tasks.

We have been discussing contracts between schools and companies, but an outside agency is not needed for a performance contract. Despite the characterization that opponents of performance contracting have been trying to instill in the public's mind, performance contracts do not require that big business take over the public schools and displace qualified teachers.[7] Performance contracts can be written internally without private business and under the complete control of the existing licensed teachers. A few experiments of this nature are now being tried.[8]

Thus, performance contracting should not be viewed as a way of linking a new outside force onto the existing educational process. It is a way to rearrange the relationships of all the participants in the educational process, new and old.

Participants who will be affected include the community, parents, teachers, teacher colleges, students, funding agencies, and educational firms. The new relationship of one participant, teachers, can indicate the legal rearrangements that are going to follow from performance contracting. School boards will undoubtedly meet teachers at the bargaining table in the next few months with specific performance objectives or accountability clauses to be written into contracts.[9] If teachers are to be held responsible for student performance, they must be delegated the decision-making authority to choose the learning approach they feel is best for each of their students. This flexibility is the "price" which private contractors demand in exchange for accountability, and must therefore be offered to teachers.

Other relationships will be affected. One can imagine the teacher saying to a parent, "I'll be accountable in the classroom by doing certain tasks if you will perform certain tasks at home." Where money passes directly between a parent and supplier of educational services, that will become an element in the contract. With student performance as a goal, students might withhold performance until demands for a curricular change, for example, are met. Funding agencies may make performance a basis of their relationship with schools. Funds could be required to be related to a measurable output and would be cut off if their use did not appear to make a difference. Thus, the dramatic feature of performance contracting — no results, no pay — which schools have enjoyed in their relationship with private companies, will become a very solemn responsibility of schools vis-a-vis funding agencies. Testing and evaluation will play a crucial role, and the test manufacturer will be asked to guarantee the validity of his instrument much as firms are now asked to guarantee the effectiveness of the instructional approach.

Thus, the performance contracting-turnkey approach will have a lasting legal implication for the school's relation with others in the educational process. The basic relationship will become one of consumer versus supplier of educational services, with the contract as a primary instrument in this educational revolution leading to consumer sovereignty. The application of contractual law to educational reform may seem to many to be a slow process, but once it begins, it cannot be stopped. And it began this year.   □

Reed Martin is an officer of Education Turnkey Systems, Washington, D.C., which provides management support to school systems experimenting with performance contracting in 30 cities across the country. He is an attorney and former editor of the *Texas Law Review* who has drafted and aided in negotiating the majority of performance contracts in the country. Charles Blaschke is president of Education Turnkey Systems.

---

[1] Dean Ringel, unpublished memorandum, "The Legal Status of Educational Turnkey Programs."

[2] The difficulty in keeping policy and administration separate is explored exhaustively by Carl F. Stover, in "The Government Contract System as a Problem in Public Policy." Menlo Park, Calif.: Stanford Research Institute, 1963.

[3] Letter dated July 28, 1970, from Commissioner J. W. Edgar to Attorney General Crawford C. Martin.

[4] Opinion No. M-666, August 20, 1970.

[5] See Norman Hearn's "Research Notes," *Phi Delta Kappan*, September, 1970, p. 59, for comments on adoption rate of one federal program.

[6] See "The Performance Contract-Turnkey Approach to Urban School System Reform," *Educational Technology*, September, 1970. One of those changes must certainly be the incorporation of a monitoring system that provides constant feedback on performance and costs. This would be essential during the demonstration phase to indicate whether any success was being demonstrated; and it is essential afterwards so that a newly adopted system can continue to be changed. This is the second major difference in turnkey. Rather than locking a successfully demonstrated program into the system and forgetting it, the turnkey approach continues to evaluate that program as an input leading toward a total goal. Thus turnkey includes the capacity for continual change.

[7] See resolution opposing performance contracting passed at American Federation of Teachers National Convention, August, 1970.

[8] Two of the sites in the Office of Economic Opportunity nationwide experiment in performance contracting are Stockton, California, and Mesa, Arizona, where the contracts are between the school board and the teachers' association.

[9] Myron Lieberman discusses the New York City accountability clause in "An Overview of Accountability," *Phi Delta Kappan*, December, 1970, pp. 194-95.

XIV

ACCOUNTABILITY AND PERFORMANCE CONTRACTING

by James R. Forsberg

". . . teacher associations, may be expected to attack both account-ability and performance contracting with renewed vigor as current programs progress beyond the experimental stage to practical application."

The concept of accountability and one means of its implementation, performance contracting, are subjects of increasing debate within the educational community. While supporters justify and critics attack the concept, the demand grows for some way to measure the responsibility of educational managers for the outcomes and products of educational systems. Legislators and taxpayers insist, for example, that programs must achieve what their initiators claim they will achieve.

Presently, the theory and application of accountability is in a period of rapid development and change. New experiments are being conducted and refinements added as school districts decide to try some degree of accountability. As a result, the mainstream of the literature reflects a trial and error approach, but also reveals an increasing sophistication in proposal requests and evaluations.

In reviewing the literature concerning this innovative concept, this paper will gather definitions and dimensions of accountability and performance contracting, survey causes of and demands for accountability, identify supporters and critics, and cite current projects. Subjects covered include the issue of accountability and governance, the use of management systems and safeguards, the problems of measurement, and the legal aspects of performance contracting.

Reprinted from ERIC Clearinghouse on Educational Management, University of Oregon. Analysis and Bibliography Series No. 13, October 1971: EA 003 680.

Definitions and Dimensions

A term classic in management theory but new to education, *accountability* is defined by Kruger (1970) as the responsibility to provide effective educational programs and to employ efficiently the resources allocated for this purpose. Rhodes (1970) considers accountability a goal-directed management process that permits both the present and the desired operation of a school to be viewed from a common frame of reference, with priority placed on the learner. Accountability provides the means for dealing with process and product together.

Probably the most well-known definition of accountability is that of Lessinger ([1970]), who calls it the product of the process of performance contracting (see below). In a 1971 publication Lessinger maintains that accountability helps to counter the Peter Principle that bureaucracy tends to be self-regulating, cut off from control and assessment by those outside it and, therefore, not accountable to the client or citizen. In contrast, accountability promotes competence and responsiveness in a bureaucracy by reporting publicly, through the medium of an outside agency, an independent and continuous review of results promised by the bureaucracy.

Under *performance contracting* a local educational agency contracts with private enterprise to achieve specific goals, within a specific period, for specific costs. According to Lessinger ([1970]), "At its most basic, it means that an agent, public or private, entering into a contractual agreement to perform a service will be held answerable for performing according to agreed-upon terms, within an established time period and with a stipulated use of resources and performance standards."

A performance contract has been interpreted by Estes (1971) as a procedure by which a school district contracts with a private firm for certain instructional services, usually including reading or math programs, or both. Terms and conditions of the contract are such that the contractor receives a set compensation if designated pupils achieve specified educational gains as a result of contractor-administered activities. If pupils do not meet the specifications, the contractor receives less reimbursement and may even be penalized. If pupils exceed specifications, the contractor receives additional reimbursement.

According to Lessinger ([1970]), the purpose of a performance contract is to catalyze and foster institutional reform within a school system. A major concept of performance contracting is the "turnkey" provision whereby methods, materials, and practices resulting from the contractor's intervention can be incorporated in the regular operations of the school or school system. As yet there is little literature on the provision; however, most contracts now contain a "turnkey" clause.

Performance contracting is representative of the approach that tries to foster accountability by relating "input" to educational output" in a meaningful way. However, Lieberman (1970) warns that accountability should not be defined solely in terms of performance contracting. Another approach to accountability, he indicates, is to allow consumer choice of schools. The competition created by consumer choice would force schools to become more accountable or lose clientele. The voucher system represents this approach parents are given a specified sum of money and allowed to select, with certain restrictions, the schools to which they send their children.

Causes and Demands

Educational accountability has many causes, a few of which are briefly described here. The federal government has increasingly demanded accountability for money issued under its programs, such as Titles II and VIII of the Elementary and Secondary Education Act of 1965. For example, Title VIII's Dropout Prevention Program provided the impetus and funding for the Texarkana contract and a number of succeeding contracts. The Model Cities Program has also provided fudning for contracts. Another cause of the federal government's insistence on accountability is the increasing emphasis on evaluation and assessment, as evidenced by the National Assessment Program.

The demands of the disadvantaged for adequate education and the trends toward decentralization and community control place additional pressure on educators to focus on the outputs of the educational system. Finally, increased sophistication in evaluation and management systems, together with more accurate measuring devices, have made it feasible to relate inputs to outputs.

Supporters and Critics

Leon M. Lessinger and Charles L. Blaschke are considered by

some as creators of the concept of educational accountability and performance contracting. Other strong supporters include:

1. congressmen, federal administrators, governors, and state legislators, who demand evidence of educational outputs for dollar inputs
2. corporations in the growing educational industrial complex, who want an opportunity to demonstrate their new teaching materials and techniques and hope that lessons learned in performance contract experiments will lead to more profitable contracts
3. administrators of inner-city schools and school board members and associations, who are anxious to find ways of more efficiently using diminished funds to satisfy their constituencies
4. minority groups and other disadvantaged groups, who demand that their children be educated to a minimal level of competency and that schools remedy the causes of high and accelerating dropout rates

Among the critics and skeptics influential congresswoman from Oregon and a former teacher. She objects to the overemphasis on skills inherent in an accountability project and believes there are too many external environmental and health factors beyond the teacher's control to hold a teacher responsible for outcomes. She also distrusts the motives and abilities of the educational industrial complex. Bob Bhaerman and the American Federation of Teachers (AFT), Helen Bain and the National Education Association (NEA), and local teacher associations have also criticized accountability for reasons discussed below.

Current Projects

Hall and Stucker (1971) note the diversity of programs in operation. Programs may differ in the content of the educational programs in the portions of the programs under contract in the contract terms and in the characteristics of the contractors' learning programs. Few contracts go beyond reading and math skills because of the problems in measuring achievement in other areas of learning.

Hall and Stucker classify the programs in four groups. The

first group contains the 1969-70 programs. The second comprises the 1970-71 programs for student achievement. The third contains programs unique for their concern with the education of teachers rather than with the education of students. The final group contains programs in the structured experiment being conducted by the United States Office of Economic Opportunity.

Projects range from the controversial Texarkana project to the Gary, Indiana, school district, which contracted a whole school to Behavioral Research Laboratories.

A comprehensive listing of current projects involving performance contracting is provided by Hall and Stucker, and another by the New York State Education Department (1970).

Accountability and Governance

One of the first questions asked is, *"Who* will be held accountable?" At least three answers to this question can be found in the literature, depending on which of three groups the writer belongs to. Teacher associations as a group demand various degrees of governance or decision-making in policy matters before they will accept accountability. Another group focuses on the school level and would hold the principal responsible. Yet a third group is researching to develop models and methods for determining the effects of various inputs by parents, administrators, and teachers on specified educational outputs.

Representing the first group, Harland (1970) has capsulized the views of the NEA in its demand that governance precede accountability. The NEA requests self-governance in such areas as the right of the teaching profession to approve programs, issue licenses, enforce standards of ethics and practices, promote studies and research designed to improve teacher education, and in general delegate responsibilities concomitant with accountability. This participation in decision-making, Harland argues, would remove the reluctance of the profession to being held responsible.

The AFT has opposed both accountability and performance contracting. Bhaerman (1970), in his critique of Lessinger's views, states that teachers have not been made sufficiently aware of new technology and materials, nor have they been given adequate preservice and inservice training. He proposes that strengths and weaknesses of teachers be identified so that continuous growth experiences can be provided.

Another facet of the question of governance is brought up by Wilson (1971) in a discussion of the views of the American Association of Classroom Teachers (ACT), which stresses the right of teachers to speak on matters relating to curriculum and instruction. Although school boards have the right to set policy, the ACT maintains that development and implementation of policy remain the responsibility of professionals and their organizations. Wilson delineates specific matters for which teachers should be held responsible and insists that classroom teachers, through their professional associations, should be involved in decision-making processes in performance contracts.

In some instances teacher organizations are working closely with contractors and administrators on various programs. The Chicago Model Cities Program involves the Chicago Teachers Union in what it calls the Performance Contract Management Committee, an overall management group of administrators and community organizations engaged in preplanning and long-range planning. The Dallas Project (Estes 1971) uses a similar group called the Planning Advisory Group. Albert Shanker of the New York United Federation of Teachers has agreed to develop, with the New York City Board of Education, objective criteria of professional responsibility.

English and Zaharis (1971) offer an alternative to teacher association objections by suggesting that accountability and governance are incompatible since the increase in teacher power at the bargaining table restricts the ability of the public to hold teachers accountable. In the authors' view, the solution is internal contracting, such as the system now in progress at Mesa, Arizona, where teams of teachers contract with the school board for services.

Meade (1968) is representative of the second group, which holds the school principal responsible. He maintains that there has been a shift away from holding individual staffs and schools responsible for their effect on educational outcomes. Those who propose this theory compare the principal to an industrial plant manager who is responsible for all that goes on in his plant.

The third group attempting to assign responsibility are researchers who develop methods and models relating input variables to specific outputs. Barro (1970), for example, has written a sophisticated analysis of the information and methodology required to determine the extent to which teachers or administrators can affect outcomes within their own spheres of responsibility, given the environments in which they must work and the constraints placed on them. He recommends statistical analysis of the effects on a pupil's progress in a given classroom of such variables as ethnicity, socioeconomic status, and prior educational experience. Barro's methodology for measuring the individual agent's contributions to pupil performance is a multiple regression analysis of the relationship between pupil performance and an array of pupil, teacher, and school characteristics.

Dyer (1970), on the other hand, emphasizes not individual contributions, but the joint responsibility of the entire school staff. He advocates recognizing and measuring four school variables: input, educational process, surrounding conditions, and output. These variables must be measured and appropriately interrelated and combined to produce readily interpretable indices by which the staff can know to what degree its own efforts produce the desired changes in pupils. He calls such indices School Effectiveness Indices (SEIs) and describes their derivation, suggesting short- and long-range plans for operation.

Management Systems and Safeguards

Accountability systems and performance contracting have drawn on the theory and applications of management systems, systems approaches, systems analysis, and evaluation procedures. Management support groups, a feature of most performance contracts, provide many of the management services required by a contract and supplement school staff management experience. Evaluators function as monitors by assisting in management and seeing that the instructional contractor meets specifications. Additional safeguards are provided by independent audit teams, who verify that a contractor has met his contract guarantees.

Kruger (1970) identifies ten critical factors of program design, operation, and management: community involvement, technical assistance, needs assessment, management systems, performance objectives, performance contracting, staff development, comprehensive evaluation, cost effectiveness, and program audit.

Community involvement provides one of the more effective safeguards in an accountability program. Accordingly, community priorities and resources must be considered in both the planning and operating stages. Farquhar (1971) discusses the information systems needed to determine these priorities and resources and al also to keep the public informed of the performance of the program. In a work published soon after the adoption of the Model Cities Act, Campbell, Marx, and Nystrand (1969) discuss the importance of community involvement in model cities projects. Both the Chicago and the Dallas performance contracts involve community groups in planning procedures.

Describing evaluation as one of the most important aspects of a performance contract or accountability program, Kruger urges that an evaluation plan be made prior to the commencement of project operations, that the plan have adequate scope, that it provide evaluation of objectives-accomplishments at both operational and management levels, and that, within these levels, it pay attention to product and process. The evaluator must be skilled in both educational evaluation and management operations analysis.

Hall and Stucker (1971) recommend a broad perspective to evaluate effects other than the narrow objectives listed for a performance contract, since there will likely be affective or volitional impacts on students and both positive and negative impacts on teachers and school officials.

Andrew and Roberts' (1970) evaluation report on the Texarkana project points out the errors and weaknesses of that experiment and provides a good example of the problems that may face an evaluator. One of the rpoblems in that project was that the internal evaluator was hired *after* the project had begun.

Lessinger ([1970]) has outlined the general functions of the various groups in a performance contract:

- The local education agency (LEA) employs a management support group (MSG).
- The MSG draws up a set of general specifications called a request for proposal (RFP).
- The RFP is the subject of a prebidding conference.
- The LEA, with the aid of the MSG, selects the best bid and negotiates a performance contract.
- The LEA employs an independent audit team to monitor execution of the performance contract and to certify results for purposes of payments.

Actual requests for proposals provide a clearer idea of the role of management support groups and independent auditors.

(Chicago Board of Education 1970, Texarkana School District 7 1970, and Estes 1971).

Measurement Problems

Accountability presupposes some measure of inputs and outputs. Because the evaluation of achievement is no better than the measurement instruments used, the identification of appropriate instruments to measure the attainment of the objectives specified in the performance contract is essential. The instruments and systems used for measurement are critical, not only in determining the amount of the contract payments, but also in evaluating the conduct and effectiveness of the program.

The instruments for measuring these outputs have generally been the standardized norm-referenced achievement tests for reading and mathematics skills, together with their subtests. In his thoughtful analysis of the measurement process and problems, Lennon (1971) questions the validity of the standard achievement tests, noting that these tests are concerned with a wider range of content and outcomes than the narrowly defined, specific areas of contract intervention. Moreover, achievement tests on reading skills do not correlate perfectly with one another and may even vary on subtest composition and relative emphases. Similar problems exist in the mathematics tests.

Another problem, reliability, involves the difficulty of measuring the gains of an individual pupil. Since the highest reliability of any test is .90, the error of measurement of a gain score may very easily equal or exceed the amount of gain guaranteed in a short-term contract intervention. One solution Lennon offers is designing projects of longer duration.

As an alternative or supplement to the norm-referenced test, Lennon suggests the use of criterion-referenced tests. However, it is not yet clear how results of a series of criterion-referenced tests can be translated into units that will yield measures of gain or growth. Criterion-referenced tests have ben recommended by other authors. Harmes (1971), for example, maintains that use of behavioral objectives increases the options for development of many different specific procedures, instead of limiting the process to one test or combination of uncorrelated tests. Some requests for proposals are already specifying a certain percent—usually 25 percent—of the payment to be based on criterion-referenced test items taken from pools of items developed by the instructional contractor (Chicago Board of Education 1970, Texarkana School District 7 1970).

Byrd (1970) discusses current testing problems, including the time lag between events and curricular changes and new test construction, and the use of test results as a method of evaluation in accountability.

Andrew and Roberts (1970), the internal evaluators for the first Texarkana contract, describe that contract's notorious problem of teaching test items. The effect of such teaching was to make evaluation of the contract meaningless. Although Educational Testing Service, the auditor for that contract, attempted to analyze the effects of teaching certain test items and hence salvage some meaningful evaluation, it did not succeed. To avoid this problem, local education agencies use criterion-referenced test items, to establish stricter procedures for monitoring contracts in progress, and to cease telling instructional contractors what achievement tests or forms of those tests will be used.

Legal Aspects

Local education agencies desiring to draft performance contracts must obtain expert legal assistance to make sure the contracts are legally valid. A lawyer assisting in this drafting should be knowledgeable in educational matters as well as in the law.

Some legal offices serving boards of education have questioned the ability of school boards, under state constitutions and laws, to contract with outside, private firms. For example, the counsel to the New York State Education Department has stated he does not believe boards of education in that state have authority to enter into agreements with third parties to provide instructional services in public schools (New York State Education Department 1970).

Martin and Blaschke (1971) divide the problem into two issues: the authority to contract and the improper delegation of policy-making powers. A school's authority to contract may be limited if it is under a duty to perform a task imposed on it by constitutional declaration or statutory delegation. In such instances, an attempt to contract for the performance of this duty may be void.

To decide the issue of improper delegation, the courts must

determine what is within a board's policy-making responsibility. There are indications the courts will construe this very strictly. To determine if a school is improperly delegating policy matters, school districts should consider: (1) the degree of specificity on requests for proposals, (2) the sufficiency of expertise of the school staff or additional personnel hired to fulfill its monitoring and management function, and (3) the specificity of the period the contract is to run before it is abandoned or absorbed by the school.

Future Trends in the Literature

The literature on performance contracting may be expected to follow three differing trends. The first group, directed to decision-makers, will consist largely of evaluations of current projects and practical treatises on how to implement performance contracting or accountability in schools.

The second group, written by theoreticians such as Barro and Dyer, will continue to develop methods and means to determine the precise effect of inputs on pupil performance. Since research designs and methodologies are not yet sufficient to relate inputs to outputs with precision, temporary intermediate methods for evaluating teacher and administrator performance will be required.

The third group, presenting views of various teacher associations, may be expected to attack both accountability and performance contracting with renewed vigor as current programs progress beyond the experimental stage to practical application.

The first of three reports in a comprehensive study of performance contracting sponsored by the United States Department of Health, Education, and Welfare has been published by The Rand Corporation. The report is in two parts. In part 1, Stucker and Hall (1970) explore the basic issues in performance contracting, addressing their discussion to education decision-makers. The second part (Stucker 1971) is a technical appendix of mathematical models of interest mainly to theoreticians and model builders.

A later report will analyze the outcomes of some programs after 1970-71 results are available, and the final report will be a Performance Contracing Guide, combining concepts of the first report with conclusions drawn from program results in the second to produce a general guide on how to plan, conduct, and evaluate performance contracting programs.

Conclusion

Many writers are concerned that educational accountability and performance contracting will join the long list of innovations that have been debated with a great deal of fanfare and then quietly discarded. Chandler (1971), noting this phenomenon, suggests that performance contracting can go one of two ways. Through abuses, exaggerated claims, unreliable evaluations, and unethical practices, performance contracting could end in disrepute. On the other hand, if performance contracting is carried out with patient, careful, and intelligent testing and experimentation, it could become a highly effective tool for education. The next few months may provide the answer.

Even when well conceived and implemented, performance contracts are usually considered only temporary or stopgap devices to be used until schools can adopt the techniques and technology of the contractor through turnkeying. Consequently, as performance contracts are phased out, it may be expected that more attention will focus on the basic concept of accountability, If that stage is reached, the persons or groups who are held accountable may become vociferous in their disapproval—as teacher associations threaten to do—if the accountability programs are not carefully planned and worked out with the affected groups.   □

Bibliography

Andrew, Dean C., and Roberts, Lawrence H. *Final Evaluation Report on the Texarkana Dropout Prevention Program.* Magnolia, Arkansas: Education Service Center Region 8, 1970. 118 pages. ED 044 466 MF $0.65 HC not available from EDRS.

Barro, Stephen M. "An Approach to Developing Accountability Measures for the Public Schools." *Phi Delta Kappan,* 52, 4(December 1970), 196-205.

Bhaerman, Bob. *Response to Lessinger: The Great Day of Judgment.* Washington, D.C.: American Federation of Teachers, 1970. 6 pages. ED 045 568 MF $0.65 HC $3.29.

Brain, George B. "National Assessment—Evaluation and Accountability." Paper presented at meeting of the National Association of State Boards of Education, October 1970. 14 pages. ED 046 064 MF $0.65 HC $3.29.

Byrd, Manford, Jr. "Testing under Fire: Chicago's Problem." Paper presented at the Conference of the Educational Records Bureau, "Testing in Turmoil: A Conference on Problems and Issues in Educational Measurement," New York, October 1970. 15 pages. ED 047 013 MF $0.65 HC $3.29.

Campbell, Roald F.; Marx, Lucy Ann; and Nystrand, Raphael O., eds.

"Educational Problems in the Urban Setting." Chapter 1 in *Education and Urban Renaissance,* (Book based on papers presented at the National Conference on Education, Dimension of the Model Cities Program, University of Chicago Center for Continuing Education, 1967.) New York: John Wiley & Sons, 1969. 19 pages. ED 031 793 MF $0.65 HC $3.29 (Complete document, 148 pages, available from John Wiley & Sons, Inc., 605 Third Avenue, New York, New York 10016, $5.95.)

Chandler, B. J. "What School Boards Should Know about Performance Contracting." Paper presented at regional conference of the National School Boards Association, New York, 1971. 10 pages. ED 049 519 MF $0.65 HC $3.29.

Chicago Board of Education. *Model Cities: Guaranteed Reading Achievement.* Chicago: 1970. 118 pages. ED 045 332 MF $0.65 HC $6.58.

Coleman, J. *Measures of School Performance.* Santa Monica, California: The Rand Corporation, 1970.

Cronback, L. J., and Furby, L. "How Should We Measure Change—Or Should We?" *Psychological Bulletin,* 74, 1 (July 1970), 68-80.

Culbertson, Jack A. "Evaluation of Middle Administrative Personnel: A Component of the Accountability Process." Paper presented at annual convention of American Association of School Administrators, Atlantic City, February 1971. 11 pages. ED 051 543. MF $0.65 HC $3.29.

Cunningham, Luvern L. "Our Accountability Problems." *Theory into Practice,* 8 4(October 1969), 285-297.

Dyer, Henry S. "Toward Objective Criteria of Professional Accountability in the Schools of New York City." *Phi Delta Kappan,* 52, 4(December 1970), 206-211.

Educational Testing Service. *Proceedings of the Conferences on Educational Accountability.* Princeton, New Jersey: 1971. 108 pages. ED 050 183 MF $0.65 HC $6.58.

Education Turnkey Systems, Inc. *Performance Contracting in Education.* Champaign, Illinois: Research Press, 1970.

English, Fenwick, and Zaharis, James. "Are Accountability and Governance Compatible?" *Phi Delta Kappan,* 52, 6(February 1971), 374-375.

Estes, Nolan. "Education Performance Contracting: The Dallas Project." Paper presented at the annual convention of the American Association of School Administrators, Atlantic City, February 1971. 16 pages. ED 049 517 MF $0.65 HC $3.29.

Farquhar, J. A., *Accountability, Program Budgeting, and the California Educational Information System: A Discussion and a Proposal.* Santa Monica, California: The Rand Corporation, 1971. 34 pages. ED 050 498 MF $0.65 HC $3.29. (Also available from Communications Department, Rand, 1700 Main Street, Santa Monica, California 90406, $2.00.)

Green, Norman S. "Whither Performance Contracting?" Paper presented at annual convention of the Pennsylvania School Boards Association, Pittsburgh, October 1970. 6 pages. ED 047 380 MF $0.65 HC $3.29.

Hall, George R., and Stucker, James P. "The Rand/HEW Study of Performance Contracting." *Compact,* 5, 1(February 1971), 6-9.

Harland, D. D. "The Profession's Quest for Responsibility and Accountability." *Phi Delta Kappan,* 52, 1(September 1970), 41-44.

Harmes, H. M. "Specifying Behavioral Objectives of Performance Contracts." *Educational Technology,* 11, 1(January 1971), 52-56.

Hegedus, Rita. *Educational Vouchers.* Dover: Division of Research, Planning, and Evaluation, Delaware State Department of Public Instruction, 1971. 14 pages. ED 048 674 MF $0.65 HC $3.29.

Jung, Stephen M.; Lipe, Dewey; and Wolfe, Peggy S. *Study of the Use of Incentives in Education and the Feasibility of Field Experiments in School Systems. Final Report.* Palo Alto, California: American Institutes for Research, 1971. 152 pages. ED 051 547 MF $0.65 HC $6.58.

Kaufman, Roger A. "Accountability, A System Approach and the Quantitative Improvement of Education—An Attempted Integration." *Educational Technology,* 11, 1(January 1971), 21-26.

Klein, S. P. "The Uses and Limitations of Standardized Tests in Meeting the Demands for Accountability." U.C.L.A. *Evaluation Comment,* 2, 4(January 1971).

Kruger, W. Stanley, "Implications of Accountability for Educational Program Evaluation." Paper presented at the Invitational Conference on Measurement in Education, University of Chicago, April 1970. 14 pages. ED 043 665 MF $0.65 HC $3.29.

Lennon, Roger T. "Accountability and Performance Contracting." Paper presented at annual meeting of American Educational Research Association, New York, February 1971. 21 pages. ED 049 520 MF $0.65 HC $3.29.

Lessinger, Leon M. *Engineering Accountability for Results into Public Education.* [1970]. 32 pages. ED 040 155 MF $0.65 HC $3.29.

_____. *Every Kid a Winner: Accountability in Education.* New York: Simon and Schuster, 1970.

_____. "Robbing Dr. Peter to Pay Paul: Accounting for Our Stewardship of Public Education." *Educational Technology,* 11, 1(January 1971), 11-14.

Lieberman, Myron. "An Overview of Accountability." *Phi Delta Kappan,* 52, 4(December 1970), 194-195.

Martin, Reed, and Blaschke, Charles. "Contracting for Educational Reform." *Phi Delta Kappan,* 52, 7(March 1971), 403-405.

Maryland State Department of Education. *Evaluating Compensatory Education Accountability.* Baltimore: Division of Compensatory, Urban, and Supplementary Programs, [1971]. 21 pages. ED 047 068 MF $0.65 HC not available from EDRS.

Meade, Edward J., Jr. "Accountability and Governance in Public Education." Adapted from paper presented at the annual convention of the National Association of Secondary School Principals, Atlantic City, February 1968. 14 pages, ED 031 807 MF $0.65 HC not available from EDRS. (Available from Ford Foundation, Office of Reports, 320 East 43rd Street, New York, New York 10017, free.)

Millman, J. "Reporting Student Progress: A Case for a Criterion-Referenced Marking System." *Phi Delta Kappan,* 52, 4(December 1970), 226-230.

New York State Education Department. *Performance Contracting in Elementary and Secondary Education. A Report Showing the Developments on a Nationwide Basis and the Implications for New York State.* Albany: Division of Evaluation, 1970. 44 pages. ED 049 525 MF $0.65 HC $3.29.

Office of Economic Opportunity. *A Proposed Experiment in Education Vouchers. An OEO Pamphlet.* Washington, D.C.: 1971. 19 pages ED 048 667 MF $0.65 HC $3.29.

Rhodes, Lewis A. "Educational Accountability: Getting It All Together." Background paper for seminar on accountability of the annual Texas Conference for Teacher Education. October 1970. 14 pages ED 045 566 MF $0.65 HC $3.29.

Stucker, James P. *The Performance Contracting Concept, Appendix: A Critique of the Theory. A Report Prepared for the Department of Health, Education, and Welfare.* Santa Monica, California: The Rand Corporation, 1971. 56 pages. ED 050 497 MF $0.65 HC $3.29.

Stucker, James P., and Hall, George R. *The Performance Contracting Concept in Education. A Report Prepared for the Department of Health, Education, and Welfare.* Santa Monica, California: The Rand Corporation, 1971. 81 pages. ED 050 496 MF $0.65 HC $3.29.

Texarkana School District 7. *[Dropout Prevention Program. Request for Proposal No. 2.]* Arkansas: 1970. 77 pages. ED 043 950 MF $0.65 HC $3.29.

Wilson, Donald F. "The Practitioner and Accountability." Speech presented at annual meeting of the National School Boards Association, Atlanta, March 1971. 11 pages. ED 049 528 MF $0.65 HC $3.29.

Wohlferd, Gerald. *Quality Evaluation through Nomographs.* Albany: New York State University System, 1970. 34 pages. ED 047 006 MF $0.65 HC $3.29.

James R. Forsberg is a research analyst at the ERIC Clearinghouse on Educational Management, University of Oregon.

XV

SCHOOL ADMINISTRATION BY CONTRACT

by Charles H. Wilson

"Why cannot a local board of trustees contract with a respectable management firm to provide all administration for a given period of time, as it presently contracts with an individual superintendent?"

A new type of school administration could be in store for us, if it is not already just around the corner. It will utilize the best features of industrial and business management without eliminating the cherished virtues of local control. It will bring an element of competitiveness into a profession heretofore marked by degrees, years of service and even favoritism. The outline of its future may be seen emerging in the large consulting or managerial firms being organized—and reorganized—throughout the country.

Today it is a rare school district that does not rely to some extent upon the recommendations of outside management or educational consulting firms. Sometimes these recommendations are sought simply to reassure local citizens on proposed bond issues. Increasingly, however, the local district, large or small, requires the expertise of managerial specialists who are prepared to make recommendations ranging from site selection to curriculum development.

All of which leads to a quite simple question: If expert management is desirable in school operation, why is it not purchased outright by a district rather than superimposed on an already costly administration? Why cannot a local board of trustees contract with a respectable management firm to provide all administration for a given period of time, as it presently contracts with an individual superintendent?

If this be heresy, then so be it. But before I am nailed to the wall as a traitor to my profession, let's examine the reasons why this proposal makes sense from the standpoint of the school district *and* the school administrator.

In the first place, there has always been an element of the macabre in educational administration. Presumably, superintendents have been head teachers chosen to lead the teaching staff because of their outstanding classroom ability. But they are nothing of the kind. Teachers have no voice in the selection of their so-called leadership. Superintendents are employed by boards of trustees and are responsible solely to boards for their salaries and continued employment.

But superintendents, when employed, are expected to administer the schools through an established, on-going hierarchy of subordinate administrators that comprise an almost unmovable bureaucracy. I do not exaggerate greatly when I say that the superintendent is dependent solely upon the goodwill of his subordinates to tolerate him in office. Any efforts on the part of the superintendent to "get things done" will go for nought without the support of his associates, assistants, directors, principals, supervisors and what-have-you. Indeed, if a superintendent were so inclined, and some are, he could simply float along for years on the shoulders of his administrative bureaucracy without making serious decisions or solving critical problems.

Even this, however, fails to touch the hard-core reality of American school administration—the fact that it is the largest and most costly of any in the world. The State of New York, for example, is reputed to have more administrators than all of France. I know from personal experience that a school in Great Britain managed by one head master and a secretary would require a superintendent, three or four principals, a buildings and grounds director, a business manager, a curriculum supervisor and a half dozen counselors if it was relocated in a typical American suburb.

Why all this proliferation of administrators? There are several reasons. The nature of local control, for one thing, places the major burden for raising tax money on the administration. Every principal, if he is worth his salt, is a good public relations agent, a sort of educational ward healer. More than this, however, administration provides status and financial rewards for teachers otherwise tied to poor salary schedules. Then, too, the complicated nature of

modern education and financial support demands specialists of
many different kinds.

This last factor, in my opinion, may hasten the coming of the
managerial firm. For instance, a superintendent simply must have
on his administrative staff today, in addition to the customary financial and building specialists, a person to prepare federal reports
and another to negotiate with teachers. Now unless the district is
exceedingly large, it is unlikely that either position is a full-time
assignment. It is still more unlikely that one person can serve in
both capacities. Therefore, we employ two people and fill up their
time with whatever busy work we can find. Eventually this work
becomes so burdensome that there is not enough time for the
original assignment, thereby requiring, with Parkinson's Law predictability, the employment of an administrative assistant and an
additional secretary.

I know of no district where there are not far more administrators than are really needed if personnel could be used efficiently.
Actually, the situation is so bad that in some districts over half of
the certificated (professional) employees are in non-teaching assignments. And all, or nearly all, are frozen into position by a combination of tenure and tradition.

Nor am I, as a superintendent, able to make any significant
reduction in the non-teaching staff. Every year or so, when someone retires or leaves the district, I can possibly consolidate two
positions into one or spread the retiree's duties among several
people. But I get only suspicious glares from those remaining, who
step up the pace of their busy work to protect their own jobs and
avoid additional assignments.

What advantages?

How many of these problems could be eliminated with professional management employed by trustees for a period of three
to five years as the superintendent is presently employed? And
what would be the benefits?

First, there would be the benefit that would result from competitive bidding. The trustees would specify in broad terms the
character of administration they desired, whereupon the competing firms would appear for interview and bid upon a contract.

What exactly would the trustees buy, and how would this
differ from existing practice? Today, as I pointed out, the trustees

employ only a superintendent, who is obliged to accept an administrative staff which he knows little or nothing about and cannot dismiss or transfer except at great peril to himself and the system by which he is employed.

Under a managerial contract system, however, the trustees would employ a managerial team. The director (superintendent) might or might not be specified in the contract. In either event, he would be appointed by, and responsible to, the managerial firm, as a school building architect is responsible to and paid by the architectural firm that assigns him to a specific job. Indeed, the parallel is pronounced. When school trustees build a building, they employ an architectural firm, which assigns a member of the firm to be in charge, who in turn uses his firm's engineers, draftsmen, architects and other specialists to the best possible effect. No one has ever questioned the loss of "local control" in the process.

We should think it madness if a board of trustees employed a single architect, however competent, to direct the board's own engineers and draftsmen in designing a new building. Similarly, no one should find it in the least surprising that a firm employed to manage a school district appoint its own director, who in turn would choose his own managerial team.

Later, I shall say something about why the lives and welfare of existing administrators need not be unduly threatened in the transitional process. Before I do, let us see what advantages an independent managerial system would have over our existing practices.

One thing that immediately comes to mind, of course, is that every managerial firm, large or small, would be obliged to recruit the best administrators it could find, and to pay these people whatever is necessary to retain their services. It is conceivable that particularly able superintendents or business managers would be offered bonuses and stock options on top of high salaries. Certainly, we should see an end to salaries and promotions based upon the length of service in a school district or the attainment of an advanced degree.

Next, and equally important, we should witness a higher order of efficiency introduced into school administration. No longer would an individual be employed to fill a particular slot and be expected to perform dozens of functions he is incompetent to perform. A firm would not employ a business manager, or a

maintenance supervisor, or a personnel director, or a data processing director, or a teacher negotiator for every school district it
serves. Rather, it would have specialists who would serve many districts. Unburdened by rigid tenure laws and seniority rights, the
management firm, pressed to maintain profits, would employ only
the minimum number of executives to get the job done.

As employees and representatives of a particular firm, desir-
ous of obtaining a renewal contract for that firm, the administrative team would be universally solicitous to work with teachers
and citizens of the community. No longer would we see the au-
thoritarianism for which many administrators, protected by tenure, seniority and tradition, are known throughout the land. That
school principal, long suffered for his fuddy-duddy paternalism,
would become as polite and cooperative as a rising young bank
executive.

Furthermore, when that principal or other administrator un-
expectedly encountered a situation he could not handle, a management firm would not have to wait until the end of the year, or
until the poor man reached retirement age, to offer a replacement.
That could be done in a fortnight with a temporary or longterm
substitute.

Let's face one fact squarely: whatever the strengths and
shortcomings of those who enter school administration, there's
not one in a thousand with the skill and fortune to avoid all disaster. Any one of us deserves at least a second, if not a third, fourth
or fifth chance before permanent discard! And who is best qualified to assess an administrator's talents—an elected board of trustees or a group of professionals with their reputation on the line?

Out in the cold
This brings me back to the matter I referred to a moment
ago: why the lives and welfare of existing administrators need not
be jeopardized by such a change. How would this be possible?
How can you avoid disastrous treatment of a run-of-the-mill administrator, who, through no fault of his own, finds himself out in
the cold when a board of trustees decides to employ a management firm?

Some people would say, of course, that if a man is run-of-the-
mill or incompetent, he deserves to be put out to pasture. Isn't
this the way business and industry operate? Well, yes and no.

Many enlightened and socially responsible commercial firms take adequate care of individuals who have given long-time service to the enterprise, even when time has passed them by. Besides, when an executive is dismissed from a company, there is an endless number of companies for the executive to apply to. Where would the released school administrator turn?

First, one must keep in mind that most of us would find employment with the managerial firm, as many have already done.

Second, an administrator generally has a degree of tenure protection that a business executive does not have; while he may be dismissed from his $15,000 a year principalship, he does have tenure as a $10,000 or $12,000 a year teacher.

Third, we must remember that the new managerial concept, if it does materialize, will not come about all at once. It will be a gradual process that may require a decade or two to complete. And herein is still another element of competition that will be intorduced. Where a management firm may be employed in school district A, school district B next door may continue to rely on the traditional administrative bureaucracy. Both the public and the trustees will have a good opportunity to compare the two systems.

Will the managerial firm face opposition from universities and legislatures? Obviously, any change meets with resistance. However, I would predict less resistance than might be expected. The firm-employed administrator would still require certification, just as the firm-employed architect or lawyer requires certification. Universities would continue to provide this training; but it would become a more precise and professional sort of training rather than the broad, ambiguous and somewhat directionless training that attempts to make all things out of all administrative candidates.

Personally, I can foresee little resistance from economy-minded and business-oriented legislatures. Whatever technical changes in the law might be required should be forthcoming with little opposition. After all, who could object to more efficient administrative practices at less cost?

How will a start be made? A start has already been made by a number of large consulting firms, who are admirably staffed by ex-administrators, college professors, architects, data processors and a host of other specialists. I have a suspicion that most of these firms are competent right now to take over the management of any school district, whether large or small.

Where it will start

I would guess, however, that the first significant inroads in firm-management will be made in small school districts where an inadequate jack-of-all-trades administrative staff might be unprepared to cope with the contemporary world of computers, negotiations and the growing complexity of federal and state financing.

Let me be among the first to admit that without a fairly large staff of administrative specialists, I could not begin to administer a school district today.

But while I cannot survive without a business manager, a building and grounds director, a personnel director, a public relations coordinator, a curriculum assistant, a data processing director and at least two people in charge of state and federal reporting, I will admit that this is something like double or triple the administration I need. My problem is that a highly skilled public relations coordinator cannot direct the data processing division. As a consequence, I run something of a managerial firm myself, seeking other districts who can use the services of these two specialists.

Do I hear someone suggest that administrators might soon come from professions other than teaching? Yes, possibly a few, such as accountants and data processors. But what better training ground is there for educational administration than teaching? The great majority of administrators would continue to come from the classroom.

However, they would not necessarily be talented teachers or aging football coaches to be rewarded with administrative assignments. Aside from the fact that competent teaching and coaching are needed the same as good administration, our schools have tended to drain the best teachers from the classrooms for administrative assignment.

Under the system that I envision, a teacher interested in administration would train specifically for employment with a managerial firm. Here he would serve in a variety of administrative capacities and rise within the firm as a junior executive rises to corporation president. No longer would he be thrown directly from the classroom or the gridiron into a full scale administrative assignment for which he may have had little training, experience or talent.

Do I hear the objection that competent administrators may not be willing to accept assignments where they must travel and move around a lot? But why not? Many of them do now. Our own building consultant lives 500 miles to the north. Our architects live in another state over a thousand miles distant. A large consulting firm from New York is handling a major assignment for some California schools.

By and large, of course, administrators would live in the general area where they work, as architects and engineers presently do. It is probable that most of them would serve a single district for many years.

But no longer would an administrator, whatever his rank or age, be subject to the whims of changing board of trustees or superintendent. As an employee of a firm, he might be able to transfer from one assignment to another, even in another state, without loss of rank, salary or retirement benefits. In view of the hopelessly chaotic differences that presently exist among the states, retirement benefits alone should be enough to attract most would-be and practicing administrators to a managerial firm.

How would teachers receive this new breed of administrator? I am tempted to say—what difference? Haven't teachers, in their current militancy, asked for it? But, in matter of fact, I have a suspicion that teachers would welcome a more efficient and professional management. In the long run, it is to the advantage of teachers everywhere to have effective and economical administration.

Would local boards of trustees lose any degree of control? No faster than they are losing it now to the state and federal governments with the fantastic inefficiencies they are obliged to tolerate. "Local control" in the United States has always been something of a myth perpetuated by trustees who relished, and thought they had, power. Local boards have no power whatsoever except that granted to them by the state. As many people are coming to see, there is only one board of education in every state—the legislature.

Therefore, if the myth of local control is to be preserved (and there are good reasons why it should be preserved) it is essential that trustees seek to obtain the highest form of managerial direction at the least cost. And where can this best be obtained—from a haphazard system of teacher trained administrators, or from a professionally trained and skilled administration?

Educational arthritis
Perhaps the point I should stress is this: we are a young

nation turning arthritic before our time. Painfully and grudgingly, we are making progress in the area of human rights; but we are remaining hopelessly arthritic in education.

I would not pretend that a professional, business-like administration is the cureall for our educational arthritis. In theory, at least, I believe that teachers must ultimately be responsible for the management of schools, as doctors are largely in charge of the administration of hospitals. Buf if, and when, that day arrives, there will still be a need for skilled and specialized administrators.

For that matter, I would not pretend that it is ever possible to maintain a satisfactory system of education. No generation can conceive that its successor is equally well educated, let alone superior. Yet it must be obvious that we cannot correct a fundamental weakness in a system by doubling, tripling or quadrupling the weakness.

If it has beén an error, as it surely has been, to separate and relieve teachers from administrative responsibility, we cannot correct the situation with more and more administrators. For the time being at least, the best we can do is to provide an efficient administration. Once that is established, perhaps next we can talk in terms of a teaching profession—a group which selects, polices, dismisses and governs its own ranks.

And when this day arrives, what professional group would not desire the best management? Again, every dollar less for administration is a dollar more for teachers. And every dollar for good administration is overwhelmingly likely to produce more dollars for teaching.   □

XVI

PROPOSING A NATIONAL BOARD
TO ACCREDIT TENURED PROFESSORS

by Henry Saltzman

"Performance criteria, discipline, and a sense of individual account-
ability are imperative if some tenured faculty members are to
continue performing at professional standards and the public's
confidence in the university is to be restored."

A dean or department chairman in a university develops so close a
relationship with his faculty over the years that ambitious, energet-
ic, qualified teachers who earn tenure are frequently permitted to
age like fine wine, without being disturbed. I suggest that in the
best interests of the academic community the professional work of
tenured faculty members must be objectively reviewed on a periodic basis according to established standards and criteria.

 If it is not surprising that many tenured professors acquire a
"What, me worry?" attitude, then it is also not surprising that the
practice of granting tenure—permanent possession of one's place in
a faculty—is being challenged by students, their parents, legislators,
taxpayers, and university administrators. In fact, the abuse of tenure by a few is now threatening to overshadow the real benefits of
this important guarantee of academic freedom.

 The general charge seems to be that a sinecure hardly encourages the continued effort that produces intuitive discoveries, inspired teaching, a willingness to look at old ideas in new ways, and
the intellectual vigor that had marked a man for tenure. But this
formulates the issue inaccurately.

 Attacks on tenure based on alleged attitudes among some
tenured faculty members simply overlook the chief shortcoming

Reprinted with copyright permission of The *Chronicle of Higher Education,* November
8, 1971.

of the tenure system. The nub of the problem is not tenure itself, nor the present procedures leading to loss of tenure, though these might be streamlined.

The Key Is Supervision

Rather, the behavior and attitudes of supervisors of tenured faculty–deans and department chairmen–are the key to the matter. These members of "middle management" (corporate though the term may be, that is precisely their role) are either unwilling or incapable of properly supervising, evaluating, and disciplining the tenured faculty. This weakness gravely threatens the tenure system.

Poor monitoring of the tenured faculty results not from ill will or conspiracy. It is a reflection of a problem in human nature. Deans, chairmen, and tenured faculty have worked and virtually lived together for a long time. Often they are good friends. Indeed, senior members of a faculty often constitute an extended family system: Chairmen become godfathers to the children of tenured faculty members and frequently hlep each other in times of illness or other serious difficulty. After a while, a familial, rather than a managerial, relationship is established.

Such intimate bonding can provide great strength in an institution. In the interest of achieving good management and better performance, it would be foolish and futile to impose upon a familial, collegial relationship a system that is potentially punitive.

Nonetheless, performance criteria, discipline, and a sense of individual accountability are imperative if some tenured faculty members are to continue performing at professional standards and the public's confidence in the university is to be restored. High standards, appropriately enforced, will enhance the quality of education.

Is not better education, after all, the principal aim of university teaching and a prime factor in research? It could be deleterious to the university community to force exacting administrative responsibility into the present middle management system (or non-system).

Proposal for an Accreditation Board

Therefore, I propose establishment of a national independent tenure accreditation board. This is how it would work:

As a parallel to the regional accreditation associations now examining higher education institutions as a totality, the board would formulate objective, balanced, reasonable standards and criteria as its basis for evaluating the performance of each tenured faculty member, for recommending necessary improvement in performance, and for advising on continuance or separation.

The board, named the National Tenured Professor Accreditation Board, would assign teams composed of distinguished scholars, lay members interested in education, university trustees, and students to visit the campuses of member colleges and universities. With only the power of recommendation, the teams would be backed by the public's confidence in their judgment and the public value of their recommendations. Normally, a visit to a school would occur at five-year intervals.

During a visit, a team would examine dossiers that deans and chairmen would be expected to maintain on each tenured faculty member within an academic area. Ideally, the dossier would reflect the faculty member's continued effort to meet the board's standards, and it would function as a record of the guidance toward that end provided by the dean and/or chairman. Such evidence as always-current reading lists, appropriately revised lecture notes, active professional memberships, knowledge and use of new equipment, contributions in one's field, publications, and outside activities—including community service—could partially constitute performance criteria. Criteria would be weighted to account for professional differences among teachers, writers, researchers, and others.

5 Categories of Evaluation

The visiting team would interview the tenured faculty member, his chairman and dean, students, and administrators. As much objective evidence on professional performance as possible would be gathered and evaluated. The aim is to determine periodically the extent to which tenured professors satisfactorily maintain professional growth and bring to their teaching relevant current developments.

The evidence taken together would describe the nature and extent of a tenured person's contribution to his profession, his students, and the college community in a given period of time. The criteria established should undercut the nefarious doctrine of "publish or perish" and restore a balance by looking at performance based upon a variety of factors. It would give greater weight in the priorities of judgment toward demonstrated competence and currency in one's field as these can be evidenced by the professional's teaching and working.

The evaluation team, like its counterpart that now examines higher education institutions, would submit a draft report to the institution's trustees, administration, and campus community. Of course, each tenured professor would receive an advance copy of the report for his comment as to its factual content. His dossier would always be open to him and he could enter replies or rebuttals as he deemed necessary. The team would take these statements into account before submitting its final public report, which would be circulated on the campus.

The report would state which of five categories, based on the evidence, the tenured professor has been placed in:

(1)   Surpasses all criteria.

(2)   Meets all criteria satisfactorily.

(3)   Meets most criteria, but should improve performance in one or two specified areas, and is recommended for continued tenure.

(4)   Meets some but not most criteria, and tenure is recommended for the following two years, subject to a re-evaluation.

(5)   Fails to meet most criteria, and discontinuation of tenure is recommended. (This would be tantamount to a recommendtion of dismissal for cause.)

The report also would suggest to deans and chairmen steps they should take to improve the quality of work among tenured faculty, compared with the criteria and based on the evidence.

The National Tenured Professor Accreditation Board would be supported by institutional memberships. Its findings would apply to tenured faculty members only. Member schools would continue to set their own standards for providing tenure. The board would embody a voluntary system of self-discipline, self-development, and individual accountability that would enhance the likelihood of better education for students.

A self-policing system such as I suggest must be instituted before other groups within society move to impose standards that may be harmful to the community of scholars. If the nation is to preserve its tradition of academic freedom, scholars must impose upon themselves an objective system of accountability under established professional standards and criteria.

Such a system would produce other benefits: Public confidence in teachers and the schools would grow, professional norms would be set for junior professors, qualified tenured professors would have sound evidence to support requests for increased pay, and the abuse of tenure would be significantly reduced.

The National Tenured Professor Accreditation Board is anything but anti-intellectual. The notion that a teacher is beyond professional standards of accountability is silly. A board of peers relying upon objective evidence accumulated over a reasonable period of time will identify the inspired teacher, imaginative researcher, and serious scholar. It also will identify the professor who hides behind his tenure and does little to warrant it.

For tenure, like a good reputation, must be earned over and over again.   □

Mr. Saltzman is president of Pratt Institute.

XVII

COLORADO'S 1971 ACCOUNTABILITY ACT

SENATE BILL NO. 33. BY SENATORS Schieffelin, H. Fowler, L. Fowler, Minister, and Strickland; also REPRESENTATIVES Fentress, Bain, Byerly, Dittemore, Friedman, Fuhr, Johnson, Lindley, Miller, Moore, Munson, Sack, and Strang.

CONCERNING THE ESTABLISHMENT OF AN EDUCATIONAL ACCOUNTABILITY PROGRAM, AND MAKING AN APPROPRIATION THEREFOR.

Be it enacted by the General Assembly of the State of Colorado:

SECTION 1. Chapter 123, Colorado Revised Statutes 1963, as amended, is amended BY THE ADDITION OF A NEW ARTICLE to read:

Article 41

EDUCATIONAL ACCOUNTABILITY

123-41-1. **Short title.** This article shall be known and may be cited as the "Educational Accountability Act of 1971".

123-41-2. **Legislative declaration.** (1) The general assembly hereby declares that the purpose of this article is to institute an accountability program to define and measure quality in education, and thus to help the public schools of Colorado to achieve such quality and to expand the life opportunities and options of the students of this state; further, to provide to local school boards assistance in helping their school patrons to determine the relative value of their school program as compared to its cost.

(2) (a)   The general assembly further declares that the educational accountability program developed under this article should be designed to measure objectively the adequacy and efficiency of the educational programs offered by the public schools. The program should begin by developing broad goals and specific performance objectives for the educational process and by identifying the activities of schools which can advance students toward these goals and objectives. The program should then develop a means for evaluating the achievements and performance of students. It is the belief of the general assembly that in developing the evaluation mechanism, the following approaches, as a minimum, should be explored:

(b)   Means for determining whether decisions affecting the educational process are advancing or impeding student achievement;

(c)   Appropriate testing procedures to provide relevant comparative data at least in the fields of reading, language skills and mathematical skills;

(d)   The role of the department of education in assisting school districts to strengthen their educational programs;

(e)   Reporting to students, parents, boards of education, educators, and the general public on the educational performance of the public schools and providing data for the appraisal of such performance; and

(f)   Provision of information which could help school districts to increase their efficiency in using available financial resources.

123-41-3.   **State board of education – duties.** (1) (a) The state board of education shall develop a state accountability program, which:

(b)   Describes and provides for implementation of a procedure for the continuous examination and improvement of the goals for education in this state.

(c)   Identifies performance objectives which will lead directly to the achievement of the stated goals.

(d)   Adopts a procedure for determining the extent to which local school districts accomplish their performance objectives. Evaluation instruments, including appropriate tests, shall be developed under the authority of this article to provide the evaluation required, but standardized tests shall not be the sole means developed to provide such evaluation.

(c)   Recommends a procedure and timetable for the establishment of local accountability programs.

(2)   The state board of education shall adopt rules and regulations for the implementation of this article.   □

Chapter Three

WHO IS ACCOUNTABLE?

I

WHO IS ACCOUNTABLE?

by Frank J. Young
PSBA President

"Everyone wants to jump on the bandwagon of accountability. But it also appears that most advocates of accountability seem to think in terms of accountability by someone else."

As I have traveled throughout the Commonwealth and in other states on behalf of the Association, I have increasingly puzzled over the question, "Who is accountable?"

There is every evidence that the general society that education serves wants to hold someone accountable—accountable not only for financial resources and how they are used for education, but accountable also for educational results. It seems, also, that everyone wants to jump on the bandwagon of accountability. But it also appears that most advocates of accountability seem to think in terms of accountability by someone else, not by the particular interests that they represent. Let me explain.

College level educators seem to perceive accountability as something that should happen in elementary and secondary educational programs. Not many college level people seem to want to extend this exploration of accountability to such questions as, "Is what we are doing at the college and university level really bringing about some of the problems we see at the elementary and secondary level?"

Educators and others at the federal level seem to view accountability as something that applies to state and local programs, and not very often — if, indeed, at all — does one hear much about accountability related to federal programs despite the fact that

Reprinted with permission of the *PSBA Bulletin,* the magazine of the Pennsylvania School Boards Association, November/December 1970.

some of the most heavily financed such programs seem to have been questionable in effectiveness or have been generally consider- ed ineffective.

Semi-official agencies, such as accrediting agencies and testing or screening agencies, very often view their roles as assigning ac- countability to someone else. Seldom, if ever, do they ask the question, "Are the procedures we are using appropriate for the cir- cumstances?" A good case in point on this score is the manner in which accrediting agencies carry out their function of reviewing and accrediting secondary schools. This whole procedure needs careful re-evaluation. Internal auditing of educational practices and procedures is a necessary part of assessment or accountability re- view. But true accountability will never result from peer evaluation within the same general community of interests. Instead, what is likely to happen is a reciprocal arrangement whereby if "I accom- modate your views and interests, I can expect you to treat me in a like fashion when it is your turn at bat." That just isn't an inde- pendent audit and will not give a true measure of accountability!

Teacher leadership talks about greater "internal control" within the profession, and generally views overall accountability as being someone else's problem. While greater internal control is a laudable objective, there is no fundamental reason presently exist- ing which prevents teachers as a group from exercising this control or demand for increased accountability from their peers. But here again, I sense that teacher leadership views accountability as being applicable to someone else, not to teachers. Also, there is little reason to believe that effective accountability really results from peer review and judgment. Effective accountability really calls for review and judgment by a non-vested interest!

Recent data from the federal government indicates that the United States will spend a record $114.6 billion for food in the current year. During this same year, Americans will dedicate some $73 billion for education, or more than 64 per cent of the amount that will be spent for food. This certainly says that America has placed a high value on education. Thus, it is not surprising to find increasingly that accountability is being demanded for such an order of expenditure.

School boards, and school administrators on behalf of school boards, can expect that the pressure for increased accountability will gorw, not diminish. In their role as representative of general public interest and society's children, school boards need to assemble effective evaluation instruments and resources that can objectively perform independent audits of today's educational programs. School boards can expect to be held accountable, not just for finances but for educational effectiveness as well. This is an appropriate role for school boards, and they must move in the direction of satisfying this increasing responsibility. This is not a function that can be neatly assigned to someone else, for this is an inherent part of the overall responsibility of a school board!   □

II

EDUCATIONAL ACCOUNTABILITY STARTS AT THE TOP

by Dr. Terrel H. Bell
Acting U.S. Commissioner of Education
Department of Health, Education, and Welfare

" 'Accountability' may be an overworked word as applied to teachers and school administrators, but it is virgin soil where school boards are concerned."

Executive Secretary, Mr. Darld Long, asked that I speak on a subject that has gotten a great deal of exposure in the educational press recently — accountability. At the outset I want to make it clear that I come with no illustrated, step-by-step, how-to-do-it government accountability manual. The best I can do is to offer my views on the ways in which this interesting new concept applies to your concerns as school board members and to list a few questions that seem to need answering.

Actually, accountability in education as practiced by school boards could be a very down-to-earth thing. It calls for no complex and expensive hardware, but merely the introduction of measurement and control practices that have been in operation for years in virtually every sound business establishment.

We have fairly good measurement and control practices on the financial management side of education. However, we have a void where measurement and control are needed most, on the learning accomplishment side. This is the point I want to make tonight: that school boards will not be accountable until they audit learning output the way they audit dollar output.

Contemporary pressures demand that school boards become more than administrative groups primarily concerned with budgets

An address by Dr. Terrel H. Bell before the annual convention of the Utah School Boards Association, Salt Palace, Salt Lake City, Utah, Thursday, November 19, 1970. Reprinted with permission of the author.

and construction. As trustees to the community, school boards are now being forced to look more searchingly and intently at the educational welfare of the pupils within their jurisdiction. This, of course, is part of a growing movement toward grassroots government taking place all over the country. School boards are the most "grass green" of all such movements.

And that is where "accountability" enters the picture. "Accountability" may be an overworked word as applied to teachers and school administrators, but it is virgin soil where school boards are concerned. We know that in any organization the most logical place to begin the application of performance criterion is right at the top — the school board.

Before I develop this concept further it is only fair that I explain why I feel this new point of view is worth your consideration. As you all know, in an era of social unrest such as we are living in today, education tends to become the key to the solution of many diverse problems. People of all types turn to educational institutions for guidance and help. This begins in the kindergarten and carries through to higher education.

Today, for example, parents send into our schools children who seem to need more help than they did in the past. On the surface they may appear more independent. That is, many of them no longer accept things on faith, as we did. Whether it's television or parental permissiveness that has made them more skeptical, today's children have to be hit with gut issues that emotionally involve them or they'll tune the teacher out. This of course has its advantages from a purely educational point of view. There's certainly nothing wrong with relevancy in teaching. But it also forces today's teachers to carry additional burdens. Teachers must compete not only against the excitement and lure of television entertainment, but must also compensate for an increasing lack of home training.

This runs all through primary education. Teachers become arbiters for all the problems not solved at home. In a growing number of cases, they also find themselves having to rebuild the personalities of children with wounded egos, again the result of parental neglect. Today's teachers, in addition to teaching, must play the roles of doctors, psychologists, actors, or what have you? Guiltily or ignorantly, many parents today give their children a morning shove in the direction of the school and hope for the best.

I recognize that this does not typify the actions of most parents but it is representative of a significant number.

On a higher level the dependence on educational institutions is equally patent. We all know the great hue and cry that went up throughout the country when the Russians sent Sputnik into the sky. "Make our schools teach more mathematics and science subjects," the citizens demanded as our effort to catch up with the Soviets in space. Today we find similar examples in the social sciences, where people feel that education is the answer to all their environmental problems.

This dependence of the public on educational institutions has of course burned the spotlight directly into the hides of the educators. No longer do they operate a cloistered establishment. Parents now demand specific performance results. This may be an unconscious expression of self-inadequacy on the part of parents. But regardless of the cause exciting their sudden interest in education, the interest is there, and it is growing more intense with each passing year.

As members of school boards, you are well aware of one way — a rather painful way — this parental interest in education is expressing itself. Increasing numbers of parents are now demanding of the schools that they demonstrate their effectiveness before asking for more funds.

Recent polls taken by Gallup bear this out. Parents are insisting that they be informed of their children's status in comparison with the rest of the country. Three-quarters of the adults recently polled by Gallup said they want students in local schools to be given national tests for their educational achievement so that the results can be compared with students in other communities. When asked if they would favor or oppose a system that holds teachers and administrators more accountable for the progress of students, some 67 percent said they favor the idea.

All of this indicates the growing importance of accountability in education. It directly involves the teacher, the superintendent, and, in my opinion, now reaches the school board. As educational trustees of the community on questions concerning the ultimate welfare of your schools, you find that the buck stops with you.

What would constitute an adequate list of performance measures for a school board? Well, I personally feel that the most fundamental characteristic of a good school board member is reflected in his attitude. His concern for education and learning should never be overshadowed by his interest in administrative matters such as budgets, buildings, transportation, and the numerous other items that plague him.

I know that some of you will claim a foul right here by saying you are not qualified to intrude into professional educational matters. Before I consider this aspect, let us take up the more conventional performance measures for a good school board.

Your first task, of course, is to create conditions that make for the success of the Superintendent and his staff. This means putting up a fight for an adequate budget. It also means overseeing the budget to the extent that there is a balance of funds to provide for all the wider aspects of education — innovation, experiments, adoption of new methods, and the opening of new directions that will keep the school system up-to-date in a fast-moving world.

It also means giving psychological support to the administrative staff when you feel its members are in the right. This calls for getting the facts on controversial issues and not buckling under to pressure groups. It means not committing yourself to a decision until all the facts are in and studied. In other words, bearing the Superintendent and staff out before reaching your conclusions.

The response of school boards to pressure groups is becoming an increasingly important factor in modern education. Our highly organized society is composed of all kinds of special interest bodies and many of these groups, sad to say, are attacking the schools. Constructive response and sophisticated management of frustrating pressure from many sources will make school board accountability in this area a vital element to success in the future.

Except for added pressures, there's nothing really new in these requirements. Most of you face them throughout the year. I mention them only to keep the picture in balance. For though we see your shadows, as members of school boards, constantly lengthening in terms of potential accomplishment, we nevertheless recognize that there is a certain routine necessary for making the machine go.

Switching from here into a more subtle area of accountability, the school board must ask itself whether it is supporting conditions for the school's governance to operate as an "open" system. For some time now, American public schools have been moving to become more responsive to major changes in our society and economy. We have been more consciously and practically involved with the goal of providing equitable education for all children regardless of race, creed, or economic-social background. This has placed a greater burden on our educational system. It has had to attain increasing flexibility so that it could respond not only to the demands of the middle class, but to those of the newly emerging minority and disadvantaged and handicapped people as well.

To be able to cope with these new challenges, a school board must now ask itself just how "open" is its system. Are channels being established within the school for parents to express their concerns under sympathetic conditions? The struggle that occurred to make the Brooklyn, New York, Public School system more responsive to the community should be studied closely by all of us. In that case, the inability of parents to reach the top of the educational hierarchy, either through normal channels or "direct action," eventually produced an explosive situation that threatened to rip as under the entire public school fabric. A school board should ask itself if its school is facing this community challenge.

Teacher input should also be welcomed as part of the "open" system. In every school there is a yearly influx of young new teachers carrying young new ideas. The Board should be aware to what extent its schools are giving serious consideration to these contributions. In the trade, schools are known as backward or progressive. Some are considered good, others bad. Certainly an alert school board should be sophisticated enough to discern where its schools stand — locally, countywise, Statewise, and even in the national pattern.

Students' rights should also not be overlooked, or slighted by the school board. We have learned that small things, considered ridiculous by the administration of the school system but terribly important to the student, can often grow into major tests of authority. In devising a plan of accountability, members of school boards certainly should ask themselves whether their schools are really "open" to the consideration of such claims. Teachers' rights are equally important, and of course there should always be protection for the right to appeal.

If you will look into some of these factors, I think you will find that no great professional educational know-how is needed to assess the extent to which your schools are "open," and thus in a more strategic position to cope with the problems of the new age.

As a matter of fact, most of these accountability requirements fall into the area of good common sense.

Something that touches more of the professional, however, also should occupy a key position in your accountability appraisal. Here I am referring to teaching and learning performance accountability.

A school board today must insist that it be provided, by the professional educators it employs, a student progress surveillance system and evaluative processes broad and comprehensive enough so that the Board knows at all times the relative strengths and weaknesses of its schools.

This is a rather tall order, but something which no one can afford to close his eyes to, least of all a member of a school board. In Utah, overall, we are not in such bad shape, but let us consider what has turned up in the national situation under the glare of professional surveys and evaluation.

In reading, the results are disturbing.

About seven million public school pupils in the United States (16 percent of the enrollment in grades 1-12) require special instruction in reading.

In those of the Nation's public schools in which at least half of the pupils come from poor homes, more than one out of five of the elementary, and more than two out of five of the secondary pupils, require special instruction in reading.

Board members should also keep a close eye on their dropout statistics. Nationally this is another rapidly deteriorating situation.

In the 1969-70 school year, there were around 800,000 dropouts from high school, an increase of 100,000 from the previous year. This 800,000 figure is based on the number of fifth graders in school in 1962.

Youth unemployment is directly related to dropout rates and presents still another dismal aspect. Twice as many dropouts are unemployed as high school graduates. Jobs calling for high school graduates have increased 30 percent while jobs for non-graduates decreased 25 percent. The unskilled are the last to be hired and the first to be fired.

Among the disadvantaged the educational statistics are equally disturbing. Here disparity widens as age increases. When at the twelfth-grade age level, the ghetto child may be as low as the sixth grade in actual achievement.

At least once a year each school board should sit down with its staff and perform an educational accomplishment audit. This exercise should include a review of dropouts, youth unemployment, reading failures, and other easily measured outputs. Such an appraisal on a school-by-school and also on an age-level basis is part of a school board's accountability to the community that elected it. Appraisal, of course, should be followed by *action,* plans by which the system can grow to a higher level of educational excellence. A system of renewal and recognition for accomplishments of schools and of individuals in the system would be another quite obvious outcome of a performance-oriented school system.

As I look at it, the greatest mistake a school board could make is not to comprehend the gaps existing between what "is" and what "ought to be" in the school system. Industry has long ago faced up to this challenge by devising a plan of procedure known as management by objectives, or MBO, to use the abbreviated term.

The process is relatively simple in concept. Objectives or goals are established after a free flow of information pertinent to the subject has determined what areas need to be improved. This of course calls for a careful and unbiased perusal of weaknesses and strengths. Then once the objectives are clarified and put into mold, a management procedure is established to monitor for results. Through this monitoring there is early detection of any shortcomings, and it is then possible to make timely correction to set the work back on its true course.

Though I have given you the briefest abstract of Management by Objectives, its theories and procedures can be applied to education as well as to business. The results of education's failures and breakdowns in such vital areas as reading and dropouts — figures which I have just listed on a national scale — indicate that many school systems are painfully in need of a comprehensive plan to identify and correct their shortcomings. School boards are really the only people who can effectively demand that their institutions develop and implement plans adequate to coping with such situations.

It is platitudinous to assert that the problems facing the American educational system today are enormous. It is more important to find out what we can do about them. One of the first things is to obtain reliable, practical information on student progress and goals. A Management by Objectives type operation could put this responsibility for performance into the system with a minimum of expenditure and effort. Members of the Board, as educational trustees to the community, are logically the ones to make certain that such adequate monitoring and evaluation exist in their schools.

As long as education continues to be a cornerstone of our free civilization, education will remain a subject of vital importance to most Americans. The first requisite of school board performance has always been to see that quality education is developed. I urge you to evaluate yourselves as Board members so that accountability in education can start at the top, where it must begin if it is to be a success. Once the spirit of accountability begins to permeate the school boards of our Nation, it will move strongly from there through the entire educational system.

When the school board appraises itself and then holds itself to high standards of performance, the staff and students will respond in kind. Nothing is so infectious as a good example. What you apply to yourselves others are more ready to accept.

How enthusiastically Board members accept accountability as an idea applying to themselves as well as to school employees might well determine how long we will keep our present system of local control of education. My recent experiences in Washington convince me that our system of local control of education will face some strong attacks if we do not become more responsive to the educational urgencies of our era. But dramatic improvements must be made, and they will have to come primarily from you. Accountability starting at the top is one answer — perhaps one of the most sensible and practical answers we can make to the educational problems of the day.   □

III

INTERNAL ACCOUNTABILITY *(abridged)*

by Kenneth P. Mortimer

". . . it is much more difficult to apply systems analysis to an educational enterprise than it is to either a business enterprise or the Department of Defense. There are just terribly important intangibles you cannot measure."

It is difficult to know definitively who should be making internal policy decisions in colleges and universities; consequently, it is difficult to ascertain who is or should be accountable to whom for what. Legally, but within the parameters set by external forces, the board of trustees has ultimate authority to control institutional decisions. In practice, this authority is delegated to administrators, faculty, and students. The extent to which they are or can be held accountable for the use of delegated authority is the point at issue. There are those who feel that faculty *are* the institution and, as such, control ought to be vested in them rather than in a board representing nonacademic, lay interests.

    While there are many reasons for the difficulty in assessing who controls what or who is accountable for what, three factors seem of primary importance: the peculiar nature of authority in colleges and universities; lack of clearly defined goals and objectives; organizational complexity, which includes increased demands for involvement in decisionmaking. The discussion of these three factors will illustrate various approaches to increasing or decreasing accountability that are apparent in the literature on academic decisionmaking.

Reprinted from *Accountability in Higher Education.* ERIC Clearinghouse on Higher Education — The George Washington University, February 1972.

The Nature of Authority

A review of the literature on authority in organizations reveals considerable disagreement about the proper use of terms such as power, authority, and influence (Dahl, 1963; Platt and Parsons, 1970; Presthus, 1962; Etzioni, 1964; and Blau and Scott, 1962). There is, however, a degree of consensus about the bases on which authority, power, and influence rest—in other words, the ways in which an organization gains legitmacy in its authority relationships.

Peabody (1962) summarizes much of this literature by classifying authority into two types: formal and functional. The bases of formal authority are rooted in legitmacy, organizational position, and the sanctions inherent in office. An organization and the position or offices in it gain legitmacy (e.g., the acknowledged right-to-rule) through their legality, which presumably results from general social approval, and by a general deference to authority of position or office accorded to traditional practices. On the other hand, functional authority is based on such relatively informal sources as professional competence, experience, and human-relations skills. Formal authority may be supported by functional authority where, for example, a department chairman especially in colleges and universities, that formal and functional whose field is English, is not competent to control the *essential* activities of faculty members in other fields.

The distinction between the formal and functional roots of authority is useful, for it summarizes much of the concern about professional and administrative authority in all organizations (Etzioni, 1964):

> Administration assumes a power hierarchy. Without a clear ordering of higher and lower in rank, in which the higher in rank have more power than the lower ones and hence can control and coordinate the latter's activities, the basic principle of administration is violated; the organization ceases to be a coordinated tool. However, knowledge is largely an individual property; unlike other organization means, it cannot be transferred from one person to another by decree.... It is this highly individualized principle which is diametrically opposed to the very essence of the organizational principle of control and coordination by superiors—i.e., the principle of administrative authority. In other words, the ultimate justification for a professional act is that it is, to the best of the professional's knowledge, the right act....

The ultimate justification of an administrative act, however, is
that it is in line with the organization's rules and regulations,
and that it has been approved—directly or by implication—by a
superior rank (pp. 76-77).

In practice, both formal and functional authority are present
in organizations as well as a fundamental tension between them,
especially in organizations such as colleges and universities, hospitals, schools, and industrial research laboratories where a substantial number of professionals are employed (Clear, 1969; Bates and
White, 1961; and Kornhauser, 1962).

In this respect, the institution is unable to control important
aspects of professional or functional authority valued so highly by
some of its most prominent members. Recognition of expertise
and the prestige that goes with it, for example, is often conferred
on a faculty member by agencies external to the institution. While
administrative or formal authority assumes a power hierarchy, or
at least that rank and capability are closely correlated, such correlation is often not the case in colleges and universities. Of course
there are hierarchical relationships in academic organizations, but
the dilemma between formal and functional authority is particularly acute in colleges and universities (Anderson, 1963).

The university . . . if it is to exist as an organization, must enforce organizational discipline at the same time that it must foster independence or freedom for its most important group of
organizational members (the faculty). This is a dilemma neither
confined to the university nor to contemporary times. It is one
of the great philosophical issues of history. Yet it is perhaps nowhere more strikingly revealed than in university government
(p. 16).

How then are faculty held accountable for their performance? Using the term in its broadest scope—being answerable
for one's conduct—McConnell (1969) has discussed four ways
individual faculty are held accountable: (1) he is accountable to
his own conscience and especially to his own standards of scholarship and intellectual integrity; (2) he is accountable to his
scholarly peers—the quality of his scholarship and performance
as a teacher will be judged by his peers and he will be held accountable for these when promotion, tenure, and salary decisions

are made; (3) he is accountable in a variety of ways to his students —for the quality of his teaching, for permitting freedom of expression and the right of dissent in the classroom, and for the confidentiality of a student's beliefs and opinions; (4) he is accountable to his institution for the ways and procedures it adopts to administer the academic program, for the discipline of other faculty members, and for maintaining a productive educational environment.

Using the distinction drawn by Neff (1969) between accountability and responsibility, accountability to one's conscience refers to the assumption of a voluntary obligation or responsibility, while accountability to scholarly peers, students, and the institution are, or could be, matters of academic responsibility. Individual faculty members can be held accountable for much of this.

Traditionally, the standards for assessing accountability and the rights and responsibilities of faculty and students have been rather informal. Among the traditional guidelines used are (Carnegie Commission on Higher Education, June 1971):

> . . . the largely unwritten but shared understandings among faculty members and administrators about the nature of academic life and desirable conduct within it. These understandings have mainly involved collegial consensus about professional ethics and full tolerance toward the individual faculty member in his own teaching and research endeavors (p. 33).

The increased frequency of dissent and disruption on the campus have put severe strain on such informal understandings. Faculty are increasingly divided among themselves as to the basic elements of academic life (Lipset and Ladd, 1971). Pressure from external agencies and the administration has led many institutions, including the Universities of California and Illinois, and the Oregon Board of Higher Education, to draft statements of rights and responsibilities as guidelines for the control of excessively deviant faculty and student behavior.

Some attention is now being directed toward the accountability of various mechanisms like committees, senates, and faculty unions through which faculty participate in the decision-making process. Myron Lieberman (1969) charges that faculty senates and committees lack accountability—they cannot be brought to account for the advice they render. In the absence of codified grievance procedures, an individual faculty member has limited, if any, opportunity to appeal an adverse finding from a faculty personnel committee. The proceedings and membership of such committees are often confidential and the individual is denied the right to confront the evidence against him. Similarly a faculty selection committee can nominate a president, dean, or other administrator with complete immunity from having to answer for the quality of its recommendation. Lieberman (1969) refers to these practices as institutionalized irresponsibility.

Some advocates of collective bargaining in higher education argue that the process of negotiating a legally binding agreement on wages and terms and conditions of employment will result in firmer lines of accountability (Sherman and Loeffler, 1971). Codified grievance procedures will provide an avenue of individual appeal and a mechanism of external review over the decisions of administrators and faculty committees. The appeal procedure, because it may ultimately result in external review through fact finding and binding arbitration, formalizes standards to which administrators and faculty committees can be held accountable. Presumably, these standards will decrease the incidence of arbitrary administrative and faculty behavior, lack of fairness in handling personnel cases, and assure due process and the protection of basic freedoms. Both the institution and its officers can be held accountable to the system of law on which the contract is based (e.g., National Labor Relations Act, state-enabling legislation, and other relevant legal precedents).

There are two aspects of accountability in the preceding developments. Codes of conduct and ethics attempt to specify the limits of and thereby control *individual* behavior. Faculty organizations, especially those involved in collective bargaining, seek to ensure that the institution is held accountable to external standards of due process and fair play. Essentially these two developments are a long overdue recognition of some of the inadequacies of systems of functional or professional authority. Some of these inadequacies are reflected in the lack of precise goals and objectives in colleges and universities.

Lack of Precise Goals

Several observers have remarked about the diffuse functions and goals of institutions of higher education (Bell, 1971; Trow, 1970; Corson, 1971). There is some semantic confusion about the difference between functions, purposes, goals, and objectives. Peterson (1970) refers to the functions of higher education as the activities institutions perform that are related to other social institutions, such as socialization of the young and transmission of a cultural heritage. Purposes refer to stated conceptions of the mission of systems, groups, or types of institutions. The purposes of public institutions are often specified in a master plan. Goals refer to the particular, possibly unique pattern of specified ends, outputs, and priorities of a single institution. Objectives are the ends of various component units, programs, or services.

It has been noted that colleges and universities are not completely free of external pressures in establishing their functions, purposes, goals, and objectives. Determining goals and objectives that are consistent with functions and purposes is, however, one of the primary requisites for establishing internal accountability.

The literature on behavioral accountability is voluminous. Many proposals are being advanced that would specify goals and objectives in behavioral terms and result in greater accountability. Conferences have been devoted to the topic and the proceedings published (Educational Testing Service, March and June 1971). Entire issues or parts of leading educational journals have been devoted to accountability (*Educational Technology*, January 1971; *Phi Delta Kappa*, December 1970; *Junior College Journal*, March 1971; *Theory Into Practice*, October 1969) and an annotated bibliography appears in the May 1971 issue of *Audiovisual Instruction*. While the vast majority of these proposals are directed at public schools, much of it is relevant to higher education. The essential features of behavioral accountability can be summarized from this and other literature on the topic.

Behavioral Accountability

If Leon Lessinger is not the father of behavioral accountability, he certainly is its midwife. His notion of accountability has been widely adopted by those writing on the concept as it applies to education. According to Lessinger (1971a):

> Accountability is a policy declaration adopted by a legal body such as a board of education or a state legislature requiring regular outside reports of dollars spent to achieve results. The concept rests on three fundamental bases: *student accomplishment, independent review* of student accomplishment, and *a public report,* relating dollars spent to student accomplishment (p. 62).

In another reference he defines the concept in more specific terms, stating that it means much more than simple indices, such as number of dropouts or the results of reading tests (1971b).

> We must go far beyond such general outlines of general results and find out what specific factors *produce* specific educational results. We must find what specific educational results can be achieved with different groups of children for different amounts of financial resources (p. 13).

Almost all proponents of behavioral accountability urge that the effectiveness of institutions be judged not by their outputs alone but by their outputs relative to their inputs. What has a student attained relative to his capability at the starting point? This view assumes that colleges and universities are capable of having considerable cognitive and affective impact on those who pass through their doors. The assumption about affective impact has been seriously challenged by research on the topic (Feldman and Newcomb, 1969).

The proponents of behavioral accountability also argue that institutions must be efficient while they are having this impact. Requirements of both effectiveness and efficiency result in a plethora of techniques and approaches to achieving accountability. Browder (1971) cites 12 factors as critical to the process of rendering account in behavioral terms:

1. *Community involvement* is necessary so that members of concerned community groups are involved in appropriate phases of program activity. This will facilitate program access to community resources, understanding of the program's objectives, procedures and accomplishments, and the discharge of program responsibilities to community support groups.
2. *Technical assistance* is necessary for providing adequate resources in program planning, implementation, operation, and evaluation. To provide such technical assistance the institution should draw upon community, business, labor, education, scientific, and governmental agencies for expertise and services necessary for effective operations.
3. *Needs assessments* will identify the target group and situational factors essential to planning a program of action.
4. The development of effective *change strategies* for

systematic change will need to be incorporated in the
strategy of program operation.

5. The *management system* approach through such mechanisms as program evaluation and review technique (PERT),
program planning and budgeting, and management by objectives will need to be adapted to education program management at all levels.

6. *Performance objectives* must be specified in a comprehensive manner that indicates measures and means for assessing the degree to which predetermined standards have been
met. In curriculum design and instruction this usually takes
the form of behavioral objectives (Mager, 1962; and
Kapfer, 1971).

7. *Performance budgeting* will allocate fiscal resources in accordance with program objectives rather than by objects or
functions to be supported.

8. *Performance contracting* will be used in some cases. This
takes the form of an arrangement for technical assistance
from an agent on a specified compensation schedule linked
to the accomplishment of performance objectives.

9. The institution will have to determine the nature and extent of *staff development* needed to implement the related
activities.

10. Implementation of accountability requires *comprehensive
evaluation* or systems of performance control based on the
continuous assessment of a program's operational and management processes and resultant products.

11. Some measure of *cost effectiveness* is necessary to analyze
unit results obtained in relation to unit resources consumed under alternative approaches.

12. *Program auditing* or a performance control system will provide external reviews through qualified outside technical
assistance designed to verify the results and assess the appropriateness of program management and operation.

These 12 elements comprise a total institutional approach to
behavioral accountability. A program of behavioral accountability
will include man, if not all of these 12 factors in a systematic attempt to specify objectives in measurable terms, control educational outputs to coincide with these objectives, and provide external program evaluation of the extent to which these objectives
were achieved.

The proponents of behavioral accountability are not modest in asserting a wide variety of benefits that will accrue if their proposals are adopted. First, they claim that the successful implementation of accountability will shift the principal focus of an institution from inputs to outputs, from teaching to learning. Institutions will be held accountable for what students learn while they are in residence rather than what they bring with them when they enter or what the faculty *claims* they are taught. This will lead to a second benefit—reinforcement of the demand that every student shall learn, as opposed to a belief that some are incapable of learning.

A third major effect of accountability will be the development of better systems of instructional technology. Education will be less tied to the traditional systems of instruction because technology will clearly indicate that some students learn certain subjects better through less conventional instructional methods. Students and teachers will learn that technologies can help them achieve the recognized goal of education—student learning.

Fourth, accountability will result in development capital being set aside for investment by administrators in promising activities suggested by teachers, students, and others who can promise to produce results. This development capital will serve as an incentive for innovative experimentation.

Fifth, the definition of accountability requires some outside review and will lead to a greater emphasis on the modes of proof and methods of assessment. Accountability will insist upon techniques and strategies that promote objectivity, feedback knowledge of results, and permit outside replication of demonstrated good practice. In short, the scientific method will be used in the approach to educational innovation and curriculum.

A sixth major effect of adopting behavioral accountability will be to enhance educational engineering. Educational engineering is a rapidly emerging field designed to produce personnel who are competent in the technologies necessary to implement accountability. These techniques include but are not limited to system analysis, management by objectives, program planning and budgeting, and instructional planning through behavioral objectives. A common example of education engineering in public schools is the performance contract. Under a performance contract the local educational agency contracts with an outside enterprise to achieve specific goals within a specific period of time (Forsberg, 1971). The terms and conditions of the contract are usually such that the contractor receives a predetermined compensation if the students achieve a specified set of learning objectives. If the students do not meet the specification, the contractor receives less reimbursement and may even be penalized; if the students exceed specifications, the contractor receives an additional reimbursement.

It is doubtful that all these benefits will accrue to higher education even if behavioral accountability were adopted. Faculty are unlikely to be satisfied with measures of institutional effectiveness based solely on student learning. In a time of increased financial crisis, few institutions will have the risk capital needed to experiment with and evaluate different educational approaches. Many institutions are not large enough to achieve the economies of scale necessary to use instructional technologies efficiently (Smith, 1971).

It is not possible, however, in a study such as this, to cover in detail each of the 12 elements of behavioral accountability or whether it will result in the six major benefits its proponents claim. There are three major points that should be made about the limitations of and resistance to behavioral accountability. The first has to do with unmeasurable intangibles in higher education and the second is related to the application of many of the techniques of achieving behavioral accountability. The third point relates to a possible distinction between or at least a better understanding of the interdependence of effectiveness and efficiency.

The difficulties in measuring effectiveness or the impact of colleges on students are well summarized in Withey (1971), Feldman and Newcomb (1969), McConnell (1971), and Hartnett (1971). First, few institutions have determined what their goals are and therefore have few measurable criteria to judge effectiveness. To achieve more precise statements of goals and objectives will be a monumental undertaking. Second, it is fairly clear that the personal characteristics of some students make them more educable, ready or eager to learn, than others. Third, given students of varying backgrounds, skills, interests, and educability, no single measure of effectiveness is likely to be adequate. Developing multiple criterion measures may be possible over time but will certainly not be a simple task. Fourth, changes may occur in students that are not attributable to the college experience. These changes may be due to normal maturation, personal trauma, or social influences external to institutions of higher education.

Given these difficulties in measuring effectiveness, can colleges and universities still be more efficient in their operation? The answer appears to be a qualified yes (Severance, 1971).

As a former official of the Rand Corporation and former undersecretary of defense, President Charles Hitch of the University of California is eminently qualified to discuss the application of one technique, system analysis, to the university (Wood, 1971).

> There are a lot of opportunities for the university to use systems analysis. We do run quite a large number of activities that are really business enterprises: our hospital operations for example; our dormitory operations; the large fleet of cars, which we maintain and service; computer centers which are very large and expensive operations. In all these areas, we have found such basic business principles applicable. But apart from these kinds of enterprises, it is much more difficult to apply systems analysis to an educational enterprise than it is either to a business enterprise or the Department of Defense. There are just terribly important intangibles you cannot measure (p. 54).

In practice these nonmeasurable "intangibles" are one of the primary sources of resistance to greater use of systems of behavioral accountability (Spencer, 1971). Some educators believe that education should not be regarded as a commodity that one, by various means, purchases for his own benefit.

> Higher education is not a commodity. The chief beneficiary of higher education is not the person who gains its credits and degrees. . . . The beneficiary is society itself (Benezet, 1971, p. 242).

Few would argue, however, that these analysis techniques are totally inapplicable to higher education. The argument tends to be over the proper applications. Systems analysis, needs assessment, and management information systems are not so advanced in their technology that they can be transferred without modification to higher education. In order to apply the techniques of systems analysis, data of appropriate quality must be available. This is often a time consuming and expensive effort, especially in colleges and universities. Systems analysis is subject also to such biases as

asymmetry in sources of information, disproportionate attention
by the analysts to preferred information sources and selectivity in
organizational recruitment.

In discussing the relationship between program *budgeters* and
behavioral objectives in faculty instruction, Lindman (1971) says
that both have found it impossible to place dollar values upon the
behavioral objectives formualted. "Moreover they were unable to
determine the cost of achieving various behavioral objectives because the cost depended upon the methods used and the ease with
which students learn (p. B-3)." There appear to be important distinctions as well as interrelationships between a management system designed to allocate resources and an instructional and planning system designed to utilize educational resources most effectively. Budget deicsions are often geared to a fiscal period, whereas
instructional planning and evaluation is a continuous effort. The
budgetary process is primarily concerned with decisions like class
size and salaries—decisions that affect cost, whereas instructional
planning and evaluation is concerned primarily with finding more
effective teaching procedures that often have little or no effect upon annual costs. For example, some community colleges have
adopted the behavioral objectives philosophy in their instructional
efforts, yet it is doubtful whether this has increased their annual
operating costs. It may require that more faculty time be spent in
redesigning course content.

Another major factor is that basic decisions about budgeting
and instruction are made by different agents, with the administration having effective control over the former and the faculty dom-
inating the latter. This is not to say that program budgeting and
behavioral objectives in instruction are totally independent activities; however; there are limits on the interdependence of the two.
External agents and the administration may force the adoption of
program budgets, while it is difficult to see them forcing faculty to
adopt behavioral objectives in instruction.

In Chapter 2 the distinction between evaluation and accountability was discussed where evaluation was primarily related to effectiveness and accountability related to both effectiveness and
efficiency. The unanswered question is the proper balance between
effectiveness and efficiency. Colleges and universities can and
should devote more attention to both, but the relationship between the two will be determined by the value judgments of those

in positions of decisionmaking responsibility. It may be more efficient but less effective to operate large lecture sections in English
and the social sciences than in physics or the creative arts, or in
undergraduate than in graduate studies. In cases similar to those
cited by Hitch it may be possible to be more efficient without
sacrificing effectiveness; in other cases, efficiency may have to be
sacrificed to effectiveness.

   Colleges and universities need to have a much fuller understanding of the success and limitation of behavioral accountability
than now exists. Even in the public schools, where several experimental approaches are being tried, the evidence is not yet defini-
tive (Estes and Waldrip, 1971; Locke, 1971).   □

Kenneth P. Mortimer is a Research Associate at the Center for the Study of
Higher Education, and Assistant Professor of Education at Pennsylvania State
University.

IV

IN EDUCATION, ARE PUBLISHERS ACCOUNTABLE?

by Roger H. Smith

"What better way to get into the market than by "guaranteeing" performance?. . .What can a publisher, bidding his books for an adoption, say that his books will guarantee?"

Suppliers of educational materials and systems, entering into performance contracts with school superintendents, are saying, in effect, that unless their materials and systems produce educational achievement results that are measurably improved over what the school was achieving before, they will waive payment for their materials and systems or they will accept reduced payment or they will forfeit a performance bond. Details of these performance contracts vary, but the principle remains the same: the burden of educational performance rests on the supplier of materials.

There is a lot that is appealing in such arrangements, which are somewhat new in the education field. In the consumer goods field, there is a tradition, not always observed, that if a newly purchased produce does not perform as promised, it may be returned for repair, replacement or refund. The consumer has a reasonable guarantee, in short, of his money's worth.

The "money's worth" line of thinking has now entered the field of American education. As local taxes rise, in part to meet the rising costs of maintaining the local school system, the local taxpayer may be forgiven the thought that, in terms of his children's educational performance, he is being short-changed. As often as not, he is. He would like a guarantee that what his tax collar is buying will produce measurable results.

The "money's worth" line of thinking is appealing, too, to

suppliers who, believing what they read in the 1960s about the
booming education market, have tooled up to get into that market.
What better way to get into the market than by "guaranteeing"
performance? Established educational suppliers felt compelled to
follow suit with performance "guarantees" of their own. With all
these "guarantees" in force, it remained to be seen only whether
they would work. On the basis of evidence currently available
about schools' performance, the "guarantees" so far haven't meant
very much—except, perhaps, to those who entered into them and
those who have benefitted from them commercially.

Functional illiteracy is perhaps the greatest blight in contemporary society, and many of the "guaranteed" educational materials and systems are aimed at eradicating or at least minimizing it.
These are worthy aims, but how can their results be "guaranteed"?
How can a supplier, under a performance contract, be held
accountable?

Education has performance profiles, of course, and standardized tests, but they don't tell much about the goals which education and educational materials are supposed to achieve. Performance contractors can bring to school systems a body of expertise
which might be otherwise unavailable, but the purpose of the expertise remains insular, vague, confined to scores and test results.

What can a publisher, bidding his books for an adoption, say
that his books will guarantee in the way of performance? He may
know that the books represent the best efforts of the best editorial
talent available to him, that reputable educators have found them
to be worthy. But what can he say these books will perform in the
way of real educational accomplishment? In any classroom, the
books may succeed and fail at the same time. Education is full of
variables and imponderables. To think of it as something that can
be guaranteed is to take a very narrow view of human nature. Education is not like a new electric mixer, which, if it doesn't work,
can be returned for credit.   □

Roger H. Smith is executive editor of *Publishers' Weekly*.

V

ADMINISTRATORS AND ACCOUNTABILITY

by Conrad Briner
Claremont Graduate School
Claremont College

"Accountability as only a professional exercise is unrealistic. Accountability as a combined community and educator political exercise is workable."

What makes education accountable? Who determines what is being done in the schools? Who answers for its instructional and management problems?

Historically, educational policy and administration have been fundamentally the people's business. Schools are domesticated organizations: we, the public, allow little self-determination, competition, and radicalism in them; we dote on them, often being attentive, protective, and sometimes generous in our care for them. We are used to being watchful of schooling—of the behavior of personnel, of the costs and quality of activities and facilities. We watch the students, too, for the effects of schooling, especially in terms of what each of us expects the effects to be.

We, the public, are emotional about the need for good schools because schools are the means of personal success; they are the road to the future of our society.

But the public is not alone in its concern for education and its problems. School board members, legislators, congressmen, and other spokesmen for our social consciences are increasingly fostering inquiry into "who is responsible" and "what's being done."

Because of the extent to which education sorts human destinies, it must represent public sentiments. But should the public

---

Reprinted with permission of author and *Theory Into Practice*, October, 1969.

go it alone in defining the required nature of teaching and learning, governmental responsibility and educator expertise are denied. Should the educators go it alone, technology is worshipped as king. The answer to the question "who is responsible" lies somewhere in between.

Local public concern in education is illustrated by the old practice of groups of people establishing their own schools to represent their beliefs about what education should be. Schools, both public and private, represent the deeply embedded moral principles and values of their sponsors. Parents and others presume and even arrogate to themselves the power to determine the nature of schools. Educators are employed to operate schools, not to define them. This fiercely held public right to local control is mediated only by occasional deference to needs that are of general benefit in our society.

One result of the public's interest in education has been a continuation of the traditions of both common and elitist schools. Generally speaking, elementary education has meant providing common schools and secondary education has meant elitist schools. In elementary schools, each student is expected to attend and to achieve minimal achievement standards before being eligible for "release." Secondary schools have been obstacle courses designed and operated so only the fittest survive. Today these distinctions are less sharp, but they are far from being eliminated. As a result, educational accountability is faced with the special purpose of achieving equity of educational opportunity at all levels. Equity is increasingly a popular demand to improve education.

Equity is an exciting challenge for a number of reasons. Schooling today to a large degree still involves the classification of young people, sorting out those who succeed from those who fail and the various levels in between, rather than functioning to help each succeed to the best of his abilities. Students still get "turned off" in school and fail to finish in many ways what they had intended intially. But worse, some finish their schooling functionally illiterate and unemployable. This condition is inconsistent with our democratic tenets; it does not operate for the common good.

Spiraling costs represent another hindrance to better education. Revenues for education, like all governmental services, probably always will be scarce. Probably too, the demands for educational services will continue to grow and exceed any existing financing arrangements. Such are the consequences of a dynamic society. Consequently, administration must involve expressing educational needs, proposing priorities, planning comprehensively, and inventing, all within the limits of policy, expertness, and cost. An updating of management practices is long overdue.

In human terms, the need to overcome neglect of individual integrity and welfare is most at stake in achieving equity on education. There obviously exists a lack of commitment to the moral responsibility of furthering, as a democratic pledge, the emancipation of individuals from the bondages of poverty, discrimination, fear, and lack of optimism about the future. This lack of commitment is evident whenever one looks closely not at what we say needs to be done in education, but at what we actually do and what happens as a result. The typical instructional and management practices in education are in many ways inhumane; schools are intolerable to students, teachers, parents, and others.

As a consequence, popular activity in education is increasing. Attention is being focused on how to update policy processes, educational purposes, and technologies. The public demands greater involvement in the schools, in policy-making, and administrative activities to achieve basic literacy skills, fewer dropouts, and vocational education that is relevant to present and future manpower demands. Vocational education is also being questioned in terms of whether or not each student learns to believe in himself and whether or not schools have overcome the stigma, so subtly taught and learned, that preparation for work after school is less respectable than preparation for college. Some of the demands are controversial because they reflect emerging values more than traditional ones; for example, sex education in the schools, increased student determination of curricula, and planned racial and socio-economic integration of student bodies and faculties.

The public drive for accountability and equity represents a demand for constructive action to eliminate education's failures.

As a concept, accountability can only be understood as a derivative of a number of social and technological contexts. After all, learning is not only the result of formal educational experiences; it is also a matter of human conditions that reflect a broad array of societal components. The concept means more than measuring and

evaluating the outcomes of teaching: it is a mixture of social problems, political processes, and educator expertise.

Education is a basic social institution and its organizational
forms are human contrivances based not just upon an empirical
plan for schooling but also moral judgments about what is good
and bad about our society. The real nature of administration, instruction, and learning is many faceted; intertwined inextricably
are social, political, and economic forces influencing the technical
means of doing the educational job. Accountability is, thus, a matter of knowing and using cooperatively both public and governmental, as well as professional resources. I wish to argue in this
context that the responsibilities for policy, organization, and management do not reside alone with the public at large, with any governmental agency, nor with the educator. We, the public at large;
we, the governmental representatives; and we, the educators, know
too little about how to guarantee maximum educational achievement for all. The nature of human capability to learn is still something of a mystery, as are the political, administrative, and teaching arrangements required to realize individual potential.

A dramatic implication of this political-educational complexity is that instructional and management practices must go public.
This means more than people voting, courts rendering judgments,
and governments taking action. Educational accountability, geared
to the continual improvement of teaching and learning, must involve participative communication and decision opportunities both
for the public and the educator. Operationally, this can mean localizing educational administration more so than exists now, differentiating various functions to open up the educational system,
and bringing new resources into the task of improving learning. It
also means making systematically developed information about
educational success, failure, and the limits of expertise available
for all to see.

In localizing administration, the practices of each school will
become the object of lay and professional diagnosis, experimentation, and innovation. Teachers and community representatives
must be indirectly accountable for advising and counseling administrators about educational purposes and means that are to be
realized. Administrators must be accountable for stating and explaining directly to immediate publics the discharge of their responsibilities. This will require that administrators know the

dispositions of their public, including teachers and students, the quality of their educational programs, and the ways of learning how to do better the educational job.

Teachers, parents, and others apparently don't want to be fully accountable for improving education. They tend to be consumed by their typical social and professional roles. On the other hand, administrators must be directly accountable. It is their essential reason for being. They are the ones upon whom the hands of approval and disapproval will be laid. Accordingly, their roles require orientation and commitment to educational success and the elimination of failure. In their performance, they can be expected to explain both success and failure; they must be capable of proposing educational improvement to the satisfaction of students, teachers, parents, and others.

Administrators are not to be feudal lords, however. Schools should be managed with the assistance of public expression of need, teacher and student advice and counsel, and knowledge of human development. They should be managed by administrators who can accept the challenge and career risks attendant with admitting that instructional, learning, and management problems do exist, and they are difficult because we are not sure how to solve them.

There will be conflicts over policy and professional decision. Such is the nature of freedom and political process. Schools embody and thrive on these ideals, as do other social systems. The educational process is, thereby, of necessity a dynamic rather than a static arrangement for social development.

School administrators must literally take to the sidewalks. They must know their publics, programs, and operational limitations. They must be articulate and aggressive in revealing successes and failures to the public and arranging participative efforts to eliminate the failures. The administrator must be an educational planner and a statesman. He, by his actions, generates open assessment of educational need and function and, hopefully, a popular respect for schools—a respect based upon educational success.

Accountability as only a professional exercise is unrealistic. Accountability as a combined community and educator political exercise is workable.

In support of this thesis, I propose certain assumptions and strategies. First, that in one manner or another students can be taught and they can learn; second, that human and financial resources will continue to be scarce; and third, that the educational management process can include participation of various publics in determining priorities of educational needs, source and manner of allocating resources, and types and uses of evaluation. These assumptions all defer to a new management technology that involves stating instructional objectives, defining performance criteria, monitoring, auditing, and correcting instructional activities within the context of local, state, and national political processes.

The basic strategy of accountability in these terms is to employ participative decision-making to shaping educational policy and evaluation and a highly detailed plan of educational management. What should be incorporated in educational management is careful reasoning about teaching and learning that is similar to engineering work. The desired result of instruction is made explicit; known alternative ways of accomplishing this are simulated to ascertain feasibility in terms of needed public and professional approval, available personnel, space and time, and of course, cost. The activities selected are then evaluated. Should the known ways of doing an educational job not be successful enough, invention is required and, accordingly, research and development work including experimentation and innovation will be the handmaiden of the engineering-like management practices.

Tying together these two basic strategies of participation and engineering is continuing assessment of both governance and technology. This is a matter of always knowing how well any educational job is being done according to the beliefs and perceptions of the people involved. Students, teachers, parents, and others will be asked repeatedly how well the participative decision-making arrangements are working. Instructional and management technologies will be judged similarly. Where possible, formal evaluation of instructional results such as standardized testing will add significance to the effects of assessment.

These strategies are based in the traditional nature of instruction and administration. It is not possible to hold teachers accountable for the quality of learning. They are too little involved in educational management, including the allocation of resources; and surprisingly, the pronouncements of teacher organizations to the contrary, they do not want to be involved greatly. Teachers do wish to believe, however, that they have the opportunity of access to policy-making and administration processes.

For administrators, it is a different story. Their primary responsibility is educational accountability. Administrators must be the ones to acknowledge eloquently what is being done in education, what should be done and why, to strive to free hopeless educational conditions. Such boldness will require considerable personal courage. The various publics must judge administrators in terms of the clarity and sophistication of their reasoning and the morality of their explanations and proposals. Administrators cannot be sufficient masters of all forces buffeting schools, but they will be helped to overcome the liabilities because the management process will be a public affair and therefore represent all the power of the democratic political system.

Accountability in education must be the result of rational understanding and communication between the public and educators about the discharge of responsibility for determining educational purpose, defining function, judging results, and taking corrective actions to improve learning. Even the new expertise involved in modern management technology such as cost-benefit analysis and program budget planning can only function in terms of the tradition of educational government—bringing social problems and educational responses together locally. Localized popular participation—give-and-take between the public and the educators —is still the most productive way to determine educational policy and administration. Schools are the people's business.   □

Editor's Note. This article is based upon a position paper the author prepared at the request of Leon M. Lessinger, Associate U.S. Commissioner for Elementary and Secondary Education, August 1969.

VI

ACCOUNTABILITY IN THE TWO-YEAR COLLEGE

by John E. Rouche, George A. Baker, III,
and Richard L. Brownell

"Overwhelming educational inefficiency can be traced to archaic attitudes and self-serving institutional collosity. . .Accountability is inevitable because it is needed so desperately."

Accountability is becoming an increasingly popular and controversial concept among educators. Accountability is both fundamental and complex: it can be applied to the activities of an individual, a department, a division, or an institution. To some people accountability suggests finance and business operations; others think of instruction and student learning. In practice accountability can apply to these and many other activities. Judging from the growing number of magazine and newspaper articles, it is indeed an idea whose time has come.

A favorite question is, "Why has accountability suddenly become popular in certain educational circles?" After all, the concept has been around for many years. Perhaps the best explanation for the historic rejection of the concept is what might be called educational determinism and the consequent acceptance of student failure. Simply stated, educational determinism is the belief that people have a predetermined capacity for learning, a capacity best defined by intelligence quotient. This being the case, it is reasonable and acceptable that an increasing number of students will fail as they climb the educational ladder. Or, to put it in the language of Darwinism, in the educational jungle only the fittest survive. Until recently this belief in a limited and predetermined

Excerpts from *Accountability and the Community College: Directions for the '70's,* a monograph published jointly by RELCV and the American Association of Junior Colleges. Reprinted with copyright permission of the American Association of Junior Colleges, 1971.

capacity to learn precluded the idea of accountability for learning. How could anyone, with the possible exception of the learner who might be lazy and therefore fail to utilize all of his capacity, be held accountable for something determined by divine will or the chance of heredity? It would certainly be unreasonable to hold educators accountable for something over which they had no control.

Currently this belief in educational determinism is being discarded by a growing number of people. Studies have revealed self-fulfilling tendencies in the measurement of student achievement when educators are informed in advance of student "intelligence quotients" or "learning abilities." Furthermore in many colleges students have been graded in accordance with normal curve distributions, anothe way of demonstrating that only a few students can really excel at learning. But now, given the evidence of many studies and the re-examination of basic beliefs about learning, many notable educational researchers and writers are arguing that almost all students can learn if a variety of instructional approaches are available and if sufficient time is allowed each student. Now the question becomes, "Why do so many students fail?"

The re-orientation in beliefs about learning and what can reasonably be expected of students, schools, and education has led to a growing interest in accountability. No longer is widespread student failure and attrition acceptable. As Charles E. Silberman so aptly states in his recent book, *Crisis in the Classroom,* "It is only when men sense the possibility of improvement, in fact, that they become dissatisfied with their situation and rebel against it."

THE CONCEPT OF ACCOUNTABILITY
The word accountability is laden with a host of meanings. It may seem threatening and unreasonable to educators who are reluctant to accept responsibility for academically inept and poorly motivated students; it might be viewed as a fashionable slogan by those with a penchant for launching naive attacks upon academe's disordered strongholds; it has profound implications for community colleges. In the following paragraphs four essential characteristics of accountability will be discussed.

(1) *Accountability Accents Results:* Accountability aims squarely at what comes out of an education system rather than at what goes into it. If educational institutions exist primarily to cause learning, then educators should scrutinize the results of their

efforts. Teaching causes learning. If no learning occurs, no teaching has taken place!

Why speak glowingly of academic buildings and salaries when the failures of the education system contribute to social discord and violence? Educators must remove their heads from the sands of irrelevance or risk becoming irrelevant themselves.

Leon Lessinger, former Associate Commissioner of Education, has stated succinctly the urgent need for accenting results:

> . . . *the American educational commitment has been that every child should have an adequate education. This commitment has been stated in terms of resources such as teachers, books, space, and equipment. When a child has failed to learn, school personnel have assigned him a label—'slow,' or 'unmotivated,' or 'retarded.' Our schools must assume a revised commitment—that every child shall learn. Such a commitment includes the willingness to change a system which does not work, and find one which does; to seek causes of failure in the system and its personnel instead of focusing solely on students; in short, to hold the school accountable for results in terms of student learning rather than solely in the use of resources.* [1]

(2) *Accountability Requires Measurement:* Accountability suggests that we stop counting the number of volumes in the library, quit measuring square footage per full-time student, and start looking at how well students are being taught. We must use relevant criteria to evaluate teaching. Learning, the only valid evidence of teaching, can be further defined as a change in behavior. If specific behavioral objectives are established, educators can be held accountable for students who are able to demonstrate learning by acting in ways that were impossible before teaching took place.

In January 1970 Lessinger quantified accountability in easily understood terms:

> *If an air conditioning contractor promises that his installation will reduce interior temperatures 20 degrees below outside temperatures, it takes only an accurate thermometer to determine if the promise has been met. Similarly, if an educational manager promises that all children attending his school will be able to read 200 words per minute with 90 per cent comprehension on their twelfth birthday, as measured by a*

specific test, simply giving the test to all children on their
twelfth birthday will readily reveal if the promise has been
fulfilled.[2]

Although learning cannot always be measured as easily and as
accurately as in Lessinger's example, modern educational techniques enable us to achieve acceptable evidence of learning. The
concept of accountability is based on specifically defined objectives, measurement techniques that determine exactly what the
teacher intends to accomplish, and instructional methods that
guarantee most students will obtain the objectives.

(3) *Accountability Assumes and Shifts Responsibility:*
Accountability assumes responsibility for the success or failure of
individual schools and pupils.[3] Students have traditionally been
held responsible through tests and recitations for whatever they
may or may not have learned. Accountability shifts the emphasis
of that responsibility away from the student.

Another associate commissioner, Don Davies, has said:
This concept of accountability . . . links student performance
with teacher performance. . . . It means . . . that schools and
colleges will be judged by how they perform not by what
they promise. It means . . . shifting primary learning responsi-
bility from the student to the school. It also means that a lot
of people are going to be shaken up.[4]

(4) *Accountability Permeates the College Community:*
Although some people (as Mr. Davies predicts) may be shaken up,
teachers should not become scapegoats. Teachers cannot be accountable unless the concept of accountability permeates the entire spectrum of institutional responsibility.

In a broad sense accountability means that boards of trustees,
presidents, administrators, and teachers will be held responsible for
the performance of their students.[5]

Accountability implies that two-year colleges must be accountable externally to the community and that colleges must be
accountable internally to the students who pass through their open
doors. This state is achieved when students from the community
enter the college, find a program that is compatible with their
goals, persist in college until the goal is reached, and then become
productive members of the community.

In short, the entire college body including the board, the

president, the administration, the students, and the instructors will
become accountable to the community.

Conclusion
Accountability is far more than a glib term or "in" word. It is an
operational concept "that comes to grips with the notion that
schools and colleges should shoulder responsibility for . . . their
pupils."[6] Accountability is a privilege—not a burden. It calls forth
the best within us. It challenges us to examine our purposes, to
find better ways to make education responsible to the society that
pays the bills. It holds equal promise for all of education's clients,
"those who come to school well prepared to share its benefits, and
those who have nothing in their backgrounds that would equip
them for a successful learning experience."[7]

Accountability is inevitable because it is needed so
desperately.

THE NEED FOR ACCOUNTABILITY
An October 1970 issue of *Time* contained an education feature entitled "Open Admissions: American Dream or Disaster?" The
article expressed the notion that an "open access" policy could
either "invigorate colleges" or lead to "academic disaster," and
pointed out that education officials meeting at the American
Council on Education in St. Louis displayed opposing attitudes
towards a policy of open admissions. "To some it seemed a triumph of democracy; to others an omen that colleges may soon be
overwhelmed with the wrong kind of students."[8]

Are ignorant, culturally deprived, and poverty-stricken youth
the "wrong" kind of students? Should they be branded undesir-
ables because they are academically inept and need education
desperately? The American academic system is already on the
brink of disaster because of the "wrong" kind of educators. Why
fear the "wrong" kind of students? Overwhelming educational inefficiency can be traced to archaic attitudes and self-serving institutional callosity. Arthur Cohen in *Dateline '79* pictures traditional faculty members making "desperate attempts to plant sprigs of
ivy at the gates so that the barbarians will be dissuaded from
entering."[9]

The time for "planting ivy" has passed; the gates are open.
Educators must leave their comfortable retreats and become

accountable by joining the ranks of other professions in a common effort to solve national problems. A tangible expression of educational accountability in the form of honest "open door" policies supported by a willingness to assume responsibility for student learning may be the only way to prevent "academic disaster."

Historical Foundations of the Community College

The community college in the United States has been described as the only educational institution that can truly be considered an American social invention.[10] Sometimes called "democracy's college," it adopted a philosophy of equal educational opportunity for all and espoused an ideal of open admissions.

The community college is not an offshoot of classical higher education in America. Its ancestry can be traced to 19th century educational innovations developed to fill needs that traditional institutions of higher learning could not meet. The classical colleges, with their limited curriculums, existed to transmit culture and class values to a privileged elite. Those institutions were neither willing nor able to respond to 19th century industrial and social demands for broader curriculums or choice of subject matter including business, technical, and agricultural courses. The nation's educational framework had to be supplemented with additional colleges and different types of institutions. Land grant colleges, created by the Morrill Land Grant Act of 1862, gave substance to the concept that each individual, regardless of his economic or social status, should have the opportunity to progress educationally as far as his interests and abilities might permit.[11]

The belief in extending educational opportunities to all people led to a philosophy of the "open door" that has become the hallmark of the community college movement. Its democratic style, positive philosophy, and social promise appealed to the American people and won great popularity and support. The unprecedented educational benefits accompanying the G.I. Bill of Rights after World War II further enhanced and expanded the community college movement.[12]

Philosophical Foundations of the Community College

In addition to the idea that universal higher education is the right of any person who can profit from it, the community college movement was also founded on the conviction that colleges exist to serve the society that supports them.

A democratic society cannot sustain itself without a well educated citizenry capable of influencing its destiny in a responsible manner. The increasing polarization and violence of American society emphasize the need for more education for all citizens. Education's role in enhancing the civic competence of the American people is crucial to the nation's economic, social, and cultural welfare. Education helps to equalize opportunity by stressing the concept of individual worth and serving as a vehicle for personal and social advancement.

The pending crisis in American society represents a particular challenge to the community college because it is more closely identified with social needs than is any other segment of higher education.

National Need for Community Colleges
The community college movement is much more than a democratically inspired attempt to meet educational demands that have been ignored by other institutions of higher learning. In the United States today post-secondary education is a vital national need—not a luxury. Community colleges are in a unique position to answer that need.

The role of unskilled workers becomes less important as technological society grows more complex. There are few jobs available for high school graduates who possess no other training.[13] Conversely, there is an insistent national demand for manpower trained in sophisticated skills. The obsolete concept of scarcity of educational opportunity is not applicable to highly developed nations. At one point in its history, this country needed only a few highly educated persons and thus provided economic support for only a small number of students to complete advanced education. The academic system was designed to select the talented few and to reject the majority. Today the nation cannot afford to waste human resources. Educational institutions must impart essential skills to all students.[14]

In an age of burgeoning enrollments and increasingly selective admissions at senior colleges and universities, the community college's familiar role of meeting the educational needs of society becomes more and more important. While the university continues to cater to relatively homogeneous groups from a dominant stratum of society, the community college embraces a heterogeneous group that represents a cross section of the total population.[15] Two-year college students are more likely to come from the lower two-thirds of the socioeconomic spectrum. The "open door" is a matter of national concern, for the community college performs a vital service in removing barriers to education.

Geographic location of academic institutions is a crucial factor in education. (Most community college student bodies are localized within fifteen miles of the campus.) Colleges constructed within commuting distance of potential students extend educational accessibility to the total population and facilitate attainment of our national goal of universal higher education.[16] And the fact that community college fees are either modest or nonexistent removes financial barriers and provides an economical avenue to higher education. However, even if all geographical and financial barriers could be eliminated, racial minorities, women, and children from low socioeconomic classes would still be sparsely represented.[17] These groups contain human talents that cannot be wasted even though potential students might be poorly motivated. The concept of accountability demands active efforts to seek, recruit, enroll, and retain every possible student in the community; the community college must "make readily available, programs of education . . . that match a wide spectrum of community needs and relate economically to the total pattern of educational opportunity in the area."[18]

The Challenge of the Open Door

Today more than two million students are enrolled in community colleges. Over 1,000 two-year colleges already exist in this country and more are being added at the rate of one per week.[19] The community college movement has solid historical and philosophical foundations. It occupies a unique position and seems to promise a solution for many of the nation's pressing social and educational needs. The community college is now faced with the critical challenge of becoming accountable for its unfulfilled potential by translating ideals into reality.

The open-door policy of the community-junior college implies acceptance of the concept of universal higher education. The basic criteria for admission is graduation from high school; however, all individuals 18 years of age and older, who appear capable of profiting from instruction, are usually eligible for admission.

Community colleges have become the primary vehicle for social and economic advancement for the lower two-thirds of the population. The typical student body is an extremely heterogeneous and diverse group that is often drawn from backgrounds characterized by low economic and social status, low educational achievement, marginal employment, and limited participation in community organizations. Students from these environments are disadvantaged to the degree that their culture has failed to provide them with experiences typical of the youth that traditional colleges are accustomed to teaching. The community college must recognize, however, that a considerable number of disadvantaged, low-aptitude students in its student body creates diverse problems that necessitate drastic modifications in traditional instructional techniques, as well as requires an expanded curriculum.

Unfortunately, few community colleges faced with these problems have lived up to their bright promise. The "open door" is too often a glib admissions statement rather than a true concept of accountable reality.

Unfulfilled Promises

Although the community college movement should be credited with pursuing the ideal of universal higher education, accountability demands that the success of that venture be judged by results. Student success (both persistence and achievement in college) is the only accurate measure of the open door.

Attrition rates at community colleges generally are alarming. The typical urban community college reports annual student dropout rates of more than 50 percent.[20] As many as 75 percent of low-achieving students withdraw during their first year.[21] In one typical California public junior college, 80 percent of the entering students enrolled in remedial English, but only 20 percent matriculated into regular college English classes.[22] Remedial courses are generally poorly designed, poorly taught, and seldom evaluated carefully.

The problem of unacceptable attrition has led critics to refer cynically to the open door as a "revolving door." The obvious lack of accountability behind these shocking attrition rates seems particularly reprehensible when one realizes that they reflect the shattered hopes of disadvantaged youth who were led to believe that the open door offered them a chance. "There is a marked difference between allowing a student to learn and taking responsibility for the direction and extent of that learning."[23]

The glaring inadequacies of many community college programs should lead educators to seek new approaches geared to individual learning and learning deficiencies. If community college instructors can be taught to become effective teachers, and are willing to be held accountable for student learning, the promise of the open door can be fulfilled. Unfortunately, there is a decided difference between the attitudes of many community college instructors and the attitudes that must be developed if they are ever to become effective teachers of community college students.[24] A national survey of community colleges revealed the discouraging evidence that, although 91 percent of the institutions espoused the concept of the open door, only 55 percent provided programs appropriate for non-traditional students.[25]

Inappropriate Attitudes

Edmund J. Gleazer, Jr., writing in the winter 1970 issue of the *Educational Record,* stated:

> *I am increasingly impatient with people who ask whether a student is 'college material.' We are not building a college with the student. The question we ought to ask is whether the college is . . . student material. It is the student we are building, and it is the function of the college to facilitate that process. We have him as he is, rather than as we wish he were . . . we are still calling for much more change in the student than we are in the faculty. . . . Can we come up with . . . the professional attitudes . . . [necessary to] put us into the business of tapping pools of human talent not yet touched?*[26]

This clear statement of accountability strikes at the heart of the community college problem. The promise of the "open door" will never be realized until teachers change their attitudes and accept the professional responsibility of becoming accountable for students. When educators point a finger at the "wrong" kind of student, their own three fingers point back at the "wrong" kind of educators!

Accountability must permeate every level of the institution, but the individual instructor is by far the most important element in the success of community college programs.[27] Unfortunately, the typical faculty member is seldom in complete accord with the generally acknowledged purposes or with the principles of admission applying in most community colleges.[28] Although some teachers appear genuinely concerned about the high rate of student attrition, many simply attribute the dropout rate to the notion that the students were not "college material."[29] How can a unique multi-purpose institution catering to ahighly non-traditional student body be successful if the faculty—who are the key element in implementing the purposes of the institution—do not agree with those purposes?

The typical community college faculty member is a subject matter specialist. The instructor is usually male, a full-time instructor, and a former elementary or secondary school teacher.[30] His graduate education has developed his interests and abilities along a narrow spectrum. This faculty member is "academically inclined," finding his greatest satisfaction in transmitting the knowledge of his chosen discipline to able students who can comprehend and appreciate his discipline. This accounts in large part for the instructor's preference for teaching advanced and specialized courses: they afford him the opportunity to teach that which he knows best.

Few community college instructors have had any preparation for teaching in that unique institution.[31] Most have served internships in schools other than junior colleges; they do not understand the community college setting and tend to think of it in terms of their own senior college or university experience. Thus, these instructors cannot fulfill the responsibilities imposed by the open door if they insist upon "aping the practices of . . . universities which were designed in other times to provide services to different populations."[32]

Four-year institutions undoubtedly serve a necessary and valuable educational function. They are selectively geared to upper socioeconomic levels and the upper third of the student population. They are research oriented and pursue the task of advancing basic knowledge rather than providing training for immediate job application. While the defined task of the university faculty member includes teaching, this is essentially subordinate to his other functions.[33] Traditional four-year institutions are neither willing nor equipped to offer educational opportunity to all—especially when increasing numbers of those individuals seeking higher education lack the academic prerequisites for successful performance.

The community college is not a basic research institution nor a home for a "community" of scholars. The main function of the community college instructor is to teach; he must be committed to his role and specialize in instructional processes.[34] He must be willing to be held accountable for student learning.

Like their university counterparts, community college instructors are concerned about "status" and being properly identified with higher education. They "view themselves as members of a profession in which they are independent practitioners who specialize in interaction with students in groups."[35] They may believe that the "person of the instructor" has some intrinsic "worth in itself"[36] and many cherish the center stage role of dispensing knowledge to the less learned. They fail to understand that being identified with higher education does not automatically confer respect, and that "an instructor is worth only as much as he contributes to the purposes of the institution."[37]

If instructors feel that teaching specialized and advanced courses affords them prestige, while the onerous chore of teaching remedial or developmental courses is below their dignity, they certainly do not belong in community colleges.

Accountability demands that the best qualified instructors available be assigned to well organized courses of remedial instruction. Those who believe in the philosophy of the community college should seek personal and professional prestige by carrying out the promise of the open door. Yet it is the inexperienced instructor, without preparation or understanding of the basic objectives of the course, who is most often found in remedial classrooms.[38]

Many community college instructors persist in the practice of norm-referenced testing and curve-based grade-marking practices, even though these archaic mechanisms were designed to screen and sort students in the days when only a talented elite merited higher education. These traditional methods assume from the start that all will not succeed.[39] Such practices have no place in any community college that is willing to open its doors and be accountable for the learning of all students.

Research has shown that specifying learning objectives in precise terms and using well organized, self-paced instructional sequences to reach those objectives can guarantee learning for up to 90 percent of all students.[40] Yet many community college instructors resist the very methods that could help them become accountable for student learning. Some are reluctant to give up their "star" role and fear a loss of status in becoming a "manager of learning" rather than a "dispenser of wisdom."[41] Others seem unwilling to do the considerable work necessary to systematically organize self-paced instruction. They prefer to hide behind "a feeling of elitism manifest in such statements as 'Hold me accountable for their learning? They don't belong in college anyway! In my day we had to work for what we got!' "[42]

Changed attitudes are the key to fulfilling the promise of the open door.

Conclusion

If the community college is to meet the nation's desperate educational needs and fulfill the promise of the open door, a genuine acceptance of accountability must permeate all levels of the institutional spectrum. This will require changes in the attitudes of governance and administrative officials and even more drastic changes in the attitudes of instructors. "Administrators can supervise . . . and make assistance available, but instructors must implement the process. If teachers refuse to spell out ends or to accept accountability for their being achieved, the enterprise will not succeed."[43]

Community colleges can no longer exist selfishly as ends in themselves, stifled by obsolete traditions and ignoring their democratic heritage. Their calling is too dynamic and too important to be rejected in favor of posing pathetically as poor cousins of the university.

Faculty members and administrators must change their attitudes and work together to gear curriculum to student achievement, to define objectives, and to accept accountability for their efforts. By "guaranteeing some form of minimum educational achievement" they can turn their institutions into places where learning takes place. By working towards equality of educational results they can transform their communities and fulfill the unique promise of the open-door community college philosophy.   □

John E. Roueche is director of RELCV's junior college division. George A. Baker, III and Richard L. Brownell are program associates in the junior college division.

[1]Lessinger, Leon, "Accountability in Education." (National Committee in Support of the Public Schools, February 1970), p. 1.

[2]_____, "Accountability in Public Education." *Today's Education,* May 1970, p. 52.

[3]Meade, Edward J., Jr., "Accountability and Governance in Public Education." (Address to the Annual Convention of the National Association of Secondary School Principals, Atlantic City, New Jersey, February 12, 1968), p. 3.

[4]Davies, Don, "The 'Relevance' of Accountability." *The School Administrator* 1: April 1970: 11.

[5]Schwartz, Ron, "Accountability." (Special Editorial Report) *Nation's Schools* 85: June 1970: 31.

[6]Davies, p. 11.

[7]Ibid.

[8]*Time* 96: October 19, 1970: 63-66.

[9]Cohen, Arthur M., *Dateline '79 Heretical Concepts for the Community College.* (Beverly Hills: Glencoe Press, 1969), p. xvii.

[10]Gleazer, Edmund J., Jr., ed., *American Junior Colleges,* 6th ed. (Washinton, D.C.: American Council on Education, 1963), p. 3.

[11]Roueche, John E., *Salvage, Redirection, or Custody?* (Washington, D.C., American Association of Junior Colleges, 1968).

[12]Gleazer, Edmund J., Jr., "The Community College: Issues of the 1970's." *Educational Record,* Winter 1970, p. 47.

[13]Cohen, p. 54.

[14]Bloom, Benjamin S., "Learning for Mastery." *UCLA Evaluation Comment* 1: May 1968: 2.

[15]Lombardi, John. "The Challenge for the Future." (Speech given at Developmental Studies Workshop, Los Angeles City College, June 3, 1967).

[16]Roueche, *Salvage, Redirection.*

[17]Cross, K. Patricia, "The Junior College's Role in Providing Postsecondary Education for All." (Berkeley: Center for Research and Development in Higher Education, and Educational Testing Service, 1969), p. 5.

[18]Wattenbarger, James L. and Godwin, Winfred L., eds. "The Community Colleges in the South: Progress and Prospects." (A report of the Southern States Work Conference Committee on Education Beyond the High School, sponsored by State Departments of Education and State Education Associations, 1962).

[19]*Time* 96: 65.

[20]Cohen, p. 5.

[21]Schenz, Robert F., "An Investigation of Junior College Courses and Curricula for Students with Low Ability." (Ed.E. dissertation, UCLA, Graduate School of Education, 1963), p. 141.

[22]Bossone, Richard M., *Remedial English Instruction in California Public Junior Colleges; An Analysis and Evaluation of Current Practices.* (Sacramento: California State Department of Education, September 1966).

[23]Cohen, p. 8.

[24]Roueche, *Salvage, Redirection.*

[25]Schenz, p. 22.

[26]Gleazer, "The Community College," p. 51.

[27] American Association of Junior Colleges, *Selected Papers* from the 47th Annual Convention, February 27 - March 3, 1967, San Francisco. (Washington, D.C.: The Association, 1967), p. 62-63.

[28] Medsker, Leland L., *The Junior College: Progress and Prospect.* (New York: McGraw-Hill Book Co., 1960), p. 185.

[29] National Conference on the Teaching of English in the Junior College. *Research and the Development of English Programs in the Junior College.* (Tempe: Arizona State University, 1965), p. 32.

[30] Medsker, pp. 171-73.

[31] Cohen, Arthur M. and Brawler, Florence G., *Focus on Learning: Preparing Teachers for the Two-Year College.* (Occasional Report No. 11, Junior College Leadership Program, UCLA Graduate School of Education, March 1968).

[32] Cohen, p. xvii.

[33] Blocker, Clyde E. et al., *The Two-Year College: A Social Synthesis.* (Englewood Cliffs, New Jersey: Prentice Hall, 1965), p. 144.

[34] Cohen, p. 21.

[35] Ibid., p. 96.

[36] Ibid., p. x.

[37] Ibid., p. 45.

[38] Bossone, pp. 12-13.

[39] Cohen, p. 86.

[40] Bloom, p. 1.

[41] Cohen, p. 100.

[42] Ibid., p. 199.

[43] Ibid., p. 201.

Chapter Four

INDUSTRY AS THE SYMBOL OF ACCOUNTABILITY

I

INNOVATION IN TEACHING—
WHY INDUSTRY LEADS THE WAY

by Nate A. Newkirk

"The real effect of innovation in the Industrial Revolution and the Computer Revolution was job displacement, not job replacement. Stagecoach drivers learned to drive busses. Wood carvers learned to operate wood lathes. Clerks learned to program computers. Now the Teaching Revolution is upon us. What will the teachers do?"

In California, about 1961, an electronics firm introduced a new teaching method and reduced its engineering training program from six months to three months. Veteran company engineers soon asked to be allowed to enter it. They saw they were missing something.

In Nigeria, in 1964, a group of 50 Africans from six nations was seen studying 10 to 14 hours a day, month after month, using a new method.

In Belgium, in 1966, one instructor conducted two classes, covering two slightly different technical subjects in two different languages simultaneously, using a new method.

In Canada, in 1966, a young man started conducting a six-week technical class for twelve students who had a better formal education than he. He'd never taught before, and he had less than a week to prepare. Most students thought the class was a great success. The teacher enjoyed every minute of it. He used a new method.

Not more than a handful of dedicated "industrial educators" (perhaps not even the man who started it all in California) are aware of the significance of this chain of events. This new teaching method is one of the innovations produced in industry education, and will be discussed more fully later.

The Lecture Method

But first, let's look at the conventional, centuries-old method of instruction — the technique most familiar to all of us — the "teacher-in-front-of-the-class" approach. Let's call it "the lecture method." (Although the term "lecture" has certain unpalatable connotations in industry education, it's still a fairly accurate description of what usually happens in classrooms, regardless of what's being taught.)

To start with, let's consider the assumptions that a teacher is required to make before he steps in front of a class and begins to "lecture":

1. The group is ready to learn.
2. The group is willing to begin where the teacher wants to begin.
3. Each student will learn at the same pace as the other students in the group, and will be able to keep up with the teacher's presentation.
4. Students will learn the material in the sequence in which the teacher presents it.

"Unrealistic," you may say. Right! Yet, no teacher can conduct a lecture class without assuming these conditions. The instructor's success with his class depends upon his ability to cover each topic in such a way that each individual is able to learn it — now, in the given sequence — in the time allotted for the class.

Result? A tremendous variety of successes or failures, depending upon many factors: the teacher's skill, patience, and knowledge of the subject, the number of students in the class, the similarity of their backgrounds, knowledge, intelligence, etc.

Your next question might well be, "If that's all true, how come the lecture method is still the most common method of instruction?"

I think the key reasons rest with the teachers themselves, and the emotions that motivate them to become teachers.

Teachers are smarter than most people, and they're strongly motivated to leave their mark on society by contributing their knowledge in the way that seems to affect the most people. They get their greatest satisfaction from seeing their students grow, change, and improve under their guidance. The vast majority of teachers thrive on their emotional role in the personal teacher-student relationship. Being human, they usually love to lecture. It seems the easiest way to prove that they know their subject. (Incidentally, for those who really know their subject, and who have been teaching it for a long time, lecturing requires very little pre-class preparation. That leaves time for study, research, student counseling, and other, less dedicated pursuits.)

Naturally, when someone comes along who advocates that teaching might be more effective by using other methods, most teachers react negatively.

Educational Systems

But the teachers are not the only ones to blame. Consider the entire public educational system. It still places emphasis on the very valid idea that a student must not be sent to college, or out into the world, until he is mature enough to cope. (One obvious alternative, to teach a lot more in those thirteen years of preparation for college or leaving school, has been exploited considerably in the past decade, to be sure.) This objective is fine. But how do you evaluate a student's education with this intangible objective as a criterion?

Let's switch our thinking now to what we will call the industrial education system, the system of adult education usually provided by an employer. To avoid clouding the issue, I won't attempt to differentiate between education and training.

Industrial Education Methods

How is industrial education different? To the casual observer, the differences seem to be largely the subject matter and the age of the students. Plus the depressing fact that industrial teachers are often higher paid than the best paid teachers in our nation's public schools.

To the experienced educator, there are still greater differences. In industrial education, there is great emphasis on the quality of instruction. But the purpose of industrial education is "high quality, at the lowest possible cost, and with the greatest possible speed." And in industry you can usually measure your results.

280 Industry as The Symbol of Accountability

Quality

Take the quality factor. Since most industrial education means teaching a specific skill, it's usually easier to determine if the student is able to do the work when he's finished. Either he can operate a lathe or he can't. Either he can use a desk calculator or he can't. Not all subjects being taught in industry are be any means as "yes or no" as those examples; but it's regularly easier to judge the effectiveness of industry teaching than it is to determine if a youngster is ready for college.

I am not saying that the industry educator does not face problems. Here are some factors that tend to complicate the quality judgment in industrial education programs:

1. Since education is frequently regarded as a "necessary evil" (that means it's not a direct revenue producer), it's hard to find a top executive who is willing to pay much more than lip service to the activity.
2. Not very many companies have an "Education Department". The function often rests with a particular department manager, or one of his designees, who regards education as an additional duty.
3. Even in some of the best organized industrial education departments in the world, it's not easy to find someone who's had formal training in schools of education. (Before you become too concerned about that fact, however, remember that only a small percentage of university teachers have had such training.)

Cost

What about the factor of cost? In public education, the taxpayer is at the mercy of the school officials (although they would have us believe it's the other way around). "Sure," you say, "but our town has turned down school budgets and bond issues." Let me express it this way. As I see it, the taxpayer is thoroughly boxed in. He wants his Johnny and Susie to have the best education possible. But the real problem is — he knows nothing about education. He is forced to rely, for the most part, on elected officials to represent him. If his local school board consists of people who are trained or experienced in school administration, his community is fortunate indeed.

In industry education, costs are also difficult to control, but there's one all-important difference. There's frequently a comparison available between the total cost of hiring people who have the required skills, and the total cost of educating people who don't. That comparison is continually being made, and it doesn't require any education expertise. It serves nicely, moreover, to keep the industrial education honest.

Speed in Industrial Education

What about the factor of speed? It's clear that time is the greatest contributor to cost. Total teaching salaries, student salaries and classroom space are affected. But there are more subtle items also. What about student living and travel expenses if they must visit a distant location for training? That cost alone can easily become 50% of a company's total "per student" training costs. But by far the most subtle and important consequences of the speed factor may lie in its effect on the size and cost of a company's workforce. If in a company 500 technicians must at present spend four weeks per year in school to keep themselves up to date, and if a new education method can cut that time to two weeks, a reasonable estimate of the saving is $300,000 (see Chart 1). To generate a similar amount of net profit, most companies would have to sell at least $3,000,000 more of their products and services.

Speed in Public Education

Let's speak again of public education, for the moment. We've commented on the good job the schools have done since Sputnik in 1957 woke us up to the need for better education. But if you want to contemplate a really significant effect on teachers, students, and your annual school tax bill, how about having society accept the idea that a youngster is as adult today at 17 as he was 50 years ago at 18? It should follow then that he can enter college at 17. (Plenty of them are doing it right now.)

So why not bring the speed factor into public education? Let's eliminate one calendar year of school, but let's not do it by shortening the holidays, or by working longer hours, as recently announced by a Long Island school. Let's do it, as a well-known IBM executive is fond of saying, "By working smarter, not harder." If that sounds like a ridiculous idea, keep in mind that eliminating one entire school year constitutes an overall reduction of only about 8% in total school time required for our youngsters.

Chart 1

Company F's maintenace staff includes 520 technicians, who must spend 4 weeks per year in school to keep themselves up to date. How many technicians are required if this schooling can be cut to two weeks — all other factors remaining equal? At present, 520 workers x 48 work weeks = 24,960 total work weeks. If such technician can work fifty weeks, instead of 48:

$$\frac{499}{50 \quad 24,960} \quad \text{technicians required}$$

The expense of keeping those 21 extra technicians on the payroll can easily look like this:

21 salaries @ $8,000	$168,000
2 supervisors @ $12,000	24,000
Fringe benefits @ 15%	28,800
Floor space for 23 people, 100 sq. ft. each @ $5.00 per sq. ft. per year	11,500
Tools, equipment, etc. @ $200 per technician	4,200
	$236,500
Miscellaneous overhead (10%)	22,650
	$259,150

And what about training costs:

Eliminate 500 students for 2 weeks each	1,000 weeks
Then —	
Eliminate 21 students for 4 weeks each	84 weeks
Savings =	1,084 weeks

A cost figure of $50.00 per student week would be very low for most training operations, not including travel and living expenses.

	1,084
	x$50
Training cost saving	$ 59,200
Payroll cost saving	259,150
Total Saving	$318,350

New Teaching Methods

Earlier, I commented that most teachers react negatively when it is suggested that there might be teaching methods which are superior to the lecture method. But, on the other hand, many top educators do realize the need for innovation. Dr. Mark Scurrah of the New York State Education Department Center on Innovation said in a recent speech, "We are terribly unimaginative as teachers. We seem to feel that talking is the only way to impart knowledge."

Why is it, then, that much more innovation occurs in industry education, especially since so few industry educators are trained as educators?

I believe that one important reason lies in "the system." (Don't forget the purpose of the industry education game: "High quality, at the lowest possible cost, with the greatest possible speed.") Every true educator is striving for quality, in public or industrial education. Cost and speed are simply more important in industry than in public education. Let me add two more examples that illustrate the importance of speed.

The Value of Saved Time

Company A has an 18-month training program for newly hired salesmen. The sheer length of that program may have a direct bearing on that company's efforts to hire top candidates. Few fresh college graduates, especially those holding advanced degrees, are interested in entering an 18-month training program if they can avoid it. Usually, it simply means more delay in starting to earn "the big money". A substantial reduction in the length of that program, provided quality is maintained, might do more than any other single thing to raise the quality of that newly hired sales trainee, and thus, eventually improve the quality of the entire sales force.

Company B produces a specialty electronic product. It has a highly trained staff of technicians to service and maintain its product. The engineering department has developed a greatly improved version, and it is estimated that, when they start shipping it, profits will increase by $1,000,000 in the first year. But before it can be released to customers, the technicians must be trained. All else being equal, if the training program can be cut by one week, it might mean as much as $20,000 added profit, since shipments can begin one week earlier. Not to mention the cost savings resulting from the reduction in the training program.

Nearly all large organizations can cite better examples than these which will show the dramatic impact of reducing the length of their training program. Why not develop a similar rationale regarding public education?

The Difficulty of Bringing Students Together

The second important factor spurring innovation in industry education lies in the simple idea that it's frequently extremely difficult to bring students together for a class. After all, they have jobs, family responsibilities, and other demands on their time. Then too, there's the continual problem of the company "crisis du jour", that arises to prevent a key person from attending a class. These complications lead to all sorts of interesting methods to make certain that students make it to class as scheduled. One company often gives a student a day or two off, prior to class. They tell him they want him to be "fresh and alert". The fact is, however, it's nearly a foolproof method to get him away from business problems that might prevent him from attending class.

A third factor in encouraging innovation in industry education is the sheer physical problem of assembling students. That may involve high expenses in student living and travel and more lost time due to travel.

Unlike public education, industry education is frequently a "crash program", for many reasons like Company B's problem of preparing to market a new or improved product. There's also the frequent requirement to take a segment of a company's staff and give it a "one-shot program."

- Example: A company manufactures radios. They switch from tubes to transistors. A new technology must be taught.
- Example: A company introduces electronic data processing. Every executive and manager, not to mention every employee in affected areas, must be given an orientation program.

In these cases, adequate classrooms are frequently not available, and instructors are almost never ready and waiting.

The Student Himself

A fourth factor is the student himself. He is frequently unprepared, unmotivated and uninterested (just like some youngsters of our acquaintance), but the adult student is usually much quicker to react vocally to poor instruction.

Also, to complicate things further, the older we are the slower we learn. Therefore, the teaching method must be more challenging. If you don't believe this, try a little research in a typical education department. Examine two or three classes where the students were ranked in performance. Compare those rankings with the "age ranking" of the students. The youngest will often be grouped at the top of the class, and the oldest at the bottom.

A fifth factor that contributes to the urge to innovate in industry education is the character of the education staff itself — the managers, developers and teachers — whose motives may be considerably different than public educators. Let's examine this factor carefully:

1. Few industry educators consider education as their "career." For most, it is another in a series of diverse assignments.
2. Industry teachers seldom spend more than 50% of their time in class, actually teaching. For some assignments, 20% is considered a "full-time" teaching load.
3. Only a small percentage of industry teachers have taken education courses at the university level. Even fewer are, or have been, certified to teach in primary or secondary schools.

Let's imagine what goes on in the case of a bright businessman who is selected for a teaching assignment in his company's education department. First, he is aware that most of his predecessors have stayed in education for a relatively short time, perhaps only two or three years. The good ones have then moved on to better jobs. He also realizes that he's never taught before, except perhaps as an incidental part of a former job. Finally, if he's ambitious and bright, he knows that he must do something extraordinary in order to assure recognition and commensurate reward. This last thought is common to nearly every known situation. But remember, the industry educator is in a system that allows him to exploit his opportunity to excel. In that sense, he's in a considerably different position than a public school teacher. He realizes that to excel in teaching is expected. Perhaps, therefore, he begins to seek new and better ways to teach.

Innovative Methods of Instruction

What methods can he choose? A whole host of new and different techniques have come into being in the past 15 years or so. Most famous for several years was Programmed Instruction (P.I.), developed by B. F. Skinner of Harvard. Today it is Computer Aided Instruction (CAI) that makes the headlines. In between were many variations on the theme, each with some applicability in the education scheme.

Through nearly all of these innovations in instruction are some common threads:

- The student can learn on his own, rather than in a group.
- The student sets his own pace.
- The material is carefully structured in order to minimize the time required for learning a given amount of information.
- The student is actively involved in the learning process — he's not just sitting there listening.
- The student is kept abreast of his progress, or lack of progress.

At this point, think of a "new" teaching technique you are familiar with, in terms of those five factors. Do they all apply to the technique you picked? Probably. (How about "the book" as a means of learning? It fits every factor, except possibly the last one.)

There's another characteristic I didn't list that is common to nearly all of these techniques (including "the book"). There's no personal interface with a human teacher.

Job Security of Teachers

It's not hard to understand why teachers might resist these new methods. Their resistance should ring a bell with lots of us. Let me explain why by asking you a question. What is the usual reaction when employees hear that their company's getting a computer? Any fleeting worries about job security? Of course! With some it's more than a fleeting worry.

When the job security of any group is threatened, for whatever the reason, there is a natural resistance from the group. Why
should teachers react differently when a new concept seems to
threaten their security? I think I can hear you saying, "But very
few people lost their jobs because of computers. In fact, there are
more jobs now than ever, and unemployment is very low."

Right. And new teaching techniques will undoubtedly, in
time, produce the same results. A result that is common to nearly
every innovation introduced since the first prehistoric man hooked
up a crude wheel to a cart.

But let's think back to another fundamental point that goes
beyond job security. Remember our earlier discussion about the
motives that teachers have, and the satisfactions that they derive
from being teachers? Guiding students in their growth. The personal student-teacher relationship. The love to lecture. Now we're
arriving at what I believe is the true source of teacher resistance to
new teaching methods.

The real effect of innovation in the Industrial Revolution and
the Computer Revolution was job displacement, not job replacement. Stagecoach drivers learned to drive buses. Wood carvers
learned to operate wood lathes. Clerks learned to program computers. Now the Teaching Revolution is upon us. What will the
teachers do?

Did you nod in agreement when I said that teachers are
smarter than most people? If so, you might now agree that if a
teacher can continue to gain personal satisfaction from his work,
he'll probably continue to teach. So, let's consider one more factor. Dedicated teachers are often frustrated by their inability to
give adequate attention to each student, especially in these days of
over-crowded schools. They would love to pull the under-achiever
up by his bootstraps, and push bright ones on to greater heights.
But the class is too big, and the teachers have more material to
cover than ever before.

Learner-Controlled Instruction (LCI)

These same positive and negative factors existed in California,
in Nigeria, in Belgium and Canada. And in each case, an industry
educator decided to try something new, a technique which at first
glance doesn't seem new at all. Dr. Robert Mager pioneered this
technique at Varian Associates in California in the early 1960's.

He called it Learner Controlled Curriculum. I introduced it in IBM
in 1963 and labeled it Learner Controlled Instruction. Here's how
LCI works:

Each student is given a detailed list of specific "learning objectives." He is given suggestions for reading, reference, observation, inquiry, practice, or experimentation. He is told precisely
how he must demonstrate that he has learned the subject at various stages (if appropriate) and when he has finished. He is advised
that he may direct specific questions to the instructor in private,
and that he will receive a specific answer. He is informed that
there will be no formal class session, and that he may being to
learn in any manner he chooses. Finally, the student is told that,
when he has completed all requirements, he is free to return to his
job. He is then directed to a quiet place to study and the instruction establishes himself in a convenient location.

Please read that paragraph again carefully. In it, the essential
ingredients for the success of LCI are stated precisely. The same
technique applies equally well, by the way for groups of students.

Categories of Subjects to Be Learned

Before we go on, let me remind you that there are two broad
categories of subjects that we learn in life. One broad group consists of specific skills — mathematics, engineering, the sciences,
machine operation, and computer programming, to name a few.
The other broad group generally centers around the idea of changing a person's attitude or outlook — music appreciation, salesman-
ship, and public speaking, for example. The technique I've described is remarkably well suited to the "skills" group of subjects, but
the "attitudes" group of subjects may be taught best by some
form of active voice communication between teacher and student.
A natural tendency is to consider most borderline subjects as un-
suitable for LCI-type techniques. That may well be the same kind
of error that was often made when determining if a certain task
could be done by a computer. We're still amazing ourselves with
the things computers can do.

Why a Student Likes LCI

Why does a student like LCI? That's easy. He studies when he
feels like it, and he day-dreams when he feels like it. (The fact that
he may leave whenever he finishes, is sufficient motivation for

99% of the students.) He can proceed at his own pace, in other words.

He can select his own best method of learning. He might choose to read, experiment, observe, ask questions, or, more likely, a combination of those methods.

The student can start his learning at whatever point he wishes. And he may choose any sequence of topics that he wishes (where appropriate). These two points are extremely significant, and they are based on the simple idea that no student is completely ignorant of a subject to be learned. Each student, in other words, has some point of departure that is unique to him. That puts him in the position of being the only person who knows at what point, and in what sequence, he should begin to fill in the gaps in his knowledge of the subject. These two points also are the key items that are not taken into consideration by any other "automated" teaching method with which I am familiar, although Computer Aided Instruction (CAI) has the potential to assist the student in this regard.

Computer Aided Instruction

Speaking of computers for the moment — let's ask the question, "Does the LCI technique exclude the use of automated instruction techniques"? Not at all. Variety is the spice of student life, too. An industrial education center in San Francisco is using computer terminals, video tape, programmed instruction, and audio tape in various combinations for various subjects. The student comes to regard these devices as simply another reference source. He may find himself turning to any one of them to watch, or listen to, a short description or explanation of a particular subject, in the same manner as he turns to a book or a reference manual. The important difference is that he chooses the medium, and that he has the instructor to turn to when he's stuck. Programmed instruction (PI) and CAI does not usually accommodate those two ideas. I look forward to the day when it does.

What is the reaction of the student to LCI? Nearly every student I've talked with dreads the day when he must return to "conventional" learning methods. Enough said.

Why a Teacher Likes LCI

What is the effect of LCI on the teacher?

From the start, the teacher never concerns himself with preparing his lecture. Rather, he is deeply involved in defining what is to be learned, in stating it clearly and logically, and in gathering materials that will contribute to the student's ability to learn. He soon discovers that a well-written definition of the learning objective leads him almost automatically to the point where tests, or other methods of verifying the student's knowledge, can be prepared relatively easily.

The teacher also discovers that his concptual knowledge of the subject is more important than recalling precise details. I once taught a complex technical subject in LCI mode, which I hadn't studied or worked on for four years before walking into that class. But because my conceptual knowledge was sound, I could answer questions easily.

Still another effect on the teacher, of course, is the idea best expressed by a man who pointed out that LCI enabled him to concentrate his efforts on the individuals in the class who most needed the instruction. This deceptively simple point scores highest with teachers who scorn PI and CAI.

Selection of Teachers

There's another important effect, not only on the teacher, but on the selection of the teacher. When using LCI, the main prerequisites for teacher selection change considerably. The principal emphasis should be on locating someone with a high level of competence in his subject (I didn't say "education," I said "competence"). The LCI teacher does not lecture. Therefore, his ability to stand up in front of a class and articulate is simply not important. Every public and industry education administrator will appreciate the impact of that difference. His job of finding qualified teachers is different, and easier.

How can we summarize the choice of methods up till now available to a teacher? On one side of the teaching ledger is the lecture method. On the other side are Programmed Instruction and CAI. On the one side, the teacher feels that he is everything — on the other side he feels that he is nothing. In the middle lies Learner Controlled Instruction and other new methods, with much fertile ground for improvement.

The challenge of the next decade requires that all educators concentrate on researching and developing instructional methods that stress a closer personal relationship between student and teacher. If that goal is made clear, I believe nearly all teachers will join in the search, since they won't be worried about developing methods that essentially eliminate their lecturing jobs. Further, more competent persons may be attracted to the teaching profession, because the prerequisites will undoubtedly change.

Learner Controlled Instruction is only one innovative technique. There are many more, yet to be discovered, that serve the specific mutual interests of both student and teacher. The consequences of using such teaching methods could be a marvelous and revolutionary change for the better in education.   □

Nate A. Newkirk is Vice President and Managing Director of Computer Usage Education, Inc., 51 Madison Avenue, New York, N.Y. 10010.

II

WANTED: EDUCATIONAL ENGINEERS

by Henry A. Bern

"In the heart of a metaphor often lies a view of the universe. In the heart of the metaphor 'educational engineering' lies a view of a new universe of education now taking shape."

In the heart of a metaphor often lies a view of the universe. A case in point: "God does not play dice," said Albert Einstein, summarizing his view of the cosmos. The appearance of a new metaphor is therefore an event worth noting, for it may be an invitation to discovery. The discovery will rarely affect the cosmos but, if it is at all significant, it will surely affect a universe of discourse.

My thesis here is that in the heart of the metaphor "educational engineering" lies a view of a new universe of education now taking shape. First I examine the evidence of an increased literalization of the metaphor: the current language of education, new courses in the teacher preparation curriculum, heightened interest of business and industry in education, and "the engineer" in the Office of Education. Then I look at some of the suggested "causes" of this literal interpretation: money, the damned Russians, and the *Zeitgeist.* Finally, I express my own bias by proposing a two-step program for coping with the new universe.

In the Beginning

In 1945 W. W. Charters wrote an article entitled "Is There a Field of Educational Engineering?" Charters said he had been playing with the question for 20 years. And it seems reasonable that thoughts of educational engineering arose in the 1920's when Dewey, Thorndike, and Judd were discussing the validity of a

science of education.   In subsequent decades, the metaphor appeared only occasionally and superficially. F. L. Whitney, in his
popular research textbook, referred to employment of an outside
specialist and expert surveyor as a "consultant educational engineer." Using railroad engineering as a referent, F. Bobbitt's textbook on curriculum construction called for the "educational engineer" to lay out the "curricular tracks" for students. In discussing
"Learning" in the *Encyclopedia of Educational Research,* W. K.
Estes perceived the entire field of education as "this 'engineering
discipline.' "

The Language of Education

A number of developments within the past few years, however, can now be described to support the thesis that the "engineering" aspect of the metaphor is being more literally interpreted.
The most subtle of these developments is the change in the *language* of education. Technical words drawn from the terminology
of information and communication theory and engineering permeate educational journals: feedback, input, output, information
channels, bits, entropy, redundancy, lag, lead, etc.

Although educators are seldom aware of the origin of these
terms, they find them useful. This is particularly noticeable in the
efforts of some audio-visual educators to update their field. An old
hand but young mind in this field, C. F. Hoban, justifies the use of
the new vocabulary in this manner:

> The least that can be expected from the use of in-
> formation and communication theory in media re-
> search is an improved technical vocabulary that permits
> the researcher to deal with relevant variables. An ade-
> quate technical vocabulary is not available elsewhere.

And in a special journal supplement sometimes referred to as the
New Testament of the audio-visual field, we find that the main
section describes the field itself in this extended engineering
terminology.

Engineering in Teacher Education

A second and more structured development is the introduction of courses oriented toward human engineering and technology
in schools of education. For example, a recent textbook states an

explicit human engineering bias, proclaims the need for a technology of learning, and predicts that the educational psychologist of the future will be a psychologist-engineer. It attempts to develop this "eningeering approach" in the major portion of the text and then concludes:

> In short, educational technology is a direct movement to increase learning efficiency. When problems are conceived in terms of efficiency, then the methods of problem solving take on engineering characteristics. Traditional research in education has not emphasized the engineering approach.

In the first chapter of another textbook for teachers, the first section is entitled "Human Engineering" and expresses the author's basic view as follows:

> Education may need a new orientation that can best be described under the head of "human engineering." This approach, sometimes labeled "engineering psychology," is one of which every teacher should be thoroughly cognizant.

At Indiana University as long ago as 1959 at attempt was made to extrapolate an educational aspect of human engineering. It was labeled "instructional communications systems engineering." More recently a number of colleges and universities (e.g., San Francisco State College, University of California, Wayne State University, Syracuse University, and Indiana University) have listed courses described as "educational technology." Most of them introduce elementary analogical communications engineering principles. Last June Catholic University issued a lengthy news release announcing and describing a new graduate program of master and doctoral level training in educational technology. According to the release, "the primary concern of the new program in educational technology at Catholic University will be to train 'program engineers.' "

It should be especially noted that the term "human engineering" is generally no longer the figurative term of decades gone by. It is *not* the study of the management of the "psychic" forces (interest, will, and motivation) of workers in industry. It is *not* Korzybski's idealistic reconstruction of man through "the science and art of directing the energies and capacities of human beings to the advancement of human weal." Nor is it the fatherly advice given by the renowned professors of the Massachusetts Institute of Technology chair of humanics on how to get along as an engineer with non-engineers. Nor is it Stevens Institute of Technology's aptitude testing program conducted by its Laboratory of Human Engineering.

Today's referent of human engineering is literally physical equipment (hardware) engineering. Today's human engineers are predominantly engineers or engineering psychologists whose professional training and efforts are intimately and ultimately related to complex electro-mechanical information and communication equipment design problems and applications.

Industrial-Publishing Combines

A third and perhaps most significant development supporting our thesis is the effect of near frenetic efforts of business and industry to relate to educational enterprises. In some of the more significant cases the interest has expressed itself as powerful combines of industrial and publishing giants. Among these can be listed General Electric and Time, Inc., Radio Corporation of America and Random House, and Raytheon and D.C. Heath. I.B.M., Zerox, and Litton Industries are other giants which have purchased one or more organizations producing educational texts and materials. For an illustrated summary of these.mergers and acquisitions, see the figures in adjacent columns. Whatever questions may exist about the consequences of these transactions, there is little question about *one* consequence—the infusion of an engineering orientation and of engineers themselves into vital operations of education. The infusion of a systems engineering orienfation can be seen in a statement following purchase of D.C. Heath (for $40,300,000) by Raytheon's president, Thomas L. Phillips:

> Busy educators should not have to assemble the various components and fragments of learning equipment from a multitude of sources. We will now be able to build an integrated capability —a systems approach.

The engineering perspective is more clearly expressed in the advertisements to be found in weekly news-magazines. One recent advertisement shows a mountain of books threatening to overwhelm a bright-eyed tot. The lower half of the page explains what Sylvania, a subsidiary of General Telephone and Electronics, is doing for this tot, the "target of the knowledge explosion." Sylvania is designing "electronic systems for education . . . completely integrated systems of educational communications."

Engineers for Education

Nor is the engineering know-how of industry being brought to bear solely on the design and manufacture of educational products. Making sure that the product gives satisfactory performance to the customer in the field via its field service engineering staff is a well established function of industrial organizations. Some of the organizations already in the field now servicing the Office of Economic Opportunity include General Electric Company, U.S. Industries, Inc., Litton Industries, Burroughs Corporation, and Packard Bell Electronics Corporation. In fact, these field service engineering contractors outnumber such conventional professionally oriented educational contractors as Southern Illinois University, the University of Oregon, Northern Michigan University, and the Pinellas County (Florida) Board of Public Instruction.

Who are the "field services" engineers for these enterprises? We do not have much data to answer this question. From occasional news releases, however, they appear to be persons with some technical engineering training and experience. For example, the director of the new Job Corps Center at Clinton, Iowa, operated by General Electric, is Wilfred A. Lewis, an electrical engineering graduate of Purdue University.

The Engineer in the USOE

The increasing literalization of the metaphor of the educational engineer is most appropriately symbolized by a recent addition to the high command of the U.S. Office of Education, Associate Commissioner of Education and Director of the Bureau of Research Richard Louis Bright. Bright is the controller of the mighty reservoir of research funds which is to generate the educational defense power needed to electrify our coal and gas era school system. Bright can indeed be considered forerunner of the ultimate breed of educational engineer. He is a bona fide electrical engineer, with a master's and a doctor's degree from Carnegie Tech, with prizes (Alfred Nobel Prize of the American Institute of Electrical Engineers), honors (Fellow of the Institute of Electrical and Electric Engineers), patents (semiconductor circuitry), and an outstanding record in industry (Westinghouse) to testify to his engineering capability.

But what has he done in the field of education? Well, for one thing, he has taught in a university while working for his master's and doctor's degrees. For three years thereafter, before going to Westinghouse, he taught at Carnegie Tech. Did he teach courses in the field of education? No, he taught electromagnetic field theory, servomechanisms, electronics, and machines. Anything else a little more closely related to education? Yes, in 1964 Westinghouse gave him the title of director of instructional technology and he was assigned to work with the newly formed Learning Research Development Center at the University of Pittsburgh until he was appointed Associate Commissioner in January, 1966. Is that all? Apparently yes.

Does this mean that in all of the United States, among the thousands of educational psychologists, educational researchers, college presidents, deans, etc., there were so few qualified candidates for this central role in the development of the future of U.S. education that we must choose a man whose major contracts with the broad field of education consisted of a bare two years as a Westinghouse engineer in contact with a university research center? Again, apparently yes, for as *The Educational Researcher,* official newsletter of the American Educational Research Association, points out, "Dr. Bright did not *seek* the job of heading up the Office of Education's new research bureau. It sought him.

Then some extremely unusual qualifications must have been required. Precisely. For, as *The Educational Researcher* continues, "it is clear that Commissioner Keppel wanted a research chief who had *rapport with the industrial research community. . . .*" (Italics added.) There is our clue, the "felt need" of an educator who, as Commissioner of Education and former dean of the School of Education at Harvard University, could claim the right of leadership. He wanted a man who could cope with the new view of the educational universe, namely, an industrial research engineer.

Money, the Root of . . . .

The literalization of educational engineering describes but does not explain the events just detailed. What has brought about this accelerated approximation of engineers and education? The explanations will undoubtedly range from the simple and obvious (like money) to the complex and perscrutative. With respect to money, according to the *Phi Delta Kappan,* "Experts estimate that the educational technology market in the U.S. has already reached the $500 million a year mark with a potential of $5 to $10 billion within a decade." This first figure refers only to "hardware" technology. If one were to include the monies for "software" and for design and implementation of training programs using both hardware and software (e.g., the funds of the Office of Economic Opportunity for Job Corps centers previously mentioned and the funds forthcoming from the Department of Defense to be described below), the total is already at the multi-billion-dollar level.

The money motive is occasionally publicly admitted by the business "outsiders," as in this statement by one industrial official: "When Congress passed a series of education bills last year, it awakened many outsiders to the profit potential in publishing." In general, however, more altruistic motives are offered. In assuming operating control of the Clinton, Iowa, Job Corps center, Richard L. Shelter, a former General Electric vice-president now president of the General Learning Corporation (a joint enterprise of General Electric and Time, Inc.), said:

> One of the original goals of General Learning was to make a contribution toward helping educators and government solve the problems of the school dropout and the chronically unemployable citizen. The Clinton Center . . . is a realistic laboratory for the development of new techniques which we expect will give significant help to the traditional American educational system in meeting the staggering challenges of the next decade.

Some months earlier the chairman of General Electric, Gerald L. Phillippe, had described the motives for engineering the education of 600 young women at Clinton, Ohio, in the following terms.

> What we see in Clinton is a chance to contribute to our society, a chance to help some people lead more useful and economically independent lives, and a chance to learn something important ourselves.

Those Damned Russians
One may well wonder why the unprecedented flood of money from federal headwaters should occur at this particular time in

history. A frequently heard reply, amusing in its ambivalence, is that "It's all because of those damned Russians." Silly as this explanation may sound, it has much factual evidence to support it. There is little doubt that an immediate effect of Russia's first Sputnik was to make us blink incredulously and indignantly at the suddenly glaring deficiencies of the American educational system. Among these deficiencies was the failure to recognize that the technology of national *defense* rests upon the technology of national *education.* Congress immediately responded with a correction signal, Public Law 85-864, appropriately entitled the National Defense Education Act. Since then other laws have been passed to produce additional correction signals and the Office of Education has been given sums of unprecedented magnitude for grants and contracts to provide some minimal control elements to the otherwise unintegrated components of our national educational system.

It is easy to see that industrial contractors, already doing business with the Department of Defense and familiar with the principle of industrial diversification, can readily diversify their technological potentials and interests to include educational technology, which under Public Law 85-864 *was* a component of national defense. An excellent example of the current relationships among education, defense, and industry can be seen in a joint conference held last June in Washington, D.C. According to the flyer describing the conference, its endorsers include the Department of Defense, the Office of Education, and the National Security Industrial Association.

The conference was called to order on its first day by Chairman Roy K. Davenport, Deputy Assistant Secretary, Research Office of the Secretary of Defense. Overviews of the conference were provided by such notable speakers as Thomas D. Morris, Assistant Secretary of Defense; Harold Howe II, Commissioner, Office of Education; and, for industry, by George L. Haller, Vice President, Advanced Technology Services, General Electric Company.

> The purposes of the conference, as described in the flyer, were:
> To brief industry on the magnitude and kinds of Office of Education and Department of Defense education, training, and related support activities and the procedures for formulating policy related to these specific areas.

To inform industry on DoD and OE major problems and priority areas and to advise industry of possible solutions to education and training problems.

To give industry an idea about what areas they might explore in terms of future market potentials in the four billion dollar a year DoD education and training program and in areas supported by OE.

To develop rapport between industry and DoD and OE in seeking solutions to education and training problems.

On the second day, the conference was chaired by Colonel Gabriel D. Ofiesh, USAF, OASD. Col. Ofiesh was the initiator of the largest single effort in programmed instruction in the military. Upon retirement from the Air Force last fall he became the director of Catholic University's previously described department for the output of educational engineers.

Little wonder that the conference was entitled "Engineering Systems for Education and Training Conference."

Mechanization of World Picture

Historically, the ramification of the engineering viewpoint and the penetration of its branches into the issues of other areas is a logical necessity of "the mechanization of the world picture." In a book bearing this title, E. J. Dyksterhuis, professor of the history of science in the University of Utrecht, attempts an objective historical account of how this world picture came into being.

According to his description of the various views of the world offered by science, none has been more significant in its practical effects than those which contributed to "mechanicism," the system of thought which accepted "experiment as the source of knowledge, mathematical formulation as the descriptive medium, mathematical deduction as the guiding principle in the search for new phenomena to be verified by experimentation." The success of this system of thought first in chemistry, astronomy, and physics, and then in the development of the technology which characterizes our modern industrial society has led to its inspection for possible adoption in wide realms of knowledge, remote as they may be from the commonly accepted physical and technological realms.

Up to this point, except in the title, I have tried to avoid expressions

of personal bias, even bending backwards to stick carefully to the
documentable facts as they relate to the major thesis. In what follows, I wish to state why I, personally, support the described development of educational engineering and to indicate where we go
from here. In the first place, the growth of what Dyksterhuis calls
"mechanicization" is supported by the historical facts. It is indisputable that the-concept has now penetrated most aspects of professional behavior. What is debatable is the major course of action
to take in the light of this concept. Here the decision rests upon
the personal values of the evaluator. And as Dyksterhuis recognizes,

> Some commend it as a symptom of the graduate clarification of
> human thought, of the growing application of the only method
> that is capable of producing reliable results in every sphere of
> knowledge and whose value remained unimpaired when physical
> science, in the form in which it has lately developed, was obliged
> to abandon some of the fundamental principles of classical
> mechanicism. Others, though recognizing the outstanding impor-
> tance it has had for the progress of our theoretical understand-
> ing and our practical control of nature, regard it as nothing short
> of disastrous in its general influence on philosophical and scien-
> tific thought as well as on society; they consider that for other
> branches of science to copy the working method of physical
> science is anything but a methodological ideal. They are inclined
> to look upon the domination of the mind by the mechanistic
> conception as one of the main causes of the spiritual chaos into
> which the twentieth-century world has, in spite of all its tech-
> nological progress, fallen.

It is my contention, however, that the fear which keeps us
from welcoming the scientists and engineers who can help us control human behavior is irrational. The fear is a product, precisely,
of that lack of behavioral control which we wish to overcome. The
hydrogen bomb is at one and the same time a symbol of the
heights of success and the depths of failure of the human mind.
On the one hand it expresses the almost boundless control of the
human mind over the physical world; on the other hand, the perhaps fatal lack of control of the human mind over the social world.
   But the greatest threat to civilization is not The Bomb. More
devastating weapons than The Bomb have already been conceived
by the minds of men. The greatest threat lies in the lack of control
of the social direction, development, and output of those minds.

And how is this control to be achieved? As it has been achieved for the control of the physical world, through science and technology —but the science and technology of education.

Education, if not as yet the science, is at least the technology of control of the direction, development, and output of the human mind. If we could today trace a parallel history in the development of the control of the behavior of the mind as we can for the control of the behavior of the atom; if in education we had had the equivalent stages of development leading from a Democritus to a Fermi, from a tallow flame to a laser, from a wheel to a Gemini Eleven—would we not now be more confident of our ability to control the problems of illiteracy, of overpopulation, and of interracial and international hatreds which threaten our survival?

The history of the past few hundred years tells us clearly that there is something wrong with the control systems of the developed nations. There has been no feedback to signal that the battle with physical nature for an open route for food, shelter, and health is won and that a "switchover" is required for a new mode of operation—an operation directed towards the battle with man's own nature. The symptoms and malfunction are clear. The troubleshooting must concentrate on the control systems of the mind itself.

For thousands of years, despite all experience, it had been assumed that "self-control"—the control of the mind over its own behavior—was merely a matter of "exposure" to a liberal education. Only 50 years ago we discovered control functions buried deep in man's unconscious which seemed to offer, for the first time, some empirical meaning to self-control. Only within the past few decades have we found reliable psycho-technological and psycho-pharmacological methods of achieving minimal behavioral control. These remarkable achievements have immediately raised the old familiar specter of loss of individual personality, will, and thought, whereas in fact we are for the first time at a starting point for achieving the heart's desire of civilized men—self-control. The point is that only because we know how to control atomic reactions do we have the potential of extending, almost limitlessly, man's power resources; only because we know how to control physiological reactions do we have the potential of extending man's physical life expectancies; only as we discover how to control mind-behavior will we be able to extend man's control over himself and consequently over his social life expectancy.

Meeting the Engineer Halfway

Now, assuming we are going to design complex and sophisticated control systems (we are, in fact, doing so) whom else should we call upon but those experts most knowledgeable about designing control systems—the rare expert like Bright, for example. In the beginning, of course, even the expert is going to make mistakes. Bright is most welcome at this time. But he is the breadboard model, not the prototype, of the educational engineer to come. I rejoice to hear that he has taught graduate courses in theory of servomechanisms, for it will enable him to help struggling educators who have caught only a glimpse of the significance of the concepts of information and communication control theory. On the other hand, his limited experience in education can have enabled him to catch only a glimpse of the significance of educational concepts. He will undoubtedly have much to learn from professional educators who have literally expended their lives teaching graduate courses on these less tractable concepts.

I find the growing acceptance of engineering in education exciting and encouraging. What are even more encouraging, however, are other signs, signs showing that engineering can meet education halfway in its humanistic and social requirements.

These signs can be seen, for example, in a paper by James R. Killian, Jr., chairman of the board of the Massachusetts Institute of Technology. Killian describes the new role of the engineer as increasingly one of general public responsibility. This role goes beyond design and production, research and development. Killian says:

> [The role extends to] responsibility to help society appraise, assimilate, and wisely use the torrent of new technology . . . to administer great teams of people that both use and create this advanced technology . . . to serve as an indispensable consultant and adviser to government and private organization, thus helping to shape both public and private policy . . . to deal with men as well as things.

He then shows how this responsibility is being met, citing facts and figures of engineers in all echelons of government and public service. In concluding, he accepts essentially the humanistic goal for his field: "The great opportunity for engineering today is *to help humans to be more human.*" Not more efficient, not more productive, not more economical, but more *human*. Surely, the field of education can accept this "password" as a preliminary distinction between friend and foe.

More important that the password, however, will be the behavior of engineers inside the camp. Not all fields of engineering have equal potential for contributing to education. Evaluating the potential of various fields will be an initial step and continuing process. Among those that show immediate promise, however, are some of the newer fields and subfields which, even among themselves, show an overlap of orientation. This very overlap, briefly described below, constitutes one of the characteristics of the contemporary engineering point of view which make an alliance with education possible.

According to the American Institute of Industrial Engineers, industrial engineering is concerned with the design improvement and installation of integrated systems of men, materials, and equipment. Depending upon the problem posed in integrating the system, it draws not only upon mathematicians and scientists in the physical sciences but on the social sciences as well. As a consequence, industrial engineering has developed subareas such as management, engineering, administrative engineering, and systems engineering. Let us consider but one of these, systems engineering.

Says Simon Ramo, of Bunker-Ramo and Ramo-Woolridge fame:

> Systems engineering is concerned with the creation of the entire aspect of some real life problems. . . . It is appropriately defined therefore as the design of the whole as distinct from design of the separate part. . . . The systems engineer must find ways to go from the requirement of the user . . . the individual who is asking for the solution—to the overall answer.

As a result of this perspective, the systems engineer must answer not only technical questions in his own field but must face and find answers to vexatious questions impinging upon social, economic, and political areas.

Keep in mind some educational problem, e.g., the need for a mobile meeting room and specialized library to promote participation by citizens of small communities in discussion and study of local problems, and ask yourself these questions: Is the "product" really needed? What are the assumptions upon which this need is based? Are the assumptions organizational "policy" questions? Can policy be modified or changed? What is the decision structure of the existing system into which the system under development must be fitted? How much can the "customer" afford to pay? Is the "industry" necessary to produce the "product" ready to "go," or does it have to be developed? Do we have enought of the critical personnel, professional and nonprofessional, required for the task? How are we to decide upon "contributor-participants" in the task? Must we consider participation on a "political" basis? Can we use this basis—or any basis other than competence—when, for some of the "components," even the most competent participant may not be able to produce? How much time is to be allowed for the various stages of development?

You can recognize that many of these questions are relevant to the solution of the problem. Yet these are the kinds of questions that are asked by the systems engineer involved in the production, let us say, of a missile. And this is the point; the questions are answered with tools which are not presently in the kin of education, but can be modified and developed therein.

A Two-Step Program

A brief look at fields such as systems engineering will be sufficient to prompt even further inquiry. This inquiry can hardly be continued in the present paper. To advance its rank as a science via the route of engineering, education must do more than flutter a broad pennant labeled "research," must do more than go about like Diogenes, in the broad post-sputnik daylight, with a recruiting lantern looking for an "honest" engineering man. A systematic and long-range campaign is required, and it might begin with the following simple two-step program:

1. *Consultation with and study of educational institutions such as M.I.T., military organizations such as the U.S. Naval Training Devices Center, research and development centers such as System Development Corporation, and education and training research laboratories of industrial organizations such as the Hughes Aircraft Company.* In effect this would be a survey and analysis of areas where considerable cross-fertilization of education and engineering has already taken place and where it is therefore likely that the seeds of educational engineering of the future are germinating.

2. *The development and institution of courses and a curriculum leading to a professional degree in educational engineering.* Less than 10 years ago, the number of schools offering degrees in the interface between engineering and biological sciences could be counted on the fingers of one hand, as they say. Now, almost every day another school announces the establishment of courses or degree programs in biomedical engineering, biotechnology, life science engineering, engineering biophysics, biomedical electronics, bionics, and similar fields whose names denote this engineering approach to biological problems. A similar movement in education can be anticipated following an initial impulse.

In an earlier part of this paper we have already described an interface between engineering psychology and education. This is minimal, however, as are the various courses, also previously mentioned, subsumed under educational or instructional technology. There are indications, however, that educators are willing to face more extensive and more direct contact with engineering behavior. As an example, we refer to symposia and conferences inviting engineers to discuss systems engineering, operations research, communications engineering, and the like which have been supported and reported by educational institutions and organizations.

The time is now to begin removing the large sign in the educational skies that has been written by Sputnik: "Wanted: Educational Engineers!"   □

Mr. Bern (2139, Indiana University Chapter) has been close to the technological-instruction interface as a communication officer in the Air Force; as a field service engineering instructor for the Sperry Gyroscope Company; as a research associate on the bombing-navigational computer K-System project (in the Institute of Educational Research, Indiana University); as a research psychologist, Office of Naval Research (U.S.N.) Training Devices Center, Port Washington, L.I., New York; and as head of the Research Department, Audio-Visual Center (Indiana University). He is a member of the Society of Engineering Psychologists (American Psycological Association) and the American Educational Research Association.

III

COMPARISON OF HISTORICAL AND CONTEMPORARY MOVEMENTS FOR ACCOUNTABILITY

by Paul Chapman

"A call for educators to initiate reform in the schools by adopting more rigorous, more efficient methods of measuring and evaluating output is not new. Business-education links have grown steadily since the beginnings of the public school system."

"The term educational accountability, as used most recently by certain economists, systems analysts, and the like, has frequently been based on a conceptualization that tends, by analogy, to equate the educational process with the type of engineering process that applies to industrial production. It is this sort of analogy, for instance, that appears to underlie the proposals for "guaranteed performance contracting" as exemplified in the much-publicized Texarkana project. The analogy is useful to a point. But there is also a point beyond which it can be so seriously misleading as to undermine any sensible efforts to develop objective criteria of professional accountability.

It must be constantly kept in mind that the educational process is not on all fours with an industrial process; it is a social process in which human beings are continually interacting with other human beings in ways that are imperfectly measurable or predictable."

Henry Dyer
PDK, December 1970

"If to these are added instructional technology and modern educational management theory, a new and valuable interdisciplinary field emerges. This body of knowledge, skill and procedure can be called educational engineering. Why couple the term "engineering" with education? Why more apparent dehumanization? . . . Engineering has traditionally been a problem-solving activity and a profession dedicated to the application of technology to the resolution of real-world difficulties and opportunities. While the teaching-learning environment differs from the world of business and industry, some rationalization of the two subcultures may be beneficial."

Leon Lessinger
PDK, September 1970

". . . the era of contentment with large, undefined purposes is rapidly passing. An age of science-is demanding exactness and particularity.

The technique of scientific method is at present being developed for every important aspect of education. Experimental laboratories and schools are discovering accurate methods of measuring and evaluating different types of educational processes. Bureaus of education measurement are discovering scientific methods of analyzing results, of diagnosing specific situations, and of prescribing remedies. Scientific method is being applied to the fields of budget-making, child-accounting, systems of grading and promotion, etc."

Franklin Bobbitt
The Curriculum, 1918

"Shall we turn education over to corporate enterprises which has avariciously exploited and depleted our resources with no eye to the future? Shall we turn education over to corporate boards of directors who are still reluctant to consider the terrible blights they have created on the ecological landscape? Shall we turn our children over to profit-motivated business managers who have a long record of sacrificing human values to the almighty dollar? Shall we allow a fragmentation of the school population, leaving the establishment of educational values to the vagaries of persons whose basic motivations may be at complete odds with the well-being of society?"

Larry Sibelman
The American Teacher, 1970

The statements by Lessinger, Dyer, and Sibelman document the current controversy about the appropriateness of the business-efficiency model in education. But as the passage from Bobbitt's landmark work suggests, a call for educators to intitiate reform in the schools by adopting more rigorous, more efficient methods of measuring and evaluating output is not new. In fact, recent literature on the history of U.S. education indicates that the business-education link has grown steadily since the beginnings of the public school system. According to studies by David Tyack and Michael Katz, [39, 40] the bureaucratization and centralization of the common school in the late 19th century followed the lines of business corporate organization. Hugh Hawkins has also investigated the relationship of industry and the emerging university at the turn of the century.[41]

Early Demands for Efficiency in Education

Raymond Callahan's *Education and the Cult of Efficiency,* more than any other study raises striking comparisons between the early 20th century use of business methods in education and the accountability surge of today.[42] He traces the tremendous impact of the book *Principles of Scientific Management* (1911) by Frederick W. Taylor, whose organizational ideas were applied to virtually all phases of U.S. society. Callahan believes that "very much of what has happened in American education since 1900 can be explained on the basis of the extreme vulnerability of our schoolmen to public criticism and pressure" and that "this vulnerability is built into our pattern of local support and control."

What advantages and disadvantages can we expect from our new efficiency experts? How "vulnerable" are school administrators today to the pressure for accountability and efficiency? Will the current quest for efficiency result in yet another "descent into trivia" and a second "tragedy of American education?"

The current trends are most dramatically illustrated by the sudden emergence of performance contracting. Much has been written and said about performance contracts in the past two years, continuing the old debate over the appropriate relationship between business and education. The passage from Bobbitt's 50-year old work puts a current dialog between two schoolboard members in a different perspective:[43]

> They (the public) don't give a damn about those administrative niceties. They want results and it's *our* boardroom they storm when they don't get them. If performance contracting can provide us with a means of demonstrating the results the public wants—and is entitled to—then I'm for it.

> Performance contracting . . . can never be allowed to become one more of those terrible infusions that are making education less humane and less child-centered, at the very time that education needs to address itself more singularly than ever to the human needs of the individual child.

At lease since the Civil War, the U.S. business community has influenced in varying degrees the membership, content, and aims of the educational system. The recent development of performance contracting is a new and potentially radical phase of the business-education symbiosis, but the concept of the schools borrowing techniques and philosophies from business managers to achieve greater rigor and productivity is not new. We can gain a valuable perspective on the accountability issue by comparing the current period with the early 20th century reform era on five counts: (1) the substance of business techniques in the schools, (2) the reform climate, (3) the nature of school criticism, (4) efficiency as a panacea, and (5) efficiency's effects on education.

The Role of Business in Education: Principles and Mechanics

Taylor's *Principles of Scientific Management* was not directed exclusively at the schools, but rather dealt with general rules for an efficient system of management in industry. His theory was derived from three case studies of manual-labor—bricklaying, work at a ball-bearing plant, and loading pig iron at the Bethlehem steel yards. First brought to public attention during Interstate Commerce Commission investigations into the causes of railroad bankruptcy, the system was quickly and enthusiastically applied to many areas as diverse as the army, navy, law, church, home and education. When applied to the schools, Taylorism meant that a great deal of attention had to be paid to the many mechanical and often superficial aspects pertaining to the organization and day-to-day operation of the school. Since the ideas were originally developed in relation to the industrial work process, the theory had nothing to say about curriculum and instruction. But the decision of school administrators to accept what was in essence a "factory model" for school management implicitly subordinated the strictly educational aspects of the institution to those concerned with plant, maintenance, and operation.

When the efficiency experts of this period *did* conduct their analysis in terms of students and "educational output," the results were usually trivial exercises in number pushing. One example is a study of "retardation and elimination" in city school systems entitled *Laggards in Our Schools,* published in 1909 by Leonard Ayres. The work purports to arrive at an "index of efficiency" for the public schools of 58 different cities, based on the percentage of "raw materials" (entering students) that they are able to retain, process, and "get out."

The analogy between performance contracting and scientific management is not strained. The underlying purpose of each is to gain greater productivity from human labor. Each relies on a "one best method," whether it concerns purchasing school supplies or learning to read. Taylor's management system used five basic steps —time and motion studies, improvement of tools, analysis by experts, standardization for the entire system, and task-reward motivation. Performance contracting operates analogously—development of a science of reading, improvement of educational materials such as programmed reading machines, educational technology companies offering expert advice, standardization of the system, and task-reward motivation.

When and how have educators adopted these systems? What effect have they had on the instruction of the child?

The Reform Ethos

The rise of the educational efficiency expert in 1911 and again in 1969 rested on three preconditions: (1) prevailing sentiment in favor of reform, (2) a vogue for business techniques in all areas of society, and (3) *economic pressure* which made efficiency a prime concern. In 1911, Progressivism and the Square Deal had created a climate for change. Specific school developments also paved the way for this efficiency expert. The newly-created, centralized boards of education sought to reduce inefficiency by consolidating functions, reducing membership, and "taking education out of partisan politics." Industry pressured educators for a more practical curriculum to serve business' rising manpower needs.

Also, around 1911 scientific management was applied to a variety of governmental and social institutions. Thus, according to Callahan, several factors created a situation ripe for Taylor's "gospel of efficiency"—the dominance of businessmen and their values, a new cost-conscience and reform-minded public, an attack on the mismanagement of all American institutions, and the rising cost of living.[44]

Similar factors seemed to be operating early in 1969. The legislative change during the Kennedy-Johnson years created an ethos of reform, while the Vietnam War and the inflationary depression since 1968 produced the dual desire for change and efficiency. Since the decline of progressive education in the 1950s and the shock of Sputnik, business and technological values have gained a new legitimacy for the schools. PPBS and the cost-effectiveness were instituted by Robert McNamara in the Department of Defense, suggesting that perhaps the public was ready to accept business solutions for the mismanagement of U.S. institutions. Raymond A. Ehrle recently made the connection between reform and efficiency:[45] "In this day of increased competition for national resources . . . it is expected that performance contracting will be increasingly relied upon to meet the vast number of priority projects and problems which must be addressed." Thus while performance contracting appears to be a new historical phenomenon, it rises out of conditions very similar to those that produced the first cult of efficiency.

The Criticism of the Schools: Muckrakers and Vulnerability
        In 1911 and again in 1969 the unique combination of intense criticism of the schools and the extreme "vulnerability" of school board members and superintendents accounted for the rapid acceptance of industrial technology in the schools. Witness, for example, the kind of criticism leveled at the New York schools in the very year Taylor's *Principles* was published. Why, asked Simon Patten, a well-known educator and economist, should New York support "inefficient school teachers instead of efficient milk inspectors. Must definite reforms with measurable results give way that an antiquated school system may grind out its useless products?"[46] And witness, too, the process by which efficiency experts made changes that the public rapidly sanctioned. Jesse B. Sears, a leader of the school survey movement, described how criticism brought the business model to education:

> With a critical public opinion demanding economy and efficiency, and with a new conception of education growing rapidly into a science of education, we had both the motive and the means by which the survey movement could take form. . . . Naturally, then, when boards of education called upon *educational experts* to help point the way out of difficulties, the idea was promptly understood and sanctioned by the public, *and the school survey movement had begun.*[47]

The intense pressure for school reform has resulted in part in the rapid development of performance contracting. Recall the first board member who said, "If performance contracting can provide us with a means of demonstrating the results the public wants—and is entitled to—then I'm for it." A recent survey (December 1970) showed that although 89 percent of administrators surveyed thought their teachers were "doing their jobs well today," 72 percent were also in favor of "making teachers formally accountable in some way for the academic performance of their students."[48] Compelled on the one hand to defend the status quo, forced on the other to demonstrate results, administrators naturally look for a means to alleviate the public pressure—and performance contracting is a likely avenue to pursue.

The climates in 1911 and 1969, while similar in the mere presence of hostile criticism and schoolboard vulnerability, were not entirely analogous. For one, the nature of the criticism was different. Muckrakers in the early 1900s called for better resource allocation and lower expenditures. They had no quarrel with the free enterprise system—they just wanted to oil the machinery. The critics of the 1960s called for this and more. For the first time they wanted better results. Their criticism probed to greater depths and questioned the validity and legitimacy of the public school itself.[49] The administrators in 1911 also were less well organized as a profession, and teachers were only beginning to unionize. Overall, school personnel were more vulnerable in 1911 and consequently responded to pressure more rapidly. By 1969 school administrators had closed ranks, and while sensitive to criticism they did not demonstrate as rapid a response as 50 years earlier. Their respect for the increasing militancy and political strength of teachers' unions has also been a sobering factor.

The Great Panacea

Differences in the reform climate, the nature of criticism, vulnerability, and the extent of support and opposition accounted for the varying speed of responses. The earlier adoption of scientific management was lightning fast and all-encompassing. According to Callahan, it became a "great panacea" for U.S. educators and public. Although the initial support for performance contracting has been equally sudden in many school districts; how long lasting the effect will be still looms as a very large question.

Scientific management's supporters were both numerous and influential. Businessmen, "efficiency agencies," superintendents, most school board members, professional educators and administrators (e.g., Frank Spaulding, Franklin Bobbitt, and Ellwood P. Cubberly) all backed scientific management with evangelical fervor. The advocates claimed it provided an enriched program *and* saved tax dollars, but says Callahan, "It is also clear that the economy feature was the primary factor in its appeal."[50]

The opposition was scattered, unorganized, and for the most part "unavailing" in its dissent. Samuel Gompers spoke for the fledgling American Federation of Labor in 1911 when he protested that efficiency experts were just one more management device to "get the most out of you before you are sent to the junk pile.[51] Robert Hoxie, investigating the system for the U.S. Commission on Industrial Relations in 1921, warned that many efficiency experts were "fakirs" and "industrial patent-medicine men."[52] A few renegade administrators like William E. Maxwell of New York City noted the faddism involved:

> In the first stage, everything hitherto done in the schools is wrong; in the second stage, if the new theory receives any popular support, everything will be well; the new subject or the new method is a panacea that will cure all educational ills; in the third stage, the practical teachers have divested the new theory of its superfluous trappings, have swept away the preposterous claims of its advocates, and have discovered and used whatever small kernel of truth it contains or conceals. . .[53]

A few teachers in cities where unions were strongest ventured to oppose scientific management. Benjamin C. Gruenberg gave the strongest rebuttal in 1911 when he said:

We have contested to measure the results of educational efforts
in terms of price and product—the terms that prevail in the factory and the department store. But education, since it deals in
the first place with organisms, and in the second place with in-
dividualities, is not analogous to a standardizable manufacturing
process. Education must measure its efficiency not in terms of
so many promotions per dollars of expenditure, nor even in
terms of so many student-hours per dollar of salary; it must mea
measure its efficiency in terms of increased humanism, increased
power to do, increased capacity to appreciate.[54]

Will performance contracting bring a new cult of efficiency?
At this point, it is difficult to gauge the future of industry's re-
entry into education. Plans for educational television and computers, devices that were to revolutionize education, have failed to
meet expectations, prompting one businessman to ask recently,
"Has the Education Industry Lost Its Nerve?"[55] But performance
contracting exploded on the scene much like scientific management entered Taylor's *Principles* in 1911. Launched in 1969 as a
dropout retention program in Texarkana, Arkansas, performance
contracts in the 1970-71 school year were operating in more than
170 school districts. Educational technology companies have increased ten-fold since 1969 to more than 100. In July of 1970, the
federal government increased its support by awarding $6.5 million
dollars for contracts and enlisted The RAND Corporation to study
the projects and prepare a guide for schools contemplating a future
contract. Judging from the recent flood of journal articles on performance contracting and accountability, historians 20 years from
now might well conclude that this was a new efficiency cult on
the rise.

The adamant resistance offered by the American Federation
of Teachers summarizes some of the opposition's points of contention. Robert Bhaerman, director of research for the AFT, has
called performance contracting a Nixon-big business plot designed
to absorb the new demands for work as military and space contracts are cut back. In its official news publication, the *American
Teacher,* the AFT has leveled the charges that performance contracting takes the determination of educational policy out of the
public control, threatens to create a highly potent business monopoly in education, tends to dehumanize the learning process, sows
distrust among teachers, promotes teaching to the test, subverts

collective bargaining by reducing teacher input, and is unsound in its machine orientation.[56] The AFT has threatened strikes in several cities where performance contracts, or some other accountability scheme, have been initiated, notably in Gary, Seattle and Washington, D.C.

However, the majority opinion seems to be one of wait and see. Industry remains cautious since profits are frequently uncertain. High start-up costs and single-year OEO grants have kept the larger research and publishing companies from entering the field. The average break even point, for instance, is a reading increase of 1.6 grade levels, or roughly three times the national yearly advance. The National Education Association, while deploring "the OEO performance contracting program" because it will "weaken the structure of the public school system and . . . discredit the school in the eyes of the public," has tentatively approved contracts between school systems and teacher unions.[57] School administrators, as represented by the earlier quotations, appear divided as a recent poll shows.[43]

If the "age of accountability" did dawn in Texarkana, and performance contracting is to spearhead the movement, the proof is still several years away.

A Tragedy of American Education?

Callahan concludes that "the wholesale adoption of the basic values, as well as the techniques of the business-industrial world, was a serious mistake in an institution whose primary purpose was the education of children.[58] Two major questions arise. One question is, was there a "tragedy?" Is there no room for the so-called business tools and techniques in education? Were there any benefits from the use of scientific management? The other question is whether there will be a new cult of efficiency in the 1970s?

Perhaps the best way to approach the first series of questions is to note the attractiveness of contractors' claims for their product; performance contracts promote management efficiency and intelligent cost consciousness, provide an excellent method of teaching certain basic skills, individualize instruction, can be institutionalized and integrated into the present system through the "turnkey" approach, and help to increase the student's self-concept through behavior modification and frequent rewards. Some of the smaller concerns can be easily remedied through close and accurate controls—contractor dishonesty, fake companies, teaching to the test and antiteacher bias. Deeper and more fundamental issues, however, cast doubt on the entire concept. There *is* the danger that "accountability" will become a new panacea—yet another sandbox for school officials to stick their heads in. Performance contracting rests on several questionable assumptions—that teaching skills can be fragmented, that reading skills have little to do with verbal skills and can be taught solely by programmed instruction, and that education is merely a process of absorption rather than critical thinking.

Will there be a new "cult of efficiency?" To a certain extent the first age of efficiency has never passed. A fundamental criticism of Callahan's study is that it fails to recognize the infusion of business values in schools during the 19th century, a process uncovered several years later in the research of David Tyack and Michael Katz. The events after 1911 did not represent a detour. Like the performance contracting movement, they were part of a broad history of business in education.

To be sure, there seem to be too many reluctant persons who are opposed to performance contracting to allow this particular accountability measure another conquest in the fashion of scientific management. The question is whether accountability will gradually become the order of the day in school districts across the country, i.e., whether there is enough dissatisfaction among student, parents, and educators to compel individual districts to seek out the kind of plan that is well suited to their needs. It is not generally feasible for a performance contractor to take over *all* managerial and educational responsibilities as happened in Gary, Indiana. In other words, if there is to be a new wave of efficiency in education—the growth of an era of accountability—then the change will be incremental rather than sudden and large scale. No one method such as performance contracting will win nationwide support as scientific management did a half-century ago. Only time will tell to what extent the entrenched, bureaucratic educational system—in part a product of that proliferation of Taylorism in the early 20th century—will prove capable of yielding to this or any other form of significant reform.   □

Paul Chapman is a Graduate Student, at Stanford University, California.

[39] Katz, Michael B., "The Emergence of Bureaucracy in Urban Education: The Boston Case, 1850-1884," *History of Education Quarterly,* Summer and Fall, 1968.

[40] Tyack, David, "Bureaucracy and the Common School: The Example of Portland, Oregon, 1851-1913," *The Emerging University and Industrial America,* Lexington, Massachusetts, 1970.

[41] Hawkins, Hugh, "The Relationship of Industry and Higher Education," Ibid.

[42] Callahan, Raymond E., Education and the Cult of Efficiency, Chicago, 1962, p. viii.

[43] "Performance Contracting: Is It the Tool for the New Boardmanship?", *American School Board Journal,* November 1970.

[44] Callahan, p. 18.

[45] Ehrle, Raymond A., "National Priorities and Performance Contracting," *Educational Technology,* July 1970.

[46] Callahan, p. 48.

[47] Ibid., p. 188.

[48] *Nation's Schools,* Vol. 86, December 1970, p. 33.

[49] See for example, Fred M. Newmann and Donald W. Oliver, "Education and Community," *Harvard Educational Review,* Vol. 37, No. 1 Winter 1967; and Charles V. Hamilton, "Race and Education: A Search for Legitimacy," *Harvard Educational Review,* Vol. 38, Fall 1968.

[50] Callahan, p. 155.

[51] Ibid., in note, pp. 40-41.

[52] Ibid., p. 41.

[53] Ibid., p. 123.

[54] Ibid., p. 121.

[55] Locke, Robert W., "Has the Education Industry Lost Its Nerve?", *Saturday Review,* January 16, 1971.

[56] Bhaerman, Robert, *Education Turnkey News,* December-January, 1970.

[57] *Nation's Schools,* Vol. 86, October, 1970, p. 87.

[58] Callahan, p. 244.

IV

AN EDUCATOR'S VIEW
OF INDUSTRIAL AND EDUCATIONAL GROWTH*

by Ralph A. Smith

"Should educational form follow industrial form? Or are there grounds for contesting the imputed analogy between industrial and educational enterprise?"

In American economic thought the notions of industrial and educational growth are closely related. It is assumed that continuous economic growth demands technological expansion and that the ability to apply scientific and other organized knowledge to sophisticated problem solving requires increasingly higher levels of education. To ensure that supply will meet demand, or not lag too far behind, manpower studies are diligently undertaken by practically all concerned with planning. The consequence is that education is pressed into meeting the needs of industry. As the need for educated manpower becomes greater, the government intervenes with incentives to universities to encourage entry of students into strategic disciplines and professions. The consequence of this is that industry, government, and education become functionally interdependent.

There is a further assumption, perhaps not universally shared, that industrial societies converge to roughly similar modes of organization and planning. One such point of convergence is industry's need to control markets in order to protect heavy investments in research and development. However, there are also indisputable cultural variations and this fact has given rise to a "convergence-divergence hypothesis"[1] regarding the effects of industrialization which promises to increase substantially our knowledge in this area.

Reprinted with copyright permission of *Educational Forum*, November, 1970, pp. 15-23 and Kappa Delta Pi, an Honor Society in Education.

What is already certain is that education has become more crucial to industrial growth. And as large numbers of students have come to characterize institutions of education one also hears that industrial form, so well suited to the efficient handling of large quantities, should be imposed on educational form, particularly in higher education which supplies industry and government with much of its manpower. Education, too, it is said, has a responsibility to plan efficiently, to maximize investments, to insure full use of physical plant, etc. Educational institutions can thus be organized along the lines of factories and corporations. Accordingly, Richard J. Barber has remarked that "our major universities have increasingly taken on the character of businesses. With huge budgets and large numbers of employees and students, they have assumed the character of any large enterprise, complete with a covey of vice presidents and diverse management specialists. Their enormous scientific capacity and rich human resources have made them natural allies of business and government."[2]

The attempt to rationalize educational activities has been a recurrent feature in the history of American education,[3] which should not occasion surprise given the pervasive role business has played in American life. Today it is manifested not only in "systems" approaches to educational administration but also in educational research where as a necessary condition for the assessment of educational achievement emphasis is being placed on the specification of educational outcomes in precise behavioral terms. In short, the plainly visible hand of the efficiency expert is once again reaching out into academia.

Some would say that this is the price education must pay for being taken seriously. Having become a crucial factor in a nation's economic and social achievement, education must now submit to constraints that render its performance more manageable. Of course nothing like a complete rationalization of education has occurred in the United States, nor is it likely to occur in the future. But considerable harm may be done if the purposes of different kinds of institutions—in the present case industry and education—are not understood. Should educational form follow industrial and educational enterprise? I believe there are. The structure of universities in particular is so fundamentally different from that of industries that were education to submit to industrial order it would lose its essential character. So I will first indicate why I think it is unwise to use an industrial model for thinking about institutions of learning. The latter part of the paper will speculate about the future relationship of industry and education.

Industrial Form and Educational Form

An analysis of the dynamics of mass societies reveals a tendency to rationalize any activity involving large quantities of materials and numbers of people. The rationalization of industrial processes is a well-known story. Its animating force has been technology whose imperatives are long-range planning, large capital investment, precise specification of tasks, high degrees of specialization and coordination, control of market conditions, and the creation of human wants.[4] I will not spin out the details of technology here. To do so would be tedious.

But what about education? There is initial plausibility to the belief that the logic of technology can be applied to educational enterprise. Education, as indicated above, is big business. It involves large expenditures and the structure of any large American university reveals a high degree of specialization and division of labor. As in industry so in the university parts are supposed to bear some relationship to each other, courses and programs are expected to add up to an educational product, and efforts are made to assess this product. Thus in addition to specialization, in any large university there must also be coordination and measurement. Power relations in the university also resemble the authority structure in the new corporation. Power, prestige, and status pass to those with special skills and knowledge, which has the effect of dif diffusing authority and modifying older line and staff hierarchies. But some of these similarities are more apparent than real, and the likenesses are often superficial. In other respects there is no resemblance whatsoever between industrial and educational institutions.

First, there is a greater plurality of aims and purposes in education which rules out the formulation of a single precisely defined goal or end. This situation, in which goals conflict with each other, implies that coordination consists of making innumerable adjustments among competing philosophies of education within a given university. As Charles Frankel has written: ". . . university administrators cannot create a total plan of work, define jobs within it, and then assign individual workers to them. . . . The product of a factory is a corporate product to which individuals contribute.

The product of a university is many separate, individual products, for which the corporate arrangements provide protection and support, but for which the individuals have basic responsibility."[5] Jacques Barzun adds that it is indeed a species of magic to manage the mélange of courses, programs, institutes, and centers that comprise the American university, and that it may take a new administrator two years just to learn what's going on.[6] Self-respecting industrialists and management specialists find this situation intolerable, and they would be justified if education had the same purpose as business. But it does not and can not.

As for the student, he is hardly raw material being processed for predetermined uses. Moreover, whatever is done to the student is for *his* benefit and not for that of the university or "company," and no graduating class is properly construed in profit and loss categories. If we ask in the university who the prime beneficiary is the answer must be the student. What is the benefit? Ideally, certain qualities of mind, or those educated dispositions which enable students to participate in various domains of intellectual, moral, and aesthetic value. Now qualities of mind and human dispositions, unlike industrial products, are not cultivated with a view to their rapid obsolescence, but rather for a lifetime. True, universities often fail to initiate students into the life style of the educated person, but in a mass society education will always be difficult. The task of the university is further complicated by the competition it receives from other potent educational forces—the formidable campus peer culture, for example, or the ubiquitous mass media.

But if pluralism, divergence, and tension between different domains of educational influence are in certain respects vices, especially in the eyes of those who see industrial form as the paradigm for rationalization, they are also the virtues that help to keep universities alive and vital. The almost structureless structure of the American university is what enables it to function as an important critical institution, the only one that, again ideally, owes allegiance to no extrinsic interests save those of understanding and truth. Nothing could destroy the atmosphere necessary for free inquiry more completely than the effort to rationalize educational institutions in the manner of industry. Where else but in the university can the function of scholarly inquiry be freely undertaken? Where else can tradition be continuously renewed and its insights

brought to bear on the problems of the present? Where else can
the future be projected with objective detachment? Where else can
the arts mingle so well to their mutual benefit?[7]

Perhaps I am guilty of belaboring the obvious. But there is no
little political capital being made today by those who think that
the schools and universities should begin to show explicit returns
on investments, and loosely conceived and misleading analogies
abound. But the university is not a factory or firm or corporation,
which is to say that professors and administrators are not primarily
employers or managers or production heads, nor are students essentially employees or hirelings or inanimate raw material to be
used in manufacturing. Growth rates in industry and education
mean different things. The university is an institution whose
unique business is learning and research. And for this purpose it
has evolved a distinctive structure. Technical rationality has an important role to play in running a university but only insofar as it
functions to provide the apparatus for creating the best conditions
possible for studying and learning. But now what of the future of
industry and education?

The Future of Industry and Education

It seems I have argued against any intimate relationship between industry and education, for I have tried to show that despite
the interdependence between industry and education due to the
need for educated manpower, and despite the industry-like appearance of educational institutions which "process" huge numbers of
students, differences of purpose and form make industry and education ultimately incommensurate. Industry and education are
nonetheless intimately related by their joint task of meeting what
is perhaps the greatest challenge from the future. The nature of
this challenge will be explained via a brief discussion of some critiques of proposed new directions for the economic system.

One such critique is contained in John Kenneth Galbraith's
The New Industrial State[8] —a work, he tells us, that is the structure
into which his earlier *The Affluent Society*[9] provided a first
glimpse. Praised by progressive liberals for his devotion to public
and social goals, scorned by conservaties who both understand and
misunderstand his argument, regarded with contempt by specialists who find his generalism unsettling, Galbraith demands
response.

The key to Galbraith's analysis is his description of the Accepted and Revised Sequences of economic activity.[10] In the Accepted Sequence, images of which still dominate conventional thinking, the consumer expresses his wants and preferences by giving signals to producers in an open market situation. These wants and desires are then supplied by the producers. In the Revised Sequence of economic activity, corporations reach out through extensive advertising to persuade consumers to want the goods and services produced by industry. It is the Revised Sequence that makes up by far the greater part of economic reality today, although the Accepted Sequence co-exists with it in diminished magnitude. The Revised Sequence is a response to (a) the imperatives of technology which demand the protection of heavy investments in planning and development, and (b) the diminished urgency of wants on the part of people who no longer live at a minimum subsistence level. This means that their preferences are more malleable and subject to influence by others. "Affluence," a fruit of modern technology, becomes a factor in perpetuating the system that made it possible which up to a certain point works to the benefit of many in society. To assure expansion and growth, however, industry must create and manage new wants, and under such conditions it is naive to believe that a free market situation can exist. The questions then become whether the goals of industry are congruent with visions of the good life and whether social achievement in general is to be assessed primarily in terms of ever greater economic growth rates.

Galbraith has serious doubts since the imperatives of technological expansion inhibit commitment to significant non-technological goals such as aesthetic experience. Yet more than any other institution in the United States, industry—due to its failure to control pollution and its use of a dissonant system of advertising—is responsible for the deteriorating quality of life. The use of the United States defense and military establishment as a convenient means to pace economic growth is also highly dangerous. (True, cold and hot wars are also responsible for the growth of the military sector. But defense needs to not account for all growth in this area.)[11] There are reasons, then, for questioning the consequences of a continual commitment to increased production. The issue, it should be emphasized, is not the validity of economic goals and technological expansion, but rather the rates of growth

and the appropriate control and regulation of industrial enterprise
in areas where it impinges adversely on the quality of life.

It is precisely at this point that future studies are extremely
important. Those to whom we usually attribute the ability to project images of the future—our artists, writers, poets, and film-
makers—do not at the moment seem to be responding to this challenge. As I review contemporary artistic effort, and I elaborate this
point because the arts are a powerful educational force, the principal concern seems to be with a nostalgic portrayal of a passing era
or with a future that focuses on the life styles of small technological elites. When portraying the present, contemporary artists seem
to be obsessed with sex, violence, and the adulation of youth. Rare
is the contemporary film that deals seriously with the themes of
science, humanism, and politics, or with the responsible conduct
of the industrial enterprise[12] . I talk moreover as one with a vested
interest in aesthetic studies who agrees with those who say that
when a new life style does take hold it will probably be because
large numbers of people have been seduced by persuasive aesthetic
images of it, and that the unpredictability of the conditions under
which this will occur is the primary justification for supporting
creativity and the avant-garde.[13] But for the time being alternative
images of the future are being forged not by our artists but by a
mixed bag of social and physical scientists. For the time being, at
least in the United States, we look to persons such as Kenneth
Galbraith, Kenneth Boulding, Herman Kahn, Anthony Wiener,
and Daniel Bell for ideas about the future. This is, as I said, a
mixed assortment of futurists, and I can make only the briefest
reference to some of their ideas.

Kenneth Boulding may be singled out as another economist
worth mentioning because he seems to have an approach to two of
the problems raised in this essay. For one thing, his notion of
"spaceship earth" as well as other concrete images and metaphors
are such that they can help educate men's imagination about the
future in a way that contemporary art is currently failing to do.
Secondly, his bold proposals for a new type of economic thought
might prove a corrective for many of the things Galbraith criticizes
in the Revised Sequence.

We are, says Boulding, in the middle of a transition of the
image man has of himself and of his environment.[14] We are finally
moving away from a conception of earth as an illimitable plane

offering constantly new frontiers to conquer and toward a conception of the earth as a closed sphere or system. The notions of open and closed systems are central to Boulding's concern, although several other concepts need to be introduced for a more adequate understanding. An open system is defined as one in which some kind of structure is maintained in the midst of throughput from inputs to outputs. In the economic system—the "econosphere," as Boulding calls it—"throughput" would be the specifically economic part. Throughput is everything involved in the industrial plant, the processing of raw materials into products, and the distribution and even the consumption of goods. "Input" refers to the noneconomic reservoirs of raw materials and energy, while "output" refers to the noneconomic reservoirs, such as the oceans and the atmosphere, into which wastes and pollution are discharged when production and consumption, i.e., throughput, have run their course. In the present open economic system the only accepted measure of economic success is throughput, meaning the rates of production and consumption or the amount of the Gross National Product. And this, thinks Boulding, will have to change.

Before trying to indicate what changes Boulding would advocate, it might be helpful to point out one further distinction. The econosphere as we now know it is open with respect to three kinds of inputs and outputs: information, matter, and energy. Among the many interesting things Boulding has to say about information inputs and outputs I will mention only two. First of all, the knowledge system is of fundamental importance to the econosphere, and he cites as an example the amazingly rapid recovery of Germany and Japan from wartime destruction of its industrial plant; this was possible because the knowledge system had been preserved intact. Secondly, the production of knowledge must always exceed its consumption if a nation is to continue to progress economically.

But our situation is most serious with respect to matter and energy inputs and outputs because we have too long blinded ourselves to the fact that non-economic reservoirs are exhaustible and are rapidly being depleted because of the way our open economic system operates. We must, then, attempt to approach a closed system, i.e., one in which the outputs of all parts of the system are linked to inputs of other parts. It would by a system in which all outputs from consumption would constantly be recycled to become inputs for production, and this, claims Boulding, is conceivable in the case of matter or raw material. But *any* throughput, even in a closed system of matter, requires large inputs of energy, and as long as we depend on fossil fuels and fissionable materials as sources, a closed system with respect to energy cannot be achieved and available supplies will become exhausted. Eventually we will probably have to devise ways of satisfying all energy needs from solar energy.

As this brief sketch indicates, the technological problems that must be solved in transforming an open into a closed economic system—or, to use Boulding's more colorful phrases, in abandoning an expansionist "cowboy economy" for a "spacemean economy" without unlimited resources of any kind—are staggering. But at least as difficult is the chance in attitude that must be brought about, especially in the attitude toward consumption. Production and consumption will no longer be regarded as intrinsically desirable. The measure of economic success will no longer be the quantity of throughput. On the future spaceship earth the measure of economic success will have to be the nature, extent, quality, and complexity of the total available capital stock, including human bodies and states of mind. The less consumption that is needed to maintain a given state of well being, the better off we shall be. The economy of the spaceship earth will thus have to be parsimonious, but it need not be impoverished. Heedlessness and wastefulness will have to be replaced by dedicated care to preserve the homeostasis of the total capital stock of the system. Life, says Boulding, can no longer resemble a parade ground but must assume the character of a tea ceremony.

The challenges to both industry and education—the plane upon which both must re-establish a close relationship—should now be obvious. Education, especially within the research-oriented institutions of higher learning, must of course continue to provide input for the knowledge system to keep the production of information abreast of its consumption and entropy; it will also have to supply the highly specialized manpower which increasingly more sophisticated technology will demand. But this is really not a new role for education. What will be new is that in addition to preparing young persons *for* the econosphere, education must also make them knowledgeable *about* the econosphere. Educated consumers, for instance, should not be the hapless victims of economic manipulation in the kind of system which Galbraith calls the Revised

Sequence. Moreover, persons educated about the econosphere and its precarious balance can perhaps reinstate a more enlightened version of the Accepted Sequence: they will demand of industry only those goods and services that do not endanger the maintenance of the capital stock in a closed system. In short, it will be one of education's most pressing tasks to develop responsible consumers.

The challenges to industry are at least as great and are by no means limited to following the cues received from educated and ecology-minded consumers. The utmost in inventiveness and ingenuity will be required to adjust the industrial plant to a closed economy marked by recycling and new forms of energy. But why, it will be asked by some, should industry make such gigantic efforts and start preparing for them now? Why not reap profits and let the future take care of itself? Why should so much self-discipline be exercised in order not to leave a depleted earth to posterity? Answers to these questions need not lie in the realm of philosophic speculation. Nothing more exalted than self-interest needs to be appealed to, for failure to resolve many of our current problems will affect not some distant posterity, but members of this generation and the next. As Boulding puts it: ". . . tomorrow is not only very close, but in many respects it is already here. The shadow of the future spaceship, indeed, is already falling over our spendthrift merriment."[15]   □

This is a slightly revised version of an invited address presented to the International Seminar on Industrial Soceity and Management in the Future, Tokyo, April 23, 1970 sponsored by the Nippon Office Management Association.

The author of this thoughtful article is Associate Professor of Education in the Bureau of Educational Research at the University of Illinois. Coincidentally, the last part of the paper, which seems to be very relevant to Earth Day, was delivered on Earth Day in Japan. Professor Smith's interest in Futurism represents but one side of his academic activity; one of his major concerns is aesthetic education, and he is the editor of the *Journal of Aesthetic Education.*

[1] Bernard Karsh and Robert E. Cole, "Industrialization and the Convergence Hypothesis: Some Aspects of Contemporary Japan," *Journal of Social Issues,* 24, 4:45-64 (October, 1968).

[2] *The American Corporation* (New York: E. P. Dutton & Co., 1970), p. 106.

[3] Raymond E. Callahan, *Education and the Cult of Efficiency* (Chicago, University of Chicago Press, 1962).

[4] John Kenneth Galbraith, *The New Industrial State* (Boston: Houghton Mifflin Co., 1967).

[5] Charles Frankel, *Education and the Barricades* (New York: W. W. Norton & Co., 1968), pp. 42-43.

[6] Jacques Barzun, *The American University* (New York: Harper & Row, 1968), pp. 114, 117.

[7] There are, of course, other functions which a university performs. For a brief typology that might have relevance to the future administration of universities, see Daniel Bell, "Quo Warranto?—Notes on the Governance of Universities in the 1970's," *The Public Interest,* No. 19 (Spring, 1970).

[8] Galbraith, *op. cit.*

[9] 2nd Ed. (Boston: Houghton Mifflin Co., 1969).

[10] Galbraith, *The New Industrial State,* Chap. 19.

[11] Seymour Melman, "Who Decides Technology?" *Columbia Forum,* II, 4:13-16 (Winter, 1968).

[12] There are, of course, some important exceptions. See e.g., Albert William Levi, *Humanism and Politics* (Bloomington: Indiana University Press, 1969). But the content of Hollywood films and of television in general—the contemporary art that reaches most people—does not project responsible images of the future.

[13] Harry S. Broudy, "The Artist and the Future," *Journal of Aesthetic Education,* 4, 1:11-22 (January, 1970).

[14] See especially "The Economics of the Coming Spaceship Earth," in *Beyond Economics* (Ann Arbor: University of Michigan Press, 1968) and "The Great Society in a Small World: Dampening Reflections from the Dismal Science," in Bertram M. Gross (ed.), *A Great Society?* (New York: Basic Books, 1966).

[15] Boulding, "The Economics of the Coming Spaceship Earth," p. 285.

V

DISCUSSION: THE EDUCATION INDUSTRIES

by Edward L. Katzenbach
Raytheon Company

"Industry looks upon education both as a business opportunity and as a service opportunity."

Much has been said and written over the past two years about the entry of industry into education: its significance, its potential for good, and its dangers—both real and imaginary.

Let me state at the outset my conviction that there is an enormous potential for good in the developing partnership between education and industry. Yet, as in all endeavors in which cooperation is essential to success, understanding is of primary importance.

In the interest of mutual understanding, it might be well to review briefly the various perspectives involved: the perspective of industry on education, the perspective of education on industry, and the perspective of the education industry on itself.

The perspective of industry on the field of education is not one generally encountered either on the campus or in the education association. Industry looks upon education both as a business opportunity and as a service opportunity, knowing full well that the scope of the business opportunity will be in direct proportion to the quality of the service and the understanding with which it is performed. I know of no market in which a constant orientation to the needs of the cusomter is more vital to success.

An example of the seriousness with which I believe industry is approaching its responsibility to and involvement in education, is the following statement from the five-year business plan of Raytheon Company's Education Division:

Reprinted with copyright permission of the *Harvard Educational Review*, Winter 1967.

Of all his undertakings, man's greatest success has been his extension of the universe of his knowledge. His knowledge has incredibly expanded his natural endowments—his muscular power, his dexterity and speed, his ability to hear and be heard and to see and be seen. Man's memory, too, has expanded. He can recall more things and order his knowledge as never before.

Technology has been the great transducer. Technology each year puts new demands on the specialist. His scope of activity is narrowed and he must carefully attend to few subspecialties. That such a trend will continue simply must be accepted as a fact of life.

It is no mere truism to say that a man must know more and more about less and less; it is part of the ecology of technology. This being the case, man's learning life becomes longer and longer; and the value of time in the learning process is increasing exponentially.

It is the mission of this division, therefore, to save time, and hence cost, by analyzing a problem as a problem and solving it with combinations of software and hardware. Ours is a problem-solving business, whether the problem be literacy or skill training or education. Ours is basically an intellectual product.

In defining the education market, or the knowledge market as it is sometimes called, industry views education in its broadest sense, embracing the full and ever-widening spectrum of learning situations—in the primary and secondary school classroom or on the college or university campus; in business, industry, civilian government, or the armed services. It is a most interesting phenomenon of our times that the knowledge requirements of modern society are increasingly being met beyond the bounds of formal education. And formal education is itself participating in this phenomenon.

The business-industry-government share of total annual education expenditures has increased steadily since World War II. Of the more than $70 billion now being expended each year on education, some $50 billion are being expended on formal education and more than $21 billion by business, industry, and government.

The U.S. Department of Defense alone has some 300,000 men and women on full-time duty as teachers and instructors. It has a "campus" equal in total area to the cities of Los Angeles, Chicago, and New York combined. More than 6,000 courses are taught on it. In addition, it has students at one hundred universities—from Tokyo to Geneva. A million servicemen are currently taking correspondence courses. Each year nearly 100,000 servicemen earn high school certificates, 3,200 qualify for bachelors degrees and 900 earn masters degrees.

This year, American business and industry will spend something on the order of $15 billion to educate its own. While a portion of these funds is being invested in training, the bulk is going toward scientific, engineering, and management education in highly sophisticated company schools.

General Motors, for example, has its own degree-granting institution. IBM spends almost as much on the education of its own as is being spent on public education in the District of Columbia. Many companies have extensive employee education programs raning from skill training to management development. Raytheon provides extensive services in the education and training of customer personnel in the theory, operation, and maintenance of complex electronic systems.

Many companies enroll their people in specially-tailored university courses, the content of which they specify. If a company cannot obtain what it needs in this way, it can purchase courses from a for-profit teaching company—an essentially new and uniquely American institution which has arisen in response to the growing demand for continuing education beyond the years of formal schooling.

There are several other areas in which it is important to understand the perspective of industry on education. The student, the educator, and the role of research, for example, are seen in quite a different perspective when viewed from the other side of the school-yard fence.

The student is anyone who has a learning need—whether he is in a classroom or on the job and in the need of intellectual refurbishing.

The educator-consultant, while sometimes criticized by the education community for time spent outside the classroom, is viewed by industry as an honored expert eaching elsewhere.

The distinction between on-campus and off-campus research has, with the advent of the large non-profit research institutions, largely disappeared. This is true in both the physical sciences and the social sciences.

Formal education—while sometimes referred to as lethargic, conservative, slow—looks, from the point of view of industry to be on the whole dynamic, innovative, and forward-looking. Formal education is doing a good job and has provided the base for that education which perforce must be done outside.

Of the several major elements which might be said to comprise the perspective of education on industry, three stand out in my mind as being of paramount importance and most in need of clarification if the fruits of a working partnership between education and industry are to be fully realized:

One is the educator's view of industry as being motivated solely by prospects of profit, with perhaps the lingering concern that the profit motive sees the end as more important than the means.

The second is the educator's view of the size of the companies that are now seeking to serve his field and his concern that companies, by virtue of their size, will be in position to control curriculum, the content of courses, and the methods of instruction.

The third is the educator's view of industry as being more product- than problem-oriented and his concern that, as expressed by Dean Theodore Sizer of the Harvard Graduate School of Education, education faces the risk of being inundated by products that are "technically exciting but intellectually inadequate."

These concerns on the part of educators are understandable and, I might add, they are shared by companies in the education industry. Awareness of the enormity and importance of the task, and of the social responsibility of industry to education, has caused companies in the field to study closely their perspective on themselves and their role in and potential for creative contributions to American education.

For example, my own company entered the education field after intensive study and analysis of trends in education, of the problems and needs expressed by educators, and of the scope and nature of services then available to the education community from industry.

The management concluded that, by assembling a well-rounded array of learning resources and by working closely with the education community on effective solutions to important problems, the company could make significant and creative contributions to advances in the teaching/learning process.

Our approach was pragmatic. We acquired a system or, the elements of a system: a textbook company which produces, in addition to school and college texts, a variety of audio-visual materials; a scientific apparatus company which manufactures the wherewithal to learn by doing; a company which produces a multi-media

teaching and student response system which can be used for programed, automated instruction; and a company which manufactures closed-circuit television systems, language and learning
laboratories, and dial-access and learning center systems. This
industrial complex is capable of providing both intellectual content and a variety of electronic and other means for enhancing and
enlivening its presentation.

We are well aware of the fact that our ability to earn a profit
in the education field will depend on our ability to provide a valuable and wanted service. We in industry must immerse ourselves in
the problems of education and of the individual learner. To lay
ready-made solutions or interesting but isolated pieces of equipment on the doorstep of the educator and then walk away is to
fail—both as a business and as a source of service. For industry,
there can be no difference between the motive for profit and the
motive to serve.

The education community has traditionally been supplied by
a large number of relatively small and specialized companies. We
believe that there is an increasingly important role to be played by
the larger companies with a depth and flexibility of resources that
can be brought to bear on complex education problems. There is
little danger, I believe, that companies will try to control curricula
and course content or dictate methods of instruction. Were industry to function solely outside the education community, such
might be the case. But new curricula and advances in teaching and
learning techniques developed by education with the aid of industry become the products not of industry but of education. As the
customer, the educator has the final say.

In my opinion, industry has in the past been more concerned
with products than with problems and their solutions. Our company, like others, feels that intellectual content must precede the
technological means for its presentation. A machine or a system is
only as good as the intellectual product that goes on, or in, or
through it. To be effective, instructional materials and teaching/
learning tools must be developed in concert.

We are aware that we must sell a product of high intellectual
quality if we are to sell to intellectuals and that to sell to the classroom we must know the classroom and buy from the best of those
who teach there. Those who develop new curricula, who write
texts, who develop programed instruction, who consult and advise

on the problems of education—these are the people who will establish and maintain our reputation.

We consider the teacher and the textbook, now and in the
future, to be basic to the American education process—and the
challenge to education technology to be that of finding means of
extending the effectiveness of the teacher and the textbook in the
classroom.

Raytheon's learning resources begin with problem-solving services to educators. Solutions to most complex teaching and learning problems call for combinations of software and hardware,
some of which exist outside the company's resources and some of
which may not yet exist at all. We are not wedded to any particular system or to any one technology. The nature of the problem
will dictate the means for its solution.

Competition in the education industry will doubtless be intense. It will be waged on quality not, I would hope, on price.
There will be intense rivalry for talent and for higher quality services and products with which to interest the schools and colleges.

Companies will welcome tests on and experiments with their
products. In fact, much needs to be accomplished by way of research and testing to determine the true effectiveness of new education techniques in saving time and thus dollars, in providing a
proven level of knowledge acquisition, and in advancing the teaching and learning process. It is difficult to see how education can do
other than gain from competition among companies seeking to
serve it.

Let it be quite clear, however, that the education industry is
well aware at this point that it has much to learn from the classroom, much to absorb in the research centers, and many more
questions to ask than answers to give.

On the other hand, industry has a great depth of resources in
research and development, technology, systems management, and
other areas. More important, it is, I am convinced, motivated by a
keen sense of social responsibility and the strong desire to render a
truly significant service to the American people by providing a
truly significant service to American education.

Therein lies the challenge to the education community—to
establish its objectives and to communicate them clearly to industry, to enumerate its problems and to tap the resources of industry
in the search for creative solutions, to assert its freedom of choice

among the many services and products offered, and to impose upon industry its sternest criteria for intellectual quality.

The education community will, in turn, find industry both
willing and able to meet the demands of a creative, working partnership. Such a partnership will greatly benefit the student, the
teacher, and the nation as a whole.   □

Chapter Five

PERSPECTIVES ON ACCOUNTABILITY

I

ACCOUNTABILITY IN VICTORIAN ENGLAND

by Alan A. Small

Are American educators headed for a costly rerun?

Don't be misled by authors who speak of accountability and performance contracting as modern phenomena in education, pointing to Leon Lessinger, a man in his forties, as the putative "father of accountability." Precedents appear even in the literature of ancient Greece and Rome. One familiar story tells of the Sophist who, having guaranteed to teach a student the virtue of honesty, was laughed out of court when he testified that his student had refused to pay his fee and had therefore cheated him.

Admittedly, Greek and Roman history provides little help to the modern urban school superintendent trying to placate the factions and the multitude. Fortunately, however, a historical antecedent comes to us from Victorian England, the time and circumstances of which are not far removed from our own. England, then the world's most industrialized nation, was seeking to extend some justice to its poor at minimum expense and with minimum threat to its Spencerian code of ethics. The ensuing 30-year experience with the principle of accountability in education is interesting and perhaps of some practical value.

The Newcastle Report, commissioned in 1858, was the first comprehensive survey of English elementary education. The investigators were charged with recommending "what measures, if any, are required for the extension of sound and cheap elementary instruction." For a number of years, Parliament had been granting modest but increasing sums of money to a wide variety of English schools on the basis of headcount alone. In 1851 the grant to

public education had been 265,500 pounds; in 1858, it had risen
to 973,950 pounds. This education budget had grown at a time
when frugal minds were concerned over budget balances. The major expense to the English during the same period had been the
Crimean War, which cost 78,000,000 pounds. Clearly, it was time
to reduce public costs and run a more efficient operation. Support
for popular (elementary) education was one place to lower costs.

In all, the commission recommended that public support for
popular education be continued, but in order to increase pedagogi-
cal efficiency it recommended one significant change in the manner of distributing government grants: They should go only to
those schools and teachers who could show that 1) the average
student attendance reached 140 days a year and 2) children had
attained a certain degree of knowledge, "as ascertained by the examiners appointed by the County Board of Education."

As to the virtues of the principle of payment by results, the
report argued that

> ... the examination will exercise a powerful influence over the
> efficiency of the schools, and will tend to make a minimum of
> attainment universal. ... Till something like a real examination
> is introduced into our day schools, good elementary teaching
> will never be given to half the children who attend them. At
> present, the temptation of the teachers is to cram the elder
> classes, and the inspector is too cursory to check the practice,
> while there are no inducements to make them attend closely to
> the younger children. ... Everyone who has been at a public
> school knows how searching and improving is the character of a
> careful examination, even down to the very youngest children. ...

Examinations for age-grade were developed to cover each of
the "3 R's." They were based on performance criteria, as set forth
in the revised code of 1862. W. D. Halls gives us this example of
the difficulty of the typical examination questions:

> The tests that the inspectors were obliged to make in order
> to allocate the grant a school could "earn" are ridiculous, as can
> be seen from the following examples. 1) Children had to write
> correctly from dictation: *If you twist that stick so long you will
> make your wrist ache.* 2) They had to solve the following arith-
> metical problem: *Five and one-half yards make one pole. Draw
> a diagram to show that 30½ square yards make one perch.* If the

Luckless children inquired what a diagram was, they were given
the reply: "Never mind what a diagram is — work the sum!"

It is interesting to note similarities between the kind of exams
prescribed by the Victorian code and those being drawn up today.
The English model of a century ago provides an interesting comparison with a very recent version of second-grade performance objectives in arithmetic, shown in Figure 1.

What was the net result of the English experience? Financial-
ly, the principle of payment by results was undoubtedly successful
in reducing government expenditures for education: The grant
which had stood in 1861 at 813,441 pounds fell to 76,000 by
1865. However, in promoting "sound education" it was a disaster.
Historian John William Adamson gives us this appraisal:

> Its limited application impoverished the curriculum, and,
> since the teacher's reputation and very livelihood became de-
> pendent upon a high percentage of "passes" in the three rudi-
> mentary studies, cram and an even cruel concentration upon
> work done by the dullards, with a corresponding neglect of the
> more capable children, were commonly noted in schools under
> the New Code of 1862.

In 1868, after the principle of payment by results had had six
years of trial, J. Kay-Shuttleworth, a long-time educational critic,
offered his opinion on the matter:

> The Revised Code has constructed nothing; it has only pulled
> down. It has not simplified the administration. . . . It has disor-
> ganized the whole system of training teachers and providing an
> efficient machinery of instruction for schools. These ruins are
> its only monuments. It has not succeeded in being efficient; for
> it wastes the public money without producing the results which
> were declared to be its main object.

Perhaps the best-known critic of the new code was a school
inspector, Matthew Arnold, who, in his general report for the year
1867, said that the new code had lowered the quality of education
from its 1861 level. Arnold wrote, "Our present system of grants
does harm to schools and their instruction by resting its grants too
exclusively, at any rate, upon individual examination, prescribed
in all its details beforehand by the Central Office, and necessarily
mechanical; and . . . we have to relax this exclusive stress rather
than . . . go on adding to it."

Figure 1[1]

ENGLISH MODEL
Arithmetic Standards for Grade-Levels Prescribed by Victorian New Code

Standard I:	Form on blackboard or slate, from dictation, figures up to 20; name at sight figures up to 20; add and subtract figures up to 10, orally, from examples on blackboard.
Standard II:	A sum in simple addition or subtraction, and the multiplication table.
Standard III:	A sum in any simple rule as far as short division (inclusive).
Standard IV:	A sum in compound rules (money).
Standard V:	A sum in compound rules (common weights and measures).
Standard VI:	A sum in practice or bills of parcels.

AMERICAN MODEL
Report Card Showing Criterion-Referenced Measurement of Mathematics Skills for Grade Two

Concepts:	Understands commutative property of addition; understands place value.
Addition:	Supplies missing addend under 10; adds three single-digit numbers; knows combinations 10 through 19; adds two 2-digit numbers without carrying; adds two 2-digit numbers with carrying.
Subtraction:	Knows combinations through 9; supplies missing subtrahend (under 10); supplies missing minuend (under 10); knows combinations 10 through 19; subtracts two 2-digit numbers without borrowing.
Measurement:	Reads and draws clocks (up to quarter hour); understands dollar value of money (coins up to $1 total).
Geometry:	Understands symmetry; recognizes congruent plan figures — that is, figures which are identical except for orientation.
Graph Reading:	Knows how to construct simple graphs; knows how to read simple graphs.

To the English, then, the principle of payment by results had become a national failure in spite of its intention to assure a sound minimum of academic attainment by all school children. The Newcastle recommendation to make payments conditional upon results had overlooked one predictable effect, namely, that the teachers whose professional future would depend upon their demonstrated succes would, as Arnold pointed out, concentrate all their effort at the minimum level of proficiency so explicitly spelled out by the law. This, in turn, would inevitably lower the quality of instruction of the lower classes whose well-being, ironically, had been the chief concern of the commission. F.J.A. Hort, an Anglican vicar, described the effect of the new instruction as "an unobtrusive alliance [of those] who hate and fear the education of the lower classes and, therefore, give their support to a plan which will guarantee that the poor get no instruction beyond the bare minimum in the '3 R's'."

The Victorian code overlooked another aspect of human variability in promulgating the practice of pyament by results: the pupil. In other words, it was seriously short-sighted to place the full burden of accountability on the school and the teacher. Noting that there are factors beyond the teacher's control, Professor John Grote wrote in 1862 of the role of the student in the learning process: "Success in teaching is a function of the recipient as well as of the communicator; a good deal of failure of it there must always, and in every system of education, necessarily be."

In the 1970s we should reflect upon the English experience of a century ago before we move too far in the direction of unquestioned acceptance of the principle of accountability based on performance criteria. The English arguments in support of the "payment by results" principle closely resemble our own today. Will our experience only prove to be a costly rerun? Will our faith in the salvation of education through accountability and performance be rewarded?   □

Alan A. Small is assistant professor of education, Rockhurst College, Kansas City, Mo.

---

[1] Adapted from models in J. Steward Maclure, *Educational Documents: England and Wales, 1816-1967.* London: Chapman and Hall, Ltd., 1968; and Jason Millman, "Reporting Student Progress: A Case for a Criterion-Referenced Marking System," *Phi Delta Kappan,* December, 1970, p. 226.

II

ACCOUNTABILITY AND THE REVEREND DOGOOD

by John E. Motzkus

"We have developed a system called the Religious Program Budgeting System (RPBS for short)."

With all the pressure on teachers for scientific management these days, I really envied the Reverend Dogood, our local divine.

"You should be glad that you're not in public education," I told him the other day. "The key word now is 'accountability.' We're going to start to carefully measure output in terms of pupil performance and judge teachers' competence on this final product."

"So what else is new?" he shot back. "We've had accountability in our church now for over a year. Our board and president got tired of the ministers' drawing their pay without proof that they were producing. They said that on the 'outside' people get fired if they don't produce, and that's the way it's going to be in religion."

"Is that right?" I asked in surprise. "But how in the world do they decide if you are earning your money? Evaluate your sermons? Check that you make your home and hospital visits?"

"Of course not! That would be trying to measure the *process* instead of the output. We have developed a system called the Religious Program Budgeting System (RPBS for short). With RPBS, we can spell out our objectives in performance criteria so clearly that even a nonbeliever can understand. Then the Budgeting System shows exactly how much money we spend on each objective. If we fail to meet a particular objective, then funds for that objective are reduced. Simple!"

Reprinted with the March, 1971 copyright permission of *Today's Education* and John E. Motzkus.

"Well, I know something about performance objectives," I said. "But how do you write them for religion?"

"Easy," he said. He walked over to his bookcase and pulled out a thick, loose-leaf binder titled *Religious Goals and Objectives*. "How about this one?" he said, opening the book at random: "Ninety percent of the congregation will be able to write or recite the Ten Commandments with less than 10 percent error in a four-minute period of time."

"That should be an easy one to check," I ventured. "But it requires only rote memory. Lay one on me that involves a higher level of thinking: application, analysis, evaluation, or something."

"I think that most of our cognitive objectives are of the memory kind," he replied rather shamefacedly. "You see, the lay board wrote the goals but allowed the ministers to write the performance objectives. Everybody likes to score high on evaluations."

"Oh, don't feel bad," I reassured him. "The intellect isn't the most important thing in religion anyway, is it? Aren't people's attitudes the most important? How they really feel inside?"

"Yes, of course," he said, brightening considerably. "But again, you can't go just on the basis of how they feel inside. That's not *measurable*. I'll read you an attitudinal objective," he said, flipping to another section of the book. " 'The females of the congregation will appreciate the beauty and truth of the Seventh Commandment to the extent that the illegitimacy rate will decrease 10 percent per year for the next 10 years.' " He looked up, beaming proudly.

"Well," I observed, "it sounds like you're getting it down to a gnat's eyebrow! You should be able to identify the ministers who are really working at it and those who are in it for the easy money."

"You bet! We're way ahead by giving some of these guys their walking papers and calling in private industry. You know, there are companies that will guarantee the objectives in contract form. If they don't perform, they don't get their money. Of course, there is the danger of irregularities like the company that rewarded each convert with a tape recorder and Polaroid camera."

"Well, Reverend Dogood," I replied, "I wasn't sure the whole accountability thing was suited for education. But if you're sure it works for religion. . . ."

"I'm convinced of it," he cut in. "Until I got involved in the accountability approach, I was stagnating—preparing sermons on the gospels, individual spiritual guidance, all that traditional stuff. Now my whole operation has changed. I don't think of myself much as a pastor now but more as a consultant in religious management—a sort of spiritual systems analyst."   □

John E. Motzkus, social studies teacher, Savanna High School, Anaheim, California, president-elect of the Anaheim Secondary Teachers Association.

III

THE GREAT TRAIN ROBBERY

by Peter Idstein

This is a "story" about a crime. It has a moral: The plans laid by its outlandishly stereotyped principals lead to the same end reached unintentionally by many well-meaning individuals. The story is fiction. The crime is not.

It was a cold rainy morning, just the type of morning that The Man liked. He couldn't help the feeling of excitement building within him. He had pulled off more small grants than he could remember, but this was something else. It was the first time he had dared to think in seven figures and he liked what he was thinking.

The rain continued steadily and the windshield wipers of his big limousine swayed methodically. The man listened to the beat of the wipers and heard the *click, click, click* of a train. His train was coming and there was no stopping it, *click, click.* He smiled to himself, *click, click, click.*

When he entered the lobby of the plush Marriott Motel, the manager met him respectfully and assured him that the luncheon and conference rooms were all in order and that one of his guests who had arrived early was waiting for him in the lounge.

Legs were sitting in the corner and rose to greet The Man as he approached.

"Hi, Legs, how've you been?"

"Oh I've managed to keep busy," said Legs.

"Yes, I know," said The Man. "I read about your last little caper, National Institute of Mental Health, wasn't it?"

"Something like that." Legs didn't like to talk about his "projects" to The Man. "Do you want a drink?"

"No, thanks," said The Man. "The others should be arriving soon. Why don't we check out the conference room?"

Looking at the two men standing side by side, one could easily guess why Legs was called Legs. He towered over The Man by a good 12 inches. Like so many other obvious conclusions, however, this one would be wrong. Legs was so called because of the leg work that he had done and still did for The Man. Legs was a background man, a frame of reference man, a wind reader, a seer of the *Zeitgeist,* and was good at what he did.

As the two men entered the panelled conference room with its wall-to-wall luxury they smiled knowing smiles at each other. They were both recalling more humble beginnings. "It's a far cry from the boiler room," said The Man.

Before long the others arrived and took their places around the huge oak table. While they were waiting for the waitress to bring them their drinks, they had a few moments to renew old friendships and meet new members of the group. The Man drew back from the small talk and surveyed the room. Next to Legs sat Weasel. His full nickname was Weaser Word but his closer friends called him Wessel. No one in the business could write a more ambiguous statement. He could shoot commitment out of a proposal at first glance. And he could take the most nonsignificant findings and turn them into "consistent trends" with the stroke of a pen. Yes, Weasel was a beautiful man, *click, click, click,* beautiful.

Next to Weasel sat Wheels. Formally, he was called Wheeler and/or Dealer. Whatever he was called, he too was beautiful. He was an active member of the American Educational Research Association, the American Psychological Association, Phi Delta Kappa, and the National Education Association. He presented minor papers at every major conference that he was physically able to *fundedly* attend, and over the years he had made many "friends." He was a scholar. He read widely and with purpose, always with purpose. He was able to defend the behaviorist against the humanist and vice versa. He stood by the educational technologist and anti-educational technologist with equal fervor. And he defended the Federal Evaluators against everybody. As a result, he always knew where the purse was and who happened to be holding the strings.

The natural complement to Wheels was The Accountant. The Accountant had actually set out to become a CPA but he became distracted by the big money to be had in education. He was another of the beautiful people. His was the world of the special contingency fund, the travel and expenses voucher, the planning fund, the travel and expenses voucher, the planning fund, the office supplies breakdown, the consultant fund, etc. In fact, it was The Accountant who had arranged the accommodations for the present meeting. It was being financed from The Man's last grant. Once the heist was accomplished, he and The Man would be the only two people in the world who would know where the money was buried.

Opposite The Accountant sat the only real loner in the group. It wasn't that Numbers was unfriendly. He really had trouble communicating with people. It was rumored that he didn't even speak the language, but the rumor could never be verified. All of his words could be found in standard American dictionaries. The only mystery was the way he strung them together. He had multivaried ways of digging significant relationships out of reluctant data. There wasn't a partial correlation coefficient or a covariate that could escape his keen eye. Numbers wasn't sufficient, but he certainly was necessary. *Click, click, click,* thought The Man as he appraised his confederates. Nothing is going to stop this train.

The drinks arrived and the planning session began. The Man made some preliminary remarks about the size of the undertaking and the experience that was represented in the room. The essence of his message was contained in his first two sentences.

"Gentlemen, we are not about to write a proposal. We are planning careers."

The proposal centered around a massive training program designed eventually to "do the work the Work Corps didn't." The Man gave some background on the Work Corps and made some caustic remarks about the various centers he had visited around the country. He left the specifics to Legs, who as usual had done his homework. The Work Corps had been examined, dissected, put under a microscope, analyzed, and diatribed. Its failures had been hypothesized, exposed, and documented. A plan was presented to offer a pilot porject to pick up the pieces and provide relevant training for those needing it. The proposed plan was to do this by *Tapping Resources and Initiative Now.* The project was to be called, naturally enough, TRAIN. The Man smiled comfortably at the sound of the acronym. *Click, click,* he thought, *click, click.*

After Legs came Wheeler. He wasted little time showing his talents.

"As you gentlemen know, money is tight, even in Washington. The watchword is 'accountability.' The federal boys want to know exactly what they are buying, but luck is with us. They're looking for new things through old glasses. We hit them before the new prescriptions come in." Wheeler paused dramatically to let his words sink in.

"Our proposal is guaranteed to strike a responsive chord. We will propose that only minor operating expenses be allocated for the first six months of the project. Included in those expenses will be *no* staff salaries."

For the first time murmurs of discontent were heard from a couple of new members. The Man raised his hand in a gesture calling for patience and the room quieted. Wheeler continued.

"During that six-month period we will conduct classroom sessions for 'Hard Core Unemployed.' We will pre-test, using any standardized measure of aptitude which Washington would like to see used. We will post-test with the same measure and compare our results with controls. Full funding of our TRAIN will be contingent upon our producing significant differences in our treated population."

Again murmurs were heard and again The Man signaled for calm. There was something about The Man's presence which assured the others that things were under control. Failure was not even being considered.

Wheeler yielded the floor to Numbers. As usual, not everyone understood all the words, but the message came across clearly.

"It's quite simple," he said, "we just build significant differences into our design. It's done every day. We start with a selection bias. We recruit volunteers from the population that we're interested in. We make sure not to paint too rosy a picture. This way we increase the probability of getting strongly motivated people and decrease the probability of mortality problems. Then we choose our control group from a population of nonvolunteers. We just pay them to go through the testing procedures. The pay, of course, is noncontingent. No sense in motivating *them*. Normally this would be enough to guarantee us significant differences no matter what we did with our program. However, we're playing in the big leagues now and there is no reason to take unnecessary chances. Consequently, we back our selection bias with a regression artifact."

Murmurs again went through the room, but this time they were murmurs of respect. The Man's confidence was now understood. Numbers continued.

"In recruiting our volunteers we'll be certain to recruit many more than we can handle in our small pilot program. Since we have a scarce resource to allocate, it's only 'fair' that we give it to the most needy. Naturally we take those who score lowest on the standardized measure picked by the government. We're practically assured of a regression effect."

When Numbers sat down there was little left to be said. Out of sheer reverence for the magnitude of the undertaking, no one mentioned the seven-figure total which graced the bottom line of the last budget page. There might have been some doubters before the meeting, but as it broke up the same quiet confidence that characterized The Man now pervaded the whole group. It was a happy lunch.   □

Peter Idstein (47, Glassboro State College Chapter) is an assistant professor of education at Washington College, Chesterown, Md.

IV

PRODUCTIVITY, YES. ACCOUNTABILITY, NO.

by David Selden

"Accountability advocates approach education with all the insight of an irate viewer 'fixing' a television set: Give it a kick and see what happens."

It's no mystery why teachers regard the present public outcry for "accountability" as an unwarranted slur on their motives and abilities.

For one thing, most teachers are trying desperately to fulfill their assigned tasks. The small proportion of goof-offs in education affects productivity much less than gross defects of the system stemming from years of financial malnutrition.

For another, "accountability" seems to have as many definitions as there are definers. The rationale advanced by Leon Lessinger, originator of the term as applied to education, is that education is becoming more and more expensive, and yet there is no way to show that we are getting more for our money. As a matter of fact, he says, the available evidence shows that we are actually getting less. Before more money is put into schools, equipment and personnel, he adds, a way must be found to make sure we're getting our money's worth.

Teacher scapegoats: But when we think "schools," we almost automatically think "teachers." Thus accountability offers ready teacher scapegoats to amateur and professional school-haters, from the fellow who did not get along well with his eighth-grade teacher to the corporation executive who judges schools by his company's property tax rate. It is this accusatory aspect of accountability that sets teachers' teeth on edge.

Significantly, most accountability advocates want to do away with the due process protections of teacher tenure acts established after years of hard work in the state legislatures. If a child is not learning it must be the teacher's fault, these advocates say, so teachers should "shape up or ship out." Never mind what kind of out-of-school problems the child has or any of the other possible physical or emotional impediments to learning.

An example of this "get teacher" attitude of the accountability promoters is the famous "Clark Plan" drawn up for Washington, D.C., schools two years ago by Kenneth Clark, well-known social psychologist. Clark recommended that a series of standardized tests be given to all District children at regular intervals. If students did not make equivalent academic advancement, their teachers would be "counseled with." Teacher pay would be based on student achievement.

Teachers versus tractors: The concept of accountability, of course, is not limited to education these days, and the idea is not all bad. Consumer advocates such as Ralph Nader and his student associates have been trying to force vast corporations which have long operated on a "let-the-buyer-beware" basis to become publicly responsible. But accountability in the auto industry is much different from accountability in education. If a car's brakes fail, management gets the blame. It is assumed that the design was faulty, or that the company cut too many corners in reducing costs. But if a child does not learn to read, the assumption is that his teacher, rather than the managers of the educational system, did not do a good job.

There is a great deal of "know-nothingism" in the approach of the accountabilitarians. They do not tell us how accountability will change current teaching methods. They do not even advocate any particular philosophic underpinning for their theory, nor can they diagram a reorganization of school structure or curriculum. They approach education with all the insight of an irate viewer "fixing" a television set: Give it a kick and see what happens. No consideration is given to the possibility that education — teaching and learning — may be a complex and largely unexplored region requiring the cooperative effort of everyone involved if success is to be achieved.

Performance contracting: The most egregious development of the accountability movement is performance contracting, a concept that outrages most teachers.

In the first place, teachers believe they have never been given a chance to succeed with traditional methods. "How can we really teach 30 disadvantaged kids at a time in these days of crime, drug addiction, and social unrest," they ask, "especially when we have to handle 30 classroom hours a week?" Their reasoning is borne out by experiences in the various high-staff-ratio elementary programs such as New York City's More Effective Schools, Chicago's READ program, and the Neighborhood Educational Centers in Detroit.

In these schools the staffing ratio permits class size limits of no more than 20 children per teacher, and teachers have a couple of free periods every day to use for consultation with colleagues, work with individual children, lesson planning, marshalling instructional materilas, and just plain rest. And the children learn — not just memorized "answers" but a whole range of ego-strengthening attitudes and convictions.

The rhetoric of performance contracting adherents, however, makes no allowances for such rational considerations. "Education has failed," they say. "Spending more money for richer staffing ratios is merely adding 'more of the same.' Let's try something new." The percon peddlers also promise to produce more education for the same amount of money now being spent. "Don't pay us if the pupils don't learn," they say. It is the old money-back guarantee applied to schooling. Boards of education and parents can hardly be blamed for taking a flyer on it. After all, children are not learning as things are now.

The facts show, however, that performance contracting not only costs more money but also produces insignificant student achievement gains. Not to mention the management problems it invites by employing footloose staffing procedures.

Surveillance and snoopervision: Are there other ways, perhaps less objectionable than performance contracting, to build accountability into education? One suggestion is to encourage much closer surveillance of schools by local communities. But, again, the educational results are apt to be pretty bad. A conflict between aroused community groups and teachers, for example, was responsible for the 37-day teacher strike in New York City in the fall of 1968.

Another form of teacher accountability is closer supervision. Like any other workers, teachers resent the breathing-over-your-

shoulder type of "snoopervision" which some over-zealous administrators employ. When supervision is used merely to put pressure
on already overburdened teachers, the result will be a teacher re-
bellion if the practice is widely spread.

Is there *any* sort of accountability that teachers would approve of? In the United Federation of Teachers (New York City)
contract, ratified in June 1969, the school board and the union
agreed to develop such a plan, and a fund was set aside to employ
competent resource people. The job was turned over to Educational Testing Service of Princeton, N.J. After two years of effort a
special task force, Educational Testing Service, has finally devised
an instrument which it at least is willing to put into trial operation.
However, the director of the project states that the whole question
raises extremely difficult political problems involving community,
school administrators, and educational staff.

Goodbye teacher: We are just beginning to get to the bottom
of some of the problems involved in the learning process. Conceivably it may be possible at some time in the future to comput-
erize individual teacher productivity so that the public will know
what a teacher is putting out, but when we reach that stage, few
teachers will want to stay in the profession. Good teaching is a
creative activity as well as a production process.

Much of the rhetoric of accountability seems to stem directly
from "the cult of efficiency in education." We have always treated
education as a mass production industry. One of the basic principles of mass production is to so simplify the task of each worker
that his function can be learned in a very short time without any
previous training. Our educational factories are designed to be
operated by nice young ladies working under the supervision of
somewhat sterner older ladies and gentlemen.

Although no school should refuse to adopt new methods that
will make a teacher's work more productive, it must be careful not
to use the term "productivity" as loosely as "accountability" is
used. The American educational enterprise has been marvelously
productive on a unit cost basis, but at the expense of children who
have been shunted aside because they do not conform to the educational assembly line. If the system expects to increase productivity in terms of "gross national education product," it will have to
come up with more capital investment and manpower.

Hello humanization: Instead of looking for ways to build in

incentives and other efficiency devices, we would be better advised
to discover ways to humanize the system. The British have pioneered in this direction. The British infant schools are the very
antithesis of what accountabilitarians would have us do. Yet these
schools produce good education with little strain.

Another British device that could improve teacher productivity is the "teacher center." Most people who have studied education have come to the conclusion that nothing good happens in
schools unless teachers make it happen. Productivity cannot be
improved by piling on more oppressive supervision. Rather, teachers must be given the responsibility for working out their own best
methods of teaching. In the teacher center, teachers meet and confer with each other, learn about new techniques, and watch
demonstrations.

And now we come to the real nub of the accountability question. Teachers do not mind being held accountable for things over
which they have some control. For instance, all teachers accept
the idea that they must come to school on time, must plan lessons,
must be as responsive as possible to student needs. But teachers
bitterly resent having to teach in overcrowded classrooms, handle
the emotional problems of disturbed children, and work without
proper supplies and instructional materials. These are all matters
that fall within the province of administrators, school boards, and
the taxpayers. Teachers gain a semblance of control over such conditions only by exerting great collective effort.

Accountability is a two-way street. If teachers are to be accountable to the public, the public must be accountable to teachers. James Coleman identified most of the major influences on
pupil achievement, and by far the most potent were environmental
factors. Our teachers must be given the resources to overcome the
crippling effects on children of the defects in our society — unemployment, racism, drug addiction, alcoholism, and the brutality of
poverty. If we are really interested in increasing productivity
rather than mere finger-pointing and scapegoating, let us develop
ways in which teachers can share policymaking responsibilities. We
have much more to gain by enhancing the opportunities for cooperation than by introducing the two-edged sword of accountability. □

Mr. Selden is president, American Federation of Teachers, AFL-CIO.

V

SELF-GOVERNANCE MUST COME FIRST, THEN ACCOUNTABILITY

by Helen Bain

The NEA president-elect announces a campaign to establish pro-fessional practices boards, by state statute, to give teachers more control over teacher education, licensure, in-service education, and the ethical conduct of their peets.

Currently, the National Education Association, many of its state and local associations, and dozens of other organizations are de-manding greater teacher accountability in order to improve educa-tion. But it is pure myth that classroom teachers can ever be held accountable, with justice, under existing conditions. The classroom teacher has either too little control or no control over the factors which might render accountability either feasible or fair.

Teachers constitute the greatest resource of educational ex-pertise in this country. Yet they are often looked upon as hired hands. They are expected to respond like Pavlov's dogs to rewards and punishment. As a result, their expertise is denied and the most powerful of human forces — intrinsic motivation — is thwarted.

I contend, therefore, that most, if not all, of the possibilities for educational improvement are directly related to self-gover-nance for the teaching profession. Corrective measures should be taken immediately.

As a beginning, the teaching profession must be afforded those legal rights necessary for it to assume responsibility and ac-countability for its own professional destiny. As a minimum, this includes transferring to the profession the following: 1) authority over issuing, suspending, revoking, or reinstating the legal licensure of educational personnel; 2) authority to establish and administer standards of professional practice and ethics for all educational personnel; 3) authority to accredit teacher preparation institutions; and 4) authority to govern in-service and continuing education for teachers.

Obviously, if we are to achieve these goals we will need new legal machinery at the outset. Currently, no state has delegated the necessary legal responsibilities to the profession. Teachers are kept in a perennial advisory posture, even in matters that concern them most directly. (Let us be clear, however, that the idea of self-governance for teaching does not imply control of all aspects of education, only the governance of a profession.)

The concept of self-governance is finally generating considerable interest among teachers. Hence one of the major priorities of the NEA for the 70's is the achievement of self-governance for the teaching profession. A first concern is the creation, by statute, of independent professional practices boards or commissions in each state. These boards must be broadly representative of the profession and must give teachers the legal right to do at least the following:

1. Make and enforce policy decisions related to initial licensure and advanced credentialling of all educational personnel.

2. Determine, adopt, and enforce accreditation standards for initial, graduate, and in-service teacher education.

3. Develop and adopt a code of ethics and rules of procedure in accordance with established concepts of due process.

4. Enforce standards of teaching practice and ethical conduct.

Professional practices boards for teachers should be financed through the general budget of the state, as is true of other professional boards.

Obviously, legal authorization is only the beginning of self-governance. When such boards are established, the profession must devote much study to the problems of governance, for they are perennial. Teachers will be performing new functions. They will need new training and must understand their new responsibilities.

The idea of self-governance for the profession will not be easily implemented for at least two reasons. First, the tradition of lay decision making in professional matters is deeply ingrained. It will require understanding, patience, and persistence to convince state legislatures of the need for a shift in authority. Secondly, self-governance will require a re-division of authority within the teaching profession itself. For example, consider the area of certification. Certification responsibility is now firmly vested in an established bureaucracy that will, with but a few enlightened exceptions, fight to maintain the status quo.

There is a further internal problem. Teachers are reluctant to make peer judgments in the public interest. With self-governance, they will have to face up to this responsibility. It doesn't necessarily mean judging peers in one's own administrative jurisdiction. It does mean we must develop a sophisticated understanding of competence, ethics, due process, and the public welfare.

The NEA will soon launch a phase-by-phase program to establish self-governance for the teaching profession. The association has a clear mandate to do so. Every teacher must become informed concerning the rationale and implications of this venture, not only for selfish reasons but because its potential for improving American education is so great.

To make the easy assumption that teachers are primarily responsible for the quality of education today is absurdly naive. But teachers *could be held accountable* if this society were to see the wisdom of helping the profession devise its own self-governance. Such governance would serve both the profession and the public. It won't be a panacea, but if teachers are given the power to control the professional aspects of teaching, even the most cynical critics may be surprised.   □

VI

ACCOUNTABILITY AS A NEGATIVE REINFORCER

by Barry R. McGhan

"Accountability carries the connotation of retribution. If we say that 'someone is accountable' we usually mean that 'he must suffer the consequences of his actions!' We hardly ever mean the more positive 'he will profit from the consequences of his actions.' "

Americans have long held a reputation for being able to solve many of their problems through technology. However, it has only been in the last two or three years that there has been a jump in interest in technological concepts among educators. The accompanying jargon (input/output, feedback, systems analysis, reprogramming, performance capabilities, etc.) evokes wonderful images of efficient, resourceful solutions to problems. Certain educational innovations such as performance objectives, differentiated staffing, computer-assisted instruction, programmed materials, and teacher accountability smack of this technological viewpoint and give one the "can-do" feeling that the solutions to the grave problems facing education are at hand. One almost has to wonder, given our technological accomplishments elsewhere, what took us so long to begin to apply our technological know-how to the battered and tottering public-school system.

Perhaps some of these new ideas distress you, even though you're not too conservative to be willing to change your ways. You might feel, for instance, that children can't be educated as mechanically as can openers are manufactured. Or, you might want to cry out against the fact that stressing efficiency and bureaucratization adds to the formalism of schools. Perhaps you think that the use of technological terminology and concepts may allow educators to think of students as objects to be processed. However, the public's concern for effective education seems to be mounting, and the temptation to use techniques that have proved worthwhile in business and industry will be hard to resist. No doubt some benefits to education will come from all this, which is all right, as long as the *mischief* created causes no long-lasting damage.

The concept of accountability, for example, needs careful consideration. At first blush, the notion that teachers should be held accountable for their jobs seems perfectly straightforward and reasonable. What could be more sensible than to expect teachers to do their best, and to make appropriate changes in their jobs as their success is assessed?

Judging by recent articles in the NEA's *Today's Education* of May, 1970, and a guest editorial by NEA President Helen Bain in the April, 1970 *Phi Delta Kappan,* some of the leaders of that organization feel that the notion of accountability is sound. Mrs. Bain, for instance, thinks that teachers should accept it, *if* they are given complete self-governance over their profession. Although this sounds like a gambit in a chess match, it does seem reasonable that accountability could be accepted if teachers had the power to do things the way they think is best. The important question is, is the concept of accountability sound enough to be accepted, *even* if the price is right?

Interlocking Accountability

To begin with, there are several problems with implementation of the concept. As things stand right now, the term seems to mean that teachers should be accountable *for* their jobs *to* the public. But it seems that there should be some sort of mutual accountability so that the public cannot accuse teachers of failing to do their jobs, while at the same time it fails to provide adequate funds, thereby causing many of the teachers' problems. To be fair, this concept of mutuality should be extended to a kind of interlocking accountability which includes teachers, students, administrators, paraprofessionals, school boards, parents, and the public at large. This would require enforceable guarantees that each group meet its responsibilities to each of the others, and would tend to eliminate such possibilities as administrators trying to make teachers the scapegoats for education's inadequacies.

Another problem with accountability is that of choosing criteria for successful teaching which are necessary to hold a teacher accountable. So far, most discussion in this vein has settled on student achievement as the chief measure of teaching success. But the relationship between student achievement and teaching is not conclusive. Educational research indicates that we don't know how to bring about some kinds of cognitive and affective learning, and the research is unable to show significant differences between teaching methods. [If we think of the teaching/learning act as a black box in which something happens, then we can talk of teaching methods and materials as input, and the changes in students' behavior as output.[1] The state of education today is this: there is no discernable difference in the effect of various inputs; there is no discernable relation between specific inputs and specific outputs; it is difficult to assure that specific outputs can be obtained at any given time with any particular individuals.[2]]

Even as we can eventually establish norms for the teaching/learning act, the question of worthwhile deviations arises, because some teachers will be successful in ways which vary widely from the norms. Also, students may learn worthwhile things in school which are not measured, and it would be wrong to ignore a teacher's possible contributions to students' growth apart from the formal curriculum.

A third fault is related to the problem of motivation. As a whiskery old saying goes, "You can lead a horse to water, but you can't make him drink." This adage seems to capture the spirit of one of the principles of education. Namely, that no matter how much effort is exapnded by the teacher, students will not learn unless they have an inner motivation to learn. If this is true, then of the two individuals engaged in the teaching/learning act, the student has the more important role for the act to be successful: thus, teacher accountability places the emphasis on the wrong person. This does not mean that we should ignore the quality of a teacher's performance, but if we expect to get anyplace, we must keep that concern in perspective with regard to our concern for the student's motivation and performance.

A Retributive System?

Another fault (and all the more important because it is intrinsic) is that accountability carries the connotation of retribution.

If we say that "someone is accountable" we usually mean that "he must suffer the consequences of his actions." We hardly ever mean the more positive "he will profit from the consequences of his actions." One wonders what the social and psychological ramifications might be if teachers have to carry out their jobs in a retributive atmosphere. For example, would such a work pattern encourage teachers to teach in a manner protective of their own best interests rather than a manner suited to the best interests of their students? In response to this criticism someone could say, "Industry takes this approach, and look how successful it is in accomplishing its goals." The assumption that what's good for industry is good for education is an easy one to make, but it seems unjustified. There is no necessary relationship between manufacturing and education. For one thing, it's possible that industry might be better off with another work pattern. And, for another thing, while the psychological atmosphere generated by such a competitive, pressurized work pattern can't be passed on to the products of a manufacturing process, such an unhealthy atmosphere could be passed on to children.

If the present notion of accountability becomes generally applied to teachers, we must face the possibility that it will work as a system of punishments, and may run afoul of the same pitfalls that social scientists have discovered in other systems of punishment. Furthermore, if we as educators accept the system, we will be admitting that punishing the incompetent teacher is more important than helping him to grow into a more competent professional.

The concept of accountability is a twist on the general topic of teacher evaluation, which has been a thorny problem for a long time. The application of this and other technological concepts to education may be beneficial. But the technologists have to be guided by educators who have a thorough knowledge of, and appreciation for, the social, psychological, and philosophical—the human—values of teaching and learning.   □

Barry R. McGhan teaches mathematics in Northwestern Community High School in Flint, Mich., and is a member of the United Teachers of Flint.

---

[1]Technological concepts can be used as models to aid thinking. Our earlier complaint against them was on the basis that they seemed to be used to describe how education ought to work.

[2]The following writers all discuss different aspects of the problem of assessing teacher performance:

Dublin, Robert and Taveggia, Thomas. "The Teaching-Learning Paradox." Center for the Advanced Study of Education. University of Oregon: Eugene, Oregon. 1968.

Musella, Donald. "Improving Teacher Evaluation." The Journal of Teacher Education. Spring, 1970.

Popham, James. "The Performance Test: A New Approach to the Assessment of Teaching Proficiency." The Journal of Teacher Education. Summer, 1968.

Saadeh, Ibrahim Q. "Teacher Effectiveness of Classroom Efficiency: A New Direction in the Evaluation of Teaching." The Journal of Teacher Education. Spring, 1970.

VII

ARE ACCOUNTABILITY AND GOVERNANCE COMPATIBLE?

by Fenwick English and James Zaharis

"Protest by teacher groups against accountability proposals suggests that even the possibility of an alternative is having a profound effect upon our thinking."

The AFT's flat rejection of performance contracting, voucher plans, and other alternatives in lieu of the single salary schedule, and the NEA's insistence on self-governance first, then account ability,[1] raise an interesting question: Are the two concepts compatible at all?

Teacher groups have become extremely hostile to such notions and have, in turn, invoked the public wrath of at least one government agency on more than one occasion.[2] AFT leaders point at Texarkana, where teacher cheating resulted in the desired pupil gains, as evidence that performance contracting is not workable and would destroy the integrity of the teaching profession. Teacher leaders are expressing the suspicion that such not-so-subtle attempts to introduce merit pay in another form represent a retaliatory measure by a public angered over teacher militance.

Placed in the context of social compliance theory developed by Peter M. Balu,[3] the rise of a public alternative to the monopoly of the public school must be considered as a way around teacher power at the bargaining table. This would place the two concepts at odds with one another. In Blau's context, teacher power means that in order to obtain greater rewards from the present system, teachers must deny the recipients of their services any alternatives, must coerce the recipients into furnishing the services by using the strike, and must be sure that the public cannot do without their

services. The latter condition is virtually assured with compulsory
attendance laws.

The coercive massing of the nation's instructors to obtain better wages and a greater voice through collective bargaining within
their school systems rests solidly on the fact that the public has no
real alternative except eventually to give in to the demands by
teacher groups not only for better working conditions, but for
authority to license and control entry to the profession. This
power now rests largely in the hands of laymen. If the public is
allowed to mobilize any large-scale alternative to the public
schools, the teacher power base is considerably weakened. The
threat is best represented in the current image of the giant business-education corporations such as IBM, RCA, and General Learning greedily waiting to "contract" for whole school systems if
teachers should become overly aggressive. Teachers see this possibility as far more dangerous than the argument that it would be
an injustice to hold teachers accountable in a system in which they
have no rights or authority but much responsibility. It would not
take the public too long to discover that those with more power
should be more "accountable."

How Valuable Is an Alternative?

Usually overlooked in the arguments for or against accountability are the clients themselves, that is, the students. Efforts by
school reformers to shift the basis of measuring school effectiveness from input (pupil/teacher ratio, dollars spent per child, etc.)
to output (student behaviors) are without much precedence in education. Schools have historically been teacher-centered institutions with primary loyalties centered on colleagues and institutional norms, rather than clients. The fact that salary was unrelated to
client need or satisfaction simply reinforced this historical stance.

One of the more valuable functions of the performance contract is that it forces professionals to examine the quality of their
skills and services. If dull and uninspiring teachers are allowed to
continue a mediocre performance year in and year out, and if
schools continue using outdated instructional methods and staffing practices, what wedge does the public have to change the system? Protest by teacher groups against accountability proposals
suggests that even the possibility of an alternative is having a profound effect upon our thinking.

Alternatives also serve to question the competence base of the profession. What skills are professional? If skills are not related to pupil growth, what other base is more justified or more pertinent? Most teacher training consists in housekeeping skills — lesson plans, room environments, visual aids, and general psychology. Few, if any, of the skills taught in most teacher training programs can be related to specific pupil behaviors. This has led to measuring teacher differences along factors which are easily determined but have little reliability, either in predicting teacher performance or in calculating the effects of teachers upon children.

Gagné has suggested that instead of measuring values related to the efficacy of a teacher's performance, such as the college he attended, his degrees, and his years in the classroom, the efficacy itself would be measured. The "process" variables — what application the teacher makes of the materials and opportunities at hand — could be studied.[4] An alternative so clearly rooted in pupil outcomes forces the profession to confront the issue: Can we continue to be indifferent to pupil growth?

The Internal Performance Contract

The teaching profession needs to reorder its traditional stance on the financial incentives and reward structure for teaching. While some professional detachment is necessary, the profession needs to come closer to recognizing the nature and quality of client services as the main determiner of reward and promotion. Accountability and governance may be compatible in the context of an internal performance contract. Such a system is in the process of implementation in the Mesa (Arizona) Public Schools.[5]

Under a grant from the Education Professions Development Act (EPDA), teams of Mesa teachers will submit bids to the board of education to instruct a group of students for a given period of time. Bids will contain all relevant educational costs, including salaries, overhead, materials, and subcontracts to community paraprofessionals or consultants. The board will select the appropriate bids and award money to teachers to meet the required instructional objectives. Negotiation of the bids will be handled by the teachers' association and its representative deliberations team. Initially, teacher bids would conform to a general request for proposal (RFP) with the expectancy that board RFP's would gain considerably in sophistication as the process was refined. Teachers, in turn, could subcontract for coordinating or administrative services from their own building principals or district consultants.

While differential payments and responsibilities will be simulated the first year, eventually all salaries will be compressed into much flatter ranges than at present, still taking into consideration some difference for experience and training. Beyond that, however, ceilings for teacher and administrator salaries would be unlimited. Teachers and administrators could earn considerably more than their present wages by working on a commission basis. As teachers received direct cash grants from the board, they, in turn, may subcontract themselves back to their building principals or to other teams of teachers for in-service training.

Teachers would control the type of personnel differentiation of their teams in a fluid arrangement of role separation. If roles became ranked while meeting specified objectives, they would be abolished when a new contract was accepted. The salary distribution mechanism could take one of two major forms. Teachers could establish salary criteria based upon skill differentiation and one's contribution to meeting the contract and then ask an outside agency or the school administration to implement the salary procedure. The other possibility is that the teams would distribute the funds without the outside agency participating except for auditing purposes. The board should remain impartial to the mechanism for salary distribution, their first concern being to determine if the instructional contract has been met. This process moves the board's focus from inputs to ascertaining the quality of the output. If the board feels that bids are not really meeting the needs of the clients, they can offer their contracts to outside agencies. These agencies fulfill the quality control function by providing the public with an alternative.

This flexible salary structure would mean that teachers' and administrators' salaries would fluctuate from month to month as they do in other professions. There is no reason why music or drama teachers could not subcontract with many teaching teams for the performance of their specialties. The important thing is that teachers regulate the salary mechanism toward the accomplishment of specific student objectives. For some time we shall have to accept rather crude measures for growth in the attitudinal areas, such as the concept of educational juries or audits based upon expert advice. RFP objectives should be stated in the criterion-referenced sense, that is, they represent a validated base of pupil objectives. Norm-referenced instruments would be applicable where they clearly were the most appropriate tools for measurement purposes.

The value of the internal educational performance contract is that it is regulated by teachers through their own professional organization. Governance through peer regulation and evaluation is meshed with the real reward structure. This, in turn, is rooted firmly in client growth. Such an approach may united accountability and governance at the operational level. In this context accountability enhances governance and governance is embedded in responsibility.   □

Fenwick W. English (3332, University of Southern California) is director and James K. Zaharis is associate director of the Arizona-Mesa Differentiated Staffing Project.

[1] Helen Bain, "Self-Governance Must Come First, Then Accountability," *Phi Delta Kappan,* April, 1970, p. 413.

[2] "Rumsfeld Raps Teacher Unions on Reform," *Washington Star,* September 24, 1970.

[3] Peter M. Blau, *Exchange and Power in Social Life.* New York: John Wiley, 1967.

[4] Robert M. Gagne, "Policy Implications and Future Research: A Response," in *Do Teachers Make a Difference?* Washington, D.C.: Office of Education, U.S. Government Printing Office, 1970.

[5] Fenwick W. England and James K. Zaharis, "Internal Educational Performance Contracing: A Consortium Thrust at Professional Accountability, Self-Governance, and Educational Reform," paper presented to the National Academy of School Executives, American Association of School Administrators, Dallas, Texas, October, 1970, 12 pp. (mimeographed).

VIII

ACCOUNTABILITY AND WHY IT SHOULDN'T PANIC YOU

by S. J. Knezevich

"If accountability is an idea whose time has come, neither worried boards nor confused administrators nor the opposition of organized teachers (nor any other force on earth, as the saying goes) can stop it."

Accountability. If you think it is a fad you can resist, brought on by pressures you can weather, brace yourself: You have a monumental job of resisting and weathering in front of you. If you think accountability is a brave-new-world idea that will turn your schools topsy-turvy, relax: The "new" accountability is only a change in the "old" accountability, something very familiar to you. And now that you are somewhere between braced and relaxed, here are some things you ought to know about accountability.

School board members, superintendents and teachers have all been working under an accountability plan for years. Boards have always been accountable to the public for budgeting, accounting and auditing of school resources. Superintendents have always been accountable to the board for operating the district. And, teachers have always been accountable — for teaching.

The new accountability of the early 1970s — the feared, loved, misunderstood (especially misunderstood) and "in" accountability — switches the emphasis from inputs to *results.* That's why it is exciting, and that's why it is here to stay. Accountability holds schools responsible for the *results* achieved with education dollars (in addition to the traditional accounting for how the money is spent). This, in turn, means boards and superintendents are responsible for operating the district *and* for reaching certain educational goals; teachers are accountable for teaching *and* for the results that should be achieved through their teaching effort.

On the chance that this proposition sounds radical or unreasonable, consider the following rationale: If one of your schools had a leaky roof, the contractor engaged to replace the roof would be held accountable for the input (a new roof) *and* for the final result (a roof that didn't leak). Educational accountability applies the same principle of *accountability for results* to a child's education — something most taxpayers consider more important and just as leaky as a defective roof.

An accountability system defines who is answerable to whom and for what. If you are challenged to develop accountability in your schools, you — or someone you designate — will be involved in this process of defining goals, as well as determining who should be responsible for reaching them and making sure they are reached.

Accountability — and often trouble — starts when personnel at all levels are informed of the goals they are expected to fulfill. It *is* possible to hold someone accountable for the wrong thing, and people become understandably defensive if they have any doubts about the goals they are responsible for or the impartiality of having those goals assigned them in the first place. To succeed, accountability must be fair: Persons held accountable should be told to whom their actions are answerable, how performance will be monitored, when evaluations will be made, what rewards and penalties are in store, and what feedback is expected from them.

After everyone knows what is expected of him, a monitoring program must be established to inform the board and administrators if goals are actually being reached. Monitoring should be part of a complete evaluation system that includes specifying the criteria for determining effectiveness; developing data gathering devices, procedures and schedules; determining who will do the evaluating; and determining who will interpret the information that is gathered.

These aspects of accountability — identifying objectives, assigning responsibility and evaluation — can be difficult to put into practice. You may find, however, that the greatest obstacle in moving your schools from a rhetorical plane to an operational plan of accountability will be the individual and highly emotional interpretations people often attach to accountability. To avoid these, crystallize what the plan will include and how it will be implemented. You should:

• Establish an accountability *team* — don't put it all on one person, especially if you value his or her health.

• Identify and clarify objectives to determine if they are realistic in view of the constraints under which your schools operate.

• Conduct a specific (that means person by person) review of who is to be responsible and what (exactly) he is responsible for.

• Give each level of operation both short and long-range accountability strategies.

• Develop an information system capable of fulfilling the stringent demands of an accountability operation.

• Identify sources likely to resist accountability — if this resistance springs from confusion or ignorance, your information system can help alleviate it.

If your accountability plan works, it will supply you with information showing how well resources have been employed (and how better they *can* be employed) to achieve the goals that have been set for your schools. Accountability, then, can be thought of as a way to obtain the most productive use of available resources in pursuit of objectives. Here are four techniques for achieving objectives:

1. A Planning, Programming, Budgeting System (P.P.B.S.) helps your board decide how to allocate resources among competing interests within the district.

2. School personnel, your most valuable resource, can also be the force behind a "dump accountability" movement. To motivate this resource in your favor, initiate and maintain a review of the reward system, and keep trying to get your employees to recognize the importance of reaching certain specified objectives.

3. The full scope of resources available in the private and public sectors should be utilized — this may mean employing private contractors for services when it is prudent and practical to do so.

4. Cover all bets: To increase the possibilities for achieving objectives, establish alternative systems to long established education approaches.

The design of any accountability system should take into account the mood and educational objectives of the community. Accountability is as much a state of mind as a set of techniques — it is a point of view that, to succeed, must prevail in the entire school system.

Even if you don't like accountability, there are major social forces that may not allow you to abandon the idea. Citizens are paying more for schools now than they ever have, and they expect results for their money. And, increasingly, they are demanding results for their *children*. The federal government's involvement in local education efforts is only beginning. If school boards are serious about wanting to preserve local decision making, they are going to have to establish a relationship between program results and federal grants. Today, vast numbers of individuals, groups and organizations are genuinely concerned with the quality of education and see accountability as a way of determining whether schools are doing what they should be doing.

If accountability is an idea whose time has come, neither worried boards nor confused administrators nor the opposition of organized teachers (nor any force on earth, as the saying goes) can stop it. And if accountability can really help us achieve better education for our children — something for which we've always been morally accountable — then the greater question becomes, why oppose it at all. □

S. J. Knezevich is professor of educational administration at the University of Wisconsin.

IX

PREFACE TO THE CATALOGUE OF CURMUDGEON COLLEGE

by John Fischer

"All students are welcome to sit in any classroom as long as they like, for the standard lecture fee of one dollar an hour, payable at the door."

Our Philosophy

No student should be compelled to attend a college he doesn't like. So if you disapprove of something here, don't bother to demonstrate. Just leave.

Our Policy

Absolute freedom, tempered with occasional expulsions.

Dormitory Rules

We don't have any. As a matter of fact, we have no dormitories. Our founder and president, Henry J. Curmudgeon, can't see why an educational institution should be distracted by running a hotel business on the side. Consequently our students live anywhere they like—motels, boarding houses, brothels, or communes. How they behave there is a matter that concerns only them, their landlords, their parents, and the local police.

Sports

For the same reason, we have no sports program. Why should a college mess around with show biz when Joe Namath can do it better? Any undergraduate who feels in need of exercise can apply to the maintenance department for a broom, or can go to Jocko

Sullivan's Gymnasium and Pugilistic Parlor, conveniently located near our downtown campus. Obsessive exhibitionists are free to hire their own basketball court or football field.

Sit-Ins

All students are welcome to sit in any classroom as long as they like, for the standard lecture fee of one dollar an hour, payable at the door. Any attempt to sit in the administration building will be treated as criminal trespass by our town sheriff, Knucks McGrory (6'3", 280 lbs.). Undergraduates, in fact, have no occasion to enter the administration building, or even to go near it except on the first day of each term, when enrollment fees are payable at the drive-in cashier's window. No checks accepted. It is pointless to try to intimidate President Curmudgeon. He does not engage in confrontations; they bore him.

Governance

The college is governed by President Curmudgeon, period. He hires and fires the faculty, fixes salaries, sets the curriculum, and makes final decisions on the admission and expulsion of students. As in all colleges, the president is held responsible—by the public, alumni, professors, and undergraduates—for everything that happens. Obviously he cannot discharge this responsibility without commensurate authority.

He may from time to time consult members of the faculty on administrative matters, but feels no obligation to take their views seriously. Early in his career President Curmudgeon learned that the typical professor can't administer his way out of a paper bag. As he observed in his now-famous paper on collegiate governance:

"The true scholar is inherently incapable of running anything. By temperament, he loathes the very concept of authority; hence he is always opposed to the administration, but is even more opposed to the idea of exercising authority himself. When confronted with the necessity of making a decision, he habitually falls into a spasm of self-doubt, takes refuge in a faculty committee which argues for three months, and then resolves to defer action until further information becomes available. He can never learn Rule No. 1 of management: 'A good executive is one who always acts promptly and is sometimes right.'

"Consequently our faculty is limited to its proper functions:

teaching and research, in that order. Managerial decisions are
handled by the responsible executive, *i.e.* me. Students participate
in governance the same way that customers participate in the governance of Macy's. If they don't like the goods offered, they can
go to Gimbel's."

Pot, LSD, and Liquor

What a student ingests on his own time and in his own quarters is his own affair. But if he snores in class, breaks laboratory
equipment, gets busted by the police on campus, freaks out in the
halls, or otherwise disturbs his teachers and fellow students, he
gets shipped out on the next plane.

Tenure

None. Each faculty member signs an undated resignation the
day he is hired, and henceforth serves at the pleasure of the
president.

In the early days of the college it was widely believed that
this somewhat unorthodox arrangement might make it difficult to
attract first-class professors. This proved untrue. In the sellers'
market which has long prevailed in academia, a talented man needs
no job protection because he can always take his pick of a dozen
chairs; tenure, therefore, merely shelters the incompetent.

Nevertheless, to make sure that it gets the best men available,
Curmudgeon has from the beginning paid salaries twice as high as
the normal scale. In addition it offers certain unique fringe benefits. Professors never have to waste their time in committee meetings or the deliberations of an Academic Senate. They also are
freed from the demeaning obligation of cranking out so-called
"scholarly works" in order to demonstrate their "productivity."
On the contrary, they are discouraged from writing anything for
subsidized publication: that is, by a scholarly journal or university
press. When a professor has something really worth putting into
type, any number of commercial publishers will be delighted to get
their hands on it. To be sure, this means that our faculty have to
learn to write English, a rare skill among people who have been
marinated in academic jargon—but it pays off in hard cash, as John
Kenneth Galbraith, Loren Eiseley, Samuel Eliot Morison, John
Maynard Keynes, and other distinguished scholars have clearly
demonstrated.[1]

The most attractive fringe benefit, however, is our Professori-
al Piece-of-the-Action Plan. Instead of enrolling for formal courses,
our students simply attend any lectures or seminars which they
consider rewarding—basing their choices on the catalogue descriptions, the "Student Appraisal of Faculty" published each term,
and the campus grapevine. Such choices are not made lightly, since
undergraduates have to drop a dollar into the toll box every time
they enter a classroom.[2] The resulting cash flow indicates accurately which teachers are meeting the felt needs of the students.
Consequently, it is only fair to reward those who consistently produce above-average gate receipts with a percentage of the take.
Our star performers, as a results, are the only faculty members in
America who earn more than football coaches.

On the other hand, any professor who cannot attract enough
paying customers to cover his own salary, plus a share of the overhead, is encouraged to take up some other calling.

Since students are incapable of judging academic quality—
how can they tell whether old Dr. Chips is really giving them the
latest dope in his field?—some teachers feared that the cash-flow
system might reward the merely entertaining lecturers at the expense of the more profound and demanding scholars. To avoid
this, all classrooms are monitored with television cameras, con-
nected by closed circuit to our Inspector General's office. There
the inspectors, each a recognized authority in his discipline, periodically evaluate each professor's classroom performance, to make
sure that he comes up to scratch both in substance and in peda-
gogical technique. Thus our teachers are the first in academic history to be held strictly accountable for the quality of their work,
just like professionals in other fields. Yet at the same time we observe the time-honored convention that no administrator or academic superior can ever enter a classroom without an invitation
from the teacher.

Admission Policy

Elitist. No student is admitted unless he demonstrates his
ability to write a page of coherent, correctly spelled English prose,
and to do basic arithmetic; this rule automatically eliminates about
75 per cent of all high-school graduates. Moreover, this college is
designed only for those undergraduates who already know what
they want to do with their lives, and want our help in preparing

themselves for it. Youngsters who prefer to put in four years of intellectual finger-painting while they "find themselves" can go elsewhere; we offer no courses in social psychology, literature appreciation, oriental philosophy, or art history.

Curmudgeon, furthermore, does not accommodate draft dodgers or students who merely want the prestige of a diploma. Since we are not accredited, our undergraduates are not sheltered from the draft; and we award no diplomas. Instead a student may, if he wishes, ask his professors for a Certificate oc Competence in his chosen field—engineering, ecology, journalism, teaching, or whatever. He may request such a certificate whenever he thinks he is ready for it, and can persuade his teachers to sign it; in some cases this may require two years of work, in others seven, depending on the student's ability and the difficulty of the subject. A Certificate of Competence, we have found, is of considerable interest to future employers, but it confers no social prestige.

Examinations and Grades
If a student feels that an examination will help him measure his progress in any given subject, he may ask his teacher to give him one at any time. Similarly, if a teacher is in doubt about a student's progress, he may call for a written or oral examination. Otherwsie no exams are required.

Neither are grades. If an undergraduate is goofing off, his teachers soon know it; and when any three of them decide that he is wasting their time, and his own, he is expelled forthwith. This seldom happens. Since our regular fees plus the pay-at-the-classroom-door system make Curmudgeon an expensive institution, which offers nothing but a chance for education, it usually attracts only those youngsters who are eager and able to do the work.

Financial Aid
Available on request to all students, on a lifetime reimbursable basis.

We cheerfully advance whatever money an undergraduate may need to cover his fees, living expenses, and door tolls. In return, he promises to pay us one per cent of his annual income for the rest of his life, beginning one year after graduation. He also signs a form authorizing the Internal Revenue Service to collect this money on behalf of the college, by the simple method of adding one per cent to his yearly income tax.

This arrangement has proved highly satisfactory both to students and to the college. Any bright youngster, no matter how poor, can get an education without financial strain. Moreover, the one per cent reimbursement is the best investment he can ever make, since a practical, profession-oriented training of the kind we offer normally multiplies his lifetime earning capacity by at least ten.

For the college, this system produces a dependable—and steadily rising—flow of revenue. The president is thus relieved of the humiliating and onerous chore of constantly begging for money, a duty which consumes up to 50 per cent of the time of most college presidents. He can therefore devote his full attention to running the place, to the obvious benefit of both students and faculty.

The Curmudgeon One Per Cent Plan also has a Robin Hood side effect. Those of our graduates who become millionaires—a gratifying percentage—automatically pay high for the training which was so markedly responsible for their success. Hence they subsidize other graduates who never make such money, or who deliberately choose the less lucrative professions, such as poetry or politics, and therefore can never repay the full cost of their education.

Faculty

Curmudgeon is proud of the fact that it employs a smaller percentage of Doctors of Philosophy than any other college in the country.

This does not mean that we do not value advanced degrees, in their proper place. A teacher of ecology, for example, not only needs a Ph.D. in biology, but also some postgraduate study in several other disciplines, including economics, climatology, and urban studies. A doctorate also can be a useful tool in teaching the physical sciences and certain other subjects, such as economics and history.

In many fields, however, it not only is unnecessary; it may be a positive handicap. Witness those hapless wretches who earn Ph.D.s in English Literature. Their ordeal, coupled with years of exposure to the *Publications of the Modern Language Association,* frequently cripples their prose style for life, so that they are unfitted for anything except teaching another generation of Lit.

students and writing criticism for nonpaying journals. Curmudgeon
has no place for these self-maimed scholars. We do, of course, encourage our students to read and enjoy literature, but not in class;
it is properly a leisure-time activity, like listening to music, making
amateur films, and chasing girls.

Our only English courses are designed for undergraduates
who hope to become professional writers. They are taught by men
who have made their living in the trade for at least ten years; none
ever had time to get a Ph.D. because they were too busy writing
novels, biographies, and magazine articles.

Most of our other departments also are staffed with Old Pros.
Political science is taught by retired mayors, governors, and senators; public administration by high-ranking civil servants; business
administration by seasoned executives who once managed their
own firms with indisputable success.

We also feel free to ignore the traditional departmental
boundaries, which often are as anachronistic as feudal baronies—
and as stoutly defended by the faculty who man them. We are
now in the process, for instance, of merging our political-science
and economics courses into a single Department of Political Economy, on the grounds that economics is what politics is all about:
"Who gets what, how, and from whom."

The new department also will include all courses on city and
regional planning. This subject has fallen into disrepute on most
campuses because it traditionally has been an adjunct of the
School of Art and Architecture. Its graduates were trained to draw
lovely maps and sketch monumental building projects, which almost invariably came to nothing because they had no relation to a
city's economic and political realities. Thus the filing cabinets of
bureaucracy from coast to coast are filled with plans that never
had a chance, forgotten by everybody except the heartbroken
aesthetes who drafted them.

The few plans that actually have been carried through with
some success were conceived and put into operation by men of a
different breed. They are money men, with their hands on a spigot
which controls the flow of public funds. Often they are budget
officers, with desks next door to the mayor or governor whom
they serve. Sometimes they are bureaucrats who direct the hoses
carrying federal money to local communities—as in the case of the
Appalachian Regional Commission, which probably has produced

more effective planning than any other agency in America. For the heart of any plan lies in capital investment: in the decisions which fix priorities, and also release money to build a highway here, a housing project there, a sewage-treatment plant somewhere else. Basically, such decisions are both political and economic, and the men who make them will not long survive unless they are skilled in political economy. They should, of course, be advised by archi-tects—and by ecologists, engineers, and a lot of other specialists— but they themselves are specialists only in the public business. For the Acropolis we have to thank Pericles, a politician. Who now re-members the names of the architects he hired?

If this college can produce even a small-size Pericles now and then, we shall regard the experiment as a success.   □

Mr. Fischer was editor in chief of *Harper's* 1953-67, and is now a contributing editor. A collection of his Easy Chair columns and other articles was publish-ed in 1964, with the title *The Stupidity Problem, and Other Harassments.*

X

A PERSPECTIVE ON ACCOUNTABILITY

by Vito Perrone and Warren Strandberg

"In its most basic form, accountability responds to the questions: How much are we (taxpayers) getting for our money? Can our children read, perform mathematical computations, get a job, successfully compete at a higher level of education? These are appropriate questions. Schools should have asked them seriously decades ago, but not to the exclusion of broader concerns."

With the decline of public confidence in our schools has come a plethora of devastating critiques. Serious discussion of alternatives such as voucher plans, free schools, and de-schooling has grown enormously. (What was a "radical" posture a few years ago today has credibility across the entire political-social spectrum.) A decade of promise in which billions of dollars were expended for education has born limited fruit for Americans. Too many schools have failed, not only to assist children in their learning of basic skills, but also to provide a vision of a humane and sensitive life.

How do we explain the deficiencies outlined in Charles Silberman's *Crisis in the Classroom?* His poignant indictment of the schools for "mutilation of a child's spirit . . . of spontaneity, of joy in learning, of pleasure in creating, of a sense of self"; as places that are too often "grim, joyless . . . oppressive and petty . . . intellectually sterile and esthetically barren . . . lacking in civility . . ."[1] has heightened the defensiveness of school boards and their professional staffs. In their defensive posture, school officials have eagerly embraced accountability as a contemporary educational engineering concept.

In its most basic form, accountability responds to the

Reprinted with copyright permission of authors and *Teachers College Record*. February 1972.

questions: How much are we (taxpayers) getting for our money? Can our children read, perform mathematical computations, get a job, successfully compete at a higher level of education? These are appropriate questions. Schools should have asked them seriously decades ago, but not to the exclusion of broader concerns.

It is interesting to observe how quickly accountability has caught on. In our own efforts at creating open classrooms we are increasingly confronted by school officials who say: "All that you advocate is fine but we have to be accountable." What they mean is that children must be at "grade-level" on various standardized achievement tests and exhibit some predetermined level of growth during the school year. Can an open classroom with an integrated curriculum be "risked" when school officials have such concerns? Administrators do not like to discuss issues such as whether children can be trusted to initiate more of their learning, or the community become a major learning environment. Instead, they question whether setting such directions will cause children to produce appropriate scores on a first grade standardized reading test or a third grade achievement test in social studies, mathematics, or science. Local education leaders feel obligated to report results of such testing to taxpayers who, they feel, deserve to know how children are performing in relation to state and national norms. They believe parents are demanding that kind of accountability. School officials have long justified their evasion of challenges and issues by announcing that a particular position is what "parents want." Accountability may provide another such "opportunity."

If school districts really knew what parent concerns were, the issues would be quite different. However, three years of rather intensive discussion with several thousand parents in communities throughout North Dakota and other parts of the United States has made us skeptical of the knowledge most school officials possess of parental interest in education. Some of our initial meetings with parents were awkward—it was the first time many of them had talked about educational issues. But interaction with these people has provided us with more insights into education than we ever gained in our professional training. They clearly recognize that children are different, that they learn in different ways and have different interests, and they believe that schools should affirm this basic understanding in practice. They are sensitive to the effects on children of rejection and failure. Their awareness that a separation

existed between the school and the home—that what children were
about in school did not carry over into the home, and that children's interests at home were not beginning points for study at
school—was enlightening. For them, it was simply "common
sense" that such activities should intersect, and that such an inter-
section would cause their children to become more interested in
school.

Parental Contributions

Those who are primarily concerned with accountability have
yet to deal seriously with parents and the concerns they have for
their children's education. The significant intervention of parents,
we believe, will stimualte more creative reform efforts in education. Those efforts, in turn, will enlarge our conception of accountability. But if parents are to become more involved in the
life of their schools, schools will need to become more open institutions. Parents will then be able to assume a larger role in defining
the outcome of their children's education.

During one informal discussion we had with a group of parents, a mother began to take the University to task for not preparing her son's fifth grade teacher properly. It seemed that her son
was absorbed in a self-initiated study of astronomy, which he was
not permitted to pursue in school. The mother's solution was to
send the teacher back to the University to learn astronomy so she
would be qualified to teach it to the child. When asked how her
son had come to know astronomy, the parent realized that he had
learned it independently of the formal educational structure. It became obvious that a more reasonable solution to this problem was
possible: create a school environment that encourages children to
pursue those things in which they are deeply interested.

Within this context, what did accountability mean to this
particular parent? She was concerned about the level of her son's
involvement and the intensity of interest he exhibited in school. It
would have made little sense to talk to her about performance contracting or skill-oriented tests in reading, math, etc. Such discussion simply would have negated her intuitive sense of what the educational encounter is all about.

We often assume that parents are not in a good position to
contribute to the direction schools will take, or to evaluate what
transpires there, and, in fact, many parents do not feel they are in

a position to define the areas in which the schools will be accountable. The parent cited in the above example did not have a very
clear sense of what was occurring in the school, except as she
viewed her child's reactions to school. Yet even this limited awareness does provide a basis for judgment.

This awareness is manifested in different ways. For example,
a reporter asked a group of parents who had children in classrooms
with New School interns if their children were learning anything in
school. After a long period of silence one parent replied, "I don't
know if my child is learning anything, but I do know that each
morning for four years I have literally pushed my child off to
school. This year I have had trouble keeping her from leaving
home too early." That parent, in spite of her lack of specific
knowledge of her child's learning, did have a good sense of her
child's response to school. It is this latter knowledge that is seldom
tapped by teachers and school officials as they define the limits of
accountability.

In spite of what has been said above, we acknowledge that
the accountability movement has gained considerable support
from parents. However, where parents have made demands for accountability, the demands have been centered on a narrow range
of abilities (for example, the confrontation over inner-city children's inability to read). Parents turn to those things with which
they are most familiar (the three R's) because they have had few
opportunities to consider other possibilities. Our experience suggests that, when parents gain accessibility to schools, they can expand their own educational horizons. Increased sensitivity to the
options open to children in a classroom leaves them dissatisfied
with defining accountability in terms of test performance. Instead
they have become more interested in supporting such broadly
based concerns as independence-in-learning and joy-in-learning.
Such objectives are not easily articulated or measured. Growth is
often slow. Yet where schools are accessible to parents such limitations have been tolerable and manageable. In contrast, these limitations are much more difficult for the performance contractor to
handle. The performance contractor, so much a part of today's accountability scene, has difficulty in responding to objectives that
move beyond the narrow range of skill development, since his reimbursement is often based upon the kinds of growth that can be
measured over a short term.

While school officials claim that their schools are open to parents, our experience has shown that many parents feel ill at ease when in the school building, as if they didn't belong. They find it difficult to become active participants in the life of a school especially if they do not have a professional background. For active participation to occur, a learning environment must be created that will facilitate parental interaction with children. This simply is not possible, beyond a limited level, in traditional classrooms. Nor is it possible in a setting where the highest priority is given to assessment of performance measured in specific and limited terms such as word-recognition skills, adding two column numbers, and recognizing properly spelled words. Is it more possible where the school district is paying a contractor for predetermined performance improvement? In a highly structured classroom setting with limited objectives it becomes difficult for parents to become significantly involved with children. Where parents are encouraged to devote time to such settings, special training is usually demanded. Obviously, special training is less necessary in informal classroom settings. As a result, parents are taking part in such activities as wood working, cooking, sewing, arts and crafts, reading stories, listening to children read stories, leading field trips, and just being with children. Such participation has increased parents' understanding of the classroom and its possibilities for enhancing children's educational and personal growth. And in the process their perspective on what schools should be accountable for has changed.

Council

We must begin to think of ways of opening entire school systems to broader parental participation. One method would be to establish at each school a participant council consisting of constituent parents and teachers which could interpret the school to the community, represent it in its relations with the board of education, and keep the principal and staff informed of community needs and concerns. Equally important, the council could join in organizing parents and others who wished to contribute to the life of the school. Because they would be in close touch with their constituents, the members of the participant councils would be in a better position to respond quickly and effectively to the educational concerns and aspirations of teachers and parents. The school board would maintain its constitutional responsibility for the over-all budget and major decisions which affect the entire school system. However, it would relinquish to the participant councils a high degree of responsibility.

Accountability tends to limit the opportunities open to children, creating more rigid systems of schooling. This tendency is illustrated by another informal conversation we had with a parent and her son's fourth-grade teacher. We were discussing the youngster's lack of interest in school. The parent, having described in some detail her son's intense interest in working with radios on winter·days when school was not in session, then turned to the teacher and asked why her son could not spend time with radios in school. In response, the teacher indicated that she felt accountable for the child learning, among other things, American history, and in general being "prepared" for the next grade. Similar incidents could be cited that would underline the limitations created by the current accountability movement.

In spite of the claims that accountability will make the schools more open, more humane, and more accepting of diversity and alternative patterns of education,[2] we feel that in practice the situation has been vastly different. The pressures placed upon children, teachers, administrators, and school boards by the demands for accountability have only reinforced the artificial divisions found in most standardized curricula. Accountability is certainly not responsible for the division of knowledge and skills into subject matter areas which have long been with us. But it has had the effect of discouraging recent attempts to build a more integrated curriculum.

A number of educators are beginning to explore the integrative qualities of knowledge, skills, appreciations, and understanding, out of an enlarged awareness that knowledge has a personal dimension and that the disjunction between subjectivity and objectivity is artificial. In addition, there are those who do not see the traditional disciplines treated in isolation from one another as having a significant connection with contemporary social, political, and economic concerns. Both groups have stimulated, not only the exploration of new relationships among traditional subject matters, but also new ways of looking at knowledge in relation to learning. In becoming accountable, we should not turn away from these new directions. Recent efforts have narrowed those areas in which we seek to become accountable.

Accountability's Limits

The "break-up" of the curriculum into smaller, more isolated, limited units is due in large measure to a growing dependence upon behavioral objectives and systems analysis. It has been
argued that to be accountable goals and objectives must be translated into specific behaviors that can be observed and measured.
But in doing this, an essential quality of human action, as distinguished from behavior, is lost. It is the intentional or purposeful
nature of human action that distinguishes it and makes it intelligible. All normal people, including children, act primarily out of a
sense of purpose. Recognition of this fact, we believe, rules out a
strictly "behavioral" account of human action. Our sense of purpose gives learning whatever integrative quality it has. Achievement tests, typically used to measure accountability, simply are
not sensitive to the intelligible quality of human action. They are
not able to capture the intentional aspect of learning. Most of
those who advance the notion of accountability would argue that
you simply start with performance criteria, specifications of what
student behaviors are desired, and then develop a systematic educational program designed to produce those behaviors. But to conceive human action as separate and isolatable behaviors which are
caused by certain temporal antecedents introduced by the teacher
reduces student opportunities for integrative experiences arising
out of goal-seeking action. In creating instructional programs that
inhibit the cultivation of purposeful action, we limit a student's
freedom. "A man becomes more and more a free and responsible
agent the more he at all times knows what he is doing, in every
sense of this phrase, and the more he acts with a definite and
clearly formal intention."[3] Education must be about nothing less
than nurturing free and responsible persons. In being accountable
to children (something educators talk about very little), we can do
no less than evaluate their success in relation to the intentions they
themselves form.

Perhaps a practical example will illustrate the above point.
Not long ago we observed a school resource teacher giving a physical education demonstration to other teachers. Using a group of
her children for demonstration purposes, she showed how various
large and small muscles could be developed systematically. The
children were put through a variety of coordinated but isolated exercises which would probably accomplish what they had intended.

Yet, the children clearly lacked enthusiasm for what they were doing. Their bored expressions changed when they were allowed to
play a game. They became exuberant. The game had a "wholeness"
about it that was lacking in the skill-oriented exercises. In the
game there was more clearly a fusion of natural ability, skill, and
purpose that exemplifies human action.

There is no need to assume that "accountability" necessitates
a narrow focus. But, because of our limited conception of human
behavior and our likewise limited ability to measure it, evaluation
quickly turns to those things that are easily conceived and measured over short periods of time. Broader, more diffuse goals dealing with human action are difficult to translate into specific behaviors. Even where the translation is accomplished the inferential
leap from behaviors to objectives tends to be great and, in the process, the intentional quality of human action is lost. The aims
associated with accountability make it much easier to narrow our
vision and limit our objectives.

Throughout our discussion of accountability we have inti-
mated that our present notions of curriculum are quite limited and
often bear little relation to the lives of children. In our own efforts
at creating more open classrooms we have recognized the need to
enlarge our conception of what are acceptable and significant areas
of involvement for children. To do this we have had to break out
of the traditional subject matter mold. In emphasizing the need to
create alternative learning environments, we would not want to
suggest that basic skills are unimportant. They are fundamental,
but they must be seen in relation to the more encompassing need
to nurture in children a higher level of personal motivation and involvement in learning. The skills of literacy—reading, writing,
speaking, and thinking—develop more effectively when they are
not treated as academic exercises which exist in a vacuum. They
should be taught tin settings which stimulate children's imagination and thought, and thus foster their desire to communicate. In
this sense all forms of creative expression are important and should
be an integral part of every program.

In this age of the "knowledge explosion" there is probably no
sacred body of information to which all children must be exposed.
What is taught in each community should reflect the local environment to a high degree. Children must learn to cope with unknown
complexities they have not specifically been taught to manage.

Thus our concern is not so much the specific content of instruction as it is the process by which children are taught. We think it particularly important that children be able to initiate activities, that they be self-directed and able to take responsibility for their own learning. Children should feel intense involvement in learning, and that intensity should arise out of their wonder, imagination, and curiosity, leading ultimately to concern and commitment. In addition teachers should cultivate a setting in which children are honest and open, and where they are respectufl of themselves, adults, and other children. In such a setting we believe children will learn responsibility as an integral part of freedom.

Directions for Accountability

Our belief that we need to expand our idea of what are acceptable and significant areas of involvement for children suggests not only a desire to be accountable for the outcome but a direction for accountability that is not part of the current literature. This leaves us and others interested in classrooms that foster some of the foregoing dimensions with the issue of evaluation. Inasmuch as I.Q. and grade level equivalency scores, the typical "hard data" for many educational researchers and performance contractors, are not critical to what we want to measure, new tools are necessary.[4] Evaluation instruments for dealing with some of the broader dimensions outlined above are not particularly well developed; however, considerable pioneering efforts are being made.

In our efforts in North Dakota we are depending to a high degree on observation and individual diagnostic conferences. And we are becoming convinced that such activities can provide the kinds of evaluative data that will respond to what we wish to be accountable for. Trained observers can certainly answer questions such as: To what degree do individual children initiate their own learning? To what degree are interactions among children, and between children and the teacher, becoming more open? Individual diagnostic conferences, in addition to a teacher's records and children's, can respond to such issues as: What has the individual child accomplished? What has he understood of his experience? In what ways has he extended his learning?

The increasing interest in the foregoing types of measurement is encouraging. The Columbia Teacher's College *Indicators of Quality* has been used by teachers, and in many cases parents, quite successfully. It provides an observational mechanism for analyzing what teachers and children do that is most productive in learning, analyzing individualization, interpersonal regard, creativity, and group activity. The Personal Record of School Experiences (PROSE), an Educational Testing Service instrument used initially in Headstart evaluation, also appears to have good potential. (We are using it in a number of schools in which we have instructional responsibility.) PROSE is designed to yield a record of experiences the individual child has in school, including such dimensions as instructional content, adult role, level of participation, peer interaction, level of involvement, and activity level. In addition, there are two promising efforts that are influencing our evaluation program and to which we would like to call attention. *Analysis of an Approach to Open Education,* a study conducted by the Educational Testing Service, is a significant attempt to translate an educational position, "one which embodies a philosophy of learning, a craft of teaching, a vision of life . . . into terms which . . . have implication for psychological assessment and research."[5] While it does not present an observational instrument, it does suggest a variety of cognitive and affective dimensions of learning which can be analyzed by trained observers. Since its publication the ETS staff has developed several interrelated observational and interview instruments which they are testing in the field. Furthermore, TDL Associates in Newton, Massachusetts have just completed an impressive study, *Characteristics of Open Education: Toward an Operational Definition.*[6] An outgrowth of the study has been a Classroom Observational Rating-Scale and a Teacher Questionnaire which add considerably to our ability to evaluate what teachers do as they teach and children do as they learn.

One of the clear advantages of observational evaluation is that it enlarges the numbers of individuals, including parents, who can be significantly involved. The tie to accessibility should be clearn.

As schools become more accessible we are convinced that issues such as accountability will take on a more creative direction; testing, in traditional terms, will diminish in importance and schools will become more supportive of the integrative educational dimensions that enhance children's ability to deal with themselves, with others, and with a world of change.   □

Vito Perrone and Warren Strandberg have gained their "perspective" on accountability through their work as Dean and Program Coordinator of the New School for Behavioral Studies in Education at the University of North Dakota which was established in order to reorganize the elementary school system of North Dakota into informal schools by training teachers for such schools.

---

[1]Charles Silberman. *Crisis in the Classroom.* New York: Random House, 1970, p. 10.

[2]See Leon Lessinger, "Teachers in An Age of Accountability," *Instructor,* June/July 1971; and Leon Lessinger. *Every Kid A Winner.* New York: Simon and Schuster, 1970.

[3]Stuart Hampshire. *Thought and Action.* New York: The Viking Press, 1960, p. 91.

[4]Henry Dyer, Vice President of Educational Testing Service, has made a number of interesting observations about traditional testing that we feel are relevant to this discussion. About the I.Q. and grade equivalency scores, he says: "[They are] psychological and statistical monstrosities. I have defined the I.Q. as a dubious normative scale wrapped up in a ratio that is based upon an impossible assumption about the equivalence of human experience and the opportunity to learn. A grade level equivalency score has many of the same properties, and as such it lures educational practitioners to succumb to what Alfred N. Whitehead called the 'fallacy of misplaced concreteness.' " The *United Teacher,* April 14, 1971, p. 15. Dyer's point becomes even more relevant after noting how few additional correct responses it takes on most popular achievement tests to raise the grade level equivalency one full grade level. See Robert Stake, "Testing Hazards in Performance Contracting," *Phi Delta Kappan,* June 1971, pp. 583-588.

[5]Anne M. Bussis and Edward C. Chittenden. *Analysis of an Approach to Open Education.* Princeton, New Jersey: Educational Testing Service, August 1970, p. 1. The study is a preliminary effort to evaluate the Educational Development Center's Follow Through Program, "A Plan for Continuing Growth."

[6]Herbert Walberg and Susan Thomas. *Characteristics of Open Education: Toward an Operational Definition.* Newton, Massachusetts: TDL Associates, May 1971. This study also focuses upon the EDC Follow Through Model and uses *Analysis of an Approach to Open Education* as a starting point.

XI

SOME UNEASY INQUIRIES INTO ACCOUNTABILITY

by Dennis D. Gooler

"Accountability is deeply rooted in economics and politics. It addresses itself to the phenomenon of alienation, to the sense of lack of control of the citizen over the institutions that govern his life and his conduct. In times of tight money, accountability will flourish. And the politics of education shall not go unaffected by the move to formal accountability. One wonders if the education of the young man and woman, the boys and girls, will finally be related to accountability at all. And one wonders what criteria, standards, and indicators we will employ to determine the worth and the outcomes of accountability itself. What will be gained, and what lost?"

In a recent study by Gallup the author makes a strong case for recognition of the changing mood of the public toward education:

People continue to have a high regard for the schools of their community and they believe firmly that education is the royal road to success in America. Yet there is undeniably a new mood in the nation with which educators must reckon.

Up to this point in history, the majority of citizens have been quite willing to take the word of the school board and of the teachers and administrators that the schools are doing a good job. They have looked with pride on the community's school buildings and its winning football or basketball teams. These have been good enough to convince many that the local schools are good. But evidence in the present study indicates that this way of judging the quality of education may be in for a change.[1]

Gooler, Dennis. "Some Uneasy Inquiries into Accountability." *Accountability in Education.* Edited by Leon Lessinger and Ralph Tyler. Worthington, Ohio: Charles A. Jones Publishing Company, 1971. Reprinted with permission of NSSE, author and publisher.

Adults included in Gallup's study were asked: Would you favor or oppose a system that would hold teachers and administrators more accountable for the progress of students? The study reports that 67 percent of the adults voted in favor, 21 percent opposed the idea, and the remaining 12 percent had no opinion.

But what shape shall this accountability take? Robinson asks, "Accountability for whom? For what?"[2] And Lennon echoes the spirit of that inquiry: What are the schools to be accountable for" Who shall be accountable? How shall accountability be established? By whom shall accountability be determined?[3]

There are many definitions or descriptions of accountability in the literature, yet most definitions are strangely ambivalent. The dictionary definition uses words such as "answerable," or "explainable." One response to the question, "What is accountability?" was developed at the Center for Instructional Research and Curriculum Evaluation (CIRCE), University of Illinois. The response, contained in an introduction to *The Accountability Notebook,* is reproduced in full below:

Accountability is doing what is supposed to be done.

Accountability is often unknown because it is difficult to find out what is being done and because different people have different ideas as to what is *supposed to be* done.

Full accountability depends on people agreeing about what the goals are and on people knowing the progress toward these goals. Full accountability is impossible, but a high level of accountability can be attained.

An Illinois school that is accountable is one that is doing what it is supposed to do. It needs to keep teachers, students, parents, and other citizens advised as to what it is doing. It needs to continue to resolve—to find the best compromises for—the different needs and expectations these people have.

Accountability involves an assessment or estimation of what is, a judgment of effectiveness and/or worth of what is, and some form of attribution of responsibility to someone or something. Accountability requires disclosure of information by school people to those who demand such disclosures. Accountability is different from *responsibility*. We may not be required to offer disclosure of all those things we are *responsible* for, yet we continue to be responsible for those things. This writing addresses the problems of disclosure.

In this discussion, some inquiries into the question of criteria and standards used in accountability will be made. In addition, an inquiry into how we perceive what *is* will be pursued. This is a way of asking about the nature of accountability. The intent is to probe, not prescribe; it is generally easier to criticize than create, of course: it is hoped these inquiries will be responsible ones.

On Criteria

Educational accountability is concerned with determining how *well* the school is doing what it does, *and* whether it is doing those things it should. There is a need for a clear delineation of goals and activities, together with a clarification of the reasons for selecting some goals and not others.

The areas in which schools may be held accountable, by various citizens or professional groups, may be determined in part by perceptions of what things these groups of individuals think are important. That is, people may try to determine not only how well the school is accomplishing its goals, but also whether or not the school seems to be giving high priority to those goals it *ought* to be giving high priority to.

By what criteria shall we judge the effectiveness of our schools? The most popular criteria for determining success are those criteria concerned with certain specified cognitive learner outcomes. In performance contracting, for example, success is determined (and rewarded) by assessing gain as indicated by scores on standardized tests in specific subject matter areas. The problems of measurement related to this kind of criterion are numerous— Lennon[4], Stake[5], Stake and Wardrop[6], Barro[7]. Cognitive achievement gain, as indicated by changes in performance on specified tests, appears to many to be more amenable to measurement than any other criteria, such as the measurement of self-concept, or alienation or logical thinking.

The criterion of cognitive gains certainly cannot be dismissed as irrelevant. If we could adequately measure learner outcomes (particularly in terms of some kind of gain) would we have captured the essence of what schools are all about? Would we have identified *the* criterion upon which the school should be held accountable? Not entirely, particularly if we place and credence in such data as that provided by Gallup[8] who indicates that any thought about the curriculum (meaning, presumably, learner

outcomes, methodologies, content, etc) is relegated to only the
seventh most important school problem, as viewed by a variety of
kinds of people. Many regard so-called "non-cognitive" attributes
such as love, sensitivity, or feeling as important goals for the
school. Should these goals be reflected in judgmental criteria, and
in our attempts to be answerable?

Few people would reject the notion that the school should be
accountable for more than cognitive outcomes. Despite a general
feeling that the school exists to do more than just promote certain
specified cognitive outcomes, however, we may find ourselves
judging the school only on that basis, because the cognitive outcomes criteria may be the only criteria about which we have tried
to collect empirical data. In the absence of data on success in
achieving other school goals, we may, for accountability purposes,
consider *only* the cognitive outcomes criteria.

What are some alternative (or additional) criteria by which
the school might be judged and held accountable? The call for
change proposed by Holt, Goodman, Illich, Silberman, and others
is, in part, a call for different criteria of judgment. Further indications of the need for change are reflected in much of the "student
unrest." Students are telling us we are not using the right criteria
to judge their worth. They would hold us accountable for our
failure to establish some goals they think are important, and for
our inability to reach still others.

A number of people are beginning to think about the various
needs in which the school has some responsibility. One example of
attempts to conceptualize the broad nature of accountability is
found in the CIRCE *Accountability Notebook.* The *Notebook* is
intended as an aid to school personnel, to remind them of the
various areas in which they might be required to disclose information about what they are doing. Figure 1 outlines four broad areas
of responsibility and potential accountability (school audit, student performance, teacher performance, and administration performance), and lists within each broad area, certain specific areas.

Part of the importance of this work likes in the expansion of
ideas as to what should be the range of accountability criteria. The
school cannot and should not be judged on the basis of one or two
criteria alone. In reality, it is likely that different kinds of people
will use different criteria for holding the school accountable. The
CIRCE effort set forth a collection of possible criteria. There are

Figure 1: Four Broad Areas of School Responsibility

(From the CIRCE Accountability Notebook)

AREAS OF RESPONSIBILITY CONCERNING:

The School
  Fiscal
  Legal
  Moral

Student Performance
  Cognitive
  Affective
  Psychomotor

Teacher Performance
  Curricular content
  Teaching
  Support facilities and resources

Administration
  Routine operations
  Decision making and communication
  The school as a social institution

undoubtedly others. The substance of the *Notebook* will have to be supplemented with many other perceptions of accountability, and, perhaps more importantly, it will have to be continuously updated as new issues emerge. The authors must have had this in mind when they determined to use a three ring notebook. Tomorrow may bring new and different criteria.

Some readers may regard all of this as a plea to return to no accountability, for certainly we are not very good at measuring many of the alternative criteria suggested in *Accountability Notebook,* nor are we particularly good at defining the *rationale* for why we should measure certain things. It is likely that we may have to set priorities; we may not be able to attend to all things. Deterline argues:

Education requires some form of commitment to a set of criteria. Unless, we are willing to commit ourselves to a specific set of criteria, no "complete and objective evidence" can be obtained indicating that our students have or have not attained them! If we don't care about all of our students attaining at least some uniform minimum level of competence, then we can do without criteria, and quality control and accountability. We can then continue to present information and grade on a curve and let it go at that. Once we commit ourselves, however, and agree on a set of criteria—even if it is necessary to establish a tentative set of criteria, planning to improve that set as we collect relevant data—we can make accountability a viable concept and methodology. Obviously, I am referring here to the use of instructional objectives.[9]

Possibly true. The potential danger, however, is that agreement will be agreement among a selected few, and that those things agreed upon as criteria will be those presumably most easily measurable learner outcomes.

Judgment of worth, and subsequently accountability, is inexorably linked to goals and priorities. If we are at the moment very concerned about discipline in the schools, we will be little satisfied with data and explanation about student gains in spelling *until we have learned about the discipline problems.* At the same time, however, we may also hold the school accountable for maintaining a certain level of student spelling abilities. This suggests that accountability is a dynamic phenomenon. The predominant or important-for-today criteria for judgment change as goals and priorities change. If we honor in fact, as well as in rhetoric, the goodness of plurality, the desirability of multiple goals, we must necessarily consider plural criteria; there is also likely to be a number of criteria that appear in response to a given situation, and these criteria will constantly change as we succeed at some things, and fail at others.

In short, I have argued for the necessity of many criteria for accountability. We must begin to develop methods for telling how well we are doing in some areas, without losing sight of other relevant areas. But having a set of criteria is not the only problem. Accountability involves standards as well.

On Standards

Criteria represent variables about which people, looking at a program from various perspectives, might demand disclosure. Judgment involves not only the selection of variables, but the determination of benchmarks of excellence, or *standards.* Accountability requires the setting (implicitly or explicitly) of standards by which someone can define acceptability or excellence. Four salient characteristics of standards will be outlined below.

First, most standards are very difficult to explicate. Most of us have standards in very vague ways, standards which we find difficult to state, yet we feel them strongly. The extent to which we can explicate our personal standards depends in part on the issue being discussed. It is probably easier to state our standards concerning ice cream, than to state standards concerning desirable attitudes. Implicitly held standards do not seem to me to be any less legitimate or important than explicated standards: the point is that it is very difficult for a school official to deal with implicit standards, particularly when those standards are used as the basis for accountability demands.

Second, it appears that different people have different standards. What is excellent to one is poor to another. The significance of this characteristic of standards has been summarized by the well-worn phrase, "you can't please all the people all the time." The activities of the school involve so many people that accountability is necessarily very complex because of "non-standard" standards.

Third, standards change as do criteria. Standards are scales to be used with criteria. Standards seem to be closely related to expectations, as well as accomplishments. As we attain more goals, as we learn to do some things better, our expectations change, and so do our standards. We may not find our present telephone service very acceptable; thirty years ago our present service would have been regarded as phenomenal. And so in countless other situations. We have little documentation to suggest how much education standards have changed (indeed, even what they were or are) although we have a general feeling that standards are changing rapidly now. It can be expected that the demands for accountability will change as well.

Finally, I would speculate that standards are, for the most part, statements of a range of acceptability, as opposed to discrete points of good-not good. There are extremes: total rejection, and total acceptance—but most things are roughly categorized as acceptable or non-acceptable. Accountability, then, may be concerned with the school's ability to perform within a range of acceptability. The difficult part (for school officials) is trying to determine where the parameters lie.

The use of standards involves comparison. The comparison may be relative—the standard for one program may be another program. The comparison might be more absolute—the standard by which a program is judged may be a set of personal values held by the person judging. People make judgments using both kinds of comparisons. Just how these comparisons are actually made is somewhat uncertain; the process appears to be rather complex.

The point, of course, is that the use of standards is far from a simple undertaking. As standards are used in accountability, there may be a tendency to rely on few and simple standards of performance. Such a tendency should be resisted. We are again faced with multiples. Attempts to reduce the multiplicity to simplicity to continuously seek the lowest common denominator will necessarily lose something in the process.

Many would reasonably argue that our society must agree on some standards if we are ever to have a system of accountability. The potential difficulty is that we may get agreement on a level of specificity so general as to be of little help in making operational comparisons of output (or input) to standard. The situation *is* complex; we fool ourselves if we adopt some (arbitrary) standards for a few cognitive outcomes, and say we have solved the accountability problem.

The issue of standards has been stated elsewhere more eloquently than in this short treatment, but the intent of this brief look was twofold: to re-emphasize the notion of multiple perspectives of accountability (and thus to warn again of the dangers of oversimplification), and to forecast the probability of conflict arising because people will employ different standards in their assessment of what a school does.

On Getting It Together

There is a need to consider many criteria, and it is most likely that standards will change, and they will be different for different people. Those are powerful enough ideas, yet alone they would not seem to capture the spirit of accountability.

Fishell (personal communication) argues that the missing component is something called, for want of a better term at the time, "interaction accountability." That is, what are the operational implications of accountability when it is recognized that there exists some kind of interaction among the many criteria and standards that might be regarded as legitimate aspects of the examination of a school?

If attention is given to any one part of an educational program, less attention must necessarily be given to some other parts of that program. School resources are finite: it is impossible to attend 100% to more than one thing. Accountability requires the allocation or distribution of attention or concern among possible foci of concern. If you are demanding that the school be accountable and disclose information about X, you are of necessity requiring the school to invest less concern in Y, unless Y is a subset of X.

It appears that accountability is highly correlated with crisis. That is, if discipline appears to be of great concern to, let's say, a group of parents, because they see a lack of discipline, or they see it as a major problem (i.e., Gallup study), then that group will be likely to place the criterion of discipline very high on the list of accountability criteria. When discipline is no longer perceived to be a major problem, other criteria will be regarded as more important accountability criteria.

What is evident, however, is that discipline does not cease to be regarded as something the school is accountable for. Discipline will not be focused upon with concern *as long as discipline is not perceived to be a problem.* If the efforts and resources of the school, as well as the demands for accountability, are so directed to some other problem that discipline is neglected, then discipline will again become a problem, and will again become the focus of an active accountability. Here is where the notion of interaction, or displacement, seems important: there is some kind of relationship among the various elements of school operation, and notions of accountability must attend to these relationsips. The school should not show evidence of accountability in one area to the exclusion of accountability in other areas as well.

It is possible that many of the school's activities and outputs may be regarded as routine, at least as perceived by observers. Activities are routine when they fall within some parameters of acceptability. The school is accountable for these routine activities and subsequent outcomes, but accountability in this case means not exceeding these parameters. As long as expectations are met, the public will not actively draw attention to those elements considered routine. Should expectations not be met, however, various

publics may actively demand school accountability in the areas of
those unmet expectations. The goal is often to "keep things running." The difference between running and not running is more
discernable than the difference between running and running *well.*
In addition, new problems may enter the scene, problems which
present an individual with an unfamiliar situation, or with a situation about which he has not formal expectations or experience.
These situations may become the subject of accountability
demands.

The difficulty is that schools must, in developing an accountability plan, consider both those foundational (or basically static)
areas of responsibility, as well as those situational (or dynamic)
areas of responsibility. The weightings to be given to aspects of
each remains a formidable economic, political, and educational
problem.

It will not do to consider criteria or variables in isolation
from one another. In our accountability efforts, we must be able
to show what we gain (and what we lose) by establishing certain
priorities. We must be able to show the pay-offs and trade-offs resulting from the patterns of emphasis we adopt. We must be able
to document what happens to other disciplines, or attitudes, or
skills development if the school decides to launch a major (re-
source-consuming) assault on reading deficiencies. Or what happens if the school opts for a more independent environment.

Accountability, then, must utilize more criteria for judging
the school. Accountability must also take into account the intricate influences of action or attention in one area on other areas.
To do so requires a much more comprehensive and complex view
of criteria and standards. Given the inevitable levels of interactions,
what kinds of criteria shall be employed? How can standards be
determined? Difficult questions, to say the least.

But even if we could decide on what criteria should be used
to judge the school, and if we could agree (or operate without
agreement) as to what the benchmarks of excellence (or acceptability) should be, we have a third problem: What will be accepted
as indicators of what is happening in a school?

On Indicators

Many of the decisions made in education are made on the
basis of indicators, or some kind of behavior, idea, or phenomena

thought acceptably representative of reality. Judgments of a program are usually made in response to an observation or description of something that seems to indicate what is happening in or as a result of a program. Some of us find comfort in saying that indicators often do not reflect reality, but it is difficult to know what reality *is*. Is performance on a standardized reading test indicative of a student's ability to read? Does a certain behavior indicate an attitude? The indicators relevant to accountability would seem to be dependent in part on the criteria being used to examine a program. That is, if the school is being held accountable for how well a student can read, some indicator of reading ability would be needed. For this criterion, skill in playing basketball might not be an appropriate indicator of reading ability. Parenthetically, it might be noted that the preoccupation with a certain indicator of performance (i.e., reading skill) may blind us to indicators of unintended outcomes. For example, in the process of learning how to read, the student develops a negative attitude toward reading, and thus reads only what he is required to read. Any notion of accountability ought to include accountability for unintended outcomes, negative and positive.

Indicators have some characteristics about which questions might be raised. Is a particular indicator an *appropriate* indicator of the state of something? A rather simplistic question, but one responsible for some debate. If I want to know if the school has accomplished goal X, is performance on standardized text Y an appropriate indicator? What is an appropriate indicator of an attitude held? Or a skill possessed? Or content mastered? Appropriateness, of course, is individually defined. We may need to seek agreement, or at least understanding, of what constitutes an acceptably appropriate indicator of the trait or behavior we wish to make some judgment about. Appropriateness is a particularly difficult concept when applied to indicators of the general well-being of an entire educational system.

How *sufficient* is an indicator? That is, does a given indicator adequately encompass the nature of what we are trying to look at? Too often, educators are prone to want to accept something very simple (or singular) as being indicative of something much more complex. The traditional example is the IQ. The danger is that the single indicator may shed light on only part of the behavior or idea being studied, and that that part may be regarded as the whole.

Edward Kelly and Robert Stake have pointed out a passage that was appropriate to some of their work, and seems appropriate here also.

A century ago the Swiss Historian Jacob Burckhardt foresaw that our would be the age of "the great simplifiers," and that the essence of tyranny was the denial of complexity. He was right. This is the single greatest temptation of the time. It is the great corrupter, and must be resisted with purpose and with energy.[10]

Finally, how *observable* is the indicator? Are we presently capable of measuring or describing the indicator? Should we be trying to develop methods for measuring some indicators we can only vaguely see now? Here again is the recurring theme: Shall we restrict accountability because we do not now have the means of measuring or observing an indicator? Shall we say the school should be held accountable only for those things we think we are good at measuring? Or that we have time to measure? Or that we have the inclination to measure? Accountability may demand that we concern ourselves less with preciseness than with breadth, with approximating the whole of things. The call for new indicators is not restricted to education, but may be particularly *relevant* for education.

A plea for broader conceptualization of what accountability should be has been made. Questions, not answers, constitute the plea. What remains is to ask what will be done with accountability, where it will take us.

On the Uses of Accountability

Accountability may reduce waste. Lessinger writes:

If educators can master the process outlined above—a process for enginering programs that work—overburdened educators will regain a spirit of excitement and mastery that has flagged in recent years. It can save society the long-term cost of allowing its schools to define millions of children as "failures."[11]

But it is possible that when "waste" goes, so may go the relevance of which Collins writes:

What do the accountability people think of those who desire to develop children's abilities to think independently. How do you measure, how do you "performance contract" for relevance, love, and independent thinking?[12]

Accountability may force us to examine our goals, and our methods of achieving those goals. But accountability may force us to pursue goals most easily attained, or most easily stated. Accountability may force a kind of naive simplicity on a complex pehnomenon.

Accountability may demand the best from all of us. We may need to clarify, the experiment to work harder to make things work. Teachers and administrators may need to be more sensitive to the broader community of which they are a part. And the community may need to become less passive, less willing to take the general world of the educator that all is well.

Accountability may take the best from us. It may ask us to refrain from the creative, the spontaneous, the unexpected. We may need to become more mechanistic, more specific-goal oriented. The educator may find his direction provided by others, not by himself.

Accountability enables us to show our merit. We can do our job, and assume our responsibility, because we know what it is. We can defend and justify our existence on the basis of our ability to enable learners to learn.

Accountability may make us up tight. Responsibility for gain and responsibility for failure is upon us, even though we may not be able, as individuals, to control many of the variables contingent upon student learning. We may be susceptibel to political pressure; if we are different, if we espouse different values, we may be removed through some kind of misuse of accountability.

Accountability may enable us to show what we do with our dollars.

Accountability may force us to use our dollars in ways that we do not deem desirable.

Accountability may, for the first time, let us really see what we are doing.

Accountability may deceive us by making us think we are doing what we are not.

Accountability may force us to refine our techniques for measuring and judging what we do.

Accountability may force us to depend only on those things we can now measure.

Accountability may work for us.

We may work for accountability.

These are extremes, of course. How and for what accountability will be used remains to be seen, although it is likely that
actual use will be characterized by a comination of some of the
above.

Some have said that educators have never been held accountable for what they do or do not do, as lawyers or doctors reported-
ly have. But how do we determine when anyone or anything is
being held accountable? Hasn't the student unrest on college and
high school campuses demonstrated a demand for accountability?
Aren't the schools told something when parents demand control
over local schools? Haven't accreditation agencies fostered an accountability over the years? And don't I signal an awareness of accountability when I ask my daughter whether she enjoyed school
today?

Isn't it possible that the school does reflect societal expectations, and is thus accountable? Isn't it possible that all of us have
some undefined but real boundaries that tell us what the proper
domain of the school includes, and don't we react when we feel
those boundaries have been exceeded? Isn't *that* accountability?
When we are silent, or only a little discontent, haven't we in fact
said to the school, "We've judged your performance, and it falls
within our range of tolerance." Have the schools ever *not* been
accountable?

Accountability is deeply rooted in economics and politics. It
addresses itself to the phenomenon of alienation, to the sense of
lack of control of the citizen over the institutions that govern his
life and his conduct. In times of tight money, accountability will
flourish. And the politics of education shall not go unaffected by
the move to formal accountability. One wonders if the *education*
of the young man or woman, the boys and girls, will finally be related to accountability at all. And one wonders what criteria, standards, and indicators we will employ to determine the worth and
the outcomes of accountability itself. What will we have gained,
and what lost?   □

---

[1]George Gallup, "The Public's Attitude Toward the Public Schools." *Phi Delta
Kappan* 52 (1970): 100.

[2]Donald Robinson, "Editorial: Accountability for Whom? for What?" *Phi Delta
Kappan* 52 (1970); 193.

[3]Roger Lennon, "Accountability and Performance Contracing," Paper read at the
AERA Annual Meeting, New York, 1971.

[4]Lennon, *op. cit.*

[5]Robert Stake, "Measuring What Learners Learn." (Urbana: Center for Instructional Research and Curriculum Evaluation, 1971): mimeographed.

[6]Robert Stake, and James Wardrop, "Gain Score Errors in Performance Contracting." (Urbana: CIRCE, 1971): mimeographed.

[7]Stephen Barro, "An Approach to Developing Accountability Measures for the Public Schools," *Phi Delta Kappan* 52 (1970): 196-205.

[8]Gallup, *op. cit.*

[9]William Deterline, "Applied Accountability," *Educational Technology* II (1971): 15-20.

[10]Daniel Moynihan, Remarks made to the Cabinet and Sub-Cabinet, East Room, The White House, December 21, 1970. (Press release.)

[11]Leon Lessinger, *Every Kid a Winner: Accountability in Education* (New York: Simon and Schuster, 1970).

[12]Donald Collins, "Accountability of Relevance," *American Teacher* 55 (1970):12.

XII

THE ETHOS OF ACCOUNTABILITY – A CRITIQUE

by Robert J. Nash and Russell M. Agne

"Who are the people most forcefully imploring educators to be accountable? Who has the most to gain, politically and economically, from a large-scale adoption of accountability in public education?"

The accountability movement is generating an ethos among educators that must not go unchallenged. This ethos—whose governing principles are based on a technological-economic world-view—is distinguished by its frenzied insistence on the large-scale transportation of attitudes and practices from the world of business, engineering, and science to the world of education. One result of this slavish dependence on the beliefs and procedures of other fields has been to reduce the total educational endeavor to a tired litany of achievement, performance, and production characterized by the blank torpor of systems analysis, technological engineering, quality control, and replicability. The creeping extrusion into education of an ethos which defines the successful educational experience primarily in terms of systems engineering and measureable outputs signifies a tragic loss of larger vision and purpose among educators. The unsettling implication is that the nearer we come to the realization of accountability in our educational institutions—as accountability is presently being defined and huckstered—the greater will be the cleavage between our educational ideals and our actual practices; and the greater will be the consequent clamor for sweeping educational reform.

Reprinted with copyright permission of authors and Teachers College Record. February 1972.

The Case for Accountability

Leon Lessinger has argued eloquently for accountability in education.[1] He has asserted that each child has an inalienable right to be taught what he needs to know in order to be a productive, contributing citizen. Furthermore, each citizen has a right to know what educational results are being produced by specific expenditures. Finally, the schools have a right to draw upon talent, enterprise, and technology from all sectors of society, instead of relying exclusively on the "overburdened" resources of professional educators.[2] From these basic premises Lessinger has concluded that educators must guarantee the acquisition of basic skills to all children, regardless of their background. He has compared the educational system to a malfunctioning machine and has emphasized the necessity of preparing "educational engineers" who can look for the precise causes of the malfunction, test the variables and the performance of each part of the machine to determine what has gone wrong, and then carefully define the performances which educators ought to isolate, and the changes which need to be made in order to bring about the desired learning of basic skills.[3] Lessinger believes that this type of accountability can lead to "a symbiosis of technology and humanism, wedding the skill of the one to the values of the other."[4]

Myron Lieberman has advanced another type of rationale for educational accountability.[5] His premise is that accountability ought to prevail in the schools. He warns that if public schools fail to develop acceptable criteria and procedures for accountability, they will provoke the emergence of accountability through alternative school systems. Lieberman contends that unless school systems do a better job of relating school costs to educational outcomes, they will continue to be battered by the persistent demands of disgruntled parents, critics, and youth for alternative schools. Both Lessinger and Lieberman reason that the most convincing kind of accountability to patrons which educators can produce is to deliver in tangible, demonstrable ways on the promises they have made to teach all children the basic reading, writing, communicative, and computational skills they will need to live in a demanding technological society. Kenneth B. Clark, in a similar vein, has gone even further than Lieberman and Lessinger to propose that teachers in the inner city be held accountable to the extent that they be paid solely on the basis of their abilities to teach children the fundamental reading and computational skills.[6]

And, finally, Fred M. Hechinger, the education editor for the *New York Times,* has summarized the negative rationale for accountability. He maintains that if we hold educators accountable in objective ways, we can effectively counter three impending educational trends: a widespread dissatisfaction with the public schools; an alarming frequency of performance contracting with the educational establishment and its attendant ethically questionable practices of "teaching to the test"; and the introduction of voucher plans which might result in the demise of public education in this country.[7]

Historical Background

As a guiding ideal for professional behavior, accountability is imbedded deeply in the American tradition. An anthropologist, Francis L. K. Hsu, has observed that for three hundred years Americans have remained suspicious of most overt forms of authority. In order to prevent their institutions (such as the government) from becoming unresponsive to the individual citizen, Americans have watched their "government and check [ed] it when it misbehaves or fails to deliver the goods."[8]

Historically, white middle-class Americans have demanded that schools be held accountable to the extent that they enable students to master the basic skills which will allow them to share in the rising standard of living. Richard Hofstadter documented the American tendency toward anti-intellectualism due to the traditional expectancy that schools "be practical and pay dividends." He observed that progressive education always has capitulated to the demands of its clientele for accountability in those areas which stress knowledge for its own sake.[9] Merle Curti, in tracing the response of the American educational establishment to the demands of its constituency to be accountable in life-adjustment programs, homemaking, vocational preparation, intergroup relations, and technical training, has shown, by inference, that accountability has existed, at least as an implicit educational principle, in this country for three hundred years.[10]

In spite of the historical warrant for accountability, we believe that the new accountability cult in public school education must be challenged. Amidst the paroxysms of testimony from performance contractors and educational technologists that accountability will be the soothing alembic which will purify our beliefs and procedures, there persists the unmistakable reality that we are trivializing the aims of education at a time when we ought to be examining our basic purposes and expanding our vision. In our reluctance to challenge the necessity of being held accountable for failing to teach our clients to read, write, and compute, we have failed to understand that the ethos which professional educators are generating is itself a numbing critique of the limited ends we are striving to realize.

In the sections that follow, we will be examining three tendencies in American education which have been generated by the ethos of accountability. First, we will examine what is happening as a result of the technological imperative to adopt the procedures of educational engineering, performance criteria, behavioral objectives, and assessment techniques, at a time when we ought to be raising questions about the proximate, intermediate, and long-range ends of our educational procedures. Second, we will show how we are reinforcing a technocratic value system, based on a pseudoscientific *Weltanschauung,* at a time when educators ought to be challenging the very validity of the contemporary technocratic-scientific ethos which controls so much of our lives. And third, we will demonstrate that we are perpetuating an economic and political status quo, at a time when we ought to be probing to the roots the valuational and ideological base upon which the whole system rests.

Means and Ends

The myopic fixation on the means of accountability, to the systematic exclusion of any serious concern with ends, is amply demonstrated by recent writing on the subject. Leon Lessinger, in his pioneering work on accountability, has stipulatively defined education as the mastery of a set of skills.[11] From this definition, he constructs a model of the teacher as an "educational engineer" who must help schools to obtain a "workable technology of instruction." According to Lessinger, the educational engineer must be able to convince school officials to adopt "certain managerial procedures that both stimulate the demand for performance and help [officials] to provide it."[12] Also the educational engineer must be able to report with "tables and text" how much it will cost a community to frame performance criteria for a program, obtain an independent educational audit to measure the actual performance against these criteria, and provide for an auditor to report publicly his findings.[13] Nowhere in Lessinger's analysis of accountability, vis à vis the new educational engineering, is there even the slightest concern with any purpose of the educational process beyond the teacher's transmission of a basic set of skills to students.

In another context, Leo Tolstoy once observed that the fundamental and inescapable preoccupation of any human being is "What should I do?" and "How should I live?" Tolstoy concluded that since these are questions of ultimate ends, and not means, and since science cannot answer them, it follows that science is useless.[14] Lessinger and many other spokesmen for accountability[15] are guilty of a reverse kind of syllogistic overstatement. They are saying that the fundamental concern of any educator ought to be "What can I accomplish that I can measure?" "How can I translate these objectives into performance criteria?" and "How can I effectively assess what I have tried to accomplish?" Since these are questions of means, and not purpose, it follows that other kinds of educational concerns are useless (or, if not useless, of no value since they cannot be objectively assessed).

There can be no denial of the need to identify the means by which educators strive to realize their ends. There is also an equally compelling need for educators to state more sharply and carefully the kinds of learning outcomes they hope to induce in their students. However, the danger in specifying an educational end in the language and belief system of educational engineering is that the desirable end will be subordinated to, and distorted by, that language and those beliefs. Charles Silberman, writing about the failure of educational reforms in this country, criticizes the tendency of educational engineers to model their curricula on production and computer processes.[16] Silberman warns that no engineering model is value-free. The technology we use to frame and specify a curriculum dictates its own values, and in many cases transforms desired ends. According to Silberman, The Individually Prescribed Instruction Program, based on a programmed sequence of instruction, requires such a high degree of precision and specificity of goals that students are often forced into passive learning roles. Students have no voice in specifying their own goals and they are limited to the preordained answers of the program. The weakness of the I.P.I. Program, and other programs which have been

contrived by the new educational engineers, is to make their users
so dependent on the technological system which specifies and dis-
penses what must be learned that there is very little opportunity
for an individual to realize intermediate educational ends. Silberman has shown that those educational ends which are most significant (autonomous choice-making; independent, critical judgment;
the specification of one's own goals) simply cannot be—nor should
they be—defined in precise behavioral terms.[17]

Proponents of accountability fail to realize that every educational program has at least *three* kinds of ends or purposes. The
proximate ends include the learning of basic skills, and Lessinger
deals with accountability preponderantly on this level. But there
are two other kinds of purposes which are the *sine qua non* of the
educational endeavor, and they obdurately resist being specified in
the rigorous language of educational engineering. The intermediate
ends include those educational objectives toward which the basic
skills ought to be directed, and for which the basic skills should be
applied. These are the ends which initially may have attracted
people into teaching and they are best expressed in the emotive
language of "appreciation," "understanding," "enthusiasm," "discrimination," "judgment," and "enjoyment." These ends continue
to thwart precise behavioral classification, but they are no less
important because they do so. And, finally, there are long-range
ends which galvanize the first two levels and bestow ultimate
meaning on the total educational experience. These are the sociopolitical ends which guide all educational activity serving as a constant reminder that the ultimate objective of any learning experience is to help the private person communicate with, evaluate, and
reform the public world.[18]

When the procedures of accountability result in educational
programs which fixate on proximate ends, or which reduce the
other two kinds of ends to the proximate, there then occurs a
deadly distortion of educational purpose. The New York City examination for teachers of high school English is a wrenchingly
lucid example of distorted, short-range ends. The Board of Examiners, in an effort to be accountable to the New York taxpayers,
have devised an objective, mechanical, machine-marked test that
purports to measure the competency of prospective English teachers. The questions on the most recent test were based exclusively
on the candidate's ability to recall instantly a fact such as the

month in which Chaucer's pilgrims started for Canterbury, or to remember an obscure line or word in a poem. There were no questions which required any demonstration that the teacher understood or appreciated literature, or was able to relate a poem or short story to contemporary events. Because such goals were too subjective, and resistant to rigorous test specification, the examiners were content to measure only those dimensions of the English teacher's performance which they considered testable. Unfortunately, according to a teacher who took the test, the unintended testable outcomes became skill in instant factual recall, guessing ability, and test-taking endurance.[19]

We close this section on means and ends with a passage by Ann Cook and Herbert Mack, two former public school teachers who have raised radical questions concerning the aims of education. They maintain:

> It isn't because children can't read that our country is torn by internal conflict. It isn't because our children can't add that we elect politicians who campaign on personality, not program, that the country is embroiled in a devisive war, that consumers purchase defective merchandise, that television is a wasteland and our environment polluted. These conditions are not due to deficiencies in reading and math. It is rather that our population is not being educated in critical areas: how to judge, to ask questions, to seek information, to analyze, and to evaluate.
>
> It is not sufficient to concentrate on reading and math skills. We must look beyond the "decoding" procedures that most programs are designed to teach. What is the purpose of learning such skills? Does teaching a child to discern between the *a* in cat and the *a* in fate mean automatically that the child will want to read, make meaningful sense of his knowledge, broaden his vision or satisfy his curiosity? Learning to read is really a lifetime activity based fundamentally on one's attitudes about books and is generated by curiosity and by an eagerness to explore and find enjoyment. It is critically important that children learn to question their world, to deal with the ambiguity in their environment, and to realize that not every issue has a "correct" answer.[20]

Technocracy and Science

According to Theodore Roszak, a technocracy is a social form in which an industrial society reaches the peak of its organizational integration.[21] The technocratic ethos can be identified as follows: a relentless pursuit of efficiency and productivity; an extensive rational control over every human endeavor; an organizational logic which stresses integration, modernization, and extreme systemization; an emphasis on technique, omnicompetency, and expertise; a passionate concern with objective data and predictability; and a conscious effort to transmute the beliefs and procedures of all fields to the scientific world-view.

Roszak has fulminated against the technocratic ethos on the grounds that it has become a "mechanistic imperative" which exerts an all-consuming pressure on people to conform to the prevailing value orientation of bureaucrats, managers, operation analysts, and social engineers. He maintains that modern man is becoming indistinguishable from the cybernated systems he is assisting. Modern man is cold, precise, logical, indifferent, efficient, dispassionate, and objective. He is every inch a "professional" who spends his time observing, classifying, measuring, and quantifying, and he communicates these findings through the mediation of bloodless models, mechanical gadgets, abstract schemas, and chilly jargons. The stark outcome of technocratic professionalism is the creation of a hollow, contemporary expert who has relinquished forever any kind of awesome, tender, and spontaneous engagement with the world.[22]

In spite of Roszak's caricature of the modern technocrat, one only has to look at the field of education to see how the exaggeration has become reality. The cult of accountability has given birth to a new category of educational technocrat, the systems engineer. What follows is a systems description of the school as an educational technocrat sees it:

> Any given school, or school district, can readily be seen as a system for several reasons. It has incoming energies (inputs), is organized into a structure of processes and controls (functioning subsystems), and yields energies to the larger, or, suprasystem (outputs). Further, it is bounded spatially by other institutions which are non-schools, or, not primarily educational in nature. And, it is encased in the limitation of time. For, all systems have a tendency towards entropy. Such

entropy may be described generally as the result of minimizing the energy exchange with the environment, or with other systems, thus "closing" the system. A long-term resistance toward the system results in a "death-state."[23]

When the systems engineer describes the school in the nomenclature of "inputs," "outputs," "entropy," "suprasystem," "subsystem," and "death-state," (the imagery of organizational management and physics) he illustrates an all-encompassing faith in the basic tenets of the technocratic ethos. In his controlled euphoria over predictability, accuracy, reliability, integration, and organizational tautness, he expresses a commitment to the ideals of efficiency engineering for the effective organization of men and machines.

The fallacy of the systems model resides in the assumption that a physics-management prototype can be used to explain adequately the polymorphous intricacy of an institution like the school. A corollary fallacy is that people can be considered as simple, mechanomorphic units within a structure of interactions as unique and as diverse as the educational experience. W. Ross Ashby, a cyberneticist, has pointed out the central illusion in systems engineering—the myth of *ceteribus paribus* (other things being equal).[24] Complex systems resist the wholesale application of simpler systems models. Organizations such as the school are so unique, dynamic, and unpredictable, that crude analogies to business or engineering models must ignore the special complexity of an institution whose overarching function is to facilitate purposeful, educational transactions among developing human beings. And, finally, the danger of a facile systems application to the field of education is that often a so-called "subsystem" can be successful in on one context, but when it is absorbed by a larger system, its success is mitigated. The educational reformer, the experimental school district, the innovative teacher, ahd the administrative dissident all have in common the possible enervation and dissolution of their programs once they are coopted into a larger system whose objective may be more survival than reformation.[25]

Perhaps the major misuse of the systems model is the implicit faith that a systems approach will guarantee predictability, objectivity, and efficiency in the educational enterprise.[26] Lessinger has written that the new educational engineer will be a "manager" who will function to construct a management system and support group. Together, they will develop programs, design requests for proposals based on *objective* and *predictable* performance specifications, assist in evaluating proposals, and provide *efficient* management services to performance contractors.[27] Herein lies the ultimate *reductio ad absurdum*. Simply stated, educators have failed to understand that in an enterprise like education, where human beings are always ontologically prior to the system they constitute, the technocratic values of predictability, objectivity, and efficiency are either undesirable or unattainable.

Many scientists have realized this, and have become properly chary of transgressing the natural limits of science. They avoid casting their discipline in the mold of "scientism" (the belief that the techniques of science can be applied in all areas of human investigation).[28] Human behavior is subject to so many variables that many scientists are skeptical of the accuracy of measurement. The Heisenberg uncertainty principle has led scientists to the conclusion that they can never accurately predict or measure the velocity of subatomic particles let alone the behavior of human beings. When any kind of data are collected in a dynamic system, the data can never represent the current situation. Hence predictability is almost impossible with human beings.[29]

So too, while scientists stress the methodology of objectivity in their laboratory, the wiser of them willingly suspend the methology when they enter the world of values. The scientist is unable to deal directly with human values, and consequently he can never prove objectively what ought to be good or desirable. He refuses to extend predictability and objectivity to the world of human feeling because he cannot claim certainty here. While the scientist is aware of his investigative limits, the educational engineer has yet to define his own boundaries.[30]

Efficiency is a value which has not been of much concern to the natural scientist. And yet the educational engineer has reasoned that if educators are "scientifically" efficient, then they will be accountable. Raymond E. Callahan has traced the history of "the cult of efficiency" and the tragic misapplication of business and industrial values to education during the last fifty years.[31] He concludes his study with the admonition that in the future the quest for efficiency in education must always be secondary to the pursuit of quality learning experiences—even if these are inefficiently administered and costly. The scientist has learned what the

educational engineer has not—that a concern with efficiency (max-
imizing output while minimizing input) is a technocratic value
which has produced effective guillotines, bombs, and assembly
lines, but has never created an audacious experimental insight, or
major scientific breakthroug. Efficiency is a normative term which
tends to impede rather than facilitate the creative endeavor.

Much of the current literature on accountability is filled with
the metaphor of the school as a malfunctioning machine that systems engineers can repair with massive infusions of predictability,
objectivity, and efficiency.[32] What is so often ignored in these proposals is the root question which must guide the total educational
experience: what kind of human beings do we want our students
to become? If we reconstruct the profession of education in the
image of technocracy, then we are going to produce a society of
technocrats. If we convert the school to a systems model, then we
run the risk of unconsciously establishing as our primary educational objective the maintenance of an inert, airtight system, devoid of the unpredictable sparkle which dynamic human beings
must provide if an organization is to be self-renewing.

We close this section with a warning and a question. George
W. Morgan, a philosopher, has identified the pathetic—but inevitable—human outcome of an ethos which compares human beings
to machines, and apotheosizes the quantitative properties of
timing, dimension, speed, output, and efficiency. He calls this
creation, "the prosaic mentality," and he describes it as follows:

> . . . the prosaic man is forever incapable of considering issues
> in depth. He stays at the surface; he remains with things that
> permit readily specifiable action. He entertains no questions
> with respect to life, man, or society that do not obviously
> lead to specific things to do. Everything else, it seems to him,
> is mere words—idealistic, not realistic; sentimental, not practi-
> cal. Confronted with a difficulty, the prosaic man gets busy;
> he works at one thing and works at another; he changes,
> modifies, and manipulates; he institutes projects and pro-
> grams; . . . holds meetings, collects data . . . develops tech-
> niques. And he does all this without ever asking a single fund-
> amental question, without ever attending to such basic things
> as the aims, underlying assumptions, values, or justification of
> what he is dealing with and what he is doing. Therefore, all
> his busyness—restless, nerve-racking, and exhausting—is at

bottom only tinkering with and an accelerating of what already exists.[33]

We ask to what extent will the emphasis on accountability in education prevent the "prosaic man" from becoming a flesh-and-blood reality in the world of the future? Ultimately, this will be the most crucial test, regarding the contribution of accountability to the plight of modern man.

Maintenance of the Status Quo

The current emphasis in accountability is on micro-concerns. There is no attention being given to the sociocultural norms which govern these preoccupations. Instead, as one spokesman for accountability has stated: "There is no escaping the fact that accountability is not a neutral device—it encapsulates a view of the educational function in which basic cognitive and mathematical skills are primary." He goes on to argue that "cultural, artistic, or political" learnings might still receive attention "but they would not be dominant."[34]

Throughout the literature on accountability there is a gaping absence of any recognition of the educational experience as encompassing such concerns as political reform or social reconstruction. Leon Lessinger continues to stress the necessity of educators being responsible to the "legitimate demands" of their constituents. However, there is never any doubt that for Lessinger these "legitimate demands" must always be for the "special skills" which will enable citizens to become literate, insatiable consumers.[35] Lessinger and other spokesmen[36] limit their rationale for accountability to such educational factors as cost analysis, system governance, educational management, instructional feedback, performance incentive, and data assessment. Rarely do these writers consider the possibility of expanding the parameters of accountability to include the political dimensions of the educational undertaking. At times it would seem that the reason why these writers have not speculated on the "outer limits" of accountability is that they are too busy using the school to maintain and strengthen the status quo.

But what if the existing system is in need of sweeping reform? What if accountability is stretched to include the educator's responsibility to analyze, discredit, disassemble, and reconstruct his profession so that it is more directly responsive to the cries of human beings who suffer from the iniquitous defects of the social order? Where in the present efflux of literature exhorting us to adopt accountability techniques is there a voice, like Paulo Freire's, which goads educators to be accountable to the oppressed peoples of the world? Where are we being urged to apply Freire's concept of "praxis," which directs us to help our students to reflect upon the social, political, and economic contradictions in the culture and to take systematic political action against the oppressive power blocs?[37] Who among the spokesmen for accountability would ask us to be accountable for helping students to come to the deepest possible understanding of themselves and their relationship to society? Where is the accountability advocate who speaks out against a concept of education which has been dessicated into programmatic forms and paralyzed by a dead-end preoccupation with careerism?

What is evident in much of the apologia for educational accountability is a shocking blindness to the political structure upon which the theory and practice of American education are based. The school and the society cohere in a sociopolitical unity. Whether educators know it or not, education is a ruthlessly political process. Frequently when educators are cautioned to act as "professionals," they are being reminded that their principal and exclusive function must continue to be to integrate the younger generation into the unquestioned logic of the present sociopolitical system. The more effortlessly this can be accomplished, the better. But to restrict the function of education to the mechanical fitting of young people to the economic demands of a social system is to use the schools to maintain social realities as they are.

For example, the Dorsett Educational Systems, Inc., (the performance contractor for the Texarkana schools) is basing its entire program on motivational techniques which are insidiously competitive.[38] In using token rewards such as transistor radios to motivate students toward achievement, the Texarkana schools are transmitting a value constellation necessary for the survival of the socioeconomic system. The sociologist, Philip Slater has shown that competition for marketable skills in the schools is based on a false assumption of scarcity. We have grounded our motivational practices in the larger cultural belief that the society does not contain the resources to satisfy the needs of all its inhabitants. We insist that students compete with each other to develop the skills which will enable them to win scarce resources. Those who learn the most skills are told that they will grab the largest share of the resources, and consequently the economic system manages to perpetuate itself through the schools. Slater goes on to demonstrate that the key flaw in the scarcity assumption is that the important human needs can be easily satisfied and the resources for doing so are plentiful. Competition is unnecessary and the primary danger to human beings is not the mythical scarcity of resources, but the aggression which is unleashed when human beings are forced to compete with themselves and each other for spurious, system-serving skills and goods.[39]

Ten years ago Jules Henry, an anthropologist, charged the schools with fueling the free enterprise drives of achievement, competition, profit, mobility, performance, skills competency, and expansiveness. He warned that unless the schools stopped serving the narrow interests of the economic system, and began to stress the values of love, kindness, quietness, honesty, simplicity, compassion, cooperation, critical judgment, and autonomy, then the United States would become a "culture of death."[40] Today Bertram M. Gross, an expert on urban affairs, has described the American society in terms which make Henry's "culture of death" a prophetic reality. Gross claims that the United States can best be epitomized as follows:

> A managed society ruled by a faceless and widely dispersed complex of warfare-welfare-industrial-communications-police bureaucracies caught up in devoting a new style empire based on a technocratic ideology, a culture of alienation, multiple scapegoats and competing control networks.[41]

What is so often ignored in the literature on accountability is the realization that educators are as responsible for learning outcomes which are moral and political as they are for outcomes which are skills-centered. It makes little sense to speak of accountability to our students solely because we are teaching them to read, write, and compute, if, as an unintended outcome, we are also preparing them to fit—painlessly and interchangeably—into Gross' nightmarish vision of American society. To the extent that we produce citizens who are one-dimensional in their thinking, compulsively rigid in their value orientations, and excessively competitive in their interpersonal relationships, we have produced human selves who are fractured, and for this we are accountable.

Whenever we root our philosophy of education in a belief in "stable democracy," excluding from the learning experience the possibilities of "participatory politics," we are responsible in an indirect way for maintaining a political system which is hierarchical and self-serving. Until we begin to perceive our technological society as emergent and capable of resolving its deepest dilemmas only through an alliance of all races and social classes, then we are merely perpetuating an inequitable social order which cries out for root reform. And finally, until we realize that education has been used to strengthen a class system in the Western world, and to prop up military-industrial bureaucracies which desperately need dismantling, we will continue to be responsible for adventurist wars which our government may choose to wage in the future.

Accountability in education will have meaning only when we begin to hold ourselves responsible for causing students to accept the myths of scarcity, competitiveness, American supremacy, productivity, and acquisitiveness. We must examine carefully the possibility that the technology of accountability is much more than a set of techniques and machines to attain certain objective learning outcomes. We must consider the possibility that accountability is fundamentally an ideological appeal to the means of power that enables one group to dominate another group.[42] How this power is used will determine the future direction of education in this country.

In order to make the ideal of educational accountability itself a more responsible one, we suggest that educators begin to raise certain questions. The first step in legitimizing any ideal is to ask political and moral questions about its underlying assumptions and its desired ends. We propose to take this first step by framing a set of questions which are meant to provoke controversy.

Who are the people most forcefully imploring educators to be accountable? Who has the most to gain, politically and economically, from a large-scale adoption of accountability in public education? Who is making the decisions regardint the ends toward which accountability will be applied? How will we insure that teachers, parents, and administrators will be heard and treated fairly? At this point, why have the students been silent? Will they really have the most to gain when educators are held accountable? What procedures will allow all the participants in the educational experience to be heard? And finally, who will be making the final decisions concerning accountability?

Unless educators and their clientele can challenge and reform the current ethos which is being generated by the case for accountability, the disparity which exists between our most visionary educational and social ideals and the actuality we are now living will become even more striking.   □

Robert J. Nash is assistant professor of educational anthropology and philosophy and Russell M. Agne is assistant professor of science education at the University of Vermont.

---

[1] Leon Lessinger. *Every Kid a Winner: Accountability in Education.* New York: Simon and Schuster, 1970.

[2] *Ibid.,* pp. 4-5.

[3] *Ibid.,* p. 33

[4] *Ibid.,* p. 37

[5] Myron Lieberman, "An Overview of Accountability," *Phi Delta Kappan,* Vol. 52, No. 4, December, 1970, pp. 194-195.

[6] Fred M. Hechinger, "A Program to Upgrade Schools for the Deprived," *New York Times,* July 26, 1970, p. 56.

[7] Fred M. Hechinger, "Accountability: A Way to Measure the Job Done by Schools," *New York Times,* February 14, 1971, p. 7.

[8] Francis L.K. Hsu. *The Study of Literate Civilizations.* New York: Holt, Rinehart and Winston, 1969, p. 82.

[9] Richard Hofstadter. *Anti-Intellectualism in American Life.* New York: Vintage, 1963.

[10] Merle Curti. *The Social Ideas of American Educators.* New Jersey: Littlefield, Adams and Company, 1965.

[11] Lessinger, *op. cit.,* p. 133.

[12] *Ibid.,* p. 32.

[13] *Ibid.*

[14] See F. William Howton. *Functionaries.* Chicago: Quadrangle Books, 1969, p. 39.

[15] See theme issue, "Accountability in Education," *Educational Technology,* Vol. II, No. 1, January, 1971.

[16] Charles Silberman. *Crisis in the Classroom: The Remaking of American Education.* New York: Random House, 1970, p. 201.

[17] *Ibid.*

[18] See the latest writing of the social reconstructionist, Theodore Brameld. *Patterns of Educational Philosophy: Divergence and Convergence in Culturological Perspective.* New York: Holt, Rinehart and Winston, 1971.

[19] See Flasterstein, "A Test for Teachers?" *Boston Sunday Globe,* April 4, 1971, p. B-43.

[20] Ann Cook and Herbert Mack, "Business in Education: The Discovery Center Hustle," *Social Policy,* Vol. I, No. 3, September-October, 1970, p. 10.

[21] Theodore Roszak. *The Making of a Counter Culture: Reflections on the Technocratic Society and Its Youthful Opposition.* New York: Anchor Books, 1969, p. 5.

[22]*Ibid.*, pp.1-41.

[23]Francis J. Pilecki, "The Systems Perspective and Leadership in the Educational Organization," *Journal of Education,* Vol. 153, No. 1, October, 1970, p. 50.

[24]W. Ross Ashby. *An Introduction to Cybernetics.* New York: John Wiley & Sons, 1956, p. 5.

[25]See P. Michael Timpane, "Educational Experimentation in National Social Policy," *Harvard Educational Review,* Vol. 40, No. 4, November, 1970, pp. 547-566.

[26]See Frederick D. Erickson and Eliezer Krumbein, "A Systems Approach to Reforming Schools," in James W. Guthrie and Edward Wynne, eds. *New Models for American Education.* New Jersey: Prentice-Hall, 1971, pp. 116-132.

[27]Lessinger, *op. cit.,* p. 65.

[28]Garvin McCain and Erwin M. Segal. *The Game of Science.* Belmont, California: Brooks-Cole Publishing Company, 1969, pp. 164-171.

[29]*Ibid.,* pp. 151-163.

[30]See a typical overstatement, Felix M. Lopez, "Accountability in Education," *Phi Delta Kappan,* Vol. 52, No. 4, December, 1970, pp. 231-235.

[31]Raymond E. Callahan. *Education and the Cult of Efficiency.* Chicago: The University of Chicago Press, 1962.

[32]Lessinger, *op. cit.,* pp. 3-19. See also William A. Deterline, "Applied Accountability," *Educational Technology,* Vol. 11, No. 1, January, 1971, pp. 15-20.

[33]George W. Morgan. *The Human Predicament: Dissolution and Wholeness.* New York: Delta, 1970, pp. 89-90.

[34]Aaron Wildavsky, "A Program of Accountability for Elementary Schools," *Phi Delta Kappan,* Vol. 52, No. 4, December, 1970, p. 216.

[35]Lessinger, *op. cit.,* pp. 123-137.

[36]See Roger A. Kaufman, "Accountability, A System Approach and the Quantitative Improvement of Education—An Attempted Integration," *Educational Technology,* Vol. 11, No. 1, January, 1971, pp. 21-26.

[37]Paulo Freire. *Pedagogy of the Oppressed.* New York, Herder and Herder, 1970.

[38]Lessinger, *op. cit.,* "Excerpts from Texarkana's Formal Project Application to the U.S. Office of Education," pp. 155-171.

[39]Philip Slater. *The Pursuit of Loneliness: American Culture at the Breaking Point.* Boston: Beacon Press, 1970, pp. 96-118.

[40]Jules Henry. *Culture Against Man.* New York: Vintage Books, 1965, pp. 13-15.

[41]Bertram M. Gross, "Can It Happen Here?" *New York Times,* January 4, 1971, p. 31.

[42]William M. Birenbaum has advanced a similar agrument in relation to the American university. See *Overlive: Power, Poverty, and the University.* New York: Dell Publsihing Company, 1969.

XIII

THE FUTURE OF ACCOUNTABILITY

by Edythe J. Gaines

"The question of accountability was not raised by the profession-
als. It was raised by the laity. . .The distance between not being
held accountable for everything and not being held accountable
for anything is quite a distance indeed—one that parents and
students simply cannot be expected to accept."

O what a tangled web we weave when first we practise to — to
change what educational consumers (pupils, parents, public) had in
mind when they applied the term accountability to education into
something professionals in education believe they can live with
more comfortably. Rather simple-to-understand and straightforward notions have been all but buried in a mass of calculations,
complications, protestations, and concatenations. Taking that
route, our profession is in danger of missing a grand opportunity
to save the profession, to raise it to new and higher levels of re-
spectability and of status, to bridge the ever-widening gap between
educators and their various publics, and to gain a much-needed
measure of peace across the battle-scarred fields. These in recent
times have tended to separate us from the newest claimants of our
services, that is, the "new" minority groups in this country, one of
which, Afro-Americans, is at least four hundred and seventy-eight
years "new" inasmuch as they arrived with Columbus.

Let me remind you that the question of accountability was
not raised, in the first instance, by the professionals. It was raised
by the laity. It tended to be raised in three contexts.

First, in communities where citizens vote directly on education taxes, the question has been raised in the context of school

bond issues. "Parents and taxpayers" groups, with very strong emphasis on "taxpayers," have rebelled against the rising costs of education without receiving an equivalent rise in client satisfaction with what the education dollar is buying.

Second, when legislators were persuaded to vote allocations of funds especially for programs designed to improve educational results for the "economically and educationally disadvantaged" student, they insisted upon proofs, to be provided by evaluation studies, that the money spent brought about the results intended.

Third, there were parents and students and members of the public who were the traditional supporters of education — usually supporting bond issues, higher education taxes, higher teacher salaries, and greater expenditures for education generally — who began to have serious doubts as to the ability of the public schools to educate their children effectively. The patently-easy-to-see, clearly evident massive failure of the schools to educate the children of the poor and of minority groups brought cries for accountability from these groups early on. Upon closer inspection, parents from other walks of life began to perceive that their children, too, were not getting the kind of education to which the parents aspired. Coalitions began to form — shaky but there, nonetheless — between and among a broad spectrum of parents, all demanding better performance on the part of the schools and couching their demands in terms of professional accountability. While this group traditionally has not begrudged education a full measure of financial support (quite the contrary), today it, too, is asking searching questions about the uses to which educational resources are being put, in terms of the results that are forthcoming.

It is with reference to this last-mentioned group that my remarks will deal. It is this group whose alienation should be of particular concern to public school people, for it constitutes our traditional base of support. Loss of this support base leaves us with no foundation at all on which to rest. The continued existence of public education hangs in the balance. Can anyone deny that?

Given the stakes, one must be appalled at the response our profession has made to calls for accountability on the part of this group of people. When parents asked why their children were not getting the kind of results from schooling they had hoped for and expected, the response has been one or more of the following.

One response: *There is something wrong with your child.*

The message is never given in so straightforward a manner as this. It is couched in such descriptive terms as culturally deprived, socially disoriented, linguistically handicapped, educationally disadvantaged, neurologically damaged, genetically weak, perceptually impaired, emotionally unstable. But these terms are almost never accompanied by unassailable *evidence* about the accuracy of the label as applied to that individual child. These terms tend, instead, to be group labels, and parents rightly are not about to accept such unproven labels as being applicable to their child. Moreover, parents *know* that something must be wrong with the diagnosis when too many children fall within the "problem" categories. Parents easily accept the thought that one or two percent of the children may fit one or more of these descriptions. When the figure gets to be more than 10 percent, parents begin to be concerned about the accuracy of the data. Although they may not complain, they become alert and watchful. But when the "problem" or failing children get to be 60 percent to 80 percent of the total pupil population, as is the case in several poorer neighborhoods in the city, then nothing is going to convince parents that the problem lies with the children and not with the schools — and they are right!

Another response: *There is something wrong with the surrounding environment.* Again, other terms are used — such as social disorganization, societal factors, the poverty cycle. The problem with this is that parents know *all* about the surrounding environment (after all it is *they,* not the professionals, who live there). But they fail to see, and the professionals have failed to prove, a one-to-one relationship between a child's reading retardation and whom the child's parent is sleeping with. Indeed, if sleeping only with one's *bona fide,* certified husband or wife were a precondition for learning to read, then precious few children from the upper middle to upper upper social strata would learn to read. Parents are mindful of the fact that the public schools in the case of the earlier minorities, the European immigrants, specifically accepted the responsibility of bringing the children of the poor into the mainstream of life in this country. They do not understand why the schools have lost that earlier sense of mission and the accompanying skills to carry it out.

Another response: *The schools cannot be solely responsible for all of today's ills, including pupil failure; the schools cannot be held accountable for everything.* But, dear colleagues, don't you

know that parents already *know* that; that parents are fully aware
that schools cannot be expected to do everything. However, the
distance between not being held accountable for *everything* and
not being held accountable for *anything* is quite a distance indeed
— one that parents and students simply cannot be expected to accept. We can't have it both ways, you know. We can't say to the
public on the one hand that the schools are institutions vital to the
general health and welfare of this nation, thus deserving strong and
expensive support, while saying on the other hand that the schools
cannot assure the nation that they can bring about any of the outcomes expected of institutions which are vital to the general health
and welfare of the nation.

Another response: *Standardized test scores cannot appropriately be used to judge the effectiveness of individual teachers nor
of school units.* But think a bit. Why do parents place such confidence in the value of standardized test scores as measures of success and effectiveness? The answer is that we, the professionals,
have taught them to so regard these scores. Look at how *we* have
used them. We have deemed them to be so accurate a measure that
we use them to group children; to select those who are going to
get "enriched" curriculums and those who are going to get educational pablum; to determine who will go into the "academic" track
and who will go into "commercial" or "general" tracks in high
school; to determine who will go to college and who will not. Indeed, we have used them to determine the life chances of our
youth.

Given this example on the part of professionals, is it any
wonder that parents have logically concluded that standardized
test scores are quite accurate and quite legitimate measures of success and effectiveness? Why not, then, apply these miraculous
measuring tools to a determination of the success and effectiveness
of individual educators and of school units?

No, it is we educators, not the laity, who are dealing in non
sequiturs and logical inconsistencies when we say (through our behavior if not our words) that these test scores can make clear determinations about the performance of pupils but not about educators and schools.

Again, we cannot have it both ways. Parents undoubtedly will
give up the idea of rating educators in terms of test results when
educators give up rating children by these measures. Only when

poor scores do not automatically denote a poor student (and vice versa) will parents concede that poor results do not automatically denote poor educators.

Another response: *The concept of accountability leads to the measurement of the narrowest aspects of education, those aspects that can be quantified and measured. Yet, the most important outcomes of education are human and humane, and these will not yield to an accountability scheme. Therefore let us not have one.* Methinks thou dost protest too much. Parents and students have never advocated accountability measures limited to numerically quantifiable characteristics. Quite the contrary. They are very much concerned with organizational climate, with attitudes and nonverbal communication, with the quality of the human transactions that occur in schools. Clearly, too, they want much more from schools than whatever skills are measured by standardized tests and other such tools. I repeat that such tools are much more the darlings of the professionals than they are of the laity. *We* created them; *we* gave them status; *we* use them pervasively.

No, parents are not satisfied merely with accountability with respect to the "3 Rs." Parents simply say that schools ought *at the very least* be able to teach the "3 Rs" after centuries of continuous experience. It is precisely for this reason that parents are appalled to see that schools cannot even succeed in teaching some of their pupils mastery of these ancient and basic tools for further learning.

Another response: *Since certain children are doing poorly on standardized tests, let's not administer these tests to them at all. Constant failure on these tests is destructive of the children's confidence and sense of self-worth. Let us not subject them to this unproductive pain. Indeed, let us choose to teach other things at which these children can be more successful.* I must confess that the first time I heard this argument I couldn't believe my ears. Yet, I've heard this argument advanced again and again and by people who consider themselves to be "on the side of these children." (Please note the expression, "*these* children.")

Parents hardly know what to say to this argument. It is so chock full of patronizing insult to their children. It is a clear call for goal displacement.

This is not to say that standardized tests are good or valid or well-constructed or anything else. It is to say that parents reject a double standard in education. They also suspect that behind this "kind" argument lies a desire on the part of educators to hide the evidence of their failure to effectively educate "these children."

Another response: *Accountability is an extremely complex notion. It requires knowledges and tools not presently available to us. We do not have adequate measuring tools. In fact we don't even have an accurate and agreed-upon definition of that which is to be measured; therefore, we cannot really have an accountability system at this point in time.* Here we get a circular argument. When all the limitations and restraints and complications are explained to them, parents say that they were never asking for an accountability system measured with the accuracy of calipers. They say that they'd be content to have effectiveness bear some relationship to results as seen in pupil performance. But when parents say that, educators immediately warn that student performance is a function of "countless other variables which are often uncontrollable and too multi-dimensional to analyze effectively." The author of that statement (Allan C. Ornstein in a paper called "Methods for Conducting Teacher Behavior Research: With Implications for Educating the Disadvantaged," based on his unpublished doctoral dissertation, N.Y.U.) went on to argue that there is no agreement as to what constitutes desirable student behavior; therefore, there is no way to tell whether or not a teacher is or is not getting the desired results. In other words, you can't get there from here.

Parents rejoin, "Fellows, stop making it so complicated. We didn't ask you to calibrate every aspect of our child's functioning. We just asked you to stop producing functional illiterates who not only hate school but also are frequently totally turned off to learning by the time school is finished with them. We ask you to stop chaning bright-eyed, alert, ready-and-eager-to-learn kindergarteners into glassy-eyed, surly, and turned-off secondary youth who think of school mostly as a place to 'get in, get through, and get out.' "

Parents know that it is absurd to suggest that we can measure with absolute precision and exactitude the degree to which an individual professional's input results in a specific and identifiable outcome in terms of individual pupil performance, and they know that it is absurd to suggest that we can get such exact measures with respect to the effectiveness of school units. To use this as an argument, however, to suggest that nothing can be learned about the impact of educators and schools on the performance of individual pupils and groups of pupils is to carry the argument far too far. It flies in the face of common sense and of one's sense of truth.

Every parent knows a teacher who seems always to be successful with whatever children are assigned to him. Every parent has a fair notion of which schools are more effective than others. You ask parents to deny their sense of truth when you ask them to deny that such differences exist, can be identified, and probably can be explained in terms of differentiated human input.

Another response: (This is what I call the throw-yourself-on-the-mercy-of-the-court-with-a-plea-for-clemency response.) *Yes, you're right. We educators really don't know much about why certain pupils are failing nor about what to do about it. We are failing with "these children," but there is no malice there. We are doing the best we can. We just don't know any better. So, let's devise an accountability system that will not hold us responsible for present performance, but which will show us the way to become better performers in the future.* There is something about this "we don't know" thing that bothers me as a professional. I am reminded of a scene in the motion picture *Gone with the Wind* in which Butterfly McQueen, playing the role of a house slave who got her "privileged position" in the household of the pregnant Scarlet O'Hara by claiming to be expert in delivering babies, cried out in panic, when the crucial moment came, "But, Miss Scarlet, I don' know nuthun' 'bout no babies!" So with too many of today's educators. They hardly cross the threshold before they begin to tell you that they cannot do what they profess (by title and position) to be able to do. We have, for example, the spectacle of the English major licensed to teach English declaring unashamedly that he knows nothing about the teaching of reading — as if reading were not part of English.

Parents say, "*You* called yourselves educators, I didn't. I accepted you for what you said you are. *You* told me that yours is a profession; I didn't tell you that. I merely accepted what you said. *You* said that as a professional you are entitled to professional salaries, to professional autonomy, to the other rights and privileges of professionals. I did not argue with that. I merely ask that you *do* what you profess to be able to do. This is no time to tell me that you don't know how!"

It is for this reason that I do not believe that the accountability

scheme being worked out in New York City will be at all acceptable to the groups of parents and community people who demanded it. In essence it is an educational accounting system, not an accountability system. Parents will not object to such an accounting
system, but I doubt that they will accept it as a substitute for the
accountability system for which they asked. They are likely to
consider it to be a giant cop-out, a betrayal of their trust. It is my
fervent hope that Educational Testing Service, the chief consultant
for the project, will radically restructure its design so that it does
indeed at least attempt to meet the people's aspirations for professional accountability — a concept that rests upon the notion of responsibility *that can be fixed* for the results of the educational
enterprise.

The design for New York City speaks of *collective* responsibility of the staff for *knowing* as much as it can about the pupils,
and of collective responsibility fo the staff to *use* this knowledge,
as best it can, to maximize the development of pupils toward defined and agreed-upon pupil performance objectives.

How in heaven's name can a staff be "collectively responsible" for anything? How do you operationalize that concept? What
if they "collectively fail"? Then what? Do you ultimately separate
them from service "collectively"?

Really, the public is not a collection of fools. They know that
such terms have no real meaning. They know that we know that,
too. Therefore, they suspect us of acting in bad faith. That is no
basis upon which to reestablish public trust in the public schools
and in their educators.

A final response: *Parents and public cannot be trusted with
data on school performance. They would use such data as weapons,
engaging in vigilante activities. Therefore, try to avoid giving them
such data.* No doubt fear of reprisal is the reason behind many of
the diversionary maneuvers in the accountability game. But what is
the evidence on this matter? There have been so few cases of this
kind of witch-hunting that every case has been headline news. Why
should an entire profession cower in unreasoning fear of unlikely
consequences?

In a truly useful accountability system, practitioners would
learn what they need to know in order to be successful in their
work. First they would learn what is expected of them since parents and public would, at long last, have to combine their lengthy,

over-inclusive, often conflicting set of expectations into agreed-upon goals. Next, practitioners would learn the extent to which they
are or are not meeting those goals. Finally, they could use that information to help them to search out, in a clear and focused way,
those practices and programs which hold promise of helping them
learn to behave in such a way as to more nearly successfully meet
those goals.

In such a setting practitioners could reach a new level of freedom from stress. Make no mistake about it: with or without an accountability system, the educator who is failing in his work *knows*
it and is shattered by that knowledge. Nothing equals the private
anguish experienced by such a person. However, since he perceives
it to be to his advantage not to admit to his problem, he tends to
take on adaptive modes of behavior that are not merely destructive
to the ends of education for children, but are also destructive to
the practitioner himself — both personally and professionally.

These, then, are the most typical responses of professionals to
the concept of professional accountability. They are very much
out-of-phase with parent and public perceptions, aspirations, and
expectations.

What, if anything, could get us professionals to change our
stance? I believe that a change will come only when we perceive
that there is something vital *to us* in the concept. We cannot be
motivated by fear. No one can be. We *can* be motivated by hope
and by the promise of saving solutions to our own pressing
problems.

A good accountability system would free us from the stresses
and strains inherent in trying to meet myriad, unspecified, often
conflicting expectations. It would recognize not only that pupils
are uniquely individual human beings but also that educators are,
too. Thus, it would free us to find our own personal paths to
glory, if such can be found. It would not subject us, therefore, to
the anti-human individuality and uniqueness that inheres in the
"collective responsibility" notion. Such a notion leads to collective
anonymity and conjures up an image of a long, grey line of face-
less, nondescript beings, each indistinguishable from the other —
all working, but none knowing the worth of his work, the relevance of his work to the growth and development of other individual human beings.

A good accountability system would, indeed, help to increase our professionalism, raise our profession to higher status, heal the wounds we've suffered in battles with those who should be and traditionally have been our allies, and bring us all enormous personal satisfaction and peace of mind. Then, and only then, would we be out of the tangled web we have woven.   □